ATTITUDES
and Related Psychosocial Constructs

D1452964

ATTITUDES
and Related Psychosocial Constructs
Theories, Assessment, and Research

Lewis R. Aiken

Sage Publications
International Educational and Professional Publisher
Thousand Oaks ▪ London ▪ New Delhi

#48473866

For information:

Sage Publications, Inc.
2455 Teller Road
Thousand Oaks, California 91320
E-mail: order@sagepub.com

Sage Publications Ltd.
6 Bonhill Street
London EC2A 4PU
United Kingdom

Sage Publications India Pvt. Ltd.
M-32 Market
Greater Kailash I
New Delhi 110 048 India

Printed in the United States of America

Library of Congress Cataloging-in-Publication Data

Aiken, Lewis R., 1931-
  Attitudes and related psychosocial constructs: Theories, assessment, and research / Lewis R. Aiken.
      p. cm.
Includes bibliographical references and indexes.
  ISBN 0-7619-2452-3 (c.) — ISBN 0-7619-2453-1 (pbk.)
  1. Attitude (Psychology) I. Title.
  BF327 .A35 2002
  153.8—dc21

                        2001007016

02   03   10   9   8   7   6   5   4   3   2   1

Acquiring Editor:	Jim Brace-Thompson
Editorial Assistant:	Karen Ehrmann
Production Editor:	Olivia Weber
Copy Editor:	Kate Peterson
Typesetter/Designer:	Marion Warren/Larry K. Bramble
Cover Designer:	Jane Quaney/Sandra Ng

Contents

Preface

This book provides a compact but comprehensive, research-oriented treatment of attitudes and related psychosocial constructs (values, opinions, beliefs, personal orientations). Chapters 1 through 3 are concerned with definitional, historical, assessment, and theoretical matters, with an emphasis on attitudes. The remaining six chapters cover a range of topics and issues related to the assessment of and research on attitudes, values, opinions, and beliefs in various applied settings. These topics include social and personal matters such as prejudice and discrimination, illness and disability, death and dying, poverty and unemployment, conflict and violence, schools and teachers, work and retirement, and politics, religion, and morality.

Although there are cross-references among chapters, each of the nine chapters is essentially independent of the other eight. Each chapter represents a self-contained mixture of theories, research findings, and interpretations. The nine chapters may be read in any order, but the first three chapters are more foundational in content and should probably be studied first.

The appendixes at the ends of Chapter 2 and Chapters 4 through 9 contain descriptions of representative questionnaires, inventories, and scales designed to assess the particular attitudes and related psychosocial constructs considered in their respective chapters. Appendix A at the back of the book is a list of the names and addresses of the suppliers of all psychometric instruments described or otherwise referred to in the book. Appendix B is a list of recommendations for constructing and administering questionnaires designed for surveys of attitudes, opinions, and values. A glossary of relevant technical terms, a comprehensive list of references, and author and subject indexes are also provided.

This book is written primarily as a text for a one-semester or one-quarter upper-division college course on attitudes and associated constructs, but it may also serve as a secondary text or sourcebook for courses on psychosocial assessment, personnel psychology, social psychology, educational psychology, and social problems. It should also prove useful as a professional information source for researchers in social psychology, educational psychology, sociology, and other behavioral or social sciences.

I shall be happy to hear from instructors, students, researchers, and others who read or consult this book. Please feel free to communicate your opinions, suggestions for improvement, and any errors that may have eluded the good intentions of the author, the reviewers, and the copy editor.

They will be accepted graciously and with sincere thanks.

Acknowledgments

Many individuals other than the author are involved in the production of a book such as this. In particular, I wish to thank Richard J. Harris from the University of Mexico and other, anonymous reviewers who read and provided thorough, thoughtful, and constructive commentary on particular chapters. I also wish to thank the staff at Sage Publications, which includes my production editor Olivia Weber, my editor Jim Brace-Thompson, and his assistant Karen Ehrmann, for their continual support and shared belief in my vision for the book. Finally, a special thank-you is given to copy editor Kate Peterson, whose penchant for accuracy and thoughtful suggestions contributed immeasurably to making this book as good as it is.

1

▼

Definitions, History, and Behavior Prediction

Definitions
Attitudes
Values
Opinions
Beliefs
Personal Orientations

History
Attitudes
Values
Beliefs
Opinion Polling

Predicting Behavior From Attitudes
Theory of Reasoned Action
Theory of Planned Behavior
Prototype/Willingness Model
Personality Characteristics
Accessibility of Attitudes
Attitude-to-Behavior Process Model
Attitude Representation Theory
Explicit and Implicit Attitudes

Like the terms, concepts, or constructs in many other disciplines, those used to describe the subject matter of psychology, sociology, and other social sciences are not always definable in an objective, operational manner. Unlike basic constructs in the physical sciences, the relationships among most psychosocial constructs are not expressed in terms of mathematical formulae or equations. Consequently, the meanings of social science constructs have been topics of disagreement and debate, and the lack of uniformity in how they are interpreted and used has made communication, research, and applications involving them confusing and imprecise. Such confusion has been due, at least in part, to the fact that many of these constructs have been adopted from everyday language, carrying with them various idiosyncratic and invalid connotations.

Definitions

Among the somewhat loosely defined but nevertheless useful hypothetical constructs in psychology and sociology are attitudes, values, opinions, and beliefs. All four of these constructs involve the fundamental psychological process of evaluating the objects and events in one's experience. Not only do they represent cognitive, affective, and behavioral responses to and ways of conceptualizing and dealing with the environment, but, by influencing perception and behavior, they help to create the very kind of environment that the individual desires or assumes to exist.

Attitudes, values, opinions, and beliefs are cross-disciplinary or transsituational constructs, in that they are of concern to social and behavioral scientists, administrators in industrial/organizational and educational contexts, officials in government and the military, educators and trainers, and even the roving reporter and the average person. Whether or not one is aware of it, many decisions concerning the products and services available to us and our hopes and dreams for the future are affected by the results of research on attitudes, values, opinions, and beliefs. Every politician, marketer, newsperson—everyone who wants to influence our purchases, our choices of entertainment and information, and in general how we behave, feel, and what we believe in—has an interest in understanding and influencing our attitudes, values, opinions, and beliefs.

Attitudes

The term *attitude* can be found in Western literature as early as the 18th century, but it was not introduced into psychology until the 1860s. It was at that time that the philosophers Herbert Spencer and Alexander Bain used the term to refer to an internal state of preparation for action (Cacioppo, Petty, Losch, & Crites, 1994). As is true of many other constructs in psychology and sociology, the term attitude, which was characterized by Allport (1935) as "probably the most distinctive and indispensable concept in contemporary American social psychology" (p. 798; see also Hartmann, 1939), has varied in meaning to some extent from one researcher to another. The fact that attitudes cannot be observed directly but are inferred from behavior is made explicit in Gagné and Briggs's (1974) description of an attitude as "an internal state which affects an individual's choice of action toward some object, person, or event" (p. 62). Underscoring the relationship between attitudes and beliefs is Milton Rokeach's (1968) definition of an attitude as "a relatively enduring organization of beliefs around an object or situation predisposing one to respond in some preferential manner" (p. 112). Emphasizing a tripartite (cognitive, affective, conative) classification that goes back to the ancient Greek philosophers, Eagly and Chaiken (1993) defined attitudes as "tendencies to evaluate an entity with some degree of favor or disfavor, ordinarily expressed in cognitive, affective, and behavioral responses" (p. 155). As indicated by this definition, attitudes have cognitive (beliefs, knowledge, expectations, or perceived associations between *attitude objects* and attributes), affective (feelings, moods, motives, and emotions and associated physiological changes), and performance (behavioral or action, both intended and actual) components (McGuire, 1985). As outlined in Table 1.1, each of these three structural components can be expressed in either a verbal or a nonverbal response mode.

In addition to the three structural components, attitudes may be viewed as having various motivational functions, among which are knowledge, instrumentality, ego-defense, value-expression, consistency, and uniqueness. Attitudes provide a frame of reference for organizing information about the world (knowledge function); attaining rewards and avoiding punishment (instrumentality or utilitarian function); managing emotional conflicts (ego-defense function), expressing one's sense of self, *personal values*, or *identity* (value-expressive function); viewing oneself as being consistent (consistency function); and distinguishing oneself from other people in a social group (uniqueness function) (Katz, 1960; Ostrom, 1994).

Combining elements from several definitions, attitudes may be viewed as learned cognitive, affective, and behavioral predispositions to respond positively or negatively to certain objects, situations, institutions, concepts, or persons. Attitudes may be quite individual and thereby reflective of and related to personality characteristics such as a need for closure. A need for closure is expressed as a desire to complete a task, as in finding an answer to a question or a solution to a problem.

Attitudes serve both motivational and cognitive functions. Depending on their intensity, attitudes can shorten response times to attitude-relevant stimuli, contribute to efficient organization of one's perceptions and thoughts about different aspects of the world, and facilitate planning and decision making.

TABLE 1.1 Structural Response Categories and Modes of Attitudes

	Response Category		
Response Mode	*Cognitive*	*Affective*	*Behavioral*
Verbal	Expressions of beliefs about attitude object	Expressions of feelings toward attitude object	Expressions of behavioral intentions toward attitude object
Nonverbal	Perceptual responses (e.g., reaction time) to attitude object	Physiological responses to attitude object	Overt behavioral responses to attitude object

SOURCE: Adapted from Ajzen (1988).
NOTE: Attitude object: a person, group, object, or event toward which a particular attitude is directed or expressed.

Because of their reliance on interactions with the environment, attitudes vary not only from person to person but also with nationality, culture, and other demographic variables and situations. Particular attitudes are seen as characteristic of certain individuals, as well as being representative of a group of people or even an entire population. For example, bipolar variables such as liberal versus conservative, democratic versus totalitarian, or religious versus secular may be descriptive of both individuals and groups. Attitudes are typically inferred from observable behavior, which may or may not be the result of conscious intent. It is possible, of course, that a person may harbor an attitude that is not immediately evident in his or her behavior, and hence other people, as well as the person, may not be fully cognizant of the fact that he or she possesses that attitude.

Though the concept of attitude is not totally distinct from psychological concepts such as interest, value, opinion, and belief, there are differences in the manner in which these concepts are used. An *interest* is a feeling or preference concerning one's own activities. Unlike having a particular attitude, which implies approval or disapproval (a moral judgment), being interested in something simply means that a person spends time thinking about it or reacting to it, regardless of whether those thoughts and behaviors are positive or negative.

Values

Closely related to attitudes are the *values* held by people. Scholarly interest in values, as seen in studies of aesthetics, ethics, and religion in a branch of philosophy known as *axiology*, predated formal research on attitudes. The concept of value also plays a role in modern economic theory, being broadly defined by economists as the esteem in which something is held and more specifically as power in exchange. The economic value of any material thing is said to depend on both its desirability and scarcity (Carver, 2000).

As used in social psychology, the concept of value is interpreted as an attitude toward the ideals, customs, or institutions of a society. Examples of values are beauty, equality, freedom, honesty, and order. More formally, *values* may be defined as the importance, utility, or worth attached to particular activities and objects, usually as ends but also as means in certain situations. Attitudes and values may be viewed as characteristics of groups of people as well as individuals. Both are motivators of collective or individual behavior and are related to other social and personality variables. According to Rokeach (1973), however, values are more central to personality and more basic to the expression of individual needs and desires than attitudes. Empirical evidence for the notion that a person's attitudes are related to his or her more fundamental values is provided in Rokeach's (1973) book *The Nature of Human Values*.

Raymond Cattell (1965), who defined attitudes as readiness to act, viewed them as subservient to other personality variables. Attitudes are the starting point of Cattell's dynamic lattice model of personality, but they are subsidiary to *sentiments*. Sentiments, in turn, are subsidiary to *ergs*, which are biologically based needs or drives that are satisfied by means of attitudes and sentiments. A person's interest in plays and films (attitude level), for example, may stem from his or her involvement with photography (sentiment level), which in turn may satisfy various needs (sex, gregariousness, curiosity) at the ergic level. Other writers have described a similar hierarchy of specificity or exclusiveness, with values being the least specific, interests next in specificity, sentiments even more specific, attitudes even more so, and beliefs and opinions being the most specific or exclusive of all ("Attitude," 1997).

Opinions

The meaning of *opinion*, a judgment of a person or thing with respect to character or merit, is also similar to that of *attitude*. Opinions are sometimes regarded as the overt, conscious manifestations of attitudes; opinions are also viewed as less central, more specific, more changeable, and more factually based than attitudes. A person's opinions are expressed in words, but his or her attitudes may not be. Both opinions and attitudes may be learned either by direct, personal experience or by following the example of family members, friends, and other people whom one respects or admires.

Opinions are specific reactions to certain occurrences or situations, whereas attitudes are more general in their effects on responses to a broad range of people or events. Furthermore, people are aware of their opinions, but they may not be fully conscious of their attitudes. This is particularly true of *implicit attitudes* that are automatically activated and without conscious awareness in response to some object or situation.

Not only are attitudes less conscious than opinions, but the former are typically more basic: attitudes combine with facts to produce opinions. The combination of attitudes and facts to create opinions is, however, not necessarily additive. Not only do attitudes serve to organize facts into opinions according to some frame of reference, but they also affect the facts that will be selected for interpretation.

Beliefs

Defined as confidence in the truth or existence of something that is not immediately susceptible to rigorous proof, *beliefs* are less certain than knowledge but more certain than attitudes or opinions. Of particular interest to social psychologists are *stereotypes*—beliefs concerning the personal attributes of a group of people. Stereotypes facilitate prejudice and serve as precursors and supporters of *discrimination*—treating a particular ethnic or nationality group as different from other groups.

Beliefs are similar to opinions, in that both are judgments or acceptances of certain propositions as facts. However, the factual supports for opinions are usually weaker than those for beliefs. In terms of the extent to which they are based on factual information, attitudes are in lowest place, opinions next, and beliefs at the top. Furthermore, beliefs themselves vary in the extent to which they are based on facts. Beliefs may be viewed as being on a continuum ranging from faith (least factually based) through knowledge (most factually based).

Beliefs and opinions may also be distinguished from attitudes and values in terms of how consciously aware a person is of them: people are always aware of their opinions, but they may not be fully conscious of their attitudes or values. In addition, both beliefs and opinions are less pervasive or generalized and less resistant to change than attitudes and values. Finally, like attitudes and values, beliefs can have profound effects on personal health, behavior, and one's overall sense of well-being. The influences of beliefs on physical health and performance are often referred to as "psychological factors" or "placebo effects."

Personal Orientations

Clearly related to attitudes, values, and beliefs are generalized personality dispositions such as gender role, self-actualization, and religious orientation. These *personal orientations* influence behavior in a variety of situations. *Gender role* refers to the pattern of appearance and behavior that is associated by a society or culture with being male or female. *Self-actualization* refers to a process by which a person develops his or her abilities to the fullest, becoming the kind of person he or she would ideally like to be. A number of questionnaires and inventories have been devised to measure these two personal orientations, including the Bem Sex-Role Inventory (S. L. Bem, 1974) and the Personal Orientation Inventory (E. L. Shostrum, EdITS; see Appendix A).

History

Descriptions and discussions of attitudes, values, opinions, and beliefs can be found in philosophical and religious literature well before the 19th century, but developments in research methodology and quantification in the social sciences during the latter part of that century led to scientific studies of these constructs. A frequency count of published articles containing the term *attitudes, values, opinions,* or *beliefs* in the title increases from only a handful during the first two decades of the 20th century to several thousand by the end of the century (see Figure 1.1).[1]

Attitudes

As illustrated in Figure 1.1, the number of citations in PsycINFO is highest for "attitudes," followed in order by "values," "beliefs," and "opinions." Articles on attitudes during the decade 1901-1910, and to some extent 1911-1920, showed the influence of the psychological schools of structuralism and functionalism, which were prominent at that time. The 1920s and 1930s witnessed the development of more systematic procedures for assessing attitudes and the applications of these procedures to social problems and issues (e.g., Bogardus, 1928; Likert, 1932; Thurstone, 1928, 1929; Thurstone & Chave, 1929).

During the early 1930s, LaPiere (1934) conducted his classic study of the relationship between attitudes and behavior. He found that the responses of a sample of American restaurant, hotel, and motel managers to the mail *survey* question "Will you accept members of the Chinese race as guests?" had almost no relationship to their actual behavior toward Chinese people. As illustrated in Figure 1.2, almost all of the restaurants, hotels, and motels that were visited actually served the Chinese couple, but more than 80% of the managers who were questioned in a mail survey said that they would not serve Chinese people. Because subsequent studies appeared to confirm LaPiere's conclusion that inventoried attitudes do not correlate very highly

Decade

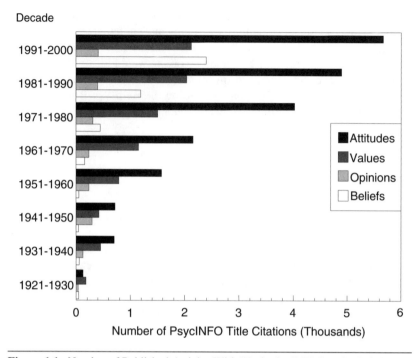

Figure 1.1. Number of Published Articles With "Attitudes," "Values," "Opinions," or "Beliefs" in Titles Listed in PsycINFO, 1901-2000

with actual behavior (see Wicker, 1969), social psychologists began to question the supposed centrality and utility of the attitude concept, and some advocated abandoning it altogether (Wicker, 1971). That this did not occur is witnessed by the subsequent flood of articles during the ensuing decades concerning measurement, *theory*, and research on attitudes.

As indicated in Figure 1.1, probably due in some measure to the greater priorities of war-related activities, a plateau in the number of professional publications concerned with attitudes, values, beliefs, and opinions occurred during 1941-1950. During the last half of the century, however, the number of publications on attitudes in particular rose dramatically. The research on which these publications were based dealt with such topics as attitude change (Petty, Wegener, & Fabrigar, 1997; Wood, 2000), attitude structure and function (Eagly & Chaiken, 1998), attitudes toward work (George & Jones, 1997; Lease, 1998), implicit attitudes (Greenwald & Banaji, 1995; Greenwald & Farnham, 2000; Nesdale & Durkin, 1998), and attitude measurement (Krebs & Schmidt, 1993). The number of publications concerned with beliefs and values also increased markedly during this period.

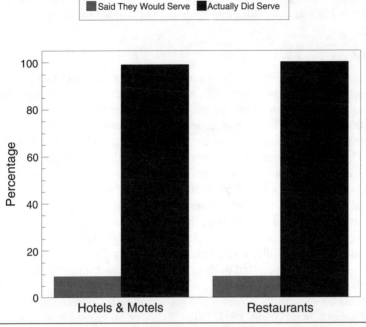

Figure 1.2. Percentage of Hotels/Motels and Restaurants That Said They Would Serve Chinese People Compared With Percentage That Actually Did Serve Chinese People

Several factors, including a pronounced rise in the number of graduate students and research professors in social psychology and related fields, the increased availability of efficient measures of attitudes, values, and beliefs, and the expansion of applied psychology beyond academia, contributed to the rise in empirical studies of these constructs.

Renewed efforts were made during the latter part of the 20th century to formulate sound theoretical ideas regarding the structure, function, development, and change of attitudes in particular (e.g., Adorno, Frenkel-Brunswik, Levinson, & Sanford, 1950; Festinger, 1957; Fishbein & Ajzen, 1975; Heider, 1958; Hovland & Rosenberg, 1960; Newcomb, 1943; Newcomb, Koenig, Flacks, & Warwick, 1967; Rokeach, 1960, 1968). These theories and associated research were concerned with such matters as the meaning and multidimensionality of attitudes, the relationships of attitudes to intentions and behavior, the effects of situations on attitude expression, the relationships of attitudes to personality, and the development of attitudes and techniques for shaping and modifying them. Studies concerned with the *assessment*, functioning, and manipulation of attitudes were conducted in schools and colleges, businesses and industries, governmental and military contexts, clinical and counseling contexts, and in other situations.

Values

As with attitudes, the design and construction of psychometrically sound measures of values during the 1930s and subsequently supported the growth of research in this area. Among the pioneers in the study of values were Gordon Allport, L. L. Thurstone, and Milton Rokeach. Perhaps the most popular measure of values was the Study of Values (Allport & Vernon, 1931), a paper-and-pencil *inventory* based on Eduard Spranger's (1928) classification of people into six types (theoretical, economic, aesthetic, social, political, religious). Following his definition of a *value* as "an enduring belief that a specific model of conduct or end-state of existence is personally or socially preferable to an opposite or converse model of conduct or end-state of existence," Rokeach (1973, p. 5) conducted extensive international and cross-cultural research on values. Psychometric instruments administered in the research of Rokeach and other social psychologists on values are described in Chapter 2.

Theories concerning *personal* and *social values* are even older than attitude theories (e.g., Urban, 1907, 1912). Research on values has not been as extensive as that on attitudes (see Figure 1.1), but numerous studies of values have been conducted in industrial, educational, mental health, and other settings since the early part of the 20th century. Studies concerning a variety of causes, consequences, and correlates of values and cultural similarities and differences between them were conducted and published in many different countries. Especially popular have been investigations of spiritual (religious), scholastic, moral, occupational, and social values.

Many unpublished or ad hoc questionnaires and published inventories of values similar to inventories of attitudes, beliefs, and interests were widely administered during the 40-year span between 1930 and 1970. However, many of these early instruments proved incompatible with later conceptions of values and are now out of print. In school situations, units or courses on "values clarification" and techniques of teaching values were introduced after 1950. Empirical studies of the relationships of values to personality, mental health, perception, and political behavior were also conducted. The increased interest in moral and ethical questions that occurred during the 1950s and 1960s, and the fear of destruction and contamination by nuclear bombs and other weapons of mass destruction, contributed to a somewhat antiscientific or antitechnology movement and a heightened concern with humanism and human values. Today, more liberal and politically oriented individuals in particular continue to be concerned with values pertaining to protection of the environment, interculturalism, and peace and happiness throughout the world.

Beliefs

Published articles with "belief" in the title can be found in professional psychological journals as far back as the beginning of the 20th century. A large number of such articles published during the first few decades were concerned with religious beliefs, including beliefs in the soul, God, the devil, life after death, immortality, superstition, magic, miracles, and taboos. Other reports focused on the relationships of beliefs to advertising, extrasensory perception (ESP), sex, academic success, personality, and science. Research on children examined their beliefs in Santa Claus, the Easter bunny, and the tooth fairy, as well as somewhat less fanciful topics. Many studies of beliefs were also conducted with college students.

The advent of more carefully designed and standardized measures of beliefs following World War II and the growing interest on the part of scholars in religious, philosophical, and intercultural topics were accompanied by a steady increase in research and writings in this area. More sophisticated theories and research methods (multiple regression analysis, multivariate analysis, structural equation modeling, etc.) also came into play to produce more complex and carefully controlled studies and perhaps more valid and generalizable conclusions. Research was conducted on the relationships of beliefs to such contemporary topics as locus of control, self-monitoring, and *Machiavellianism* (see the glossary). Also studied were the effects of beliefs on health and disease, depression, and other psychological states, and the effects of development, culture, and personality factors on beliefs. Growing interest in the characteristics and dynamics of beliefs was stimulated and supported by the "cognitive psychology" Zeitgeist at the end of the 20th century.

Opinion Polling

Although rulers and leaders since ancient times have been aware of the importance of the views, attitudes, and beliefs of the public concerning their reputations and related topics of national concern, the term *public opinion* was first used in the 18th century ("Public Opinion," 1997). Assessment of the attitudes and opinions of consumers regarding marketable products and services was in practice in the United States even before the 1920s and 1930s. However, the widespread use of statistical and other methodological procedures to determine the political and social attitudes of the public did not get under way until the third and fourth decades of the 20th century. Government leaders in democratic countries such as the United States recognized that their power depended on the consent of the governed. Consequently, to foresee potential problems and retain their power, leaders needed to know what the public thought and felt about various political and social issues.

Probably only a small percentage of adults in the Western world have not heard of *public opinion polling*. Beginning with the 1936 presidential election, George Gallup, Elmo Roper, Louis Harris, Hadley Cantril, Archibald Crosley, and other pollsters conducted hundreds of nationwide polls of the opinions and attitudes of the American public from the 1930s to the end of the century. Predicting the outcomes of political elections is, of course, not the only business of public opinion pollsters. Such polls have also been conducted to assess opinions and attitudes toward a variety of domestic and foreign issues.

During the early years of the 20th century, administering questionnaires and conducting surveys became fairly common methods for obtaining information in various applied and theoretical investigations. Extensive use of social surveys and questionnaires was made by sociologists in community studies stimulated by the reform movement of the late 19th and early 20th centuries. Among the problems emphasized by these surveys were low wages, poor housing, inadequate public health facilities, and unsafe working conditions for the laboring classes (Hoover, 1993). By the 1930s, demographers, psychologists, educational researchers, market researchers, political scientists, and other investigators of human behavior were conducting interviews and administering questionnaires to determine the attitudes and opinions of large samples of people. As seen in the activities of organizations such as the Bureau of Applied Social Research at Columbia University, the National Opinion Research Center at Denver and at the University of Chicago, and the Survey Research Center/Institute for Social Research at the University of Michigan, survey research had become part of the scientific mission of American universities.

By 1940, use of the telephone, personal interviewing, and questionnaires to determine the opinions of representative samples of the public, and by extension the population as a whole, began to provide more accurate information on the thoughts and feelings of the public regarding current events and issues. Surveys were conducted to determine the attitudes and opinions of various demographic (age, sex, race, etc.) groups toward issues such as sterilization, ability grouping, industrial strikes, prisoner parole, child-rearing practices, ESP, crime, and especially the looming threat of war. Under the direction of George Gallup, the American Institute of Public Opinion, which was founded in 1934, conducted numerous *Gallup polls*, the results of which were reported and discussed in newspapers and periodicals such as the *Public Opinion Quarterly*. Using representative samples as small as 2% of the target population, the Gallup organization maintained that the findings of their polls were accurate to within 2% (Gallup, 1936). Articles concerned with the science and methodology of opinion measurement were also published in many professional journals during the 1930s and succeeding decades.

Understandably, public opinion polls during the World War II period of 1940-1945 emphasized issues pertaining to the war and its consequences for the population. During the latter part of the 1940s and the early 1950s, polls focused on such matters as communism, loyalty oaths, prices, and nuclear war. Survey methodology was also extended to business forecasting and the assessment of employees' opinions as the nation was launched into a period of peacetime industrial production and expansion. The science and art of question and questionnaire design, in addition to sampling and statistical methods, improved during the latter part of the 20th century, making the results of opinion polls even more accurate.

Although an underlying assumption of opinion polling is that a sample of people can be selected whose opinions are representative of the opinions of a designated target population, in practice it is not always easy to obtain such a sample. One of the most famous "goofs" in the history of public opinion polling was made by the now defunct *Literary Digest* magazine in predicting that Alfred M. Landon, the 1936 Republican candidate for president of the United States, would win the election. The sampling procedure employed by the pollsters was to select every *n*th person from a list of telephone subscribers and ask that person about his or her choice for president. Unfortunately, in 1936 only about half of the families in the United States had telephones, and the average income of those families was higher than the average income of the total population. Because a larger percentage of these higher-income families voted Republican, the vote for Landon was overestimated and the vote for his Democratic opponent, Franklin D. Roosevelt, was markedly underestimated. Other polls, including one conducted by the Gallup organization, were somewhat more accurate in their predictions of the successful presidential candidate in the 1936 election. However, the tendency to overestimate the Republican vote in national elections continued to plague public opinion pollsters for many years. In the 1948 presidential election, the major polls predicted victory for the Republican candidate, Thomas E. Dewey, but the Democratic candidate, Harry S. Truman, actually won the election. Although this result was due in part to the faulty sampling procedures of the pollsters, other factors also contributed to the mistake. For example, many voters remained undecided until the last minute as to which candidate they preferred, and Truman's eleventh-hour whistle-stop tour of the country prompted many of these voters to decide in his favor.

The application of opinion assessment was extended in subsequent decades to provide information concerning the characteristics, likes, and dislikes of targeted groups of people to governments and other organizations throughout the world. Standardized psychometric and sociometric instruments were designed and administered to assess attitudes and opinions in governmental, educational, business/industrial, health-related, and public service organizations. Special types of public opinion polls known as *marketing surveys* were conducted to assess the opinions and attitudes of the public toward consumer products and advertisements. Marketing surveys of the opinions of householders toward specific programs on radio or television, a process referred to as *audience measurement*, were conducted by Hooper, Nielsen, and other organizations to provide program ratings for media decision making.

Predicting Behavior From Attitudes

It has been more than 65 years since LaPiere (1934) found that the responses of a sample of American restaurant and motel managers to such questions as "Will you accept members of the Chinese race as guests?" had a very low relationship to their actual behavior toward Chinese people. Although LaPiere's study was criticized for a number of methodological shortcomings, subsequent investigations appeared to substantiate the conclusion that inventoried attitudes have only a low relationship to actual behavior (see Corey, 1937; Wicker, 1969). Thus, general, overall measures of attitudes are not very accurate predictors of specific behaviors. The findings of later investigations indicated that attitude-behavior correlations could be improved by using aggregated, that is, multiple-item combinations, rather than single-item measures of both attitude and behavior. The resulting general measure of attitude is typically a better predictor of a general than of a specific measure of behavior. On the other hand, if the activity to be predicted is highly specific in nature, then the attitudinal measure used to predict it should be compatible, that is, specific to it. In short, attitudes are better predictors of behavior when both attitude and behavior are measured at the same level of generality or specificity (*principle of compatibility*). These two principles—aggregation and compatibility—were incorporated into Fishbein and Ajzen's (1975) *theory of reasoned action* (TORA).

Theory of Reasoned Action

Fishbein and Ajzen (1975; Ajzen & Fishbein, 1977) began with the premise that attitudes toward behaviors are derived from beliefs concerning the effects of those behaviors, and consequently that specific behavior can be predicted from specific measures of attitudes toward the behavior. Traditional attitude measures are concerned with attitudes toward objects or events, for example, "attitude toward science." Fishbein and Ajzen focused, however, on attitudes toward the behavior that was to be predicted, such as "registering for a nonrequired science course." According to these psychologists, the simplest way to predict whether people will do a certain thing is to ask them whether they intend to do it. Behavioral intentions are, of course, not always followed by behavior. The correlation between intentions and actual behavior depends on such factors as how specific the intention is, the length of time between the intention and the action, and the ability to do what one says one will do (King, 1975).

After reviewing the results of several dozens of studies, Ajzen and Fishbein (1977) concluded that attitudinal and behavioral entities consist of four elements: the action itself, the target at which the action is directed, the context in which the action is performed, and the time at which it is performed. They maintained that "strong relationships between attitudes and behavior are obtained only when there is a high correspondence between at least the target and action elements of the attitudinal and behavioral entities" (p. 888).

Fishbein and Ajzen's theory is based on the assumption that attitudes result from a combination of beliefs about the characteristics of particular attitude objects and evaluations of those characteristics. The theory involves several variables: volitional behavior (B), intention to perform the behavior (BI), attitude toward the behavior ($Aact$), the person's normative beliefs about what each of n other people (I) thinks he or she should do (NB_i), and the motivation to comply with the expectation (Mc_i) of each of the n other people. If w_1 and w_2 are empirically derived regression weights, then the functional relationship between volitional behavior and the other variables may be expressed as

$$B \sim BI = w_1 Aact + w_2 \Sigma NB_i(Mc_i), \qquad (1)$$

in which the summation is from 1 to n. Another form of this equation is

$$B \sim BI = w_1 \Sigma B_i a_i + w_2 \Sigma NB_i(Mc_i), \qquad (2)$$

where $\Sigma B_i a_i$, a measure of *Aact*, is the sum of products of n beliefs (B_i) concerning the consequences of performing behavior B and the corresponding n evaluations (a_i) of those consequences. In short, Equation 2 was proposed as a multiple regression model for determining the relative importance of attitudinal and normative components in predicting behavioral intentions. These intentions are, in turn, related to observable behavior (King, 1975). The consequences of this behavior may be utilitarian, that is, directly experienced rewards and punishments, or normative, that is, perceptions of other people's approval or disapproval of the behavior.

The results of research in a variety of settings have tended to confirm the essential features of the TORA model (see Eagly & Chaiken, 1993), although questions have been raised about its generality and the operation of certain variables in the equations. However, the model does not explain the research finding that often the best predictor of future behavior is past behavior. Suggestions for further research on the TORA model have been offered by a number of investigators. With respect to the attitudinal component (*Aact*) of the model, Bass and Rosen (1969) maintained that the salience or relevancy of the stimulus object or event to the respondent is an important *moderator variable* in predicting behavior from attitudes. Another variable that has been shown to affect the predictability of behavior from attitudes is the circumstances in which the attitudes were formed. Fazio and Zanna (1978) noted, for example, that behavior can be predicted more accurately from attitudes formed by direct experience with an attitude object or target than from attitudes formed by indirect experience. Because attitudes formed by direct experience tend to be held more confidently than those formed indirectly, Fazio and Zanna (1978) hypothesized, and their experiments confirmed, that behavior is predicted more accurately from attitudes that are held more confidently.

Theory of Planned Behavior

An extension of TORA known as the *theory of planned behavior* incorporates within it the notion of perceived behavioral control. According to the theory, a person can act on his or her intentions only if he or she has control over the behavior of concern. Perceived control varies with the individual's perception of the difficulty of performing the behavior in question. This perception is a reflection of the individual's past experience as well as the obstacles or impediments to performing the behavior.

As summarized by Ajzen (1991), the importance of perceived control in determining the relationships between attitudes and behavior has been confirmed in a number of empirical studies. These studies support the hypothesis that people with higher degrees of control tend to have both stronger intentions to engage in specific behaviors and are more likely to perform those behaviors when the conditions are appropriate.

Among the behaviors that have been focused on in research concerned with testing TORA and the theory of planned behavior are

AIDS-related risk taking

Breast self-examination

Charitable behavior

Condom use

Controlled burning policy

Coupon usage

Drugs/alcohol misuse

Exercise behavior

Fast food consumption

Health-related behaviors

Moral behavior

Smoking cessation

Testicular self-examination

Violence control

Voting behavior

Women's career behavior

Of these behaviors, the largest number of investigations based on TORA have been concerned with condom use, exercise behavior, and testicular or breast self-examination. In contrast, the largest number of studies based on the theory of planned behavior have focused on adolescent smoking, adolescent use and misuse of alcohol, health-related behaviors, condom use, and exercise. Both theories have received substantial research support (see Sideridis, Kaissidis, & Padeliadu, 1998).

TORA and the theory of planned behavior assume that behavior is the result of conscious decisions to act in a certain manner. According to this explanation, when two or more behavioral choices are present and one must be selected, a person engages in deliberative processing of information pertaining to those behaviors. The attributes of the object or situation, the relevant attitudes, and the costs and benefits of specific behaviors are all considered before acting. However, not all behavior is a consequence of deliberate cognitive processing. Some behaviors are automatic, not under volitional control, and not all involve judgment or conscious decision making. Fazio (1990) accepts the Fishbein/Ajzen TORA theory as applicable to behavior that is deliberate and judgmental, but introduces another set of processes to account for the influence of attitudes on behavior when motivation and conscious deliberation are low. In this case, the more accessible attitudes are automatically activated without conscious awareness.

Prototype/Willingness Model

Similar to TORA in its emphasis on social norms and behavioral intentions is the *prototype/willingness model* (Gibbons, Gerrard, Blanton, & Russell, 1998). According to this model, behavior is often determined by attitude toward the behavior, whether other people engage in the behavior (*subjective norm*), the person's intention to engage in the behavior, whether the person is willing to perform the behavior under various circumstances, and images of what people who engage in the behavior are like. Inherent in the model is the idea that attitudes influence both intentions to behave in ways that are consistent with those attitudes and a willingness to engage in behavior that is consistent with the attitude (Gibbons et al., 1998; Gibbons, Gerrard, & McCoy, 1995).

Personality Characteristics

A number of moderator variables, such as specific personality variables, have been shown to influence the correlation between inventoried attitudes and observed behavior. One of these variables is *self-monitoring*—the extent to which a person is sensitive to, or monitors, his or her own behavior according to environmental cues. High self-monitors are more sensitive to what is situationally appropriate and act accordingly. Low self-monitors, on the other hand, are less sensitive to external cues and act more in response to their own internal attitudes and feelings (Snyder, 1982).

Another personality variable that moderates the relationship between attitudes and behavior is the *need for cognition*. A person with a high need for cognition is more likely to process information carefully and thereby develop well-founded, strong attitudes that are predictive of behavior. Petty and Cacioppo (1986) found, for example, that the voting choices of persons who were high in the need for cognition were more predictable from their attitudes toward the political candidates than were the voting choices of those who were low on the need for cognition.

Whether or not people behave in accord with what they say they would do or are going to do also affects the predictability of behavior. Not only do circumstances change and lead people to change their minds, but people may dissimulate, or lie, on attitude inventories to make a favorable impression, or they may misread or otherwise misunderstand the questions. Furthermore, when faced with a situation that appears to call for a particular type of behavior, some people are more controlled by social norms than others and may find themselves unable to resist social pressures or potential rewards. They may also find that the situation is actually quite different from how it was described as being or how they imagined it would be.

Accessibility of Attitudes

The predictability of behavior from attitudes also depends on various features of those attitudes, namely, their strength, clarity, accessibility, whether they are the results of direct or indirect experience, and whether there are conflicting situational pressures. These variables are, of course, not independent. For example, the *accessibility* of an attitude—the speed or readiness with which it comes to mind when a particular object or event is encountered—is related to the strength and clarity of the attitude (see Fazio, 1990).

A central variable in Fazio's theorizing is direct experience with an attitude object. According to Fazio (1990), the greater the amount of direct experience one has with an attitude object, the stronger will be the association between the object and the person's evaluation of it. Attitudes that are based on direct experience are more accessible, in that they can be retrieved from memory more quickly and are more predictive of behavior toward the attitude object (Fazio, Chen, McDonel, & Sherman, 1982; Fazio & Zanna, 1981).

Attitude-to-Behavior Process Model

Direct past experience with an attitude object is particularly useful when one has little time or opportunity to weigh various behavioral options and must act quickly. This situation is incorporated into Fazio's (1989; Fazio & Roskos-Ewoldsen, 1994) *attitude-to-behavior process model*. According to this model, a particular situation, such as being approached by a stranger at a busy intersection, activates a particular attitude. Activation of the attitude influences the individual's perception of the attitude object in that situation. When combined with the person's knowledge of what behavior is appropriate in that situation (social norms), this perception automatically determines the individual's definition of appropriate situational behavior and consequently his or her expression of that behavior.

Attitude Representation Theory

Another theory representing an attempt to solve the dual problems of predicting behavior from attitudes and the inconsistency of behavioral expressions across time and situations is Lord and Lepper's (1999) *attitude representation theory* (ART). This theory is based on two postulates: a representation postulate and a matching postulate. According to the *representation postulate*, a person's responses toward an attitude-relevant object are a product of his or her subjective representation of the object or category as well as the person's direct perception of any specific attitude object that is present in the immediate environment. The *matching postulate* holds that the consistency or stability of attitude-relevant responses depends on the extent of the match between the subjective representation of the attitude object and the immediate perception of it at different times or in different situations. In short, the theory views recollection, construal, and other subjective cognitive processes as having a critical role in determining a person's behavior in various attitude-relevant situations. Research relevant to the representational postulate and the matching postulate up to 1999 is summarized by Lord and Lepper (1999). Extrapolating from the concluding comments of this summary, the research findings "point to the critical role of recollection, construal, and other subjective cognitive processes in determining how people will behave in various attitude-relevant situations" (p. 329).

Explicit and Implicit Attitudes

According to Greenwald and Banaji (1995), research on the relationship between attitudes and behavior "has established that attitudes have *predictive validity* in situations in which they are strongly activated and/or when the actor clearly perceives a link between attitude and behavior" (p. 7). Quoting Myers (1990), "Our attitudes predict our actions . . . if, as we act, we are conscious of our attitudes" (p. 40). While accepting this conclusion, Greenwald and Banaji expressed nostalgia for the time when Allport (1935) declared that *attitude* was the most dispensable concept of social psychology. They maintained that it is also true that "attitudes of which the actor is *not* conscious at the moment of action (implicit attitudes) are also strongly predictive of behavior." Greenwald and Banaji summarized research findings concerned with implicit attitudes, dealing with such topics as implicit *self-esteem* and implicit race and gender stereotypes, as well as the halo effect, subliminal attitude conditioning, and context effects. From their summary, it may be concluded that, at least in this case, the opposite of a great truth is also true: attitudes are predictive of behavior both when they are above and when they are below the level of conscious awareness.

Recommended Readings

Ajzen, I. (2001). Nature and operation of attitudes. *Annual Review of Psychology, 52*, 28-58.

Eagly, A. H., & Chaiken, S. L. (1998). Attitude structure and function. In D. T. Gilbert, S. T. Fiske, & G. Lindzey (Eds.), *The handbook of social psychology* (4th ed., Vol. 1, pp. 269-322). New York: McGraw-Hill/Oxford.

Eiser, J. R. (1994). A brief history of attitude research. In *Attitudes, chaos and the connectionist mind* (pp. 1-31). Oxford, UK: Basil Blackwell.

Fazio, R. (1995). Attitudes as object evaluation associations: Determinants, consequences, and correlates of attitude accessibility. In R. E. Petty & J. A. Krosnick (Eds.), *Attitude strength: Antecedents and consequences* (pp. 247-282). Mahwah, NJ: Lawrence Erlbaum.

Greenwald, A. G., & Banaji, M. R. (1995). Implicit social cognition: Attitudes, self-esteem, and stereotypes. *Psychological Review, 102*, 4-27.

Jones, E. E. (1998). Major developments in five decades of social psychology. In D. T. Gilbert, S. T. Fiske, & G. Lindzey (Eds.), *The handbook of social psychology* (4th ed., Vol. 1, pp. 3-57). New York: McGraw-Hill/Oxford.

Lord, C. G., & Lepper, M. R. (1999). Attitude representation theory. In M. P. Zanna (Ed.), *Advances in social psychology* (pp. 265-343). San Diego, CA: Academic Press.

Maio, G. R., & Olson, J. M. (2000). Emergent themes and potential approaches to attitude function: The function-structure model of attitudes. In G. R. Maio & J. M. Olson (Eds.), *Why we evaluate: Functions of attitudes* (pp. 417-442). Mahwah, NJ: Lawrence Erlbaum.

Manstead, A. S. R. (1996). Attitudes and behaviour. In G. R. Semin & K. Fiedler (Eds.), *Applied social psychology* (pp. 3-29). London: Sage.

Note

1. Both the singular and plural, for example, attitude and attitudes, were entered into the PsycINFO system for search purposes.

2

Assessment Methods and Instruments

Attitude Assessment Methods
  Direct (Overt) Methods
  Indirect (Covert) Methods
  Traditional Attitude-Scaling Procedures
  Other Attitude-Scaling Methods

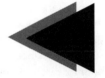

Reliability, Validity, and Norms
  Reliability
  Validity
  Standardization and Norms

Illustrative Instruments and Sources

Sound knowledge concerning attitudes and related psychosocial constructs depends on the care with which scientific research on these topics is conducted. Critical to the conduct of valid research are (a) definitions of relevant variables; (b) acceptable procedures for measuring those variables; (c) hypotheses, models, or theories based on assumptions concerning the relationships among the variables; and (d) the ability to derive plausible explanations and to make reasonable predictions from the hypotheses or theories regarding the phenomena of interest.

Hypotheses or theories are based on the results of prior research combined with logical reasoning about the relationships among the variables of interest and the research findings. For example, theories of attitudes or values may provide reasonable and valuable explanations of how attitudes or values are formed and changed; their effects on perception, cognition, and other psychological functions; and how they influence the interactions among various groups of people. Unfortunately, as with most psychological and sociological theories, those that are concerned with the constructs of attitudes, values, opinions, and beliefs have not yielded very accurate predictions or explanations. As demonstrated by the theories described in Chapters 1 and 3, however, theory can provide a stimulus and guide for research and explanation in a particular conceptual domain.

This chapter is concerned with the *measurement* or *assessment* of attitudes, values, and associated evaluative constructs. Decisions on how to measure relevant variables are a fundamental and critical part of research design and analysis, in addition to the application of research findings to the solutions of practical problems. Throughout human history, advancements in science and technology have relied greatly on improvements in measurement techniques and instruments. This has been as true in the social or behavioral sciences as it has in the physical and natural sciences. Observational, survey, correlational, *developmental*, and *experimental methods* (see the glossary) of answering theoretical and applied questions all depend on the availability of accurate methods for classifying and quantifying data. Consequently, the construction and selection of reliable and valid psychosocial assessment instruments and procedures are crucial to the results of both research and practice in the behavioral sciences.

Attitude Assessment Methods

This section focuses on the design and analysis of attitude assessment instruments, but the discussion also applies in large part to the assessment of values, opinions, beliefs, and related psychosocial constructs. The design and construction of questionnaires, *opinionnaires*, and inventories for measuring opinions and personality variables are covered at length in *Questionnaires & Inventories* (Aiken, 1997). Design, construction, and analysis of other psychometric instruments—*checklists*, *rating scales*, tests, and so on—are given thorough coverage in *Rating Scales & Checklists* (Aiken, 1996) and *Tests & Examinations* (Aiken, 1998).

Research on attitudes has been conducted on hundreds of variables involving many different topics over the past century. Table 2.1 is a representative list of concepts with which published research on attitudes has been concerned. Like research on other psychosocial constructs, the findings of investigations involving measures of attitudes are no more accurate than the instruments and procedures that serve as measures of the independent, de-

---

TABLE 2.1   Topics of Representative Research Papers Concerned With
Attitudes

Attitudes toward the following:

Abortion	Mathematics
Aging	Mentally ill people
AIDS	Minority groups
Alcohol use/abuse	Overweight people
Bisexuality	Physician-assisted suicide
Capital punishment	Polygamy
Childbearing	Rape
Christianity	Religion
Death	Science
Disabled people	Sex offenders
Drug use/abuse	Sexual harassment
Dying people	Smoking
Elder abuse	Special children
Elderly people	Spelling
Electroconvulsive therapy	Spouse abuse
Environment	Substance abuse
Euthanasia	Suicide
Gay/lesbian parenting	Taxes
HIV infection	UFOs
Homeless people	Women's rights
Imprisonment	Work
Love	

---

pendent, and concomitant variables observed and manipulated in the investigation.

Direct (Overt) Methods

The most direct way of determining attitudes toward specific objects or events is to observe how people behave toward them. That is, what a person actually does or says in a situation where the object or event is present or occurs may be interpreted as representative of his or her attitude toward it. Examples of such behavioral measures of attitudes are willingness to do a favor, sign a petition, or make a donation to some cause. Because it is not unusual for people to play a role or in other ways attempt to deceive others, even direct behavioral observation may not always be a valid indicator of a person's attitude in a given situation or on a particular occasion. Taking a representative sample of behavior across different occasions and situations would presumably eliminate this objection, but such a procedure is time-consuming and expensive. Time and expense notwithstanding, it may be necessary to employ direct observations to assess the attitudes of certain groups of people, such as young children, or when other, more obtrusive procedures influence the very behavior that is being observed.

More common than direct observations of behavior are interviewing people and asking them specific questions about an attitude object or event. So-called *explicit measures* of attitudes such as interviewing and questionnaires are based on the assumption that respondents are aware of their attitudes and are willing to reveal them in an *interview* or on a questionnaire. It is also assumed that these procedures are *unobtrusive*, in other words, that the process of asking people what their attitudes are does not influence or change those attitudes.

Indirect (Covert) Methods

As with psychological assessment in general, some researchers have been so dubious of the assumptions underlying questionnaires, interviews, and direct observations that they have opted to use more covert or disguised measures that are less influenced by the need to present oneself is a positive or socially desirable light.

Wrong-Number and Lost-Letter Techniques

Illustrative of covert or unobtrusive procedures that are sometimes employed in field research on attitudes are the wrong-number technique (Gaertner & Bickman, 1971) and the lost-letter technique (Schwartz & Ames, 1977). As an example of the *wrong-number technique*, suppose that you receive a telephone call from someone whom you don't know. After he asks to speak to a mechanic, you explain that he has called the wrong number. He apologizes but explains that he has no more change to make another call and would you do him a favor and call the telephone number that he gives you. He asks you to tell the person who answers that his car has broken down at such and such a location and would they please send a repairman or tow truck to that location as soon as possible. The telephone number you are asked to call is actually that of the researcher. Whether or not you agree to make the call presumably depends on your attitude toward the person who makes the request.

In the *lost-letter technique*, a researcher prepares a set of letters in addressed, sealed, and stamped envelopes. The name of an organization with known positions on major issues is typed on each envelope, but the street address is that of the research organization. The letters are dropped in areas of high pedestrian traffic and perhaps watched to see who picks them up and what they do with them. In any event, the number of letters that are mailed and therefore received at the research address is considered to be a measure of the attitudes of the finders toward the organization identified on the envelopes.

Psychophysiological Techniques

Nonverbal measures of attitudes such as patterns of facial expression (e.g., Cacioppo, Petty, Losch, & Kim, 1986) and brain waves (e.g., Weinstein, Weinstein, & Drozdenko, 1984) are occasionally used as *covert measures of attitudes*. Other psychophysiological techniques that have been used for this purpose are changes in the electrical conductance of the skin (*galvanic skin response*, or GSR) and in pupillary diameter (*pupillometrics*). For example, differences in the GSR or pupillary response to pictures of people in different ethnic groups may be used to assess ethnic group prejudice (Cooper & Pollock, 1959; Hess, 1965). These techniques are, however, fairly expensive and inefficient when applied to large groups of people. In addition, they are probably indicators of arousal, attention, interest, or the orienting response rather than attitudes per se (Woodmansee, 1970).

Projective and Other Disguised Techniques

Projective techniques such as *word association, sentence completion*, and picture stories, which were devised primarily for *personality assessment*, have also been used on occasion as indirect or covert measures of attitudes. For example, a group of people may be asked to make up a story about each of a set of ambiguous pictures. Because the objects or events depicted in the pictures are subject to various interpretations, the stories told by the respondents may provide information on the direction and intensity of their attitudes toward something. Also of interest is a combination projective technique and traditional *attitude scale* that uses two series of faces constructed to represent feelings from extremely positive to extremely negative. The faces have been quantified so they can be scored in the same manner as any other form of attitude measurement (Kunin, 1998). Another indirect or disguised measure of attitudes is a knowledge test that deals with matters relevant to the attitude being assessed (Korman, 1974; Moyer, 1977). Evidence that these procedures are less obtrusive or more valid than attitude inventories or scales is, however, not compelling.

Measures of Implicit Attitudes

Physiological, perceptual, and projective techniques are appropriate when the respondents are aware of their attitudes but reluctant or unwilling to reveal them. These techniques may also be useful in revealing *implicit attitudes*, which are activated (by particular objects, events, persons, or situations) and influence behaviors without conscious awareness of those attitudes. However, other procedures, including priming and the Implicit Association Test, have often been used in research on implicit attitudes.

In the *priming* technique (Fazio, Jackson, Dunton, & Williams, 1995), which was adapted from research on implicit memory, a prime word that is the name of an attitude object (e.g., *snake*) is presented briefly and then followed by presentation of a negative or positive evaluative adjective (e.g., *disgusting* or *beautiful*). If presentation of the prime automatically activates a negative evaluation and the target adjective that is subsequently presented is also negative, then the respondent indicates the connotation by responding fairly quickly. But if the target adjective is positive, the respondent will react more slowly. The reverse is true, of course, when the prime activates a positive evaluation. It is not difficult to see how this procedure might be applied to research on social prejudice and other interpersonal attitudes.

The Implicit Association Test (IAT; Greenwald, McGhee, & Schwartz, 1998) measures the differential association of two target concepts with an attribute. The two concepts are presented in a two-choice task (e.g., flower vs. insect name) and the attribute in a second task (e.g., pleasant word vs. unpleasant word). Either highly associated categories (e.g., flower + pleasant) or less associated categories (e.g., insect + pleasant) share a response key. The participant's response time to a paired stimulus is more rapid when the two concepts are highly associated than when they are less associated. The difference in response times for the two kinds of paired stimuli is a measure of the differential association (attitude difference) of the concepts. The IAT has been used to study ethnic group prejudice by pairing the names of different groups with pleasant or unpleasant evaluative stimuli and in other attitudinal studies (e.g., Greenwald & Farnham, 2000; Rudman, Greenwald, Mellott, & Schwartz, 1999; Swanson, Rudman, & Greenwald, 2001).

Traditional Attitude-Scaling Procedures

An attitude scale consists of a series of statements expressing positive or negative feelings toward an institution, a group of people, or a concept. Total score on an attitude scale is determined from the aggregated responses of the examinee to the statements; the specific scoring method depends on the type of scale. Traditional techniques for constructing and scoring attitude scales include cumulative scaling, paired comparisons, equal-appearing intervals, summated ratings, and scalogram analysis.

One of the earliest formal approaches to the measurement of attitudes was the *method of social distances*, which was used to construct the Social Distance Scale (Bogardus, 1925). The objective of this approach was to determine the most proximal behavior, that is, the closest distance to a person of another racial or nationality group at which the respondent was comfortable. In administering this *cumulative scale*, respondents were instructed to indicate the degree to which they accepted various social or religious groups in various capacities. The selected *items*, which were arranged randomly on the questionnaire, in reality constituted a hierarchy so that a positive response to a given item implied a positive response to all preceding items in the hierarchy. The Social Distance Scale provided a somewhat crude method for studying the relationships between racial prejudice and other variables, but further developments in cumulative scaling of attitude items did not occur until Guttman's (1944) work on scalogram analysis.

Bogardus's (1925) approach to attitude scale construction proved useful in research on regional differences and other variables associated with ethnic group prejudice, but it permitted measurement of attitudes only at an ordinal level. In *ordinal-level measurement*, the numbers refer to the ranks of objects or events arranged in order of merit (e.g., numbers designating order of finishing in a contest of some kind). L. L. Thurstone (1928, 1929) experimented with a similar approach to constructing attitude scales, but he hoped to improve on this approach by measuring attitudes at an interval level of measurement. In *interval-level measurement*, equal numerical differences imply equal differences in whatever is being measured (e.g., Fahrenheit or Celsius temperature scale as a measure of heat energy). The two methods with which Thurstone proposed to accomplish the interval scaling of responses were labeled *paired comparisons* and *equal-appearing intervals*. Construction of an attitude scale by either procedure begins with the collection or preparation of a large number of items or statements reflecting a wide range of positive and negative feelings toward something. The next step in the method of paired comparisons is for a large number of "judges" to compare the statements with each other and indicate which statement in each pair expresses a more positive attitude toward the attitude object or event. Because making the numerous comparisons of the n statements (viz., $n(n-1)/2$) required by this procedure is rather cumbersome and time-consuming, the method of equal-appearing intervals proved more acceptable as a method of constructing attitude scales.

Equal-Appearing Intervals

The first step in constructing an attitude scale by the method of equal-appearing intervals is to collect or construct 200 or so statements expressing a wide range of positive and negative attitudes toward an attitude object or event of interest. Next, each member of a group of "judges" is directed to sort these statements into 11 response categories, ranging from least favorable (Category 1) to most favorable (Category 11) attitude. The judges are told to think of the 11 categories as lying at equal intervals along a continuum. After all judges have sorted all statements, a frequency distribution is constructed for each statement, listing the number of judges who placed the statement in each category. The responses of the judges are then compared, and those of unreliable judges are excluded. Finally, the median score (*scale value*) and semi-interquartile range (*ambiguity index*) are computed from the overall frequency distribution of each statement for the remaining judges (see Box 2.1). The finished attitude scale consists of approximately 20 statements selected so the scale values of the statements are approximately equal distances apart, with the range being as wide as possible and the ambiguity indexes of the statements fairly low. A person's score on the complete attitude instrument is the median scale value of the statements with which he or she agrees.

Thurstone (e.g., Peterson & Thurstone, 1933; Thurstone & Chave, 1929) and his coworkers constructed some 30 attitude inventories by the method of equal-appearing intervals, most of which had reliabilities in the .80s. Twelve statements from one of these scales, which was designed to measure attitude toward capital punishment, are listed in Form 2.1. Note that the scale values of these statements range from .1 (*highly negative*) to 11.0 (*highly positive*), with a total score computed as the median of the scale values of the statements checked by the respondent. Remmers (1960) generalized the equal-appearing intervals procedure in his nine Master Attitude Scales, which measure attitudes toward any school subject, any vocation, any institution, any defined group, any proposed social action, any practice, any homemaking activity, individual and group morale, and the high school.

Despite its popularity as an attitude-scaling procedure, a number of criticisms have been directed at the method of equal-appearing intervals. One objection, which does not appear particularly serious in the light of contemporary labor-saving devices, is the great amount of work required by the procedure. A more serious shortcoming is that a respondent's score on an inventory constructed by this method—the median of the scale values of items checked—is not unique. That is, the same score may be obtained by checking different combinations of items, such as two neutral items or one positive and one negative item. A final objection is that the scale values of the items may be influenced by the attitudes of the judges. As Thurstone appears to have recognized by requiring "expert judges" to sort attitude items into the 11 categories, not everyone is capable of acting as an unbiased judge of attitude statements. For example, it was found in one study (Goodstadt & Magid, 1977) that nearly 50% of the college student judges who participated in the study responded to a pool of attitude statements in terms of their own personal agreement or disagreement with the items. However, when people are instructed carefully on how to complete the judgment task, bias in rating attitude statement does not appear to seriously distort the equal-interval properties of the scale (Bruvold, 1975). Be that as it may, it is generally conceded that Thurstone-type attitude scales represent measurement at only an ordinal rather than an interval level, or at best somewhere between an ordinal and an interval level of measurement.

Box 2.1
Equal-Appearing Intervals Worksheet

As an example of the procedure for constructing an attitude scale by the method of equal-appearing intervals, suppose that each of 50 judges sorts 200 attitude statements into 11 piles. The numbers of judges who place Statements A, B, and C into each of the 11 categories are given in the three frequency distributions listed below. Using the pile number $(1, 2, \ldots, 11)$ plus .5 as the upper exact limit of the interval, compute the scale value (median) and ambiguity index (semi-interquartile range) of each statement.

Pile Number	Statement A	Statement B	Statement C
1			8
2			17
3		6	10
4		10	9
5		13	6
6	3	8	
7	7	6	
8	9	4	
9	13	3	
10	10		
11	8		

The following formula may be used to compute the scale value (median), the 25th percentile (Q_1), and the 75th percentile (Q_3) of each statement:

$$L + (pn_t - n_b)/n_i,$$

where L is the lower exact limit, p is the proportion (.25, .5, or .75) of scores falling below the desired percentile, n_t is the total number of scores in the distribution ($n_t = 50$ in this example), n_b is the number of scores falling below the interval containing the desired percentile, and n_i is the number of scores falling on the interval containing the desired percentile. The following formula may be used to find the ambiguity index (Q or semi-interquartile range) for each statement:

$$(Q_3 - Q_1)/2.$$

Verify that the scale values of Statements A, B, and C are 8.96, 5.19, and 2.50 and the ambiguity indexes are 1.14, 1.22, and 1.01, respectively. These three statements cover a rather wide range of attitudes and are fairly unambiguous in meaning.

FORM 2.1 Twelve of the 24 Items on a Scale of Attitude Toward Capital Punishment

---

Directions: This is a study of attitude toward capital punishment. Below you will find a number of statements expressing different attitudes toward capital punishment.

    ✔   Put a check mark if you agree with the statement.
    ✗   Put a cross if you disagree with the statement.

Try to indicate either agreement or disagreement for each statement. If you simply cannot decide about a statement, you may mark it with a question mark. This is not an examination. There are no right or wrong answers to these statements. This is simply a study of people's attitudes toward capital punishment. Please indicate your own convictions by a check mark when you agree and by a cross when you disagree.

1. Capital punishment is wrong but is necessary in our imperfect civilization. (6.2)[a]
2. Every criminal should be executed. (11.0)
3. Capital punishment has never been effective in preventing crime. (2.7)
4. I don't believe in capital punishment but I'm not sure it isn't necessary. (3.4)
5. I think the return of the whipping post would be more effective than capital punishment. (3.9)
6. I do not believe in capital punishment under any circumstances. (0.1)
7. Execution of criminals is a disgrace to civilized society. (0.9)
8. Capital punishment is just and necessary. (9.6)
9. I do not believe in capital punishment but it is not practically advisable to abolish it. (5.8)
10. Capital punishment gives the criminal what he deserves. (9.4)
11. The state cannot teach the sacredness of human life by destroying it. (2.0)
12. Capital punishment is justified only for premeditated murder. (7.9)

SOURCE: Peterson and Thurstone (1933).
a. The scale values at the ends of the statements are not included when administering the scale.

Summated Ratings

Even more popular than Thurstone's method of equal-appearing intervals is Likert's (1932) *method of summated ratings*. This method also begins with a large number of statements expressing a variety of attitudes toward a given topic. Unlike the statements on a Thurstone-type scale, however, those on a Likert-type scale need not have an obvious surface relationship to the topic under consideration. In general, the selected statements should refer to the present rather than the past, not be factual or capable of being interpreted as factual, not be interpretable in more than one way, be relevant to the psychological object under consideration, and not be endorsed by almost everyone or almost no one. Furthermore, the statements should be simple, clear, and direct; be short, rarely exceeding 20 words; contain only one complete thought; and be written in simple sentences rather than compound or complex sentences. The scale constructor should avoid statements containing ambiguous universals such as *all, always, none,* and *never;* double negatives; words not likely to be understood by respondents or words having more than one meaning; and nonspecific adjectives or adverbs (e.g., *many* or *sometimes*). Words such as *only, just,* and *merely* should be used with care and moderation. And slang and colloquialisms, which tend to make statements ambiguous and unclear, should also be avoided.

After the statements have been selected, the next step in constructing a *Likert scale* is to instruct a group of 100 to 200 people, who do not have to be unbiased or expert judges, to indicate on a 4- to 7-point scale the extent to which they agree or disagree, approve or disapprove, with each of the statements. It should be emphasized that the particular numbers of attitude statements and response alternatives (4-7) are not an inherent part of Likert's method of attitude scale construction but may vary from one attitude instrument to another.

On a 5-point scale, which is typical, responses to positively worded items are scored 0 for *strongly disagree,* 1 for *disagree,* 2 for *undecided,* 3 for *agree,* and 4 for *strongly agree.* Responses to negatively worded items are scored 0 for *strongly agree,* 1 for *agree,* 2 for *undecided,* 3 for *disagree,* and 4 for *strongly disagree.* Total score on the initial set of attitude items is the sum of the numerical weights of the responses checked by the examinee. After the responses of all people have been scored, *item analysis* procedures (*t* tests or item discrimination indexes) are applied to find the 10 or so positively worded statements and an equal number of negatively worded statements that most closely distinguish between people whose scores fall in the upper 27% from those whose scores are in the lower 27% of the total score distribution. A person's total score on the finished 20-item inventory is the sum of the numerical weights of the items checked by him or her (see Form 2.2).

Not all published attitude inventories labeled as Likert-type scales were constructed by using item-analysis procedures. Many so-called Likert scales consist merely of a set of declarative statements with five agree/disagree response categories per statement but no discernible underlying theoretical construct and no accompanying evidence that they were designed by the procedure outlined by Likert (Gardner, 1975; Poetker, 1977).

FORM 2.2 A Scale of Attitudes Toward Mathematics

Directions: Write your name in the upper right corner. Each of the statements in this opinionnaire expresses a feeling or attitude toward mathematics. You are to indicate, on a 5-point scale, the extent of agreement between the attitude expressed in each statement and your own personal attitude. The 5 points are *strongly disagree* (SD), *disagree* (D), *undecided* (U), *agree* (A), *strongly agree* (SA). Draw a circle around the letter(s) that best indicate(s) how closely you agree or disagree with the statement.

1. I have a definite positive reaction to mathematics; it's enjoyable.　SD　D　U　A　SA

2. I do not like mathematics, and it scares me to have to take it.　SD　D　U　A　SA

3. I feel at ease in mathematics, and I like it very much.　SD　D　U　A　SA

4. I am usually under a terrible strain in a math class.　SD　D　U　A　SA

5. Mathematics is very interesting to me, and I enjoy math classes.　SD　D　U　A　SA

6. I am happier in a mathematics class than in any other class.　SD　D　U　A　SA

7. I have never liked mathematics, and it is my most dreaded school subject.　SD　D　U　A　SA

8. Mathematics is fascinating and fun.　SD　D　U　A　SA

9. It makes me nervous to even think about having to do a math problem.　SD　D　U　A　SA

10. My mind goes blank, and I am unable to think clearly when working math problems.　SD　D　U　A　SA

11. Mathematics is a school subject that I have always enjoyed studying.　SD　D　U　A　SA

12. I really like mathematics.　SD　D　U　A　SA

13. I feel a sense of insecurity when trying to do mathematics.　SD　D　U　A　SA

14. The feeling that I have toward mathematics is a good one.　SD　D　U　A　SA

15. When I hear the word mathematics, I have a feeling of dislike.　SD　D　U　A　SA

16. I approach mathematics with a feeling of hesitation, resulting from a fear of not being able to do math.　SD　D　U　A　SA

17. Mathematics is something that I enjoy a great deal.　SD　D　U　A　SA

FORM 2.2   Continued

18. Mathematics makes me feel like I'm lost in a jungle of numbers and can't find my way out.	SD	D	U	A	SA
19. Mathematics is stimulating and makes me feel secure.	SD	D	U	A	SA
20. Mathematics makes me feel uncomfortable, restless, irritable, and impatient.	SD	D	U	A	SA

NOTE: Score responses to Items 1, 3, 5, 6, 8, 11, 12, 14, 17, 19 as SD = 0, D = 1, U = 2, A = 3, SA = 4; score responses to Items 2, 4, 7, 9, 10, 13, 15, 16, 18, 20 as SD = 4, D = 3, U = 2, A = 1, SA = 0.

Despite frequent misuse of Likert's procedure, Likert-type scales possess several advantages over Thurstone-type scales. Likert-type scales are easier to construct, and, unlike Thurstone scales, items that are not clearly related in the context of the attitude of interest can be used if they correlate with total scores. Likert-type scales also tend to be more reliable than corresponding Thurstone-type scales having the same number of items.

Among the shortcomings of Likert scales are that the scores represent only ordinal measurement at best. Also, like Thurstone scales, many different patterns of scores on Likert scales can produce the same score. This makes it difficult to assign a uniform meaning to a given score and creates problems with respect to the validity of the scale. Various proposals have been made to improve the psychometric qualities of Likert scales (e.g., Andrich, 1978a, 1978b, 1978c; Spector, 1976), but they have not been widely adopted. In many cases, more complex, computer-based approaches have also replaced the traditional item-analysis procedures recommended by Likert.

Another change that might improve Likert-type attitude scales is to use, rather than the traditional five levels of agreement responses to attitude statements, frequency response categories such as 1 = *never*, 2 = *once*, 3 = *two to five times*, and 4 = *more than five times* responses to attitude statements such as "How often have you picketed a Planned Parenthood Clinic?" Roberts, Laughlin, and Wedell (1999) argue that this is one way of ensuring that the Thurstone and Likert procedures are measuring the same thing. As things now stand, the differences between the Thurstone and Likert types of attitude-scaling procedures can lead to differences on the two types of scales in estimating the attitudes of respondents having extreme attitudes. The results of real and simulated comparisons made by Roberts et al. of the Thurstone and Likert procedures prompted them to conclude that, at the very least, researchers should devote more attention to the empirical response characteristics of the items on Likert attitude questionnaires, and at the very most they should use other methods to derive attitude estimates from disagree-agree responses.

In the 70 years since Likert's original paper was published, the method of summated ratings has undoubtedly been used more than any other attitude-scaling technique. Samples of attitude scales constructed by this procedure may be found in various sources (Mueller, 1986; Robinson, Athanasiou, & Head, 1974; Robinson, Shaver, & Wrightsman, 1991, 1999; Shaw & Wright, 1967; see also Appendix 2.1 at the end of this chapter). Nevertheless, the psychometric theory underlying the method has not been laid to rest, and attitude scale constructors can look forward to further changes involving item response theory and other advanced statistical methodology.

Scalogram Analysis

A major purpose of *scalogram analysis* (Guttman, 1944, 1947) is to determine whether the responses to the items selected to measure a given attitude fall on a single dimension. If the items constitute a true, unidimensional Guttman scale, a respondent who endorses any item will endorse all items having scale values lower than that of the item. As with Bogardus's social distance procedure, scalogram analysis is designed to yield a cumulative, ordinal scale. Conditions for a true cumulative scale can occasionally be found with cognitive test items, but they rarely occur with attitude statements and other affective items. Guttman knew this, but he felt that the conditions for a true scale could often be approximated. The extent to which a true scale is obtained by scalogram analysis can be determined from a statistic known as the *reproducibility coefficient* (R). R is a measure of the degree to which the statements answered by a respondent in the positive (+) and negative (–) directions can be estimated from the total number of positive responses made by the respondent.

Box 2.2 is an illustrative response matrix for computing the reproducibility coefficient for a seven-statement Guttman attitude scale administered to 10 respondents. We begin by arranging the respondents (rows) in order according to the total number of "+" responses given to each statement, where "+" indicates agreement with, acceptance, or approval of a particular attitude statement and "–" indicates the opposite. The number (p) of "+" responses in each of the statement columns is then counted, and a dividing line is drawn under the row corresponding to the pth response from the top of the column. For example, there are nine "+" responses in the column for Statement 5, so a

---

Box 2.2
Response Matrix for Computing the Reproducibility
Coefficient of an Illustrative Seven-Item Guttman Scale

	Statement							
Respondent	*3*	*1*	*7*	*6*	*5*	*4*	*2*	*Number "+"*
I	+	+	+	+	+	+	+	7
B	+	+	+	+	+	−	+	6
A	−	+	+	−	+	−	+	4
E	−	+	+	−	+	−	+	4
H	−	+	+	−	+	+	−	4
J	−	+	+	−	+	−	+	4
D	−	+	+	−	+	−	−	3
C	−	−	+	−	+	−	−	2
F	+	−	−	−	−	−	−	1
G	−	−	−	−	+	−	−	1
Number "+"	3	7	8	2	9	2	5	
Errors	2	0	0	0	2	2	2	

line is drawn under the ninth entry in that column. In a perfect Guttman scale, all responses above this line would be "+" and all those below it would be "−." Because the "−" response in the ninth row and the "+" response in the 10th row are deviations from this perfect pattern, they are counted as errors. Consequently, there are two errors for Statement 5. The number of errors for the remaining statements are determined similarly, yielding a total of $E = 8$ errors for all seven statements combined. Next we compute the total number of responses as the number of statements (rows) times the number of respondents (columns), or $N = $ rows $\times$ columns $= 10 \times 7 = 70$. Finally, the reproducibility coefficient (R) is computed from the formula

$$R = 1 - E/N \qquad (2.1)$$

as $1 - 8/70 = .886$. Because the lowest acceptable value of R for a true Guttman scale is .90, these seven statements do not form a true Guttman scale.

Other Attitude-Scaling Methods

In addition to equal-appearing intervals (Thurstone), summated ratings (Likert), and scalogram analysis (Guttman), a variety of other methods for constructing attitude inventories and scales have been devised. Among these are the semantic differential technique, Q-sort, magnitude estimation, expectancy-value scaling, facet analysis, and factor analysis.

Semantic Differential

Often viewed as yielding less obtrusive measures of attitudes than traditional attitude-scaling procedures, the *semantic differential* technique was devised originally by Osgood, Suci, and Tannenbaum (1957) to study the connotative meanings of concepts. The technique focuses on the evaluative aspect of attitudes, but it may be used to measure attitudes toward multidimensional as well as unidimensional concepts.

The data consist of ratings given by respondents to a series of concepts on each of several 7-point scales. The concepts may refer to people, institutions, sociopolitical issues, or other kinds of attitudinal targets. The 7-point scales may include such bipolar adjectives as *bad-good*, *weak-strong*, and *slow-fast*, although the evaluative dimension (bad vs. good) is most common on semantic differential attitude scales. For example, a respondent whose attitude toward the concept of *politics* is that it is fairly bad and fairly strong, but neutral in terms of its fastness or slowness might rate it as follows:

Politics

Bad	___	✔	___	___	___	___	___	Good
Weak	___	___	___	___	___	✔	___	Strong
Slow	___	___	___	✔	___	___	___	Fast

Responses on the bipolar adjectival scales can be added to obtain an overall attitude score. Alternatively, and more complexly, each of several concepts toward which attitudes are to be assessed may be scored on several semantic dimensions, such as *evaluation, potency,* and *activity,* and compared with the respondent's ratings on other concepts. A graphical plot of the respondent's scores on each semantic dimension yields a semantic space; concepts that are close to each other in the semantic space have similar connotative meanings for the respondent.

Q-Sort

In the *Q-sort* technique for assessing attitudes (Stephenson, 1953), respondents sort a large number of cards into 9 (or 11) piles. Each card contains a statement expressing an attitude—ranging from highly negative to highly positive—toward a specified object or event. The sorting procedure is similar to the first stage of the equal-appearing intervals method, but the respondent is directed to sort the statements in such a way that the number of cards placed in all piles approximates a normal frequency distribution. Although Stephenson (1953) felt that the resulting data should be subjected to factor analysis, there has been some disagreement regarding the appropriate data analysis procedure. Kerlinger's (1972) study of liberals and conservatives illustrates the use of factor analysis with Q-sort data and is recommended reading for anyone planning to assess political attitudes by means of this technique.

Magnitude Estimation

Magnitude estimation, which is based on a psychophysical procedure for scaling stimulus intensities, requires the respondent to assign a numerical value to a series of stimuli varying across a range of intensities. The averaged responses of a representative sample of people are then plotted against the actual stimulus intensities. A similar procedure has been used to scale perceptions of events such as the seriousness of various criminal offenses (Sellin & Wolfgang, 1964). The ratings given to the events are then plotted against a measure of actual values, such as the monetary cost of an offense. Magnitude estimation has also been used to scale other social perceptions or attitudes such as the popularity of political candidates, for example, by having respondents draw a line whose length reflects the strength of their feelings or attitudes toward the person, object, or event.

Expectancy-Value (E-V) Scaling

In this multidimensional approach to attitude scaling (Fishbein & Ajzen, 1975), the respondent is first asked to indicate the extent to which he or she approves of a set of affective or value dimensions (the "affective" or "value" component). The respondent is next asked to indicate the extent to which he or she believes that each of these dimensions applies to the issue under consideration (the "cognitive" or "expectancy" component). Combining each expectancy (E) with its corresponding value (V) yields an E-V score. For example, in one study preferences between various energy technologies (nuclear, fossil fuel, tidal power, etc.) were evaluated. Respondents began by indicating their degree of liking or disliking for each of the following relevant dimensions: low cost, low risk of catastrophe, low long- and short-term pollution, and favorable technological spin-off. Next the respondents indicated, in terms of a probability figure, the extent to which each of these dimensions characterized each of the technologies. Favored technologies were identified by high probabilities and disfavored technologies were identified by low probabilities being assigned on most or all of the dimensions. The product of the liking score and the probability figure was a measure of the contribution of each dimension to the overall evaluation of a particular technology.

Facet Analysis

One criticism of scalogram analysis, which applies to the methods of equal-appearing intervals and summated ratings as well, is that attitudes are complex, multidimensional states that can rarely be represented by a single score. Another criticism is that the dimensionality of an attitude scale can vary with the sample of respondents. In any event, Guttman's (1968, 1982) subsequent research on attitude measurement, which he labeled smallest space analysis or facet analysis, bears little resemblance to his earlier interest in scalogram analysis. *Facet analysis* is a complex, a priori, multidimensional paradigm for item construction and analysis that can be applied to any attitude object or situation (Castro & Jordan, 1977). The procedure has been used to construct cross-cultural attitude-behavior scales regarding a number of psychosocial conditions and situations, including mental retardation and racial-ethnic interaction (Hamersma, Paige, & Jordan, 1973).

Factor Analysis

During the past few decades, it has become increasingly apparent that attitude measurement is multidimensional in the strict sense of the term and that more complex assessment procedures are required. A trend away from unidimensional scales is evident in the increasing use of such methods as *multidimensional scaling, latent structure analysis*, latent partition analysis, and the repertory grid technique in the scaling of attitudes (see Ostrom, Bond, Krosnick, & Sedikides, 1994; Procter, 1993). In addition, the use of factor analysis in constructing attitude scales and analyzing scores on these instruments is now fairly commonplace.

Factor analysis is a statistical procedure for analyzing responses to a set of instruments (items, tests, etc.) to determine the underlying factors and their importance in accounting for the relationships among the variables measured by the instruments. There are several steps in a complete factor analysis:

1. Computation of the matrix of correlations among the variables

2. Extracting the factors that account for a large percentage of the variance in scores on the variables

3. Rotating the extracted factor matrix to simplify its structure so the factors can be interpreted

4. Computing the score of each person on each factor

The details of these steps and procedures for computing the relevant statistics are described in various sources (e.g., Harris, 2001; Norušis, 1992). The result of Step 2 is an $m \times p$ matrix of loadings of the p factors on the m variables. The magnitude of the loading of each factor on each variable is a measure of the contribution of that factor to that variable.

Although the number of common factors needed to provide an adequate description of the relationships among the p factors and the m variables are determined at Step 2, the resulting factor pattern matrix of the loadings of the factors on the variables rarely permits the most meaningful interpretation of the factors. To provide a clearer interpretation of the extracted factors, the factor pattern matrix must be simplified by rotating to achieve a simple structure in which a large number of loadings of each factor on the m variables are zero or near zero. Various methods of factor rotation have been devised; the particular method used depends on the researcher's theoretical orientation, the characteristics of the data and statistics, and whether the analysis is an exploratory or confirmatory one.

As a simple illustration of an exploratory factor analysis, let's conduct a principal axis factor analysis and an associated varimax rotation of the extracted factor matrix on the responses of a large national sample of people to the following seven questions concerned with attitudes toward abortion (Davis & Smith, 1994):

Do you think it should be possible for a pregnant woman to obtain a *legal* abortion if

Q$_1$. the woman wants it for any reason? Yes = 1, No = 2

Q$_2$. there is a strong chance of serious defect to the baby?
Yes = 1, No = 2

Q$_3$. the woman's own health is seriously endangered by the pregnancy?
Yes = 1, No = 2

Q$_4$. she is married and does not want any more children? Yes = 1, No = 2

Q$_5$. the family has a very low income and cannot afford any more children? Yes = 1, No = 2

Q$_6$. she became pregnant because of rape? Yes = 1, No = 2

Q$_7$. she is not married and does not want to marry the man?
Yes = 1, No = 2

The loadings of these seven questions on the two extracted factors are listed in Table 2.2. These two factors account for over 80% of the variance in the scores on the seven variables.

To interpret the rotated factor matrix in Table 2.2, we begin by identifying those variables having high loadings (greater than .50) on a factor. Variables Q_1, Q_4, Q_5, and Q_7 have high loadings on Factor 1, whereas variables Q_2, Q_3, and Q_6 have high loadings on Factor 2. Referring to the seven questions listed above, we see that the four variables with high loadings on Factor 1 involve nonmedical or nontraumatic reasons, whereas the three variables with high loadings on Factor 2 involve medical or traumatic reasons. Therefore, the construct measured by Questions 1, 4, 5, and 7 may be labeled "nontraumatic reasons" for abortion, and the construct measured by Questions 2, 3, and 6 may be labeled "traumatic reasons" for abortion.[1]

Reliability, Validity, and Norms

As with any kind of psychological assessment instrument, the practical value of measures of attitudes depends on their reliability, validity, and adequacy of standardization. In view of the careless way in which many attitude inventories and scales have been constructed, it is not surprising that adequate psychometric information on these instruments is unavailable.

Reliability

Reliability, the extent to which the scores obtained by administering a psychometric instrument are consistent and thereby relatively free from errors of measurement, is a critical characteristic of an attitude scale. As is true of most measures of affective variables, the *reliability coefficients* of attitude scales are usually lower than those of cognitive measures. However, test-retest and *internal consistency* coefficients of .80 and .90 for Thurstone- and Likert-type scales are not unusual. These relatively high reliability coefficients may be attributable in part to a strong general factor in what these scales measure. Reasonably accurate estimates of reliability for attitude scales that are fairly homogeneous with respect to item type may be obtained by computing internal consistency (*split-half* or *alpha*) coefficients as well as coefficients of *stability* (test-retest) and *equivalence* (*alternate forms*).

In addition to actual changes in attitudes produced by some manipulated condition, a number of situational and procedural variables can affect the reliability of an attitude instrument. Among these are conditions of

TABLE 2.2 Rotated Factor Matrix for Seven Abortion Questions

Question	Factor 1	Factor 2
Q_1	.90004	.20859
Q_2	.28142	.82166
Q_3	.11874	.87146
Q_4	.89823	.23640
Q_5	.88661	.25674
Q_6	.28216	.80809
Q_7	.90344	.23362

administration, number of response categories, and method of scoring. Standardization of a psychometric instrument implies standard, uniform conditions of administration. Nevertheless, it is frequently impossible to keep conditions of administration constant when attitude data are collected in many different situations. Because reliability implies consistency of differentiations among persons, the reliability of a psychometric instrument tends to be lower when the conditions under which the instrument is administered have different effects on the scores of different people. For example, the scores of younger children are affected more than those of older children by variations in conditions of administering attitude scales. Consequently, it is not surprising that the obtained reliability coefficients of attitude scale scores increase with the chronological age of children and adolescents.

Another factor that may influence the reliability of an attitude scale is the number of response categories. Scores on instruments with a larger number of item response categories tend to have larger variances, and hence higher reliabilities, than scores on instruments with smaller numbers of response categories. This is one possible reason why scores on Likert-type scales tend to be more reliable than those on Thurstone-type scales. There is, however, a limit to how much reliability can be raised by increasing the number of response categories. Although it may seem reasonable that increasing the number of response categories beyond 5 would have a significant effect on reliability, this it not generally true. Likert-type scales with 6, 9, or even 19 response categories do not have appreciably greater reliability coefficients than those with the traditional 5 categories. It appears that when an attitude scale has a large number of categories, respondents are unable to make the finer discriminations required and therefore use only some of the categories.

A possible exception to this rule occurs when the range of attitudes toward the content being measured is small, in which case increasing the number of response categories to 6 or 7 can have a small enhancing effect on reliability (Masters, 1974).

It has also been suggested that increasing the number of response categories can improve the overall reliability if responses are transformed to normal deviate (z) scores (Wolins & Dickinson, 1973). This technique is one of the many efforts to raise the reliability and validity of attitude measures by some kind of item-weighting or component-weighting procedure. Unfortunately, none of the various differential weighting schemes have been found superior, with respect to their reliability, to more traditional scoring procedures. This is particularly true when the number of items on the single-score instrument is large.

On certain kinds of attitude items, including some Thurstone-type scales, there is a middle or neutral response category (?, don't know, uncertain, etc.) in addition to the bipolar yes/no categories. Use of this neutral category by respondents varies with the instructions, the context, and the type of attitude object. Alwin and Krosnick (1991) found, however, that the reliability of multicategory measures of sociopolitical attitudes was not enhanced by explicitly providing a "don't know" option. On the other hand, on two- and three-category formats, inclusion of a neutral response category may improve reliability somewhat (Aiken, 1983). For this reason, inclusion of a neutral response category is generally recommended on scales that otherwise would have only dichotomous item scoring.

Measures of attitudes usually consist of more than two categories, but many questionnaires administered in survey research attempt to assess attitudes, values, opinions, or beliefs toward each of a series of things by means of a series of dichotomous questions or statements (yes-no, true-false, etc.). In such cases, where each instrument consists of only one item, traditional test-retest, split-half, and *parallel-forms reliability* coefficients are inappropriate. One procedure for estimating the consistency (reliability) of responses to single attitude or opinion items on questionnaires is to repeat the items, or variants of them, at different places in the questionnaire and compare the responses to items at different locations. Coefficients such as *gamma* and Somer's *d* provide appropriate measures of consistency of responding in such cases.

To evaluate the consistency with which two or more judges or raters evaluate persons, objects, or events in terms of two or more categories, an *intraclass* (interrater, interobserver) coefficient or a coefficient of *concordance* may be computed. Another popular index of agreement among judges or other observers in their evaluations is the *kappa* coefficient. Procedures for computing all of these coefficients may be found in psychometrics or intermediate statistics books (see also Aiken, 1997).

Validity

The *validity* of any cognitive or psychometric assessment instrument is the extent to which the instrument measures what it was designed to measure. Validity depends, of course, on reliability, in that reliability sets an upper bound on validity: the correlation between scores on a psychometric instrument and true scores on the underlying conceptual variable cannot be higher than the reliability of the instrument. The *validity coefficient* of an instrument may be substantially lower than the reliability of either the predictor or criterion variable, but it cannot be higher than the reliability coefficient of either variable.

Both the reliability and validity of measures of attitudes, values, opinions, and beliefs are limited by conditions that introduce measurement errors. Among the factors that can produce measurement errors on measures of attitudes and other affective instruments are *response sets* and faking. *Response sets* are tendencies to respond in relatively fixed or stereotyped ways, such as answering "true" to ambiguous statements or questions (*acquiescence response set*) or providing what is perceived as a more socially acceptable response (*social desirability response set*) than an honest response.

As with other psychometric instruments, there are three kinds of evidence for the validity of measures of attitudes, values, opinions, and beliefs: content validity, criterion-related validity, and construct validity. *Content validity* refers to the representativeness of the sample of questions on an instrument with regard to the entire domain with which the instrument is concerned. The content validity of a psychometric instrument is determined by having a group of people who are thoroughly knowledgeable with respect to the subject matter of the instrument examine it carefully and make judgments as to the validity of its content. Information concerning the *criterion-related validity* of a psychometric instrument is obtained by correlating scores on the instrument with another measure of the variable obtained at the same time (*concurrent validity*) or at a later date (*predictive validity*). Although the resulting criterion-related validity coefficients computed from measures of attitudes or values are usually fairly modest, when combined with scores on ability tests they frequently make a small but significant contribution to the prediction of performance on the criterion. Higher correlations between attitudinal predictors and behavioral criteria are obtained when the statements on the attitude instrument are expressed in behavioral terms.

The first step in designing an attitude instrument—identification of the theoretical construct to be measured—is often neglected. Only after a construct has been identified is the investigator ready to search for a measure of it among available instruments or to design a new measure. The most general method of determining whether a given instrument actually measures the appropriate variable is to search for evidence of its construct validity. The *construct validity* of any psychometric instrument is concerned with the process by which the instrument is shown to measure a particular psychological *construct*. To establish the construct validity of the instrument, it must be demonstrated that scores on the instrument are related to scores on other psychometric instruments and to patterns of behavior in ways that are consistent with a theory concerning the operation of the particular construct.

Construct validity cannot be evaluated by a single procedure. Various kinds of evidence must be sought: expert opinion, correlations of scores with other measures of the same construct, and comparing the scores of people who obviously possess a high amount of the construct with the scores of people who have a low amount of it.

Standardization and Norms

To be meaningful, scores on attitude inventories and other psychometric devices must be interpreted with respect to the subjective standards that qualified people hold regarding good and poor, normal and deviant performance. These standards are developed by experience with the purposes of the instrument and the resulting expectations regarding high and low scores. Unfortunately, even highly experienced evaluators frequently disagree in their interpretations of scores on inventories, questionnaires, and scales.

Quite early in the history of psychological assessment it became clear that a more objective means of evaluating scores on both cognitive and affective assessment instruments was needed. Because dependence on one's unrecorded experience with the performance of a large sample of individuals on a test or other measuring instrument was found to be undependable, the practice of administering the instrument to a large sample of people who were representative of the (target) population with which the instrument was to be used was instituted. To control for differences in age, grade level, ethnicity, and other demographic variables that are conceivably related to scores on psychometric instruments, proportional samples of examinees were selected at random from the various levels or strata comprising those variables.

Because variations in examiner characteristics and other conditions of administration may have significant effects on scores, standardized tests, inventories, and scales should be administered under controlled, standard conditions. After an instrument is administered, it is scored and a frequency distribution of the scores is constructed. Finally, the scores are converted to various types of *norms*, so the performance of future examinees can be interpreted by comparing their scores with the norms. In interpreting a person's score(s), it is important to make certain that the norms tables with which the score is compared have been constructed from the scores of samples of individuals who are similar to the person in terms of significant demographic characteristics (age, grade level, sex, etc.).

Among the different kinds of norms found in psychological test and inventory manuals are age norms, grade norms, percentile norms, and standard scores norms. *Age norms* are determined by calculating the median score on a test or inventory made by persons of a given chronological age. For example, if the median score of children who were 10 years 5 months old when they completed an attitude inventory is 60, then the age norm of a person who makes a score of 60 on the inventory is 10 years 5 months.

In contrast to age norms, *grade norms* are computed by determining the median score made by students in a particular grade. For example, if the median score attained by children in the 6th month of the fourth grade is 55, then the grade norm of an individual making a score of 55 is 4.6. Note that grade norms are expressed in years and 10ths of a year, the assumption being that there is no change in the variable being measured during the summer months.

Although age and grade norms are popular ways of interpreting scores on standardized achievement tests in particular, they are rarely used in standardizing measures of attitudes or other affective variables. Much more popular as a method of converting and interpreting raw scores on measures of attitudes, values, and personality characteristics are percentile norms. A *percentile norm* corresponding to a particular raw score is equal to the percentage of people in the *standardization* group who made that score or lower. Thus, if 60% of the standardization group made a raw score of 75 or less, then the percentile rank of a person who makes a raw score of 75 on the assessment instrument is 60. It should be cautioned, however, that in converting test scores to percentile ranks one should make certain that the standardization group on which the norms were determined is an appropriate frame of reference for evaluating the raw scores of people to whom the instrument is administered.

Unlike the ordinal-level properties of percentile norms, *standard scores* are interval-level (but not ratio-level) measures. All standard scores are based on z scores, defined as

$$z = (\overline{X} - X)/s, \qquad (2.2)$$

where X is the raw score and $\overline{X}$ and s are the mean and standard deviation of the raw scores. Because z scores may be either positive or negative decimal numbers, a further conversion is usually made by multiplying them by some convenient integer and adding another integer to the product. For example, T

scores are computed by multiplying z scores by 10 and adding 50 to the products.

Because raw scores on most attitude inventories and scales represent measurement at no higher than an ordinal level, it can be argued that it is inappropriate to convert raw scores on such instruments to standard z or T scores. However, if one prefers to adhere to the letter of the statistical law, arithmetic means, standard deviations, correlation coefficients, regression analyses, analyses of variance, and all other statistical methods that assume interval-level measurements would be barred in analyzing scores on measures of attitudes, values, and other psychosocial or personality variables. However, it can be argued that the results of applying inferential statistical procedures are affected more by violations of the distributional assumptions (normality, homogeneity of variance, etc.) underlying the procedure than by the level of measurement of the data being analyzed. It may be that violations of those assumptions are more likely to occur with ordinal-level data, but parametric statistical procedures such as t tests and analysis of variance are robust, in that violations of the underlying assumptions do not typically have a profound effect on the obtained results. However, when the frequency distribution of raw scores in the population underlying the obtained scores cannot be assumed to be approximately normal or if other assumptions underlying parametric statistical procedures cannot be met, it is probably wise to transform the scores or to use *nonparametric* statistical procedures that do not assume interval-level scaling or normality of population scores.

Illustrative Instruments and Sources

Many different inventories and scales for assessing social attitudes (Robinson et al., 1991), political attitudes (Robinson et al., 1999), and occupational attitudes (Robinson et al., 1974) are described in a series of books published by the Institute for Social Research at the University of Michigan. A representative sampling of instruments is given in Appendix 2.1, and reviews of many of them may be found in the *Mental Measurements Yearbooks* (*MMYB*) and *Test Critiques* (*TC*). Many of the professional journals in psychology and other behavioral sciences also publish reviews of measures of attitudes, values, beliefs, and opinions.

Other sources of information on measures of attitudes, values, beliefs, and opinions are the *American Social Attitudes Data Sourcebook, 1947-78* (Converse, Dotson, Hoag, & McGee, 1980), *A Sourcebook of Harris National Surveys: Repeated Questions, 1963-76* (Martin & McDuffee, 1981), *Measures of Personality and Social Psychological Attitudes* (Robinson et al., 1991), and *Measures of Political Attitudes* (Robinson et al., 1999). Dozens of attitude measures in a wide range of areas are also listed in *Tests in Microfiche* (Educational Testing Service), in Volume 5 of the ETS Test Collection Catalog (Web site www.ets.org), and at the Web site ericae.net/testcol.htm. Another source of information on published inventories, questionnaires, and scales of attitudes and values consists of publishers and distributors of psychosocial assessment instruments (see Appendix A).

As with ad hoc measures of attitudes, many questionnaires and inventories for measuring values, beliefs, and opinions have been designed for specific research purposes or applications and are not commercially available. However, a number of values inventories and scales are commercially available from organizations listed in Appendix A. Several of these instruments are described in Appendix 2.1. With respect to measures of beliefs, a host of health-related beliefs scales are available, including beliefs regarding gender roles (Kerr & Holden, 1996), health in general (e.g., Bates, Fitzgerald, & Wolinsky, 1994), and specific health problems or habits such as addiction (Schaler, 1995), AIDS (Zagummy & Brady, 1998), dieting (Stotland & Zuroff, 1990), and osteoporosis (Kim, Horan, Gendler, & Patel, 1991). Measures of religious (e.g., Hunt, 1993) and spiritual (e.g., Hatch, Burg, Naberhaus, & Hellmich, 1998; Schaler, 1996) beliefs are also available. One of the most popular of all beliefs scales is the Paranormal Belief Scale (e.g., Hartman, 1999; Lange, Irwin, & Houran, 2000; Lawrence & De Cicco, 1997)

Recommended Readings

Aiken, L. R. (1996). *Rating scales & checklists: Evaluating behavior, personality, and attitudes.* New York: John Wiley.

Aiken, L. R. (1997). *Questionnaires & inventories: Surveying opinions and assessing personality.* New York: John Wiley.

Alwin, D. F., & Krosnick, J. A. (1991). The reliability of survey attitude measurement. *Sociological Methods & Research, 20,* 139-181.

Fabrigar, L. R., & Krosnick, J. A. (1995). Attitude measurement and questionnaire design. In A. S. R. Manstead & M. Hewstone (Eds.), *The Blackwell encyclopedia of psychology* (pp. 42-47). Oxford, UK: Basil Blackwell.

Himmelfarb, S. (1993). The measurement of attitudes. In A. H. Eagly & S. L. Chaiken (Eds.), *The psychology of attitudes* (pp. 23-87). Fort Worth, TX: Harcourt Brace Jovanovich.

Krebs, D., & Schmidt, P. (1993). *New directions in attitude measurement.* New York: Walter de Gruyter.

Schwartz, N., Groves, R. M., & Schuman, H. (1998). Survey methods. In D. T. Gilbert, S. T. Fiske, & G. Lindzey (Eds.), *The handbook of social psychology* (4th ed., Vol. 1, pp. 143-179). New York: McGraw-Hill/Oxford.

Note

1. Although the factor interpretation procedure described here is the traditional one, some authorities have argued that factor interpretation should be based on the factor score coefficients rather than the salient factor loadings from factor rotation (see Grice & Harris, 1998; Harris, 2001). In addition, the factor score coefficients of the jth factor ($j = 1$ to p) on the ith variable ($i = 1$ to m) may be multiplied by the standard (z) score of a given person on each variable to obtain the person's score on that factor.

Appendix 2.1

Representative Published
Measures of Attitudes and Values

Attitude Survey Program for Business and Industry: Organization Survey (NCS London House). Measures attitudes of hourly employees and first-time supervisors toward an organization. Provides an overview of the organization and reasons for low morale, low productivity, and absenteeism. Assesses acceptance of change and determines training needs.

Attitude Toward Guns and Violence Questionnaire (AGVQ) (J. P. Shapiro; Western Psychological Services). Ages 6-29 years, 26 items, 5-10 minutes, third-grade reading level. Measures attitudes toward guns, physical aggression, and interpersonal conflict.

Attitude Towards Disabled Persons Scale (H. E. Yuker & J. R. Block; Center for the Study of Attitudes Toward Persons With Disabilities, Hofstra University). Measures attitudes of students and adults toward disabled persons.

Career Anchors: Discovering Your Real Values, Revised Edition (E. H. Schein; Pfeiffer and Company International Publishers). Designed to assist in determining dominant themes and patterns in a person's life, understanding his or her approach to work and career, and finding reasons for choices made and steps taken to fulfill his or her self-image.

Career Attitudes and Strategies Inventory (CASI): An Inventory for Understanding Adult Careers (J. L. Holland & G. D. Gottfredson; Psychological Assessment Resources). Assesses employee's current work situation, including common attitudes and strategies for coping with job, family, coworkers, and supervisors.

Career Orientation Placement and Evaluation Survey (L. F. Knapp & R. R. Knapp; EdITS). Designed to measure personal values related to the type of work one chooses and the satisfaction derived from it.

Hall-Tonna Inventory of Values (B. P. Hall & B. Tonna; Behaviordyne, Palo Alto, CA). For identifying value priorities and the skills needed for future growth in this area.

Rokeach Values Survey (M. Rokeach; Consulting Psychologists Press). Assesses the relative importance of 18 *instrumental values* and 18 *terminal values* to the respondent.

Sales Attitude Checklist (E. K. Taylor; NCS London House). Measures the attitudes and behaviors of sales applicants toward selling.

School Environment Preference Survey (L. V. Gordon; EdITS). Assesses commitment to a set of attitudes, values, and behaviors that are preparatory for entry into many areas of the world of work and that are fostered and rewarded in most school settings.

Sex-Role Egalitarianism Scale (SRES) (L. A. King & D. W. King; Sigma Assessment Systems). Measures attitudes toward the equality of men and women and judgments about both men and women assuming nontraditional roles.

Study Attitudes and Methods Survey (SAMS) (W. B. Michael, J. J. Michael, & W. S. Zimmerman; EdITS). Designed to assess dimensions of a motivational, noncognitive nature that are related to school achievement and that contribute to student performance beyond what is measured by traditional ability tests.

Survey of Interpersonal Values (L. V. Gordon; NCS London House). Measures six values (support, conformity, recognition, independence, benevolence, and leadership) involving relationships with others that are important in many work situations.

Survey of Personal Values (L. V. Gordon; NCS London House). Measures six values (practical-mindedness, achievement, variety, decisiveness, orderliness, and goal orientation) that influence the manner in which people cope with problems and choices of everyday living; provides information about how people are likely to approach jobs or training programs.

Survey of Work Values, Revised, Form U (authored and published by Bowling Green State University). Designed to identify attitudes toward work by means of six 9-item scales: Pride in Work, Social Status of Job, Attitude Toward Earnings, Activity Preference, Upward Striving, and Job Involvement.

Values Inventory (W. J. Reddin & K. Rowell; Organizational Tests Ltd.). Designed to reveal a manager's value system by measures of seven value scores: theoretical, power, effectiveness, achievement, human, industry, and profit.

Values Scale (2nd ed.) (D. E. Super & D. D. Nevill; Consulting Psychologists Press). Measures extrinsic and intrinsic values related to career development and most personally satisfying career.

Work Attitudes Questionnaire (M. S. Doty & N. E. Betz; Marathon Consulting & Press). Measures commitment to work and the degree to which such commitment is psychologically healthy or unhealthy; may be used to identify "workaholics."

3

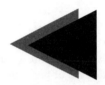

Attitude Formation and Change

Genetics and Experience
Heredity
Concepts and Theories of Learning

Consistency Theories
Balance Theory
Cognitive Dissonance Theory
Self-Perception Theory

Other Concepts and Theories
Causal Attributions of Behavior
Dual-Process Models

Practical Procedures for Changing Attitudes
Fear Arousal
Behavioral and Cognitive Techniques
Communication and Persuasion
Other Approaches to Persuasion
Resistance to Change

Chapter 1 deals with the definitions and historical background of the construct of attitudes in particular, but also with the related psychosocial concepts of values, opinions, and beliefs. Recognizing the importance, for both theoretical and applied studies, of how these constructs are assessed, Chapter 2 is devoted to psychometric theories and methods of measuring them. There are, of course, many other issues regarding attitudes and related constructs than what they mean and how they are measured. For example, what are the origins of attitudes? Are they formed mostly on the basis of hearsay, or is it necessary to have direct experience with the attitude object? Hearsay can and does have a marked influence on attitude formation, especially when the source of information is highly admired or respected. However, it seems reasonable that attitudes based on direct experience, particularly those that are extremely important to the individual and in which he or she has a personal or vested interest, would be stronger, more persistent, and more easily accessible than attitudes resulting from hearsay evidence (Crano, 1995, 1997; Kraus, 1995).

Crano (1997) reasoned that one's vested interest in a situation or issue, that is, one's view that it is personally significant or important, will affect the relationship between the individual's attitude toward the issue and his or her behavior. It was hypothesized that the higher the vested interest of persons in the issue of school busing to achieve racial integration, the more accurately would their measured attitudes toward busing predict their presidential choice—McGovern, who was in favor of busing, or Nixon, who was against it—in the 1972 election. As illustrated in Figure 3.1, the research findings confirmed the hypothesis: the higher person's vested interest in the busing issue, the more accurately did that individual's attitude toward busing predict his or her choice of presidential candidate.

The present chapter is concerned primarily with attitude development and change and the effects of attitudes on behavior. With respect to their effects on behavior, what are the consequences of accessible, strongly held, persistent, and generalized attitudes for individuals, groups, and society at large? Hardly surprising is the research finding that the stronger and more accessible attitudes are, the more likely are their effects on behavior (Petkova, Ajzen, & Driver, 1995). Of particular importance to salespersons, politicians, and teachers is the question of how attitudes, values, beliefs, and opinions can be modified or changed. For example, what are the roles of counterexperience, imitation (modeling), and persuasion in changing attitudes and beliefs?

Genetics and Experience

It is a truism that, like personality characteristics in general, attitudes and values are made, not born. But as we shall see, where and what people come from can also affect their perceptions and evaluations of their experiences and what they decide to do about those experiences. As with other aspects of human personality, attitudes are a product of heredity and environment.

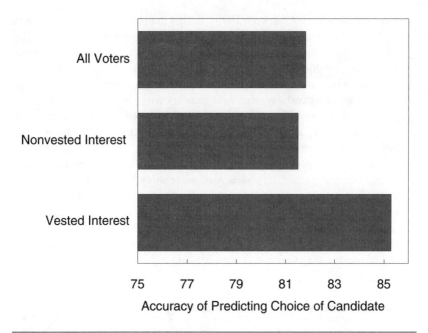

Figure 3.1. Accuracy of Predicting Voting Behavior From Attitudes Toward Busing in Groups Having Vested and Nonvested Interests in the Busing Issue

SOURCE: Based on data from Crano (1997).
NOTE: The higher the participant's vested interest in the busing issue, the more accurately did that person's attitude toward busing predict his or her choice of presidential candidate.

Heredity

Correlational evidence for the role of genetic factors on both cognitive abilities and affective variables (temperament, mood, etc.) is impressive (see Bouchard, 1994; Bouchard, Lykken, McGue, Segal, & Tellegen, 1990). Research results point to the influence of heredity in determining a variety of attitudes, including attitudes toward eating (Klump, McGue, & Iacono, 2000; Rutherford, McGuffin, Katz, & Murray, 1993; Wade, Neale, Lake, & Martin, 1999), attitudes toward jobs (Arvey, Bouchard, Segal, & Abraham, 1989; Hershberger, Lichtenstein, & Knox, 1994; Keller, Bouchard, Arvey, Segal, & Dawis, 1992), and attitudes toward religion (D'Onofrio, Eaves, Murrelle, Maes, & Spilka, 1999; Waller, Kojetin, Bouchard, Lykken, & Tellegen, 1990). Attitudinal variables differ in their heritabilities, and those with higher heritability coefficients[1] appear to exert a stronger influence on behavior and to be less changeable than those with lower heritabilities

(Crelia & Tesser, 1996; Tesser, 1998). Rather than have a direct genetic link, the heritable component of attitudes is probably mediated by personality traits, physical characteristics, academic achievement, and other individual difference variables (Olson, Vernon, Harris, & Jang, 2001).

Somewhere on the borderline between traditional personality traits and attitudes are other variables that have been shown to be subject to significant genetic influences. Among these more general variables are alienation, altruism, sociability, and traditionalism (Buss & Plomin, 1984; Tellegen et al., 1988). However, the influence of heredity on these variables, and on more object- or event-specific attitudes as well, may be an indirect consequence of heredity exerting its effects by way of more directly determined cognitive and temperament variables (general and specific mental abilities, activity level, emotionality, etc.). Attitudes, in turn, have also been found to be related to other personality variables. For example, Maltby (1997) and Lewis and Maltby (1994) documented a connection between religious attitudes and the personality variable of obsessionality.

Concepts and Theories of Learning

Although there is ample evidence that attitudes may be acquired or changed merely by repeated exposure to a novel or unfamiliar stimulus (Bornstein, 1989), most research on attitude formation has focused on the learning process. Attitudes may be stimuli or responses, causes or consequences of the learning process. They may be goads or prompters of learning, learned cognitions and feelings, or rewards or punishments administered to change someone's behavior.

The process of attitude formation is generally viewed as social learning influenced by parents, peers, and other sources of information and control. Attitudes begin developing in childhood and become crystallized to some extent in adulthood, but they may continue to undergo modification even in later life (Kuh, 1976; Tyler & Schuller, 1991). According to *social learning theory*, people learn attitudes by observing and imitating (modeling) the behavior of others (Bandura, 1977). In general, by the time a person reaches adulthood, he or she has acquired a set of subjective standards or a frame of reference for evaluating his or her experiences. These standards and attitudes are influenced by the person's emotional ties of affiliation, loyalty, and security acquired by associating with other people. The number of these associations and consequently the sources of influence on attitudes expand as a person grows to maturity. As children mature, their attitudes, although typically remaining somewhat similar to those of their parents, become more like those of their age-mates and other people in their expanding social world.

Classical Conditioning

Two types of elementary learning that have been investigated with respect to their roles in the formation of attitudes are classical conditioning and operant conditioning. The basic notion of *classical conditioning*, as applied to the acquisition of an attitude, is that a person acquires a new attitude toward something that is repeatedly paired with a pleasurable or painful stimulus *regardless of what the person does* (see Figure 3.2). Positive feelings or attitudes are developed toward stimuli that are accompanied by pleasurable experiences, and negative feelings or attitudes are developed toward stimuli that are accompanied by painful experiences. For example, a toddler is likely to develop a negative attitude toward dogs if dogs snarl and show their teeth when the child approaches, but positive attitudes if dogs wag their tails and nuzzle the child's hand. By the time the child has acquired the rudiments of language, much of the first-order conditioning of this sort has been superseded by higher-order conditioning, in which a former conditioned stimulus now becomes an unconditioned stimulus. For example, young children develop positive attitudes toward people who use "pleasant words" such as "nice boy" or "good girl" without necessarily giving presents or privileges as well.

The question of whether attitudes can be acquired by classical conditioning without conscious awareness or belief on the part of the person has been a controversial one (see Fishbein & Middlestadt, 1997; Haugtvedt, 1997; Schwarz, 1997). According to a noncognitive explanation of how attitudes are acquired by classical conditioning, affective responses elicited by an unconditioned stimulus become conditioned, without conscious awareness or intention by the individual, to any stimulus that is repeatedly paired with that stimulus. The counterposition is that conditioning cannot occur without the person being aware of the connection between the conditioned and unconditioned stimuli. Support for the latter proposition was provided by Page (1969), who found significant conditioning effects only when the participant reported an awareness of the contingency between the conditioned and unconditioned stimulation.

The results of a number of recent research investigations indicate that attitudes have both affective and cognitive components and that a purely cognitive explanation of attitude formation and change is inadequate. For example, Krosnick, Betz, Jussim, and Lynn (1992) found that subliminally presented photographs that were associated with positive affect resulted in more positive attitudes toward people in the photographs than did subliminally presented photographs that were associated with negative affect.

A classical conditioning procedure has also been used to determine whether the role of affect, or emotional feeling, in the determination of attitude is independent of that of cognitive beliefs concerning the attitude ob-

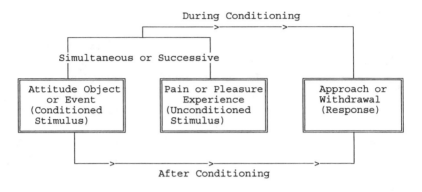

Figure 3.2. Classical Conditioning Paradigm

ject. For example, in a consumer-oriented study, Kim, Lim, and Bhargava (1998) employed a classical conditioning approach to study the impact of affect on attitude formation in the absence of product belief. From an analysis of responses to a questionnaire presented after viewing selected product stimuli shown on a television monitor, it was concluded that affect can influence attitudes even in the absence of product beliefs and that the role of affect is at least as important as that of beliefs in the formation of attitudes.

Operant Conditioning

Perhaps even more common than classical conditioning in shaping attitudes is *operant conditioning*. In classical conditioning, the unconditioned stimulus is presented regardless of what the person does after the conditioned stimulus is presented. In operant conditioning, how a person responds in a particular situation determines whether and how that response is reinforced. The concept of *reinforcement*—application of a stimulus or condition that increases the probability of an ongoing response—plays a major role in operant conditioning. In *positive reinforcement*, the presentation of a particular stimulus or condition increases the probability of an ongoing response, whereas in *negative reinforcement* the removal of a particular stimulus or condition increases the probability of the response. *Positive reinforcers* are essentially rewards, but *negative reinforcers* are not punishers. In *punishment*, a painful or otherwise unpleasant stimulus is presented whenever a particular response occurs, thereby decreasing the probability of that response. But in negative reinforcement, an unpleasant stimulus is removed whenever a particular response occurs, thereby increasing the probability of that response. A person whose actions enable him or her to escape from an unpleasant situation has been negatively reinforced, but a person whose actions lead to pain or misery for him or her has been punished. Once a particular response has been shaped by the application of a particular reinforcement schedule, the response may be brought under stimulus control by arranging for a previously neutral *discriminative stimulus* to regularly precede the response.

Although attitudes are generally viewed as cognitive/affective responses, they can, like observable behavior, be shaped by reinforcement or punishment. If the expression of a particular attitude enables the individual to obtain rewards or avoid punishment, it becomes more likely that the attitude will recur under similar circumstances in the future. For example, ego-defensive attitudes, as expressed in rationalization, denial, or projection, may serve a negative reinforcement function by leading to a reduction in anxiety that is threatening one's self-esteem. Or expressions of positive attitudes toward someone or something may lead to positive reinforcers such as social or material rewards. Finally, when applied consistently and judiciously, verbal or physical punishment for disorderly or disapproved behavior may result in a more socially acceptable attitude, or at least the expression of one, on the part of an individual.

Operant conditioning emphasizes the role of reinforcement in learning, but also important in determining whether or not an individual will respond to a particular stimulus is the perceived likelihood or expectation that a particular response will lead to reinforcement and the value that the individual attaches to the reinforcement. Reinforcement value and the *expectancy* of reinforcement vary from person to person. They are affected by the psychological relevance or meaning of the situation to the person, and this idiosyncratic meaning must be understood before the person's behavior in a particular situation can be predicted (see Rotter, 1954).

Modeling

Many attitudes are not the results of direct conditioning or reinforcement but rather are learned vicariously or imitatively by observing the activities of other people. These significant others include one's parents, teachers, peers, celebrities, or other individuals who are important to or admired by the person. *Modeling* the actions and attitudes of such people causes them to become the observer's own. From his research on modeling, Bandura (1969) concluded that "virtually all learning phenomena resulting from direct experiences can occur on a vicarious basis through observation of other persons' behavior and its consequences for them" (p. 108). Such learning includes not only verbal and motor skills but also complex, socially oriented attitudes, values, and beliefs.

Among the factors that play a role in determining the effects of a model's behavior on an observer are (a) the perceived competence of the model, (b) whether other potential models say or do the same things, (c) the perceived capability of the model to provide the observer with rewards, (d) whether the observer has previously been rewarded or encouraged by the model, (e) whether the observer perceives the model as similar to himself or herself, and (f) whether the model represents a group to which the observer belongs or would like to belong. As implied by the first factor, models who are perceived as successful in attaining their goals are more influential (see Bandura, 1977).

Also significant in determining the extent to which a particular observer imitates or models the attitudes of a source are characteristics of the observer, including more enduring cognitive abilities and personality traits (e.g., Kulik, 1999; Perry & Baldwin, 2000; Tibon, 2000) as well as more transitory states such as positive or negative moods (Barone, Miniard, & Romeo, 2000; Finegan & Seligman, 1993).

Social Comparison

Related to the modeling of behavior is *social comparison*, that is, comparing one's views of social reality with those of other people to determine whether one's own views are correct. In comparing one's attitudes with those of others, the biases, stereotypes, or other beliefs expressed by other people are not verified by the observer; they are simply adopted because these people claim or otherwise act as if they were true. Many prejudices or narrow-minded social perspectives appear to be learned in this manner (see Chapter 4). Furthermore, it is not necessary to have direct, personal interaction with a person to adopt that person's attitude and perspective. Much of the information on which social comparisons are based is obtained from the media or other secondhand sources.

Consistency Theories

Individual circumstances change, people change, and their attitudes follow suit. What seemed only yesterday to be an irrefutable certainty is reconsidered and perceived differently in the light of experience. New events, new acquaintances, and new needs lead to modified perceptions of the world and a reevaluation of one's place in it. Although changes in attitudes, values, and beliefs are not always inevitable or straightforward, for the good of the individual and society as a whole efforts may need to be made to alter those evaluations of reality. Sometimes these efforts involve positive incentives, sometimes persuasion, and at other times threats and punishment. Sometimes they are successful, and sometimes not.

Conditioning, reinforcement, and modeling are fundamental concepts of behavioral and social learning theories. Another group of influential theories that have played an important role in the study of attitude formation and change are *consistency theories*. These theories focus on a person's efforts to maintain consistency among his or her attitudes.

It is a truism, backed by research, that people tend to like others whose attitudes are similar to their own and to dislike those whose attitudes are dissimilar to theirs. It has been demonstrated, for example, that the greater the similarity among the attitudes of two people, the greater their attraction to each other (Gonzales, Davis, Loney, KuKens, & Junghans, 1983) and the longer the friendship is likely to last (Griffin & Sparks, 1990). Dissimilar attitudes and behaviors, on the other hand, can produce dissatisfaction, conflict, and disagreeable social relations (Rosenbaum, 1986). A number of attitude theorists have taken note of the role of attitude similarity in *interpersonal attraction* and the persistence of interpersonal relationships and the consequences of dissimilar attitudes for the individuals' peace of mind and for harmonious social relations. Balance theory and cognitive dissonance theory, in particular, have focused on the importance of attitude-attitude and attitude-behavior conflict in motivating changes in attitudes and behavior.

Balance Theory

According to Heider's (1958) *balance theory*, people try to arrange their relations with others so they will be internally consistent or balanced. When social relationships are imbalanced, people feel compelled to change their attitudes or behaviors to restore a state of balance in those relationships.

The concept of balance is applicable to social relationships between two, three, or any number of people. For example, if two college men who are roommates like each other and both like sports, the relationship is considered to be balanced. But if only one of the men likes sports, then the relationship is imbalanced. Because a state of imbalance is unpleasant, it motivates people to restore a balanced state by changing their attitudes or behavior. In this case, balance may be restored if one of the men changes his attitude toward sports or one of the men changes his attitude toward the other.

Now let us consider the case of balance and imbalance in a three-person group. If the relations or attitudes between one of the individuals and the other two are consistent, then that individual perceives the interaction among these three people as being in a state of balance. More specifically, if John likes both George and Frank, and George and Frank like each other, John will perceive this three-person situation as balanced. John will also perceive the situation as balanced if Frank dislikes George but John likes Frank and dislikes George. On the other hand, imbalance occurs when John likes George and dislikes Frank but George and Frank like each other. In short, as in a two-person situation, balance exists in a three-person situation when all relations are positive or only two are negative. Because perceived imbalanced relations among attitudes and behavior cause the individual to be disturbed until a state of balance is restored, when a person perceives such an imbalanced state the person will change his or her attitude or behavior to achieve balance (see Figure 3.3).

Balance theory can be extended beyond three, four, five, or *aggregations* consisting of any number of people, all of whom are sufficiently acquainted with each other to make evaluative judgments. If an accepting or approach ("like") evaluation is designated as "+" and a rejecting or withdrawal ("dislike") evaluation as "–," then the situation is balanced if the algebraic product of the signs corresponding to the various person-to-person relationships is positive (+) but imbalanced if the product is negative (–). Assigning positive algebraic signs to the solid lines and negative signs to the dashed lines in Figure 3.3 and computing the product of the algebraic signs for each of the triangles in the figure show that the relationships depicted in a, b, c, and d are balanced and the relationships depicted in e, f, g, and h are imbalanced.

Cognitive Dissonance Theory

Similar to Heider's concept of imbalance is Festinger's (1957) notion of *cognitive dissonance.* According to this theory, a person experiences cognitive dissonance whenever he or she holds cognitions (beliefs or attitudes) that conflict with each other or with the person's behavior. The presence of cognitive dissonance arouses the person and motivates him or her to reduce the dissonance. This may be accomplished by changing one's cognitions or behavior, or by minimizing the importance of the dissonant elements.

The implication of Festinger's theory is that attitudes can be changed by creating states of cognitive dissonance in people. In general, behaviors that can be induced with a minimum amount of social reward or punishment are more likely to lead to changes in attitudes.

One way in which dissonance has been produced experimentally is by getting a person to say or do something that is inconsistent with his or her attitude or belief. For example, a person who has just performed a very boring task may be promised a reward (a sum of money) if he or she tells another person that the task is really very interesting and encourages that person to participate in it. If the bribe is accepted, then, according to the theory, the person's belief and behavior will be inconsistent with each other and the person should experience a state of cognitive dissonance. This is more likely to be the result when the bribe is a small amount of money than when it is a

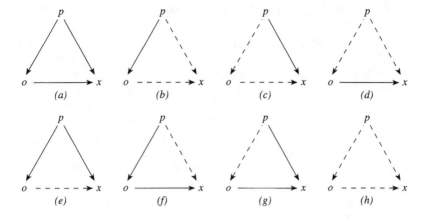

Figure 3.3. Balanced *(a, b, c, d)* and Imbalanced *(e, f, g, h)* Triads According to Heider's Balance Theory

SOURCE: Eagly, A. H., & Chaiken, S. L. (1998). Attitude structure and function. In D. T. Gilbert, S. T. Fiske, & G. Lindzey (Eds.), *The handbook of social psychology* (4th ed., p. 283). © McGraw-Hill. Reprinted with permission of The McGraw-Hill Companies.
NOTE: *p* and *o* are persons, and *x* is an attitude object. A solid line represents a positive attitude, and a dashed line represents a negative attitude toward the corresponding person or object.

large amount. In the latter case, the individual may feel that the lie was justified by the incentive, and consequently he or she experiences no conflict or cognitive dissonance. Another illustration is offering a person a reward to defend a viewpoint contrary to his or her own. The theory predicts that the speaker's attitude toward the issue is more likely to change when the reward is small, because in this case dissonance between action and attitude is greater than when the reward is a large one.

One technique that might be used to reduce the level of dissonance is to change one's attitude toward the task. Another technique is to change one's behavior so that it becomes more consonant with one's attitude. However, this strategy is effective in dissonance reduction only when incentives for continuing the behavior are low. Dissonance theory predicts that a person is more likely to change his or her attitude if the reward or inducement for a particular behavior is small than if it is large, a prediction that has been verified in a number of experiments (see Festinger, 1964). Because the incentive for the behavior is small, the individual does not view it as the primary reason for the change in behavior, but rather that his or her attitude has changed.

Subsequent research has also demonstrated that an attitude is more likely to change when the person accepts personal responsibility for the change in behavior that has occurred (Cooper & Fazio, 1984). Research has also led to the conclusion that when incentives for behaving in conflict with one's attitude are small, the individual's self-identity or integrity is threatened (Steele, 1988).

Although research on cognitive dissonance theory is not pursued as vigorously as it once was, it continues. The results of this research demonstrate that the dissonance effect is more likely when the participant is permitted a free choice between alternatives but responds inconsistently than when he or she is told what to do and responds inconsistently. Dissonance may also occur in the affective as well as the cognitive domains (Keller & Block, 1999).

The traditional viewpoint is that evaluations of selected and rejected alternatives in a free-choice situation become more divergent over time, but more recent models propose that postchoice effects vary with the attractiveness of the alternatives. In general, results show that, as predicted, when a difficult choice is made between two less desirable alternatives, participants' evaluations of the selected alternative increase. On the other hand, when the alternatives are more desirable, a difficult choice between them is followed by a large decrease in evaluations of the rejected alternative (Shultz, Leveille, & Lepper, 1999). Research has also revealed that tolerance for cognitive dissonance varies with personality traits such as extroversion ("Cognitive Dissonance," 2001).

Self-Perception Theory

Related to cognitive dissonance theory is *self-perception theory* (Bem, 1972). According to this theory, when a person behaves in a direction opposite to a given attitude in the presence of a strong inducement, the person's attitude changes because he or she assumes that the behavior was a result of that (changed) attitude. Thus, Bem argued that people infer their own attitudes, as they do with respect to the attitudes of other people whom they observe engaged in some activity, from what they observe themselves doing. For example, when a person sees himself doing something, such as helping an elderly person to cross the street, that would be interpreted as being due to altruism if he saw someone else doing it, the person concludes that he has an altruistic motive or attitude for doing so. If he really doesn't know why he did it, which may well be the case, then the altruistic explanation serves as well as any other and may be altered when supplied with better information.

Self-perception theory appears to hold up fairly well in the case of weakly held or vaguely defined attitudes or when the actor actually has had little experience with the attitude object. However, dissonance theory provides a better explanation in the case of well-defined or strongly held attitudes. As Festinger (1957) suggested, a state of cognitive dissonance and attendant arousal are produced by an inconsistency between one's behavior and one's attitude. Subsequent research has also demonstrated that the dissonance effect is increased by stimulating drugs but reduced by sedatives (Cooper,

Zanna, & Taves, 1978; Steele, Southwick, & Critchlow, 1981). However, rather than being the direct cause of the change in behavior or attitude that leads to a reduction in dissonance, the arousal simply serves to inform the individual that he or she has done something wrong and that the situation must be corrected so that his or her attitude and behavior are once more consistent with each other. In sum, when people lack information about the attitude object or situation or have no particular feelings about it, they may use their behavior as a guide to identifying their attitude. But in dissonance situations, the critical determinant of attitude change is the unpleasant emotional state resulting from cognitive dissonance produced by attitude-behavior inconsistency. This unpleasant arousal prompts the individual to do something, even something that may be contrary to a preceding attitude or behavior.

Other Concepts and Theories

Causal Attributions of Behavior

In a sense, everyone is a scientist who seeks explanations of behavior and adjusts his or her own behavior to correspond to those explanations. Although no one gets it right every time, by the time they are mature most people have a fairly good understanding, at least at a basic level, of why most people act as they do. But Everyperson's hypotheses concerning the causes of Others' behavior, or even his or her own behavior, are not always correct and are affected by fallacies, biases, and contextual variables that contribute to the incorrectness of seemingly reasonable explanations.

The study of *causal attributions* of behavior has been an active field of research in both social psychology and personality psychology during the past two or three decades. *Attribution theory*, which has important implications for attitude development and change, maintains that attitude change results not from an unpleasant emotional state engendered by cognitive dissonance but rather from a dispassionate interpretation of why one has engaged in a certain behavior.

Fundamental Attribution Error

Research on attributions has shown that, in general, people tend to overestimate the importance of traits and to underestimate the importance of situations in determining behavior of other people, a phenomenon referred to as the *fundamental attribution error* (*correspondence bias*) (Jones, 1979; Ross, 1977). Although, people have a tendency to attribute their own failures or embarrassments to variables in the specific situation, they tend to attribute the failures or embarrassments of other people to dispositional characteristics (i.e., personality traits) and attitudes (Jones & Nisbett, 1972). This error appears not to be very widespread and more likely to occur in situations where the behavioral norms are not well-defined or distinct (see Van Overwalle, 1997).

A possible explanation of the fundamental attribution error is that people understand themselves better than they understand others, and consequently they perceive more accurately that external circumstances are the principal determiners of their own behavior. Because we are likely to encounter a particular person only in certain specific situations, we tend to stereotype the person in terms of those situations: we tend to overgeneralize the appearance and behavior of the individual manifested in those situations as typical of him or her and therefore as a fairly permanent personality trait or attitude. According to Gilbert (1989), stereotyping people from the situations in which we see them, or overemphasizing the importance of traits and underestimating the importance of the situation, is also more likely to occur when a person is under stress. An explanation for this finding is that a person's cognitive resources are reduced when he or she is under stress, thereby increasing the likelihood of relying on the cognitively simpler process of stereotyping. In an extension of the notion of the fundamental attribution error, Pettigrew (1979) pointed to the tendency of people who hold strong stereotypes to attribute negative behaviors by minority group members to dispositional characteristics and to attribute positive behavior on their part to situational factors, the so-called *ultimate attribution error.*

Augmentation and Discounting

Two other concepts concerning the attribution of causation that have played a role in research on attitude change are augmentation and discounting. The principle of *augmentation* (addition rule) refers to the tendency to attribute greater importance to a potential cause of behavior that occurs in the presence of other causes that serve to inhibit it. In other words, if potential facilitators and inhibitors of the occurrence of a particular behavior are present and the behavior occurs, we tend to assign greater causal weight to the facilitators. For example, if a behavior occurs that is unique or unexpected from the contextual cues that are present, we are likely to attribute it to something else in the situation, say, something about the person (an attitude or personality trait). The augmentation principle provides an explanation of why people who engage in the unexpected response of arguing against their own personal interests tend to be more persuasive than people who argue in favor of their own interests.

The contrasting principle of *discounting* (subtraction rule) states that when the cause of a response can be explained in a number of ways, the plausibility of any one explanation is weakened (discounted). In other words, there is a tendency to attribute less importance to a particular cause of behavior in the presence of other possible causes. An illustration of discounting is the finding that participants virtually ignored an assigned essay when they suspected that the writer had an ulterior motive in writing it (Fein, Hilton, & Miller, 1990). Discounting, however, does not always occur in such situations: When a potential cause occurs first or is judged to be necessary despite the presence of other potential causes, it may not be discounted (McClure, 1998).

Dual-Process Models

Dual-process models of attitude change emphasize the importance of the recipient's perception of the arguments in a message and his or her responses to those arguments. They also maintain that attitude change may be prompted by factors other than the arguments themselves. These models emphasize that, unless motivated to do otherwise, people process information in a superficial, less detailed manner. The two most prominent dual-process models of attitude change are the elaboration likelihood model (Petty & Cacioppo, 1986) and the heuristic-systematic model (Chaiken, Liberman, & Eagly, 1989).

Elaboration Likelihood Model

According to the *elaboration likelihood model* (ELM) of attitude formation and change, certain variables can affect the amount and direction of attitude change in one of three ways: by serving as persuasive arguments, by serving as peripheral cues, and/or by affecting the extent or direction of issue and argument elaboration. Argument elaboration, that is, the degree to which one focuses on and tests the quality of an argument, mediates the route of persuasion, whether it is by the central route (conscious, detailed processing of argument quality and semantic content) or by the peripheral route. Processing by the peripheral route, where cues such as source attractiveness, emotion, social role, and impression management concerns are processed, does not require detailed thinking about the message. As argument scrutiny, ability, and motivation to process arguments decrease, peripheral cues (such as whether or not the would-be persuader is a friend) become more important determinants of persuasion. But peripheral cues become relatively insignificant as the recipient's ability and motivation to process information in a message increase. In general, emotional appeals act as peripheral cues and are most effective when the receiver's motivation or ability to process the message is low. However, changes in attitudes by way of the peripheral route are typically temporary, susceptible to counterpersuasion, and poorer predictors of behavior than changes by way of the central route. Furthermore, changes in attitudes resulting from extensive mental processing or elaboration of the content of a message tend to last longer and are more predictive of behavior or behavioral intentions.

Figure 3.4 is a flowchart of the sequence of processes and decision points in ELM. The two anchoring points in the model—the central and peripheral routes to attitude change or persuasion—are depicted in the figure.

Heuristic-Systematic Model

According to the *heuristic-systematic model* (HSM), receivers of a message reach some kind of attitude judgment about the message in one of two ways: via systematic or heuristic processing. In *systematic processing*, the message receiver relies on a content-oriented, critical examination of the message. In *heuristic processing*, the receiver develops judgments about the message by using mental shortcuts, rules of thumb, or heuristics such as cues external to the message itself (e.g., perceived credibility of the source; emotional appeals; attractiveness, status, or expertise of the source). Rather than being limited to either central or peripheral processing at any given time, as in ELM, according to HSM messages are processed simultaneously by both the heuristic and systematic channels. Although systematic processing in HSM is essentially the same as the *central route to persuasion* in ELM, heuristic processing in HSM is defined more narrowly than the *peripheral route to persuasion* in ELM. Incorporated within the latter is any non-argument-based effect on attitudes, whereas the former consists of the use of heuristics such as "experts' statements can be trusted" to form judgments and make decisions.

The Unimodel

Both ELM and HSM describe two modes of persuasion—a central or systematic mode in which attitudes and opinions are formed from carefully processed arguments in a persuasive message, and a peripheral or heuristic mode in which attitudes and opinions result from heuristics or cues that are external to the message itself. Thompson and Kruglanski (2000) contend, however, that the kinds of information provided by these two routes or modes do not involve distinctly different processes and that there is actually no need to posit separate cue-based and message argument-based channels of persuasion. These theorists maintain that "once one controls for differences in features relevant to persuasion (e.g., length and complexity), cue-based and message argument-based persuasion should be impacted similarly by various processing variables (e.g., motivation and *cognitive capacity*)" (p. 67, italics added). Although a number of other authors recognize

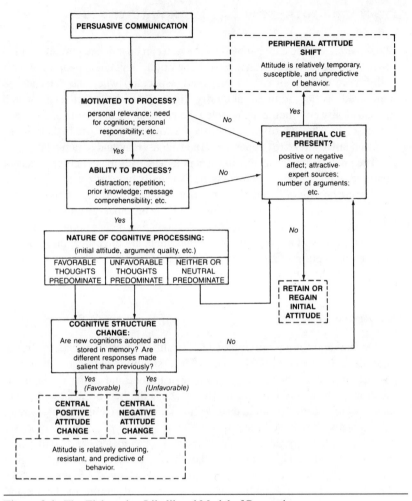

Figure 3.4. The Elaboration Likelihood Model of Persuasion

SOURCE: Reprinted by permission from *Communication and Persuasion: Central and Peripheral Routes to Attitude Change* (Figure 1-1, p. 4), by R. E. Petty and J. T. Cacioppo, 1986. Copyright © 1986 Springer-Verlag.
NOTE: The figure depicts the central and peripheral routes to persuasion.

that Thompson and Kruglanski have raised interesting questions regarding dual-process models of persuasions, they also point to some problems with the *unimodel* conception (Eagly, 2000; Lavine, 1999; Manstead & van der Pligt, 1999; Petty, Wheeler, & Bizer, 1999).

Practical Procedures for Changing Attitudes

Persuasibility is the extent to which a person can be induced or convinced to do something or to accept an idea or proposition. Dependent people are typically more gullible or easily persuaded, especially when the persuader is perceived as an admired authority figure. At the other end of the persuasibility continuum are people who are nearly impossible to convince or persuade. They are often very suspicious of authority, rigid in their thinking, and fail to attend to or understand new ideas (Hovland & Janis, 1959).

The professional propagandist, a person who tries to get people to accept a biased point of view toward an issue, is usually quite adept at persuasion. The word *propaganda* has the unsavory connotation of attempting to deceive and manipulate others. However, even the most benign and well-meaning leader is faced with the problem of convincing other people of the correctness of his or her point of view. What, then, are the procedures that are used in attempting to induce people to change their attitudes and opinions and prompt them to act on the changes?

Fear Arousal

One method commonly employed by health and traffic officials to change attitudes and behavior is *fear arousal*. The assumption of this method is that if a person is frightened enough, a change in attitude and a subsequent modification of behavior will occur. He or she will then be a slow-driving, nonsmoking, teeth-brushing, disease-free individual. Unfortunately, strong fear appeals often have little positive effect.

A classic study of the effects of fear arousal conducted nearly half a century ago was designed to discover the most effective way of encouraging high school students to brush their teeth properly (Janis & Feshbach, 1953). The effects of three different kinds of fear arousal—mild, moderate, and strong—were compared with each other and with a control condition. A lecture given to the strong-fear-appeal group attempted to arouse strong fear by vividly depicting how decayed teeth and diseased gums are consequences of poor dental hygiene. A somewhat less frightening lecture was given to the moderate-fear-appeal group, and the lecture given to the minimum-fear-appeal group was least frightening of all. The control group heard a lecture on another topic. Before and after the lecture the students filled out a questionnaire concerning their attitudes toward dental hygiene. The average attitude scores of all four groups were approximately equal before the lecture, but they were quite different after the lecture. The results show that the percentage change in attitude toward the lecturer's viewpoints was highest in the minimum-fear-appeal group (36%) and next highest in the moderate-fear-appeal group (22%), but in the strong-fear-appeal group (8%) it was only slightly higher than that of the control group (0%). In addition, the minimum-fear-appeal group was least affected by a "counterpropaganda" lecture, which took a point of view opposite to that of the first lecture, a week later. The ineffectiveness of the strong fear appeal was attributed to the fact that strong fear arousal produces a defensive avoidance reaction of minimizing the danger, forgetting the message, or staying away from situations that arouse the fear. In a later investigation, Griffeth and Rogers (1976) attempted to arouse fear in high school students enrolled in driver education classes by describing the severity of auto accidents, the chances of being involved in a traffic accident, and related effects of safe driving. The fear arousal condition in this experiment had the beneficial effect of increasing safe driving behavior.

Behavioral and Cognitive Techniques

Behavior Modification

Rather than attempting to change attitudes directly, it is assumed in a *behavior modification* approach that if one begins by changing behavior, then one's attitude will follow suit. For example, to change a person's negative attitude toward a specific ethnic group, the person may be encouraged to start by practicing accepting, supportive behavior toward members of that group. Initially, this behavior is role-played in contrived situations in which the reactions of the minority group actors are carefully controlled. Subsequently, the person practices the desired behavior in real-life situations. If this behavior is positively reinforced, or at least not rejected or otherwise punished, it will presumably increase in frequency and the person will begin to develop a more positive attitude toward the group.

Modeling

Another behavioral technique that can help to change behavior and attitudes is *modeling* the behavior of an exemplary person. For example, a child's negative attitude and fear of dental treatment may be reduced by having the child observe, at a "safe" distance, the behavior of an age-mate sitting calmly in a dental chair and undergoing a hygienic procedure. This modeling approach should, of course, be accompanied by reassurance and differential positive reinforcement for constructive behavior.

Cognitive Therapy

Unlike behavior modification, which has little to say about thoughts and other cognitive processes, *cognitive therapy* emphasizes the role of maladaptive thought patterns (specific attitudes, beliefs, expectations, etc.) in determining problems of adjustment. Using *self-monitoring*, thought stopping, and other therapeutic procedures, patients are taught how to identify and gain control over their automatic, idiosyncratic mental reactions to disturbing stimuli. Three techniques that have been demonstrated to be particularly useful in helping people cope with anxiety and stress are assertiveness training, cognitive restructuring, and stress inoculation. The goal of *assertiveness training* is to reduce the anxiety and tension experienced by a person when he or she must reject a demand made by someone else or must compete with another person. Techniques such as role-playing teach the person to make legitimate requests of others and to reject their unreasonable demands. *Cognitive restructuring* is based on the assumption that specific thoughts or self-verbalizations give rise to anxiety and that the person must modify these negative self-verbalizations by *thought stopping* whenever he or she begins to have self-defeating thoughts and to replace them with more positive self-statements (Meichenbaum, 1977). The technique of *stress inoculation* teaches people how to manage stressful situations by exposing them to small amounts of stress and providing them with suggestions for making adaptive rather than maladaptive responses (Meichenbaum, 1985).

The effectiveness of cognitive therapy is not limited to strong fears, anxieties, and depression. Both the cognitive and affective components of negative attitudes would seem to be good candidates for cognitive restructuring and stress inoculation in particular. Although behavior modification and cognitive therapy have not been employed extensively to change attitudes, there are documented studies in the literature in which various behavioral and cognitive procedures have been used to change the attitudes of patients with, for example, body dysmorphic disorder (Newell & Shrubb, 1994) and insomnia (Pat-Horenczyk, 1998).

Communication and Persuasion

A number of less orthodox procedures have also been used to modify attitudes, feelings, and behaviors, including hypnosis, truth serum, brainwashing, and subliminal advertising (e.g., Rosenberg, Hovland, McGuire, Abelson, & Brehm, 1960; Schein, 1956). All of these procedures involve some form of attitude communication under conditions of diminished vigilance or reduced resistance to the content of the communication.

It might seem as if people would be fairly resistant to verbal statements designed to induce changes in their attitudes. Since time immemorial, however, politicians, teachers, members of the clergy, and other propagandists have had noteworthy success in changing attitudes by means of persuasive communications. Three factors that play a role in the effectiveness of any communication designed to change attitudes were identified in a research program conducted by Carl Hovland and his colleagues (e.g., Hovland, Janis, & Kelley, 1953). These are the source of the communication, the nature of the communication, and the nature of the audience. Two additional factors that also play a role in the persuasibility of messages are the channel or medium of message transmission and context or situational variables. Note, however, that these are descriptive rather than explanatory categories and that not all variables within a single category affect attitudes similarly or by similar processes.

Source of the Communication

Many of the features discussed earlier in connection with modeling theory affect whether a particular source of communication will be believed. Among these are the perceived attractiveness, prestige, expertise, and friendliness of the communicator and his or her similarity to the audience. The greater the audience's perception of similarity between the communicator and them, the more effective is the communicator in convincing the audience. In addition, a communicator who is seen as having nothing personal to gain from the attitude change that he or she is promoting is more likely to be believed than one who obviously stands to profit by it.

In addition to being personally acceptable to the audience, a good communicator knows how to capture the audience's attention and stimulate interest. The communicator repeats and explains important points of the communication in such a way that they will be understood, remembered, and acted on at an opportune time.

Even when the source of a communication is perceived as having low credibility, a phenomenon known as the *sleeper effect* may occur. This effect consists of an increase in the influence of the communication as time passes and the source is forgotten. The sleeper effect may be caused by changes in the individual's personal circumstances or psychological environment, which make an attitude change in the direction advocated by the message more reasonable or justifiable.

Nature of the Communication

At least as important as the content of the message is the way in which it is presented. Messages may be presented face-to-face, by telephone or letter, or through the mass media (newspapers, radio, television, the Internet, etc.). In general, face-to-face communication is most effective, except when the appearance or personality of the communicator is distracting or disturbing. However, face-to-face advertising, selling, and other types of persuasive messages are substantially more expensive and time-consuming than the less personal media presentation techniques. Several message variables appear to promote changes in attitudes:

1. The message is inadvertently heard.

2. The message begins by stating an attitude similar to that currently held by the audience.

3. The message presents both sides of the argument if the audience is more intelligent, but only one side if the audience is less intelligent.

4. The message is repeated on several occasions.

Successful messages may also contain appeals to fear, loaded words, and suggestions. They may enable the audience to identify with successful or prestigeful people, and they may promise to satisfy the needs and goals of the audience. Depending on the cognitive abilities of the audience and its familiarity with the issue and arguments, conclusions may be implicit or stated explicitly (Bourne & Ekstrand, 1979).

Nature of the Audience

As indicated above, the effectiveness of a communication in changing attitudes varies with the source and nature of the message. An equally important factor is the nature of the audience that is subjected to the message. Audiences differ in demographic variables such as age, sex, education, socioeconomic level, and culture—all of which can influence understanding and interpretation of messages and how they are acted on. Individual differences in knowledge, intelligence, motivation, self-esteem, and other personality variables may also have an effect on message comprehension and persuasibility, and they should, whenever possible, be taken into account by would-be persuaders. The relationships of these variables to persuasibility are, however, rarely simple and direct. For example, higher intelligence might increase attention to, understanding of, and retention of a communication, but it might also cause the receiver to be less likely to yield to the argument or persuasive-manipulative features of the communication (McGuire, 1968). In any event, if the audience is seen as lacking the motivation and ability to process detailed information regarding the matter at issue, rather than spending a lot of time in presenting detailed arguments, the communicator would do well to rely on a simple approach involving repetition, positive associations, and simpler language. On the other hand, presentation of more thoughtful, detailed arguments may be appropriate in convincing a highly motivated audience with a deeper understanding of the issues.[2]

Other Approaches to Persuasion

Earlier research on attitude change was guided almost exclusively by the message-learning approach described above and inaugurated by Carl Hovland and other researchers at Yale University. Subsequently, a number of additional theoretical and methodological approaches to the study of persuasion have been introduced. One of these is the cognitive-response or information-processing approach, which begins with the notion that message recipients actively process the information in a message and relate its content to their personal beliefs and feelings about the matters of concern (Greenwald, 1968). A common technique of measuring these cognitive responses is *thought listing*, that is, exposing people to a persuasive communication and then having them list all the thoughts and ideas they have regarding the topic of the message. Evaluators then code those thoughts into positive, negative, and neutral categories, depending on whether they are favorable, unfavorable, or neither with respect to the position advocated in the message. Messages that evoke mainly positive reactions are assumed to be effective in changing attitudes toward the position advocated in the message, whereas messages that evoke mostly negative reactions will either not change attitudes at all or change them in a direction opposite to that advocated in the message. In addition, messages that evoke a greater number of responses will presumably have a greater effect in changing attitudes.

Various lines of research have provided support for the cognitive response approach to attitude change. For example, research involving *distraction*—interference with thoughts about the message—has demonstrated that it increases the effectiveness of a message in changing attitudes when the dominant cognitive response to the message is negative, but that it reduces the effectiveness of a message in changing attitudes when the dominant cognitive response to the message is positive (Petty, Wells, & Brock, 1976). The reason appears to be that distraction interferes with the recipient's ability to process information in the message and thus makes his or her response less negative when it would normally be negative, and less positive when it would normally be positive.

Another line of investigation stemming from the cognitive response approach is concerned with *involvement*—the extent to which receivers regard the topic of a message to be important or personally relevant. Because recipients who are personally involved tend to spend more time thinking about the content and issue of the message, such involvement should increase the effectiveness of a message containing strong arguments but reduce the effectiveness of a message containing weak arguments. Empirical support for this proposition up through the late 1980s has been summarized by Johnson and Eagly (1989).

Resistance to Change

Though research on attitude change, prompted to a great extent by practical problems in marketing, politics, teaching, and other persuasive endeavors, has been concerned primarily with techniques for actively shaping and modifying attitudes and opinions, ideas have also been presented and studies conducted on how to resist persuasion and other forms of psychosocial influence. Early research by Sherif and his coworkers (e.g., Sherif, Sherif, & Nebergall, 1965), for example, developed the notion that the susceptibility of a person's attitudes to persuasion is a function of whether the message falls within the person's latitude of acceptance, latitude of rejection, or latitude of noncommitment. Furthermore, persons who have strongly held attitudes about a topic because it involves their reference groups and basic values are unlikely to be persuaded to change those attitudes.

Just as people can be inoculated against disease and stress, it has been argued that they can also be inoculated against persuasion and propaganda. *Inoculation theory* maintains that resistance to arguments and to attitude change can be built up by exposing the person to weaker versions of the arguments so he or she can develop counterarguments to cope with future attacks on his or her attitudes. Some success in applying the tenets of inoculation theory to the prevention of alcohol abuse (Duryea, 1983) and to controversial issues such as the installation of air bags as passive safety devices in cars has been reported (Szybillo & Heslin, 1973).

Recommended Readings

Eagly, A. H., Wood, W., & Chaiken, S. (1996). Principles of persuasion. In E. T. Higgins & A. W. Kruglanski (Eds.), *Social psychology: Handbook of basic principles* (pp. 702-742). New York: Guilford.

Maio, G. R., Esses, V. M., & Bell, D. W. (1994). The formation of attitudes toward new immigrant groups. *Journal of Applied Social Psychology, 24,* 1762-1776.

Petty, R. E., & Wegener, D. T. (1998). Attitude change: Multiple roles for persuasion variables. In D. T. Gilbert, S. T. Fiske, & G. Lindzey (Eds.), *The handbook of social psychology* (4th ed., Vol. 1, pp. 323-389). New York: McGraw-Hill/Oxford.

Petty, R. E., Wegener, D. T., & Fabrigar, L. R. (1997). Attitudes and attitude change. *Annual Review of Psychology, 48,* 609-647.

Tesser, A. (1993). On the importance of heritability in psychological research: The case of attitudes. *Psychological Review, 100*, 129-142.

Thompson, E. P., & Kruglanski, A. W. (2000). Attitudes as knowledge structures and persuasion as a specific case of subjective knowledge acquisition. In G. R. Maio & J. M. Olson (Eds.), *Why we evaluate: Functions of attitudes* (pp. 59-95). Mahwah, NJ: Lawrence Erlbaum.

Wood, W. (2000). Attitude change: Persuasion and social influence. *Annual Review of Psychology, 51*, 539-570.

Notes

1. A *heritability coefficient*, which ranges from 0 to 1, is the proportion of a trait's (characteristic's) variance in a designated population that is attributable to heredity.

2. More recent research has pointed to an interaction between type of argument (rational vs. emotional) and type of attitude (affective-based vs. cognitive-based) in promoting attitude change (Millar & Millar, 1990). As hypothesized, it was found that affective-based attitudes were more susceptible to rational arguments but cognitive-based attitudes were more susceptible to emotional arguments.

Social Prejudice and Discrimination

Social Prejudice
   Stereotypes
   Scapegoating
   Personality and Prejudice

Social Discrimination
   Racism
   Sexism
   Ageism
   Hate Crimes

Assessment of Prejudice and Discrimination

Reducing Prejudice and Discrimination
   Legislation and Programmatic Action
   Research on Combating Prejudice and Discrimination
   Social Categorization Theory
   Reducing the Effects of Stereotypes

Not only are attitudes influenced by the people with whom one associates, but people tend to associate with those whose attitudes and beliefs are similar to their own. In this way, a person comes to belong to and identify with certain groups, so-called *in-groups*, whose values and beliefs are perceived as different from those of other groups, or *out-groups*.

Social Prejudice

Having preconceived attitudes or opinions, whether favorable or unfavorable, toward members of other groups is known as *social prejudice*, or simply *prejudice*. Used in a generic sense, however, prejudice refers to "pre-judgment," the target of which may be almost anything. Traditional out-groups, or targets of prejudice, have been members of other races, religions, ethnicities, or nationalities. Prejudice may also be expressed toward members of the opposite sex, older adults, people of other sexual orientations (e.g., *homophobia*), disabled persons, or even pro-choicers or pro-lifers. In many instances, the members of a certain group develop an active dislike for members of another group.

Prejudice has existed since time immemorial, contributing to discrimination in employment, education, housing, and social memberships, as well as acting as a stimulus for terrorism, armed conflict, and other forms of violence against persons and property. Prejudice and discrimination, which are often instigated by economic competition or other events perceived as threats, occur among almost all groups of people. According to *realistic conflict theory*, prejudice is the result of direct competition for limited resources. When people believe that members of other social groups keep them from attaining a higher standard of living, they look upon those groups in a hostile and prejudicial manner (Simpson & Yinger, 1985).

The degree of prejudice felt by middle-class residents of Louisiana, Mississippi, Alabama, and Georgia toward selected nationalities at mid-20th century was apparent in the results of a survey conducted by Prothro and Miles (1953). Five hundred middle-class adults in 30 communities in those four states expressed their feelings toward 17 nationality groups on a 9-point attitude scale. The scale consisted of nine descriptive sentences ranging from "I would accept a member of this group as my husband (or wife)" through "I would exterminate all members of this group." The consistent findings in all four states were that Northern Europeans were most acceptable, with Southern Europeans being somewhat less acceptable and Asian and African nationalities least acceptable of all. These results were approximately the same as those obtained 25 years earlier in a similar survey conducted by Bogardus (1928). The participants in Bogardus's study, however, were college men.

Stereotypes

The terms *prejudice*, *discrimination*, and *stereotype* are often used together and occasionally interchangeably, but distinctions must be made. *Stereotypes* are generalizations concerning the attributes and behaviors of people who belong to certain naturally constituted or socially determined groups. These attributes include personality traits, social roles, and physical characteristics, and the behaviors include mannerisms and other fixed ways of acting. For example, African Americans and Hispanic Americans, and to a lesser extent Asian Americans, are stereotyped by sizable percentages of White Americans as "poor, lazy, violence-prone, unintelligent, living off welfare, and unpatriotic" (Smith, 1990).

Stereotypes are not necessarily based on reality, and they are typically not the results of firsthand experience. Rather, they are overgeneralized features that are believed to be possessed by members of the group. Unlike attitudes, which have a strong affective component, stereotypes are based on beliefs, often unflattering and demeaning, about particular groups.

Though stereotypes generally have a negative connotation, they are the results of information processing and learning. They also may serve as shortcuts toward (mis)understanding and dealing with other people. The anthropologist Robin Fox (1992) maintained that stereotypes are adaptive mechanisms that promote species survival. MacRae, Bodenhausen, Milne, and Jetten (1994) consider stereotyping to be a socially advantageous automatic process. Nevertheless, stereotypes can serve as rationalizations for unwarranted *bias* and discrimination against minority groups.

Stereotypes may help to support social prejudice, but they are not always associated with it. A person may believe that certain groups possess specific stereotyped characteristics, and yet not be prejudiced against those groups. On the other hand, a person may be prejudiced against a particular group and yet not be aware of the stereotype of that group. Research findings indicate that children acquire specific attitudes and prejudices prior to age or ethnic stereotypes (Brigham, 1974; Doyle, Beaudet, & Aboud, 1988).

It is easier for prejudice to develop if its victims are readily identifiable. For this reason, people who belong to ethnic or nationality groups whose physical or behavioral characteristics are different from those of the majority or in-group are more likely to become the targets of prejudice. Prejudiced people are often more adept than nonprejudiced people at recognizing members of a group against which they are prejudiced. For example, Lindzey and Rogolsky (1950) found that compared with students who were low in anti-Semitism, students who were high in anti-Semitism were more accurate in distinguishing between photographs of Jewish and non-Jewish people.

Because there are more similarities than differences among different groups, and not all group members fit all attributes of the stereotype to the same degree, prejudiced people make many errors in social perception by failing to detect the differences among people in the out-group in question and incorrectly identifying many in-group members as belonging to the out-group.

An adult white male was approached by four white teenagers who requested money for the bus. When he refused, one of the youths said to the others,

"Let's teach this [epithet for a gay person] a lesson." The victim was punched in the face, knocked to the ground, kicked several times, and robbed of his wristwatch, ring, and wallet. When he reported the crime, the victim advised he did not know the offenders and that he was not gay. (U.S. Department of Justice, 1999)

The highly anti-Semitic students in the Lindzey and Rogolsky (1950) study labeled many more of the photographs as Jewish than did students who were low in anti-Semitism. It is also noteworthy that high-anti-Semitic students were also much more confident in their judgments of the photographs than were students who were low in anti-Semitism.

Scapegoating

The term *scapegoat*, which stems from the Biblical tradition of letting a goat loose in the wilderness during Yom Kippur after the high priest symbolically laid the sins of the people on its head (Leviticus 16:8-22), has come to refer to a person or group made to bear the blame for others or to suffer in their place. Social psychologists view *scapegoating* as a form of displaced aggression in which a person's hostility is expressed toward some person or group of people other than the direct cause of frustration. Historical data analyzed by Hovland and Sears (1940) have often been interpreted as an illustration of scapegoating on a macro level. These data, which are illustrated in Figure 4.1, indicate that during the late 19th and early 20th centuries the number of lynchings in the United States, principally in the South and of African Americans, was directly related to economic conditions. The number of lynchings was significantly higher in years when economic conditions were poor than in years in which economic conditions were better. These, of course, are correlational rather than experimental data, and other explanations of the findings than scapegoating or displaced aggression are possible.

That scapegoating is a cause of social prejudice has been verified by observation and experiment. For example, in a classic experiment conducted by Miller and Bugelski (1948), boys at a summer camp were frustrated by forcing them to take tests that caused them to miss a weekly movie where they had hoped to win a lottery. The attitudes of the boys toward Japanese and Mexicans were assessed both before and after the frustration. It was found that the experimentally induced frustration caused an increase in prejudiced attitudes toward the two nationalities. These results illustrate the principles that frustration leads to increased aggression and that aggression is often displaced onto a minority group in the form of prejudice.

Gordon Allport (1944) listed four characteristics of people who are scapegoats: easy identifiability, easy accessibility, inability to retaliate, and having been scapegoats previously. The characteristic of easy identifiability

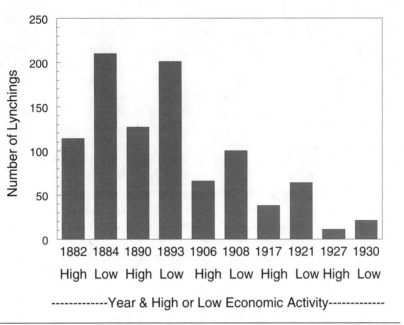

Figure 4.1. Number of Lynchings as a Function of Economic Conditions in the United States, 1882-1930: An Illustration of Scapegoating?

SOURCE: Based on data from Hovland and Sears (1940).

is seen in the fact that the more distinguishing traits that members of a group possess, the more likely they are to be victims of scapegoating. With respect to accessibility, an out-group that is easily accessible is a more convenient object against which to vent hostility induced by another object or situation. It is also important that the scapegoat be unable to retaliate or strike back, at least not with any great effectiveness. Finally, certain groups that have proved to be useful scapegoats in the past continue to be used for this purpose time and again.

Personality and Prejudice

Social prejudice has its origins in a number of variables: competition between groups, motivation to enhance one's *self-esteem*, basic tendencies to categorize and stereotype other people, and cultural learning (Monteith, 2000). Another variable that can contribute to prejudice is personality. Not all people who are members of a particular in-group are equally prejudiced, and even those who are prejudiced may be so for different reasons. Most people who express social prejudices probably develop them not because of any direct negative experiences with the targets of prejudice but simply because they have learned to behave like their prejudiced relatives, friends, and other associates. In some individuals, however, social prejudice is associated with a pattern of ethnocentric behavior and beliefs. Such people believe that the members of their culture are superior to those of other cultures, and they behave in like manner. Frequently associated with *ethnocentrism* is a complex of personality traits including rigidity, conventionality, cynicism, extreme moralizing, superstitiousness, political conservatism, a craving for power, a tendency to hold stereotypes, and scapegoating. Other traits associated with this personality pattern include dependence on authority and rigid rules, conformity to group values, admiration of powerful figures, compulsiveness, concreteness, and intolerance of ambiguity. In combination, these traits constitute what has come to be known as an *authoritarian personality*. Research on the authoritarian personality, which involved administration of questionnaires such as the California F Scale, was begun by Adorno and his associates (Adorno, Frenkel-Brunswik, Levinson, & Sanford, 1950) in the 1940s. From examining individuals of this personality type, it was found that as children they tended to have been subjected to strict parental control. Although the overcontrolled child felt resentment toward his or her parents, to express it would have resulted in severe punishment. Consequently, the child suppressed the resentment but continued to feel angry. As adults, authoritarian personalities keep their unresolved hostility toward their parents unconscious by being overobedient to authority and by displacing that hostility onto minority groups and other "safe" targets. They express their hostility quite generally—toward Jews, Blacks, and almost any foreigner or minority group—tending to be prejudiced toward all groups that are in any way different from their own.

The percentage of prejudiced people who actually fit the description of an authoritarian personality is probably not very high. Furthermore, authoritarianism is only one of many variables that are correlated with prejudice, and a person may be highly prejudiced without being highly authoritarian. For example, Pettigrew (1958) found that although Whites in South Africa were more racially prejudiced than Whites in the United States, the degree of authoritarianism in the two countries was approximately the same. Nevertheless, a positive correlation between measures of authoritarianism and racial prejudice was found in South Africa and the United States.

Additional support for the proposition that attitude toward other groups of people is frequently only an expression of a general personality trait was obtained in a study by Anisfield, Munoz, and Lambert (1963). The attitudes of Jewish high school students toward Gentiles and Jews were measured and correlated with several other variables. It was found that students who were self-accepting were also more positive in their attitudes toward their parents,

Jews, and Gentiles. In contrast, students who were high in hostility held less favorable attitudes toward their parents and toward both Jews and Gentiles. Christie and Garcia (1951) found, however, that the high correlation between ethnocentrism and authoritarianism that Adorno and his colleagues had found in California did not hold up in Texas, where ethnocentrism was more deeply ingrained in the culture (see also Christie & Jahoda, 1954).

Subsequently, Milton Rokeach (1960) developed the related notion of the closed or rigid personality characteristic of "dogmatism," which Gregory (1957) designated the "authority-dependent personality." The characteristics of this personality pattern—compulsiveness, concreteness, conformity, dogmatism, literalness, pedantry, and rigidity—overlap with those of the authoritarian personality studied by earlier researchers.

Social Discrimination

Prejudice is not the same as discrimination, but it often leads to it. *Discrimination,* defined as differential treatment of people according to race, ethnicity, gender, age, sexual orientation, disabilities, and other physical or behavioral characteristics, has been a continuing social problem in many countries. Despite the Civil War of the 1860s, the civil rights movement of the 1960s, and numerous legislative statutes designed to ensure equality of opportunity and status, Black-White relations have remained a source of concern in the United States. Blacks and Whites have different perspectives and attitudes with respect to many social issues. Data from the General Social Survey (Davis & Smith, 1994) conducted by the National Opinion Research Center showed that although both Blacks and Whites agreed that conditions for Blacks have improved in recent years, the two groups still differed in their opinions with respect to issues such as why Blacks have not progressed more, *affirmative action* in education and employment, and the role of the government in enforcing civil rights. Whites tended to feel that the poorer jobs, longer hours, and lower incomes of Blacks are consequences of their lack of motivation, whereas Blacks tended to blame racial discrimination. Only a small percentage of Whites favored preferential hiring and promotion to compensate for past discrimination in employment, but the majority of Blacks favored such affirmative action procedures. Furthermore, a substantially larger percentage of Whites than Blacks felt that the latter receive greater attention from government than they deserve.

Not only did the Civil Rights Act of 1964 and subsequent legislation and government programs promote greater economic and social opportunities for Blacks and other ethnic groups, but such measures also provided legal support for the quest for equal rights for the sexes, older Americans, and disabled persons.

Racism

Racism, the belief that certain racial groups are inferior to others and should therefore be treated as such, is, of course, not indigenous to the United States. Subjugation, slavery, and other methods of discrimination by race have occurred throughout human history in many different countries and cultures. But it is in the United States, where equality of opportunity and democracy have been eloquently preached but less often practiced, that racism has become a cause célèbre.

Put into effect after the Civil War as a compromise between Northern and Southern beliefs and interests, the doctrine of separate but equal facilities for Whites and Blacks was effective in maintaining a semblance of order and racial harmony for three generations. However, the illusory "separate but equal" doctrine was shattered by the civil rights movement of the 1950s and 1960s and ensuing federal legislation. These laws and other efforts were designed to promote peaceful integration between the races, but discrimination and de facto segregation persist in many areas and activities. African American workers are still concentrated in less desirable blue-collar jobs and earn the lowest incomes (see Figure 4.2). They live in the poorest neighborhoods, have the lowest percentage of home ownership, and have the lowest level of education, poorer health and sanitation, and a higher arrest rate than average. The values of education, hard work, and thrift, which are essential for getting ahead if one is not a gifted athlete, a star entertainer, or a skilled thief, are subscribed to by many minority families and taught to their children. Nevertheless, a large proportion of African American families, in particular, remain at or below the poverty level in the central cities where the majority reside, inviting invidious comparisons between their own material circumstances and those of a "typical" White family living in a posh suburban home or as depicted in many television programs. The lawlessness encouraged by a materialistic society polarized by "haves" and "have-nots" and the breakdown of the family structure have led to frequent confrontations and occasional riots in which African Americans are pitted against the White establishment and its enforcers—the police.

Government programs, such as Aid to Families With Dependent Children (AFDC), Social Security, supplemental security income (SSI), and food stamps, have helped ensure a minimal standard of living for many minorities, but the effects of these and other federal "giveaways" on the motivation and self-esteem of their recipients have been increasingly questioned. The situation for minorities is, however, demonstrably better than it was prior to the 1960s. There are still differences in the ways in which Blacks and Whites

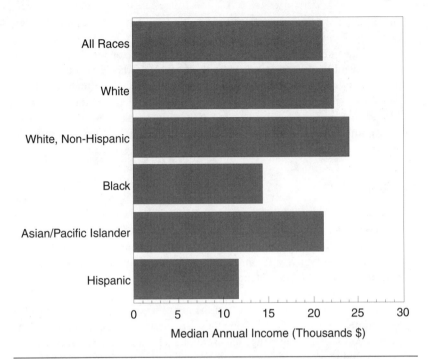

Figure 4.2. Per Capita Median Annual Income for Various Racial/Ethnic Groups in the United States, 1999

SOURCE: U.S. Census Bureau (2000a).

in general view the world, but for the most part the two groups appear to have established something of a modus vivendi—a mutual-existence arrangement in which greater interracial *tolerance* is expressed in attitudes and behavior.

Education and employment, which are passports to greater influence and power in the wider society, have become less discriminatory but still have some distance to go before attaining racial equality. Racial stereotypes are less common, and interracial friendships, dating, and marriage have increased. Young adult members of minority groups of today certainly have more opportunities than they did prior to the civil rights era.

The point has not yet been reached where everybody loves each other and can look upon everyone as a "brother" or "sister." Nevertheless, there are signs that people in American society have become more tolerant if not necessarily more respectful of members of racial and ethnic groups other than their own. Better jobs, more political power, and greater material benefits should not only provide greater harmony within but also less conflict between the races.

Despite cutbacks in federal programs targeted toward lower-income groups, in all likelihood efforts by both the public and private sectors to improve the living conditions of disadvantaged people will continue. However, those who work with these groups will be more effective if they develop a greater awareness and understanding of the culture and traditions of the people whom they serve and learn the language or dialect in which they communicate.

Sexism

If we consider all of the characteristics that serve as a basis for discrimination (gender, race, ethnicity, social class, age, etc.), the most significant in terms of economic well-being is gender. From an economic standpoint, it is certainly a disadvantage in our society to be Black, poor, uneducated, and old, but arguably the greatest material disadvantage of all is to be a woman.

Women have made demonstrable progress in the workplace and in public life during the past few decades, but the great majority remain in traditionally women's occupations. Among these are clerical and household occupations, food services, nursing, and schoolteaching. The large majority of higher-paying professional positions in business and industry, engineering, science, and technology are still occupied by men. Even in fields such as medicine and law, which have become more open and attractive to women in recent years, women tend to specialize in certain areas and men in others. Women MDs are more likely to specialize in pediatrics, psychiatry, and public health, and women lawyers tend to concentrate on domestic law and trusts rather than corporate or criminal law (Wass, 1993).

Despite some resistance from both officers and enlisted men (and sexual harassment scandals), more and more women are enlisting in the military and being trained for all kinds of duties. So far, the concerns that women are not physically or psychologically suited for combat and that their presence interferes with male bonding and morale have limited their assignment to combat positions. However, there is a great deal of political pressure to eliminate all sex distinctions in the treatment of women and men in all branches of the armed forces.

Sexism, the belief that the two sexes are fundamentally different in their abilities and that each is more suited for certain educational and vocational activities, is still quite prevalent in educational and employment contexts. Many people continue to feel that the proper place for women is in the home and that they should not try to compete with men in the world of work. In many organizations, there appears to be a kind of *glass ceiling*, a subtle barrier to the advancement by women beyond which they cannot expect to rise in an organization. It is, of course, possible that a glass ceiling exists in particular organizations because women lack the abilities, personality charac-teristics, motivation, or stamina to succeed at higher levels in those organiza-tions. There is, however, no good evidence for the validity of this supposition. Rather, it would seem that the main cause of the glass ceiling is gender discrimination.

Sexism is practiced not only in the workplace but also in the home, school, mass media, and society at large. By being discriminated against, women find it difficult to attain the knowledge, skills, and social networks that come from interacting with other executives and staff professionals. Consequently, they are not provided with an adequate opportunity to dem-onstrate the incorrectness of the negative attitudes and biases toward them.

Another illustration of the problem of women not possessing the requi-site skills for certain jobs is found among women who want or need to get back into the work force but have little or no training and therefore must set-tle for low-paying jobs with no chance for advancement and an inadequate retirement pension. Private pensions, in addition to Social Security, are made available to retired teachers and nurses, but in few other occupations that attract large numbers of women. Furthermore, for the most part women's wages, and particularly the wages of women in minority groups, are substantially lower that those of men. In 1999, the median per capita earnings of full-time, year-round workers in the United States was $26,324 for women compared with $36,476 for men (U.S. Census Bureau, 2000a). In recent years, legal attention has been given to the concept of *comparable worth*. According to this concept, pay for women should be equal to that for men in those occupations that are determined to be equivalent in importance but in which the relative numbers of men and women employees are substan-tially different. Because of the difficulty of evaluating the demands made by different jobs, thus far proposed systems for determining comparable worth have not proven very effective.

In addition to being denied equal status with men in the world of work, women are often sexually harassed and in other ways treated as sex objects rather than as individuals. Gender stereotypes abound in advertising and in other branches of the media. One illustration is *faceism*, the tendency to fo-cus on men's faces but on women's bodies when photographing or filming them. As long as sex sells and the doctrine of free enterprise prevails, such practices will probably continue. Be that as it may, men should be cautioned that women often find cross-gender touching, staring, and related behaviors offensive (Fitzgerald & Ormerod, 1991). The problem of mutual aware-ness and understanding between the sexes has led to the legal criterion of sexual harassment known as the *reasonable woman standard* (*Ellison v. Brady,* 1991). According to this standard, even if the male perpetrator of an action that allegedly involved sexual harassment did not consider it offen-sive, if a "reasonable woman" views it as offensive then in law it is consid-ered to be so.

Ageism

As defined by Butler (1974), *ageism* is

a process of systematic stereotyping of and discrimination against people
because they are old—just as racism and sexism can accomplish this with
skin color and gender. Old people are categorized as senile, rigid in thought
and manner, old-fashioned in morality and skills. Ageism allows the younger generation to see older people as different from themselves. Thus, they
subtly cease to identify with their elders as human beings. (p. 11)

Perhaps the most powerful agent that has encouraged ageism in the
United States is television (Bell, 1992). Traditionally, older adults have been
stereotyped on television as comical, eccentric, foolish, and stubborn. More
recently, portrayals of older adults on television have become more positive—as affluent, free from health problems, mentally quick, socially sensitive, active, and independent. But even these positive depictions are inaccurate representations of older adults in general. Such *positive ageism*, as it has
been labeled by Palmore (1990), overlooks the problems of poverty, illness,
and loneliness that confront many older Americans.

Ageism is more common in youth-oriented cultures such as ours than in
China, Japan, or other Asian countries that have a long tradition of respect
for age and the aged. Even Shakespeare was not immune to describing old
age in stereotyped, quasi-humorous poetry, and during the latter part of the
19th century the labeling of older people with pejorative terms became quite
fashionable (Covey, 1988). In the 20th century, negative stereotyping of
older adults in plays, films, and stories increased in frequency. Even the victims of these slurs and jokes sometimes joined in poking fun at their
age-mates, exempting themselves of course from such stereotypes. Older
people have been depicted as senile or as experiencing a second childhood,
as rigid or inflexible, sexless, unattractive, chronically ill, and fit only to live
in nursing homes.

Ageism is not limited to adults. Even young children sometimes make
racist and sexist comments and complain about having to be around old people (e.g., Bassili & Reil, 1981; Weinberger, 1979). Children, of course, learn
stereotypes of older people from other children and adults. Among the reasons for such stereotyping on the part of young adults are job competition
between the young and the old, problems with one's own parents and other
older relatives, association of old age with dying, the desire to distance oneself from the physical signs of aging and increased dependency, or any other
reason that makes one feel threatened by aging and the elderly (Hendricks &
Leedham, 1980; Kite, Deaux, & Miele, 1991). Whatever the cause may be,
ageism is based on inaccurate and overgeneralized information. On the

whole, older people view themselves as less lonely, in better health, and more useful than they are perceived by other adults (Harris & Associates, 1981). Most older Americans are fairly optimistic about their lives and want to remain active and even gainfully employed. In a recent survey conducted by the National Council on the Aging (2000), 49% of respondents between the ages of 65 and 69, 44% of those in their 70s, and 33% of those in their 80s indicated agreement with the statement "These are the best years of my life." Furthermore, 84% of the respondents said that they would be happy to live to be 90 years old.

If ageism were merely an attitude and not expressed in the treatment of older adults, it would be of less concern than it actually is. As with racism and sexism, however, ageism is manifested in the discriminating behavior of society toward older adults, and most particularly in employment contexts. Historically, older workers have been characterized as slower; less able to learn new skills; more prone to accidents; less able to get along with coworkers and customers; more resistant to supervision and change; more likely to miss work; slower in making judgments; lower in speed, strength, and endurance; less motivated; and more stubborn and overcautious (Rhodes, 1983; Sparrow & Davies, 1988). Managers who accept these unproved assumptions are more likely to discriminate against older workers in making personnel decisions. Older adults may have a lower work output volume than younger adults, but their work is generally of higher quality and performed with less wasted effort and fewer mistakes. They are also quite capable of learning new jobs, and their experience can compensate for age-related declines in the speed or strength of their performance (Rhodes, 1983; Stagner, 1985).

The civil rights atmosphere of the 1960s not only led to legislation requiring equal treatment of the races and sexes but also mandated equal treatment by age. For example, the federal Age Discrimination in Employment Act of 1967 (ADEA) banned the use of age as a criterion in hiring, firing, promotion, training, retirement, working conditions, referral by employment agencies, job announcements, or any action taken against a person with regard to compensation, conditions, or perquisites of employment. The ADEA legally prohibits employers from hiring or discharging job applicants on the basis of age alone, or segregating or classifying them in any way that is detrimental to their performance or well-being.

Hate Crimes

Sometimes prejudice gets out of hand and leads to hate crimes. The Hate Crime Statistics Act of 1990 mandated the collection of data on hate crimes, defined as crimes motivated by preformed, negative bias against persons, property, or organizations based solely on race, religion, ethnic/national origin, sexual orientation, or disability. During 1999, there were 7,876 bias-motivated criminal incidents involving 9,301 offenses and 9,802 victims reported to the FBI. Sixty-three percent of the victims suffered from crimes against persons (murder and nonnegligent manslaughter, forcible rape, aggravated assault, simple assault, intimidation, and other). The remaining 37% of the victims suffered from crimes against property (robbery, burglary, larceny-theft, motor vehicle theft, arson, destruction/damage/vandalism, and other) and crimes against society (less than 1%). The most frequent crime against persons, as well as the most frequent of all hate crimes, was intimidation (35.1% of the total). The most frequent crime against property was destruction/damage/vandalism (28.5% of the total).

The bias motivation categories associated with these hate crimes, and the number of incidents, offenses, victims, and known offenders in each category, are listed in Table 4.1. The highest percentage of these crimes occurred on residential properties. The highest percentage of offenders were White (68%), followed by Black (16%) (U.S. Department of Justice, 2001).

Assessment of Prejudice and Discrimination

Two of the earliest paper-and-pencil measures of racial prejudice were Bogardus's (1925) Social Distance Scale and Katz and Braly's (1933, 1935) adjective checklists. Since then, dozens of scales and inventories designed to assess various aspects of racism, sexism, and ageism, as well as religious, ethnic/nationality, disability, and sexual orientation intolerance, have been devised. The great majority of these instruments are ad hoc, unpublished, and unstandardized devices that have been used in only a few studies (see Appendix 4.1).

On adjective checklists designed to assess racial, ethnic, or nationality stereotypes, respondents are asked to indicate which of a list of traits they associate with a particular group of people. On Bogardus's Social Distance Scale, respondents are asked to indicate their willingness to accept individuals in particular groups at different degrees of intimacy, ranging from a very low (e.g., residing in the same country) to a very high (e.g., intermarriage) level of closeness. The *social distances* of various groups are then rank-ordered from the results. Triandis and Triandis's (1962) behavioral distance scaling procedure requires respondents to indicate the extent of their acceptance of a particular group or person on a 7-point scale ranging from agreement to rejection. On other instruments, respondents are asked to indicate the degree to which they agree or disagree with a set of statements pertaining to one group or another or the extent to which they are sympathetic or antipathetic toward the group.

TABLE 4.1   Number of Incidents, Offenses, Victims, and Known Offenders by Bias Motivation, 1999

Bias Motivation	Incidents	Offenses	Victims	Known Offenders
Single-bias incidents	7,871	9,291	9,792	7,265
Race	4,295	5,240	5,485	4,362
Religion	1,411	1,532	1,686	602
Sexual orientation	1,317	1,487	1,558	1,376
Ethnicity/national origin	829	1,011	1,040	904
Disability	19	21	23	21
Multiple-bias incidents	5	10	10	6

SOURCE: U.S. Department of Justice (2001).

Some researchers maintain that results obtained from attitude scales and other paper-and-pencil measures of prejudice and discrimination are either not very meaningful or meaningful only in certain contexts. Consequently, they recommend the use of less direct methods such as projective techniques (e.g., free association, sentence completion, picture stories, reactions to pictures of people with different features or to stories of people displaying different behaviors). *Sociometric* procedures of the sort devised by the author to measure group cohesiveness (Aiken, 1992) have also been adapted to the assessment of prejudice. Another assessment approach in research on prejudice is to obtain the reactions (aggression, helping behavior, etc.) of people in contrived situations involving different groups.

As discussed in Chapter 2, measures of implicit attitudes and physiological measures of level of activation or attention (e.g., pupillary diameter, muscle tension, heart rate) have been employed on occasion as indirect or unobtrusive indicators of prejudice. For example, in a research study conducted by Vanman, Paul, Ito, and Miller (1997), White men and women were asked to imagine working with a Black or White partner on several cooperative tasks. In addition, they were told to imagine that the rewards in each situation would be determined either by individual or joint effort of the partners. During the imaginal tasks, as a measure of the participants' feelings or affect, the researchers recorded electrical activity from the participants' facial muscles. Facial muscle activity indicative of positive feelings toward the imagery partners was greater in the individual- than in the joint-reward condition. Participants in the individual-reward condition showed greater facial muscle activity indicative of more positive feelings toward a White than toward a Black partner, whereas participants in the joint-reward condition showed greater facial muscle activity indicative of negative feelings toward a Black than toward a White partner. Thus, as predicted by the researchers, although the participants did not verbally report having more negative attitudes toward Black than White partners, their physiological reactions indicated that a greater emotional reaction, and by extension greater prejudice, was felt toward imaginary Black than toward imaginary White partners (see Figure 4.3).

Reducing Prejudice and Discrimination

No acceptable legal process can eliminate social prejudice, or it would probably have been employed by the U.S. government long before now. It has been found, however, that much can be done to reduce prejudice by removing some of the supports for it. Among these supports are stereotyped conceptions of the appearance and behavior of certain minority groups. If it can be demonstrated to a prejudiced person that minority group members do not necessarily fit his or her stereotype, then the person's attitude toward that group should change. It is ridiculous to suggest that minorities should make concerted efforts to change their appearance, but the misconception of minorities as possessing undesirable traits such as stupidity, overemotionality, or immorality can be combated by exposing prejudiced individuals to counterexamples. Illustrative of this approach are the images of minorities portrayed in motion pictures and television. For example, rather than being limited to menial and comic roles as they once were, African Americans are now often shown in the roles of higher-status individuals. Television programs expose viewers to similarities in the needs, activities, and essential humanness of different ethnic groups and provide information that may be useful in coping with people who were overlooked or actively rejected in one's everyday activities (Vrij, Van Schie, & Cherryman, 1996). For both minority and majority group members, and particularly children, exposure to appropriate role models in the media can serve as counterexamples of stereotypes and protection against prejudicial propaganda.

Legislation and Programmatic Action

During the first half of the 20th century, many people believed that one of the best ways to reduce social prejudice and intergroup hostility is to keep conflicting groups apart. For example, in the South African system of *apart-*

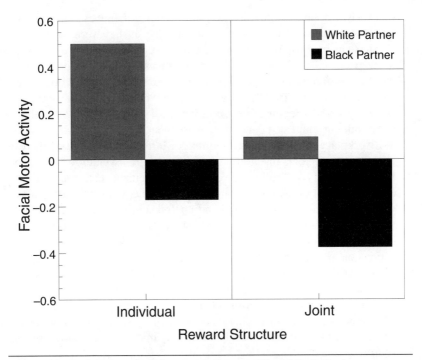

Figure 4.3. Facial Motor Activity as an Indicator of Racial Prejudice?

SOURCE: Based on data from Vanman, Paul, Ito, and Miller (1997).
NOTE: See text for explanation.

heid, Europeans and non-Europeans were segregated from each other and the latter were discriminated against—politically, economically, and socially. In the United States, the provision of separate but equal facilities was made the law of the land, a law that failed to become a reality. The separate facilities for Blacks were seldom equal to those for Whites, and in any event neither prejudice nor its effects was reduced by legalized separation of the races. The U.S. Supreme Court decision of 1954 (*Brown v. Board of Education of Topeka*) was the first link in a chain of legislation designed to eliminate segregation and discrimination in the United States. It had been demonstrated earlier in the integration of U.S. military units that prejudice was reduced when Black and White units were integrated. Many White soldiers who were initially prejudiced against Blacks changed their attitudes when they were "forced" to associate, many for the first time, with Black soldiers whose status in the military was equal to theirs. Furthermore, studies of integrated housing units (see Allport, 1954, for review) showed that White housewives became more tolerant toward Blacks when they found that the latter were as clean and as careful with property as they were.

Subsequent legislation, beginning with the Civil Rights Act of 1964, led to the extension of affirmative action programs as a method of reducing institutional discrimination by race/ethnicity, sex, religion, national origin, sexual orientation, and disability. Diversity initiatives stemming from this legislation led to a broadening of recruitment efforts, standard selection methods, skills training, enhancement of the environment, and career development in the workplace and educational settings (Murrell, 2000). Today, there is fairly wide agreement that affirmative action programs, employment opportunity laws, and court rulings have led to improvements in the occupational and educational status, living conditions, and general lifestyles of minority groups. However, though formal and open discrimination in the schools, workplaces, housing, business establishments, and other organizational contexts has eroded, subtle forms of racism, including *tokenism*—positive actions on a small scale—continue to exist in the United States and elsewhere. Furthermore, affirmative action programs have sometimes prompted accusations of *reverse discrimination*—treating members of minority groups more favorably than members of the majority (dominant) group. These charges and other indicators of continuing social discrimination become more pronounced as competition for limited opportunities and resources increases.

Research on Combating Prejudice and Discrimination

Psychological and sociological research studies of prejudice and discrimination go back to the early part of the 20th century, but they increased in frequency after midcentury. An experiment conducted by Sherif, Harvey, White, Hood, and Sherif (1961) is noteworthy because it was concerned both with creating and alleviating intergroup hostility. The participants of the experiment were 22 eleven-year-old boys in a summer camp, none of whom knew any of the others at the outset. Two groups of boys were formed in two different areas of the camp, and initially neither group was aware of the other's existence. By the end of the first 6 days, two cohesive groups calling themselves the Eagles and the Rattlers had been formed. At the end of the 6th day, each group was told of the existence of the other group, and immediately the boys clamored for intergroup athletic contests. During the second 6 days, baseball, tent-making, and tug-of-war contests between the two groups were held. Because one of the groups lost in this competitive activity, a strong intergroup rivalry and attendant hostility developed. During the third 6 days of the experiment, the researchers tried various techniques to reduce the hostility between groups. For example, it was arranged for the groups to meet together in pleasant surroundings, specifically, having them see movies and eat their best meals together. Unfortunately, this technique failed to reduce the level of hostility, and even the researchers became concerned when it failed to subside. The method that proved most effective in reducing hostility between the groups consisted of staging situations, without the boys' knowledge, in which the cooperative effort of both groups was required to attain a specified goal. For example, the researchers made arrangements for a truck that took the boys swimming to fail to start, and the efforts of all 22 boys were needed to pull the truck with a rope. Cooperative enterprises such as this resulted in the formation of a new group composed of both original groups. Although at the end of the second 6 days only 27% of the boys gave positive ratings and 63% gave negative ratings to the boys in the other group, by the end of the third 6 days 78% of the ratings were positive and only 13% were negative. In summary, the results of this experiment demonstrated that intergroup hostility can be easily created by having groups compete. After a strong intergroup hostility has developed, simply bringing the conflicting groups together in pleasant surroundings does not reduce the level of hostility, but contriving situations consisting of tasks that require the cooperative efforts of both groups is more effective.

The results of this experiment and other studies encouraged further research and theorizing concerning the *contact hypothesis* that bringing conflicting groups together can, under certain circumstances, reduce the conflict and tension between them. Allport (1954) had previously identified several conditions under which intergroup contact is more likely to produce harmony:

1. There should be social and institutional support for the measures designed to promote greater contact.

2. The contact should be of sufficient duration and closeness to permit meaningful relationships to develop among the members of the conflicting groups.

3. Insofar as possible, members of conflicting groups should be of equal status.

4. Members of conflicting groups should be required to depend on each other to achieve the desired objectives.

The last of the above requirements for effective contact—intergroup cooperation—has been examined in many field and experimental studies since the Sherif et al. (1961) investigation. For example, cooperative learning programs have been instituted in desegregated classrooms, in which children are required to work through assignments in small groups, teaching and reinforcing each other so that everyone contributes to the objectives of the lesson. The students in such "jigsaw" groups are mutually interdependent, engaging in a great deal of social interaction and thereby becoming well acquainted with each other. Research findings indicate that cooperative learning groups of this kind can increase the self-esteem, morale, interpersonal attraction, and *empathy* of students across ethnic and racial divisions; they can also improve the academic performance of minority students without hampering the performance of the ethnic majority (see Aronson, Blaney, Stephan, Sikes, & Snapp, 1978; Moskowitz, Malvin, Schaeffer, & Schaps, 1985; Singh, 1991; Walker & Crogan, 1998). However, Brown's (1986) evaluation of the *jigsaw classroom* procedure indicates that although the effects of employing the technique are statistically significant, they are generally small and open to various interpretations.

Social Categorization Theory

Reconceptualizations of research on the contact hypothesis in terms of intergroup cognition has provided a theoretical framework for understanding how social contact may change attitudes between groups. The emphasis of this theoretical framework, designated as *social categorization theory*, is on the role of cognitive representations of the contact situation in determining the outcomes of interactions between groups. Several different social categorization models of intergroup contact have been proposed, including the personalization model, the *common in-group identity model*, and the *distinct social identity model*. All three models provide explanations of techniques for reducing discrimination by changing one's cognitive representation of group membership (Brewer & Miller, 1988).

Personalization model. This "decategorization" model is based on the notion that contact with individual members of an out-group tends to break down the depersonalized categorization of those individuals and, by extension, the group as a whole (Brewer & Miller, 1984). Categorization leads to selective perception of in-group/out-group differences, reinforcing rather than reducing in-group bias. For this reason, relations between groups should be arranged so as to reduce general category differences. According to the personalization model, this can be facilitated by getting to know the out-group members as individuals rather than simply as representatives of a collectivity. Personalization of interactions can help disconfirm stereotypes and the associated tendency to perceive the out-group as homogeneous.

Laboratory studies have provided some support for the effectiveness of attending to information at the individual level in breaking down stereotypes and prejudice. However, personification may not work if positive experiences with particular out-group members are viewed as atypical and therefore not generalizable to the out-group as a whole. But if exposure to out-group members under personalizing conditions are frequent and involve several members, the importance of category boundaries is likely to be reduced and lead to increased recognition of the variability and complexity of the out-group membership (Brewer & Miller, 1988; Hamburger, 1994).

Common in-group identity model. The premise of this "recategorization" model is that intergroup bias and conflict can be reduced by processes that enable members to perceive themselves as belonging to a single group rather than to two separate groups. By coming to see themselves as members of a single, combined group, people's feelings for in-group members become directed toward out-group members (Gaertner, Dovidio, & Bachman, 1996; Gaertner, Rust, Dovidio, Bachman, & Anastasio, 1994). These positive feelings lead to more extensive between-group interaction, causing further reductions in intergroup bias. The crucial factor in developing this intergroup attitude is inducing previously separate groups to work together on cooperative enterprises. By causing disparate group members to devote themselves to shared goals, the contact situation prompts them to focus on and identify with a superordinate social category consisting of both the previous in-group and the out-group. Thus, the heretofore separate groups become conceptualized and recategorized as one.

Distinct social identity model. This "subcategorization" model of intergroup contact provides for dual identification at different levels of social categories (Hewstone & Brown, 1986). It is based on the premise that positive intergroup experiences occur when the contact situation is structured in such a way that members of the respective groups have distinct but complementary roles to play in achieving common goals. While doing so, both groups maintain their distinctive identities in an intergroup cooperative context.

Evidence for the effectiveness of the distinct social identity model has been obtained in a number of experiments (e.g., Deschamps & Brown, 1983). In an experiment conducted by Vivian, Brown, and Hewstone (1994), cooperative contact with a member of another nationality was found to be associated with a more favorable generalized attitude toward that nationality when the nationality category was obvious and important in the contact. There are, however, some negatives in this theoretical approach. For example, it may reinforce perceptions of the two groups as distinctly different and strengthen negative beliefs about the out-group.

Cross-Categorization Models

All three of the contact models described above have been shown to be effective under certain conditions. In general, decategorization, recategorization, and mutual intergroup differentiation processes can contribute to the reduction of intergroup bias and conflict (Gaertner et al., 2000). However, they also represent unstable situations that, in the long run, may increase intergroup conflict. Alternative conceptions of contact effectiveness in reducing in-group bias are *cross-categorization models*. These models are based on the observation that most people have multiple social identities that cut across social dimensions, such as gender, ethnicity, occupation, and religion. Cross-categorization models, such as that proposed by Brewer (2000), attempt to delineate the conditions under which such multiple, cross-cutting social identities reduce out-group discrimination based on a single dimension. An example of the effects of cross-cutting in real life is seen in societies characterized by cross-cultural kinship and tribal systems, which are less prone to internal feuding (Doise, 1978).

Reducing the Effects of Stereotypes

Another approach to modifying social prejudice and discrimination focuses on the process of thinking about people in terms of categories or stereotypes. Stereotypes are not always bad: they enable us to conceptualize our experiences and perhaps cope with them more efficiently. However, stereotypes are overgeneralizations, and when used to characterize entire groups of people they can interfere with a clearer understanding of the complexity and uniqueness of human beings. Baron and Byrne (2000) offer suggestions for reducing the impact of stereotypes, including the following: (a) encourage people to pay attention to the unique characteristics of others rather than simply identifying them with the groups to which they belong, and (b) avoid making inferences about other people on the basis of their outcomes, while ignoring factors that might have produced those outcomes.

Suggestions for improving intergroup relationships through contact are, of course, not guaranteed prescriptions for reducing social conflict. Contact between previously separated groups can create anxiety and hostility even when the members of both groups have good intentions and a vested interest in cooperating. Because the situation is unusual, in-group members may adopt a self-presentation style in which they become so concerned with not making a bad impression by saying or doing something that might be interpreted as prejudice that they forget about trying to make a good impression. This self-presentation style may be interpreted by members of the out-group as hostility, and they may feel that they are being victimized and evaluated negatively (Devine, Evett, & Vasquez-Suson, 1995). Research has shown, however, that although people who enter into in-group/out-group contact experience anxiety, the level of anxiety gradually decreases if the contacts are not negative (Britt, Boniecki, Vescio, Biernat, & Brown, 1996; Stephan & Stephan, 1992).

Clearly, there is no single or simple way to eliminate social prejudice and discrimination. In the interest of intergroup harmony and even enlightened self-interest, however, people should be encouraged to work toward becoming high self-monitors and self-regulators who are aware of their own socially prejudiced and discriminating behaviors and are willing to work, for the benefit of everyone, toward reducing the discrepancy between what is and what should be (see Devine, 1989; Monteith, 1993).

Recommended Readings

Brewer, M. B. (2000). Reducing prejudice through cross-categorization: Effects of multiple social identities. In S. Oskamp (Ed.), *Reducing prejudice and discrimination* (pp. 165-183). Mahwah, NJ: Lawrence Erlbaum.

Brewer, M. B., & Brown, R. J. (1998). Intergroup relations. In D. T. Gilbert, S. T. Fiske, & G. Lindzey (Eds.), *The handbook of social psychology* (4th ed., Vol. 1, pp. 554-594). New York: McGraw-Hill/Oxford.

Erdman, B. P. (1999). *Ageism: Negative and positive*. New York: Springer.

Fiske, S. T. (1998). Stereotyping, prejudice, and discrimination. In D. T. Gilbert, S. T. Fiske, & G. Lindzey (Eds.), *The handbook of social psychology* (4th ed., Vol. 2, pp. 357-411). New York: McGraw-Hill/Oxford.

Gaines, S. O., & Reed, E. S. (1995). Prejudice: From Allport to DuBois. *American Psychologist, 50*(2), 96-103.

Green, D. P., Abelson, R. P., & Garnett, M. (1999). The distinctive political views of hate-crime perpetrators and White supremacists. In D. A. Prentice & D. T. Miller (Eds.), *Cultural divides: Understanding and overcoming group conflict* (pp. 429-464). New York: Russell Sage.

Major, B., Quinton, W. J., McCoy, S. K., & Schmadser, T. (2000). Reducing prejudice: The target's perspective. In S. Oskamp (Ed.), *Reducing prejudice and discrimination* (pp. 211-237). Mahwah, NJ: Lawrence Erlbaum.

Swim, J. K., Aikin, K. J., Hall, W. S., & Hunter, B. A. (1995). Sexism and racism: Old-fashioned and modern prejudices. *Journal of Personality and Social Psychology, 68*(2), 199-214.

Whitley, B. E., Jr. (1999). Right-wing authoritarianism, social dominance orientation, and prejudice. *Journal of Personality and Social Psychology, 77*(1), 126-134.

Appendix 4.1

Illustrative Measures of Racism, Sexism, and Ageism

Racism Scales

Modern Racism Scale (McConahay, 1986). This instrument was designed to measure a cognitive component of racial attitudes of Whites toward Blacks. These attitudes are as follows: discrimination is a thing of the past; Blacks are pushing too hard; recent gains for Blacks are undeserved; racism is bad; other beliefs do not constitute racism because these beliefs are facts. This is in contrast to the old racism based on familiar negative stereotypes, support for segregation, and open discrimination. Six statements are rated on a 5-point, Likert-type scale.

Motivation to Control Prejudiced Reactions Scale (MCPRS; Dunton & Fazio, 1997). Self-report measure designed to assess those factors that account for the motivation to engage in more deliberative processing when negative racial attitudes are automatically activated. The respondent answers each of 17 statements on a scale ranging from –3 (*strongly disagree*) to +3 (*strongly agree*). Six items are reverse scored.

Prejudice Perception Assessment Scale (PPAS; Martinez, 1998). This brief scale is composed of five vignettes aimed at assessing the extent to which respondents tend to perceive prejudice as the cause of negative, interpersonal outcomes in ambiguous situations. The PPAS has good internal consistency and measures stigma vulnerability as a unidimensional variable.

Universal Orientation Scale (Phillips & Ziller, 1997). This instrument was designed to measure *nonprejudice*, a universal orientation in interpersonal relations whereby perceivers selectively attend to, accentuate, and interpret similarities rather than differences between the self and others (cognitive integration vs. differentiation). High scorers on universal orientation are more accepting and less discriminating between minority and nonminority control targets than low scorers.

Sexism and Gender-Orientation Scales

Ambivalent Sexism Inventory (Glick & Fiske, 1996). This inventory measures positive orientation toward women, male ambivalence (paternalism, gender differentiation, and heterosexuality), and negative attitudes toward and stereotypes about women. It differentiates between hostile and benevolent sexism. The inventory consists of 140 statements that are responded to on a 6-point, Likert-type scale.

Gender Attitude Inventory (GAI; Ashmore, Del Boca, & Bilder, 1995). This structured inventory is designed to assess the attitudes of college students toward a broad range of topics related to gender. It consists of 14 gender-related attitude scales totaling 109 items, rated on a 7-point, Likert-type scale; 42 of the items reflect traditional attitudes and 657 modern attitudes. The 14 scales are as follows: endorsement of female superiority, acceptance of traditional stereotypes, condemnation of homosexuality, disapproval of female sexual initiative, disapproval of female casual sex, endorsement of chivalry, acceptance of male heterosexual violence, endorsement of family roles, beliefs in differential work roles, rejection of female political leadership, opposition to women's rights, endorsement of individual action, opposition to funded day care, and opposition to abortion. Sixty-seven of the items may be used to create three second-order factor scales: stereotypes, sexual relationships, and societal organization.

Modern Sexism Scale (Swim, Aikin, Hall, & Hunter, 1995). This instrument measures the attitudes of people toward women. It consists of eight items rated on a 7-point, Likert-type scale. It differs from the traditional scales of sexism based on negative stereotypes in that it measures denial of continued discrimination, antagonism, and lack of support for policies designed to help women. The items are based on McConahay's Modern Racism Scale.

Neosexism Scale (Tougas, Brown, Beaton, & Joly, 1995). This 11-item scale was designed to measure a new type of gender prejudice: neosexist beliefs, a conflict between egalitarian values and residual negative feelings toward women. It also looks at collective interest and its impact on subtle gender bias. Items were borrowed from several earlier scales by McConahay, Gaertner and Dovidio, and Jacobson.

Old-Fashioned Sexism Scale (Swim, Aikin, Hall, & Hunter, 1995). This scale measures the attitudes of people toward women. It consists of five items rated on a 7-point, Likert-type scale. It is based on an endorsement of traditional gender roles, differential treatment of women and men, and stereotypes about lesser female competence. The items are based on McConahay's Old-Fashioned Racism Scale.

Sexism Scale (Rombough & Ventimiglia, 1981). This scale consists of 20 self-administered items in a Likert-type format that measure attitudes toward sex roles in three broad areas: internal familial division of labor, external (economic) division of labor, and perceived sex differences. The items can be used with a Guttman scoring option.

Sexist Attitudes Toward Women Scale (Benson & Vincent, 1980). This scale was designed to assess individual differences in sexism. The following seven components of sexism are reflected in the 40 items on the scale: (a) attitudes that women are genetically inferior (biologically, emotionally, intellectually) to men; (b) support for the premise that men should have greater rights and power than women; (c) support for sex discrimination (antifemale) practices in education, work, and politics; (d) hostility toward women who engage in traditionally masculine roles and behaviors or who fail to fulfill traditional female roles; (e) lack of support and empathy for women's liberation movements and the issues involved in such movements; (f) utilization of derogatory labels and restrictive stereotypes in describing women; and (g) evaluation of women on the basis of physical attractiveness information and willingness to treat women as sexual objects. On a 7-point, Likert-type scale, respondents indicate how strongly they agree or disagree with each item. Twenty-four of the statements are written from a sexist point of view, and 16 are written from a nonsexist point of view. The scale may be administered to high school students, college students, or adults.

Combined Racism and Sexism Scale

Modified Godfrey-Richman ISM Scale (M-GRISMS; Godfrey, Richman, & Withers, 2000). This scale was designed to measure stereotypes, prejudice, and discrimination toward various ethnic and religious groups, as well as sexist and heterosexist attitudes. The test items include various ethnic groups (Racism subscale), religious groups (Religion subscale), and the Heterosexist and Sexist subscales. Each of these scales is parsed into various subcategories; for example, the Racism subscale assesses attitudes toward African Americans, Asian Americans, European Americans, Hispanics, and Native Americans. Eight independent factors traverse two or more subscales.

Ageism Scale

Fraboni Scale of Ageism (FSA; Fraboni, Saltstone, & Hughes, 1990). Measures three factors—antilocution, avoidance, and discrimination, the item content of which reflects affective components of ageism. These factors also combine to form a unitary construct evidenced by a general factor revealed in a second-order factor analysis.

Sexual Orientation Attitude Scales

Attitudes Toward Lesbians and Gay Men (ATLG; Herek, 1994). Consists of two 10-item subscales, one for attitudes toward gay men (ATG) and the other for attitudes toward lesbians (ATL). The 20 statements are presented to respondents in Likert format, usually with a 9-point scale ranging from *strongly disagree* to *strongly agree*. Scoring is accomplished by summing scores across items for each subscale. Reverse scoring is used for some items. Total scale scores can range from 20 (extremely positive attitudes) to 180 (extremely negative attitudes). ATL and ATG subscale scores range from 10 to 90.

Homophobia Scale (Wright, Adams, & Bernat, 1999). This scale was developed to assess the cognitive, affective, and behavioral components of homophobia. There are 25 items, consisting of three factors: a factor that assesses mainly negative cognitions regarding homosexuality, a factor that assesses primarily negative affect and avoidance of homosexual individuals, and a factor that assesses negative affect and aggression toward homosexual individuals.

Modern Homophobia Scale (Raja & Stokes, 1998). This scale was designed as a measure of attitudes toward lesbians and gay men separately, as well as the hypothesized personal and institutional components of homophobia. It includes items reflecting the following factors: Personal Discomfort with lesbians/gay men, Institutional Homophobia toward lesbians/gay men, and Deviance/Changeability of female/male homosexuality. Although the Personal Discomfort, Institutional, and Deviance/Changeability factors are separable, they are highly correlated and show little evidence of divergent validity.

5

Living Conditions and Problems

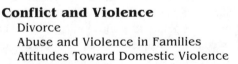

Living Conditions
Income and Poverty
Attitudes Toward the Poor
Unemployment
Housing and Homelessness

Illness and Disability
Demographic Factors in Illness
Health Psychology
Disabilities
Attitudes Toward Illness and Disability

Conflict and Violence
Divorce
Abuse and Violence in Families
Attitudes Toward Domestic Violence
Violent Crime
Attitudes Toward Crime and Deviance

Human beings have a multiplicity of needs: biological, psychological, and social. The nature of these needs and the substances, activities, and situations that satisfy them change as a person grows older and learns. Frustration of one's needs, no matter how short- or long-lasting it may be, occurs to some extent from the very beginning of human existence. But to adapt to changes in personal needs and to cope with the conditions that interfere with their satisfaction, one must learn to be patient, attentive, and tractable.

Most of the same needs are found in different people, but no person is exactly the same as any other. Each of the more than 6 billion people in the world is a product of biological and environmental factors that vary, sometimes more and sometimes less, from person to person. Such variability has increased the adaptability and hence the survival of the human species, but on many occasions it has also been a source of conflict. Because of the circumstances of birth, abilities, and living environment, some people are better equipped than others to satisfy their needs and fulfill their potential. Those who are not so fortunate may look upon these "haves" with a feeling that life has placed too many obstacles in their paths and made it unreasonably difficult for them to fulfill their needs and desires. Such is more often the case with those who are indigent, homeless, unhealthy, disabled, or handicapped in other ways. The attitude of their fellow humans toward these unfortunates is not always marked by sympathy and support. Quite often, they live a marginal existence and fail to conform to the norms and mores of the larger social in-group. The dominant social class may even perceive those who are lower in the social hierarchy as deserving of their lot, to be ignored whenever possible or to be given only superficial treatment and assistance. As history has repeatedly demonstrated, however, the social dissatisfaction and disequilibrium produced by differences between "haves" and "have-nots" are rarely solved by half-hearted, token measures. And sometimes the consequence of such oversight is malnutrition, disease, and violence in a substantial portion of the population.

This chapter is concerned primarily with attitudes and opinions concerning selected personal and social problems that occur in human society, often despite advances in science, technology, and medicine, and the efforts of well-meaning individuals. The chapter considers the needs for food, shelter, health, and safety in particular, all of which have economic underpinnings. A representative sample of measures of attitudes and opinions that are concerned with the topics discussed in this chapter is given in Appendix 5.1.

Living Conditions

Income and Poverty

Income, the most common measure of socioeconomic status (SES), is associated with a host of personal and social advantages and disadvantages. Families with below-average incomes tend to have inadequate nutrition, housing, clothing, and health care and also lack many of the necessities for education, training, and leisure-time activities. A common cause of poverty is being too ill or disabled to work, and thereby receiving no earned income. Lack of income is especially acute when an unemployed person is not adequately covered by disability or medical insurance.[1]

For purposes of poverty estimates, *income* is defined as money before taxes and does not include food stamps, Medicare, Medicaid, public housing, and fringe benefits provided by employers. Adjusting income for family size and inflation provides a measure of the family's poverty status and hence its eligibility for certain public benefits. Families having adjusted incomes below the federal poverty threshold are referred to as "poor," those with adjusted incomes that are 100% to 199% of the poverty threshold are "near poor," and those with incomes that are 200% or more of the poverty threshold are designated as "middle and high income."

The official definition of *poverty* in the United States is based on a set of money income thresholds that vary with family size and composition. The *consumer price index* (CPI) is used to adjust the poverty threshold for inflation on a yearly basis. Only money income before taxes, and no capital gains or noncash benefits (public housing, Medicaid, food stamps, etc.), is employed in defining the poverty threshold. Different poverty guidelines, and consequently different thresholds, are used for Alaska and Hawaii than for the 48 contiguous states and the District of Columbia (U.S. Census Bureau, 2000b).

As illustrated in Figure 5.1, the percentage of Americans who fall below the official poverty threshold varies with age and ethnicity. Substantially greater percentages of Blacks, Hispanics, and American Indian/Alaskan Natives than White non-Hispanics and Asian/Pacific Islanders fall below the poverty threshold. The poverty rate also varies with chronological age, place of birth, and many other factors. It is higher for children than for other age groups, higher in central cities than in suburbs or nonmetropolitan areas, and higher for foreign-born than for native-born Americans (U.S. Census Bureau, 2000b).

Despite the sizable number of people who continue to fall below the official poverty threshold, in recent years there have been marked reductions in poverty in certain groups, for example, older Americans. According to official estimates, the overall poverty rate dropped from 12.7% (34.5 million people) in 1998 to 11.8% (32.3 million people) in 1999. The number of "poor" declined for all ethnic groups, and for the "under 18" and "over 64" age groups. Poverty rates also declined in the Northwest and West, but not in the East and South, in central cities within metropolitan areas, and in seven states and the District of Columbia. However, the average dollar amount required to raise a poor family out of poverty did not change significantly from 1998 to 1999 (U.S. Census Bureau, 2000b).

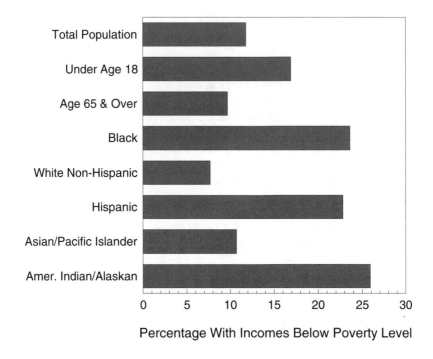

Figure 5.1. Percentage of Various Groups of Americans Falling Below the Poverty Threshold in 1999

SOURCE: Based on data from Weinberg (2000).

Attitudes Toward the Poor

Attitudes toward the poor vary with political views, social status, and religious beliefs. Analyses of opinion data from the General Social Surveys and the National Election Studies demonstrate that Biblical conservatism intensifies expression of concern for the poor, and higher education plays a role in shaping the expression of that concern (Clydesdale, 1999). Another study found that not only do poor children themselves perceive the wider society as disparaging of the poor, but they also have difficulty maintaining positive views of themselves, and they view their poverty status as a deprivation (Weinger, 1998).

Unemployment

The rate of unemployment in the United States, which is important in gauging the state of the economy, has declined during the past few years.

The unemployment rate in mid-2001 was around 4.5%, an increase from the 4.2% rate in early 2001 but a decline from 4.7% in early 1998. The unemployment rate was essentially equal for men and women, but higher for Blacks and Hispanics than for Whites and substantially higher for teenagers than for adults (Bureau of Labor Statistics, 2001).

Reactions to being unemployed depend to some extent on what a person is accustomed to or prepared for. The loss of a job, and the subsequent decline in income and status, is rarely a pleasant event at any age. However, the effects are typically greater for middle-aged adults than for their younger and older counterparts. Young adults, who have almost their entire working lives ahead of them, are typically more optimistic and realistically hopeful of finding another job, and older adults can retire and perhaps make other work arrangements. Unemployed middle-aged adults, particularly those who have worked for an organization for many years and have attained a fairly high level in the corporate hierarchy and are not ready to retire, are faced with the prospect of being unable to find a comparable position.

The effects of unemployment also depend on the reasons for the loss of a job and what it means to the individual. Unemployed men tend to perceive their status as a stigma, and they spend more time than unemployed women searching for work (e.g., Kulik, 2000). People who can rationalize the loss of a job as not being their fault and not a rejection of their value as breadwinners and human beings are more likely to take the loss in stride and deal with it effectively. This outcome is more likely to occur when an unemployed person receives strong social support from family and friends and when he or she possesses the skills needed to cope with personal setbacks and frustration (Mallinckrodt & Fretz, 1988). Most unemployed workers can distance themselves from work and learn to take advantage of other things in life, perhaps continuing to look for a job but learning to balance this pursuit with time spent in more rewarding activities.

Whether one has a negative or a positive attitude toward unemployed persons and how generalized those attitudes are varies with such factors as political orientation, occupational group, and personal experiences. Political moderates are less likely than those who are politically polarized to make generalizations concerning the unemployed. Experience with unemployed people also reduces the number of generalizations made concerning their motivations and plight (McFadyen, 1998).

Housing and Homelessness

A person's home may not be a castle, but the neighborhood in which one lives and the condition of one's home are certainly prominent status symbols. They reflect not only the resident's material well-being but to some extent what kind of person he or she is. Depending on personal income and other possessions, one may have to live on the "wrong side of the tracks" with the hoi polloi rather than with the "swells" in a posh neighborhood.

The size, construction, features, and location of housing vary not only with price but also with population density and geographical region. Housing units are different in central cities than in suburbs and even more different in small towns and rural areas of the United States. As seen in the differences between housing in the West and in the East, and between housing in the North and in the South, climate and lifestyle also have an effect on housing.

Some houses are described as "shacks" or "dumps" that are firetraps, in disrepair, and not fit for human habitation. However, the vast majority of the 53,000 housing units across the United States examined in the American Housing Survey of 1997 were in fair to good condition. Only 9% of the units were found to be uncomfortably cold for at least one 24-hour period during the winter, and about 7% had moderate or severe physical problems. These problems included such things as lack of a complete kitchen, poor building or hallway maintenance, or the absence of or frequent breakdowns in the plumbing, heating, or electrical systems. The residents of 60% of the units with moderate to severe problems were renters, whereas only 34% of all households were renters. Lower-cost rental units and those occupied without payment of cash rent were more likely than higher-cost units to have significant problems. Renters of units having one to three bedrooms spent a larger percentage of their income on housing than owners, but renters of units with four or more bedrooms spent a smaller percentage of their income on housing than owners whose houses had four or more bedrooms. Residents in the Midwest and South regions spent a greater percentage of income on housing than those in the Northeast and West (U.S. Census Bureau, 1999b).

Housing consumes a sizable portion of the incomes of most Americans, and especially those at the lower end of the socioeconomic scale. Because of relatively high rents, a large part of the small incomes of inner-city residents is spent on housing. Unlike the traditional order of importance—food, clothing, and shelter—poor people spend the largest portion of their monthly income on rent and utilities, with clothing second, and food in third place. Despite laws limiting the number of inhabitants in a house of specified size, several people often live and sleep in the same room and may share kitchen and bathroom facilities with residents of other rooms in the same building. Consequently, malnutrition and other health problems are not unusual. Health problems and malnutrition are less characteristic of the residents of publicly supported housing projects.

A common situation for less affluent people living in large cities is *single-room occupancy* (SRO) in old residential hotels. These accommodations vary in quality depending on their location, newness, and the clientele to which they cater. There is a marked scarcity of relatively low-rent facilities

of this type, which also attract many people of middle SES. The most deteri-
orated type, the residents of which are typically men, are the skid-row hotels
located in the central city. At the next level are relatively clean hotels located
in the shabbier sections of large cities. These accommodations provide
housekeeping services and cater to working-class and even middle-class
people, again, most of whom are men. At the higher end of the spectrum are
more comfortable and more expensive middle-class hotels, which provide
some activities and house equal numbers of men and women.

The facilities provided by skid-row hotels are usually barely adequate.
Meals tend to be sporadic, perhaps cooked on a makeshift hot plate fash-
ioned from an electric iron wedged between two Bibles. When they are not
in their rooms, residents of skid-row hotels tend to wander the streets or con-
gregate at large outdoor parks, at bus terminals, and in other sheltered public
places, often hustling to obtain some money. Even less fortunate than single-
room occupants are the homeless, who live in the streets, public parks, door-
ways, bus and railway terminals, or other convenient locations in metropolitan areas. They are often mentally disturbed, physically disabled, unemployed, indigent, and usually have no one to care for them. They make their
"rounds" during the day and usually find a relatively warm place somewhere
for the night until they can begin their daily wandering again.

Estimates of the percentage of the U.S. population who are homeless vary
from 250,000 to 2½ million. Homeless people belong to every ethnic, gender, and educational group. Three fourths are single adults without children,
but another one fifth consist of families with children, typically headed by a
single woman (U.S. Senate Special Committee on Aging, 2000). Some
homeless people have lost their jobs and cannot find affordable housing; others are mentally ill, alcoholics and/or substance abusers, or are plagued by
chronic health problems. Still others are battered women, petty criminals, or
disaffiliated persons (Crane, 1996).

Some cities have shelters where the homeless can find temporary lodg-
ing, but many spend their lives in the streets, trying to find something to eat,
protection from the weather, and safety. By means of the McKinney Act, the
federal government provides funds through competitive and formula grants
to sponsor programs that arrange for emergency food and shelter, transi-
tional and permanent housing, primary health care services, mental health
care, alcohol and drug abuse treatment, education, and job training for the
homeless. Hundreds of projects at the local level have been designed to assist the homeless and those who are just "one paycheck away" from homelessness to find safe and affordable housing and provide services that enable
them to continue living at home. Recognition of the global nature of homelessness is seen in programs sponsored by the United Nations and other organizations for the estimated 1 billion people worldwide who lack adequate
shelter and the 40 million or more who are homeless (Huth & Wright, 1997).

In addition to the physical problems associated with their living situation, homeless persons are often socially stigmatized and treated as mentally ill and incompetent (Phelan, Link, Moore, & Stueve, 1997). Attitudes toward homelessness are also related to personality and politics. Compared with self-identified Democrats, self-identified Republicans in one study were significantly more likely to attribute homelessness to internal rather than external factors. Republicans also expressed significantly less favorable attitudes toward publicly funded programs for the homeless (Pellegrini, Queirolo, Monarrez, & Valenzuela, 1997). Associated with this finding are the percentages of Republican, Democratic, and Independent respondents in a 1999 Gallup poll who agreed or disagreed with the following statement: "The Republican party has not been compassionate enough about the needs of the poor." Thirty-eight percent of the Republicans, 82% of the Democrats, and 70% of the Independents agreed with the statement, and 58%, 16%, and 27%, respectively, disagreed with the statement (Gallup, 2000, p. 87). Thus, whether or not Republicans are compassionate enough toward the poor, they are more likely than Democrats and Independents to see themselves as being so.

Illness and Disability

No one wants to get sick or have a serious disability. Not only do illnesses and disabilities cause pain and suffering, but they can also be disfiguring and even life-threatening. A chronic illness or serious disability can dominate one's life, absorbing time and attention, interfering with one's education, employment, leisure, social life, and activities of daily living (ADLs). When an illness is contagious or a disability is unsightly and handicapping, it can have ostracizing consequences, making it extremely difficult to interact with anyone other than a few devoted family members and health personnel. Even efforts to treat illnesses and disabilities can be disturbing and demoralizing, causing discomfort and side effects that often seem worse than the disorder itself. Depending on the effectiveness of the treatments, the patient may be subject to a long period of recovery or rehabilitation, punctuated by spells of anxiety, depression, and disappointment; false hopes; and other feelings and attitudes that contribute to the course and severity of the condition.

Demographic Factors in Illness

When questioned by survey researchers, a large majority of Americans say that their own health, in general, is good or excellent (Davis & Smith, 1994). As shown by both casual observation and careful research, however, health declines with age. For example, statistics on various diagnoses among patients with short-term hospital stays demonstrate that circulatory, digestive, and respiratory diseases; neoplasms; musculoskeletal disorders; and endocrine and metabolic disorders all increase with age (Graves & Gillum, 1996). Medical expenditures, frequency and length of hospital stays, and physician contacts and reported health are also related to chronological age. In a National Health Interview Study conducted in 1994, for example, the personal health assessments of Americans in various demographic groups tended to become more negative after age 65 (Adams & Marano, 1995).

Chronological age is, of course, not the only demographic variable associated with health. Sex (gender), race/ethnicity, and income are also important. On self-health ratings, men rate higher than women, Whites rate higher than Blacks, and people with large family incomes rate higher than those with lower family incomes (Adams & Marano, 1995; Davis & Smith, 1994). Other data support the conclusion that people who are lower on the socioeconomic scale tend to have poorer health and a shorter life span than those higher up on the socioeconomic scale (Collins & LeClere, 1997). A contributing factor is that people with lower incomes have fewer physician contacts than those with higher incomes. SES is, of course, a confounding factor in the finding that Blacks have fewer physician contacts than Whites (National Center for Health Statistics, 1995).

Heredity is a contributing factor in illness, but environmental conditions such as pollution, diet, and sanitation are also important. For example, the greater longevity of women is due in some measure to the fact that men are more likely to encounter pollution (e.g., cigarette smoke, smoke and air pollutants) in the work environment. For this and perhaps other reasons, men are more susceptible than women to respiratory disorders such as bronchitis, emphysema, and fibrosis (National Center for Health Statistics, 1991). Contributing to the inverse relationship between SES and health is the fact that poorer people also live and work in less sanitary environments, usually eat less nutritious food, and have less adequate medical care than their more affluent contemporaries. Other lifestyle factors associated with poor health and a high death rate are cigarette smoking, alcohol and drug abuse, insufficient exercise, stress, and a lack of social supports (Brannon & Feist, 1997).

Health Psychology

Health psychology is concerned with the contributions of psychology to the promotion and maintenance of health, the prevention and treatment of illness, and the identification of etiological and diagnostic correlates of health, illness, and related conditions (Matarazzo, 1980). Health psychologists are particularly interested in the role played by attitudes, emotions, and personality, not only in traditional *somatoform disorders* such as duodenal ulcers and migraine headaches but also in life-threatening illnesses such as cardiovascular diseases and malignant neoplasms.

Because their health and that of their families is very important to most people, health-related advertising and promotion are a big business in the modern world. However, many commercial health messages arouse anxiety and, as predicted by cognitive dissonance theory and other psychological theories, may prompt immediate efforts to reduce the level of anxiety (Liberman & Chaiken, 1992). Frequently, anxiety induced by health messages is reduced by simply viewing the messages as untrue or otherwise suppressing or repressing them. For example, information concerned with the importance of early detection of breast cancer or HIV infection may be overlooked, forgotten, or discounted. As discussed in Chapter 3, messages that unduly frighten people do not usually promote action. However, health messages that are worded in a more positive manner are more likely to promote constructive behavior (Rothman, Salovey, Antone, Keough, & Martin, 1993).

It is a credo of health psychologists that people are more successful in adjusting to aversive events when they believe that they have some control over those events (Thompson, 1981). Gaining such control over serious illness typically involves efforts to understand its causes and prognoses. In attempting to understand the causes of a serious illness or accident, the individual often engages in self-blame. This process may have either negative or positive consequences, depending on whether one's behavior or character (personality) is viewed as being at fault (Janoff-Bulman, 1979). In any case, blaming others for one's condition is generally viewed as counterproductive (Affleck, Tennen, Croog, & Levine, 1987).

In addition to studies of the influences on treatment progress of "self" versus "other" attributions, research has demonstrated that *self-efficacy,* or judgment concerning one's ability to deal with a situation, can, by enabling the person to deal with the stressfulness induced by the situation, have beneficial effects. Comparing one's condition with that of other people, and thereby concluding that it could be worse and will probably get better, can also be helpful.

Another area of investigation in health psychology that has shown promise is the relationship between optimism and the progress of a disorder. However, the findings on this topic are mixed. Optimism is generally viewed as health promoting, but under certain circumstances blind, Pollyannaish optimism may be health endangering (see Salovey, Rothman, & Rodin, 1998).

Other dispositional variables that have been examined for their possible relationships to stress and illness are hardiness, Type A personality, neuroticism, self-identity, and self-healing. The most extensively studied of these variables is *Type A personality*, described as "aggressive, competitive, hostile, quick-acting, and constantly striving" (Friedman, 1990, 1992; Friedman & Booth-Kewley, 1987). Evidence indicates that a personality characterized by depression, anger/hostility, and anxiety is an important factor in coronary heart disease and, in fact, in a whole range of bodily complaints (Watson & Pennebaker, 1989).

Numerous studies have been conducted on the relationships between attitudes, dispositional variables, and cancer (Derogatis, Abeloff, & Melisaratos, 1979; Levy, Lee, Bagley, & Lippman, 1988; Levy & Roberts, 1992; O'Leary, 1990; Temoshuk, 1992). It is not clear from many of these studies whether the attitudinal or dispositional variables are contributory or consequential factors in cancer, or whether they merely promote risky behaviors such as cigarette smoking, poor diet, and noncompliance with physician's orders. It has also been argued that attitudinal and personality variables are more important in the progress than in the precipitation of cancer. For example, the results of one investigation showed that people who were able to maintain a "fighting spirit"—a belief that they were going to beat the disease no matter what the odds—were more likely to recover than pessimists who resigned themselves to being "goners" (Greer, 1991; Pettingale, Morris, Greer, & Haybittle, 1985).

Disabilities

Depending on the nature of the disability, a person with a disability may have difficulty performing activities involving seeing, hearing, talking, walking, climbing, carrying, and other sensorimotor functions. Disabled persons experience problems with ADLs and/or with social roles such as schoolwork (children) and working at a job or around the house (adults). A disability is considered severe when the person is unable to perform one or more ADLs, uses assistive devices to get around, or needs the help of another person to perform basic activities.

One in five Americans has some kind of disability, and 1 in 10 has a severe disability. Among Americans aged 21 to 64, 64% have difficulty hearing, 44% have difficulty seeing, 34% have difficulty walking, and 41% have a mental disability of some kind. The percentage of Americans with any disability increases with age, ranging from approximately 9% at birth to age 14 and 19% at ages 15 to 64 to over 52% at age 65 and over. The majority of these disabilities are not severe, but an appreciable number are. The percentage of Americans with disabilities also varies with ethnicity. For example, 20% of Whites, 28% of Hispanics, and 35% of Blacks in the 55- to 64-year age range have at least one disability (U.S. Census Bureau, 1997).

Box 5.1
Physicians' Attitudes Toward Older Patients

One of the cornerstones of modern medicine is that the patient's attitude plays a significant role in the progress of an illness. The attitudes of attending physicians may also be crucial to the health of older adult patients. Unfortunately, physicians and other health care professionals tend to have less positive attitudes toward treating older patients than younger patients. Even well-meaning physicians and nurses often have difficulty communicating with older patients; they may call them by their first names and in other ways behave condescendingly or treat them like children.

Research findings also suggest that physicians pay less attention to their older patients, spend less time with them, and express less inclination to provide vigorous treatment to them (Greene, Hoffman, Charon, & Adelman, 1987; Greenfield, Blanco, Elashoff, & Ganz, 1987; Radecki, Kane, Solomon, Mendenhall, & Beck, 1988). Some of the apparent neglect of older patients may, however, be the fault of the patients themselves. By focusing on only a few symptoms, such as dizziness, pain, or high blood pressure, and raising fewer questions concerning their functioning or how the symptoms are affecting their lives, older patients demand less and hence get less from physicians (Haug, 1981).

To some extent one may sympathize with doctors who find that treating older adult patients is less personally satisfying than treating younger patients. However, the problem of physician attitudes needs to be dealt with. One recommendation is to design medical education to assist future physicians in coping more effectively with older patients. In addition, it would help if more medical students were attracted to geriatrics and family medicine as specialties. Unfortunately, geriatrics can be a difficult and unprofitable area of specialization, and specialists in family medicine usually prefer to work with younger patients who are more likely to get well and thereby reward the doctor's skill and efforts.

SOURCE: Reprinted from Aiken (2001a, p. 70).

The Americans With Disabilities Act (ADA) of 1990 makes it illegal to discriminate in employment against individuals with disabilities in the United States. As a consequence, employment of disabled persons has increased during the past decade or more. Results of surveys of managers and executives in various corporations (e.g., Callahan, 1994; Levy, Jessop, Rimmerman, & Levy, 1993) indicate a high level of favorability regarding the employability of persons with severe disabilities, as well as the advantages to disabled workers and lack of disadvantages to other workers. It remains true, however, that a smaller percentage of persons having disabilities, and to an even greater extent those with severe disabilities, are employed than individuals with no disability. Despite a lower level of employment, more than 77% of disabled Americans between the ages of 22 and

64 receive no public assistance. However, among recipients of governmental assistance in the form of cash, food, or rent, a fairly sizable portion has one or more disabilities (U.S. Census Bureau, 1997).

Attitudes Toward Illness and Disability

Among the psychological research studies conducted during the 1990s concerned with attitudes toward illness or disability, a particularly large number dealt with the topic of the disabling consequences of AIDS. Other health disorders on which research pertaining to attitudes was conducted include mental illness, Alzheimer's disease, Parkinson's disease, and cardiovascular diseases. Many of these investigations, which were conducted throughout the world, compared the attitudes toward illness or disability, in general or specifically, of various age, ethnic, sex, education, occupational, cultural, and nationality groups. Perhaps understandably, considering their "captive" status, undergraduate psychology students, medical students, doctors, nurses, and social workers were especially popular research participants in these investigations.

Attitudes toward a particular disorder are, of course, not independent of attitudes toward other personal characteristics. For example, attitudes toward HIV/AIDS are often confounded with attitudes toward gay men and/or lesbians. Thus, belief in a *"just world,"* in which people get what they deserve and deserve what they get, is reflected in the attitude that AIDS is a deserved punishment of homosexuals for unhealthy sexual behavior (e.g., Glennon & Joseph, 1993). In such cases, the effects of information, or the lack of it, on attitudes and behavior are readily apparent.

Attitudes toward persons with disabilities are expressed initially in the home, where the parents are the first to show disappointment and sometimes rejection of a disabled child. Such rejection may be manifested by parental desire to be separated from the child through abandonment, institutionalization, or giving the child up for adoption (Weiss, 1994). When disabled children remain in the home, expectations for their behavior, what they can or cannot be expected to do, and the extent to which they can be "normal" may limit their inclusion in family outings, play with neighborhood children, and school attendance (Westbrook & Legge, 1993). In cases of extreme deformity, the child may even be labeled a nonhuman "creature," "monster," or "devil." Territorial restrictions may be placed on the child, and he or she may be separated from the rest of the family (e.g., by closeting, imprisonment, or demotion to servant status; Weiss, 1994). Disabled children who attend preschool or school are also faced with the problem of rejection. Diamond, le Furgy, and Blass (1993) observed, for example, that the sample of 4-year-old preschoolers that they studied showed a decided preference for playmates who were same-sex persons without disabilities.

Although the great majority of research studies concerned with attitudes toward disabilities are not based on the attitude theories discussed in Chapters 1 and 3, Ajzen's (1991) theory of planned behavior and contact theories of attitude change have served as organizers for certain investigations. For example, using the theory of planned behavior as a guide, Roberts and Smith (1999) discovered that the attitudes of primary school children toward their peers who had physical disabilities, as well as the children's perceived control, were significant predictors of intentions to interact with those disabled children. Actual behavior was predicted to a modest extent by intentions but not by behavioral control.

Attitudes toward persons with disabilities tend to become more positive with age and experience, but these attitudes are often ambivalent and depend on the characteristics of the perceiver as well as the nature of the disability. Darrow and Johnson (1994) found that in a sample of junior and senior high school music students, the senior high students were more accepting of persons with disabilities. Among persons with disabilities, those with visible scars, heart trouble, or deafness were most accepted, whereas those with paralysis, AIDS, and blindness were least accepted. In another investigation, it was found that a sample of health practitioners working in a multicultural context had more accepting attitudes toward people with asthma, diabetes, heart disease, or arthritis and less accepting attitudes toward people with AIDS, mental retardation, psychiatric illness, or cerebral palsy (Westbrook, Legge, & Pennay, 1993).

Numerous studies concerned with the relationships of various demographic and personality variables to attitudes toward disabled persons have also been conducted. With respect to gender differences, a fairly consistent finding is that the expressed attitudes of females toward persons with disabilities are more positive than those of males (Slininger, Sherrill, & Jankowski, 2000). Examples of personality factors that are related to attitudes toward disabled persons are the self-esteem (Garske, 1996) and role identity of the perceiver (Theodorakis, Bagiatis, & Goudas, 1995).

Efforts to change attitudes toward disabled persons and disabilities in general have met with some success. Videotapes and other materials that present positive images of persons with disabilities in regular settings can help to change attitudes in a more positive direction (Beattie, Anderson, & Antonak, 1997). Mainstreaming and other procedures that promote positive contacts and information exchange between disabled and nondisabled children can also improve attitudes toward the former (Maras & Brown, 1996). When nondisabled children and adults are provided with accurate information about persons with disabilities and experience rewarding contacts with them, those who have less positive attitudes at the outset are likely to become more positive in their attitudes (Lee & Rodda, 1994; Yuker, 1994).

Conflict and Violence

Many social problems are created or exacerbated by competition and conflict. Conflict may occur on a small or large scale, or anything in between. At the micro level, conflict may take the form of a disagreement or argument between two people, say, a husband and wife or a parent and child. At an intermediate level, conflict may involve a feud between two families or two sports teams. At the macro level, conflict may break out between different religious groups, political parties, or even entire nations. Attitudes toward a particular conflict depend on whose side one is on, what information pertaining to the rights of the conflicting parties is available, personal beliefs in the rightness or wrongness of each side's position, and intense emotions that seem to defy reason.

Unresolved conflict often leads to aggression and violence, the magnitude of which depends on the individual and the support obtained from other people. Aggression is a natural response to frustration and conflict, but neither of the conflicting parties can afford to let its feelings become so intense that the result is uncontrolled violence. Disputes in the modern world are more often resolved by tact, logic, and diplomacy than by unchecked violence. As with all human actions, there are individual differences in attitudes concerning conflict and violence.

This section considers a number of examples of conflict and violence, including divorce, abuse, crime, and war. A brief introduction and some statistical information pertaining to each topic are presented, but the focus is on the opinions and attitudes expressed by different people.

Divorce

Unlike former times, when the marital roles of husband and wife were relatively fixed and men and women were expected to fulfill their vows and responsibilities in the marital union, today's couples are less apt to endure marriages beset by disagreements and conflicts. A larger percentage of today's wives, even those with preschool children, are employed and contribute to household income. They have less traditional gender role attitudes and have a greater influence on the marriage. However, these changes have come at the cost of greater marital conflict, discord, and divorce (Rogers & Amato, 2000).

A hundred years ago, marriages ended in death as often as in divorce, but divorce has become the principal cause of marital breakups. Yesteryear's legal grounds for divorce—adultery, alcoholism, brutality, desertion, and nonsupport—are still acceptable, but "incompatibility" is now more common and no-fault divorce is gaining ground.

The overall divorce rate in the United States, which is approximately 10%, reaches a peak when the disputants are in their late 40s to early 50s. The divorce rate is higher for Blacks than for Whites and higher for Whites than for Hispanics. As might be expected, divorce is more common among young women who married when they were teenagers and were pregnant or had a child prior to marriage. Higher frequencies of divorce are also found in lower income groups and among those who attend religious services infrequently (Lugaila, 1998).

The increased financial and social independence of women, the availability of welfare, and changes in public attitudes and mores have contributed to an increase in the divorce rate and the increased acceptability, if not respectability, of divorce as a means of solving marital problems and achieving self-fulfillment. Divorced people usually find, however, that a change in their marital status does not solve all their problems. Although men as well as women suffer from divorce, in the long run the reduced financial status of the ex-wife and, in most cases, the fact that she is awarded custody of any children from the marriage, create greater economic and physical hardship on her than on her ex-husband. Not only must she continue to perform the roles of homemaker and parent, but she is now responsible for taking care of all the practical and financial matters that were previously shared with her spouse. And because there are more single women than single men, a divorced woman typically has more difficulty than a divorced man in finding a new heterosexual partner.

The effects of divorce on a child depend on the age, sex, and personality of the child and his or her relationships with the parents. Young children tend to be more emotionally vulnerable, to experience greater stress, and to suffer feelings of guilt, blame, and abandonment, whereas adolescents are more likely to react with confusion and anger (Cooney & Uhlenberg, 1990). In general, teenagers cope better than younger children, especially when they have a close relationship with the custodial parent.

Studies of the effects of familial conflict on children's attitudes toward divorce have yielded conflicting results (Stone & Hutchinson, 1992; Tasker & Richards, 1994). In general, people from divorced families and/or families in which their parents' marriage was perceived as unhappy express more positive attitudes toward divorce than those who grew up in happy, intact families (Amato & Booth, 1991). Parental divorce is related to more negative views of marriage on the part of some children, especially when divorce is associated with conflict between the parents and with deteriorating relationships between parents and children. For other children of divorce, however, and particularly girls, the fact that divorce can lead to lower educational prospects, reduced socioeconomic status, earlier involvement in heterosexual relationships, and earlier departure from home may culminate in early marriage.

Sex differences in attitude toward divorce may also interact with whether the individual is from an intact or divorced family. For example, Black and Sprenkle (1991) found that in a group of undergraduate college students whom they questioned, females from intact families had a slightly more positive attitude toward divorce, but males from divorced families had more positive attitudes toward divorce.

Also of interest are the results of a study that compared the prediction of *exchange theory* with that of cognitive dissonance theory with respect to whether attitudes toward divorce affect marital quality. It was predicted from exchange theory that people who adopt favorable attitudes toward divorce invest fewer resources in their marriages, resulting in an erosion of marital quality. In contrast, the prediction from cognitive dissonance theory was that people who experience declines in marital quality adopt more favorable attitudes toward divorce as they anticipate leaving the relationship. Telephone interviews and analyses of changes in attitudes toward divorce were conducted in two nationwide surveys: one from 1980 to 1983 on a sample of 1,291 individuals who were married to the same person in both years, and a second on a sample of 1,032 individuals in 1983 and 1988. Structural equation models were used to estimate reciprocal paths between changes in attitude toward divorce and changes in marital quality in the two samples. The results provided stronger support for the prediction from exchange theory than for the cognitive dissonance hypothesis. In the long run, adopting more favorable attitudes toward divorce appeared to undermine marital quality (Amato & Rogers, 1999).

Abuse and Violence in Families

Abuse of spouses, children, elders, and other relatives in family settings is a common occurrence. Depending on the ages and circumstances of the abuser and the victim, the abuse of family members can take several forms: physical, sexual, or emotional/psychological abuse, neglect, abandonment, isolation, and financial or material exploitation. Among the physical signs of abuse are bruises, black eyes, welts, lacerations, and rope marks; broken bones and skull fractures; open wounds, cuts, punctures, untreated injuries, and injuries in various stages of healing; sprains, dislocations, and internal injuries/bleeding; physical signs of being subjected to punishment; and signs of being restrained. In cases of sexual abuse, there may be bruises around the breasts or genital area; unexplained venereal disease or genital infections; unexplained vaginal or anal bleeding; torn, stained, or bloody underclothing; and a victim's report of being sexually assaulted or raped. Signs of neglect and self-neglect include dehydration, malnutrition, untreated bedsores, poor personal hygiene, and unattended or untreated health problems (see National Center on Elder Abuse, 1998).

For years, abuse and violence within families was viewed as rare and was ignored or rationalized by medical and legal authorities. However, the incorrectness of a number of myths concerning family violence is now becoming clear. Among these myths are the following:

1. Family violence is confined to the lower social classes.

2. Alcohol and drug abuse are the real causes of violence in the home.

3. Battered wives like being hit, otherwise they would leave.

Regarding Myth 1, the truth is that police records, victim services, and academic studies show that violence exists equally in every socioeconomic group, regardless of race or culture. With regard to Myth 2, alcohol and drugs are often used by male batterers and may increase the lethality of violence, but abusive men typically control their actions even when drunk or high: they usually choose a time and place for the assaults to occur so they will not be detected. Furthermore, the battering does not necessarily end even when a batterer has completed a drug or alcohol treatment program. Finally, Myth 3 ignores the economic and social realities that face many women. Shelters for battered women are often full, and family, friends, and coworkers are often less than fully supportive. A battered woman may feel that she cannot meet the expenses of living alone with her children, and when she does leave she may be increasing the chances of physical harm and even death (National Crime Prevention Council, 1995; see also Tjaden & Thoennes, 1998).

Attitudes Toward Domestic Violence

One of the most consistent findings of surveys and other research studies of intrafamilial or domestic violence is that, at all ages, the attitudes of males are different from those of females. That women have different perceptions than men of spouse abuse and domestic violence has been documented by various studies (e.g., Kristiansen & Giulietti, 1990). In general, males' scores on measures of attitude toward violence are higher, that is, more accepting of violence against women, than those of females (Anderson, Cooper, & Okamura, 1997; Carlson, 1991; Fischer & Chen, 1994; Smith, Ellis, & Benson, 2001; Weisz & Earls, 1995).

In an experiment in which domestic violence scenarios were presented to European American and African American couples, the women, when compared with the men, placed more blame for the depicted abuse on the husband and sympathized more with the wife (Locke & Richman, 1999). Women also show greater empathy with rape victims and score significantly lower on rape myths scales than men (Brady, Chrisler, Hosdale, Osowiecki, & Veal, 1991; Ching & Burke, 1999; White & Kurpius, 1999).

Of course, not all men are superaggressive, macho types who feel that they can take what they want. There are significant differences among men in perceptions of violence against women. For example, Schaeffer and Nelson (1993) found that males who lived in coed dormitories were less accepting of rape myths than males who lived in single-sex residence halls and that males who resided in a fraternity house were more accepting of rape myths than males who chose to live in either coed or single-sex residence halls.

Women may also respond differently from men to efforts to change their attitudes toward violence. For example, Heppner et al. (1995) used the elaboration likelihood model (see Chapter 3) to examine changes in men's and women's attitudes toward rape when subjected to rape prevention messages. The results showed that women were more likely to use central-route attitude change processes, whereas men attended more to peripheral cues of the speaker and demonstration. Furthermore, the intervention produced more lasting changes in the attitudes of the women than in those of the men.

Two other demographic variables that are related to attitude toward violence are ethnicity and socioeconomic status. African Americans and Asian Americans typically score higher (i.e., more accepting of violence) than Caucasian Americans, and people with lower-SES backgrounds score higher than those with upper-SES backgrounds on measures of attitude toward violence (Anderson et al., 1997; Funk, Elliott, Urman, Flores, & Mock, 1999; Locke & Richman, 1999). Similar group differences have been found on measures of attitudes toward guns and other tools or symbols of violence (Shapiro, Dorman, Welker, & Clough, 1998).

Among other variables related to attitude toward violence are age and schooling. One study found that their attitudes toward violence became more positive as children passed through elementary school and that children attending urban public schools were more positive in their attitudes toward violence than children in other school systems (Shapiro et al., 1998). Other factors that affect children's attitudes toward violence and aggressive behaviors—peers, television, films, toys, and other environmental factors—should not be underestimated. However, the results of a survey conducted by Orpinas, Murray, and Kelder (1999) on Texas middle school students showed that parental attitude toward fighting has a greater impact on children's aggressive behaviors than any other familial variable. The likelihood that children will be involved in fighting and aggressive behaviors also depends on how well they get along with their parents, how well parents monitor their children's away-from-home activities, and whether the youngsters live with two parents or in some other living arrangement.

Violent Crime

A sizable percentage of the respondents in surveys conducted on the U.S. population view crime as one of the most important problems facing the country today (Gallup, 2000). The results of these opinion polls show that women, Blacks, and the elderly, in particular, express greater fear of crime, even in their own neighborhoods, than does the public at large.

The problem of crime in the United States is of great concern to law enforcement officials, politicians, and especially the victimized public. Despite the fact that violent crime declined during the 1990s, the media are still replete with stories of murder, rape, robbery, and aggravated assault. Property crimes such as burglary, larceny-theft, motor vehicle theft, and arson, which are three times as common as violent crimes, are also of concern, but crimes involving violence against persons are feared most of all.

As illustrated in Figure 5.2, the victimization rate for violent crime varies with gender, race, age, marital status, and family income. At almost all ages and for all violent crimes the victimization rate is higher for males than for females and higher for Blacks than for Whites. The victimization rate is also higher for teenagers and young adults than for middle-aged and older adults, for divorced/separated and never married persons than for married or widowed persons, and for persons with lower family incomes (Bureau of Justice Statistics, 2001). Rather than being the direct causes of different crime victimization rates, demographic differences are confounded with one's associates and residential location. Blacks and people with lower incomes are more likely to live, work, and play in poorer, less protected neighborhoods. Males and young people are more likely to take risks, thereby increasing the probability of being victimized. In addition, race and income and age and income are confounded with each other in their relationships to victimization rates.

Attitudes Toward Crime and Deviance

Although the victimization rate for violent crime is higher for younger adults than for older adults and higher for males than for females, older adults and women tend to be more afraid of crime than younger adults and men (Gilchrest, Bannister, Ditton, & Farrall, 1998). One reason for these gender and age differences is differential vulnerability: women are generally weaker than men, and older adults are weaker than younger adults. Even though older adults and women are not injured in criminal attacks as often as

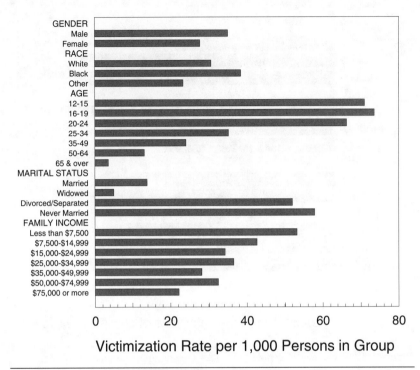

Figure 5.2. Crime Victimization Rate as a Function of Age, Sex, and Ethnicity

SOURCE: Based on data from the Bureau of Justice Statistics (2001).

younger adults and men, perception is not always identical to reality and feelings are not always reasonable. It can also be argued that because they are more afraid, older people and women are more cautious and take fewer chances than younger adults and males. They are also less likely to resist and consequently are not as likely to be physically injured as their younger and male counterparts.

As emphasized throughout this book, there is often a disparity between attitude and action, whether they are expressed by the same or different persons. The findings of a study by Sampson and Bartusch (1998) provide a further illustration of the complexity of the relationship between attitudes and behaviors. The study was concerned with racial and ethnic differences in attitudes toward social deviance, the police, and the law in 343 urban Chicago neighborhoods. Although it might be expected that because the crime rate is typically higher among Blacks and Latinos than among Whites, the first two groups would show greater tolerance of violence and other socially deviant behavior. But it was found that, when compared with Whites, greater per-

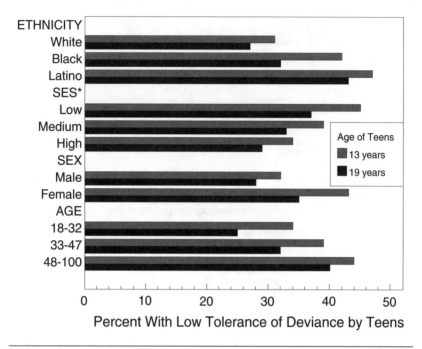

Figure 5.3. Percentage of People in Various Demographic Groups Expressing Low Tolerance for Deviant Behavior by 13- and 19-Year-Olds

SOURCE: Based on data from Sampson and Bartusch (1998).
NOTE: SES = socioeconomic status.

centages of Blacks and Latinos than Whites showed low tolerance of deviant behavior by 13- and 19-year-olds (see Figure 5.3). In addition, a greater percentage of people of lower SES than those of higher SES expressed low tolerance of deviance by teens. A greater percentage of females than males and a greater percentage of older than middle-aged and young adults also showed low tolerance of deviant behavior. On the other hand, residents of disadvantaged neighborhoods were more tolerant of smoking, drinking, and fighting among youths and in general expressed negative attitudes toward the police and the law. This was truer of males than of females, and truer of younger than of older residents.

The results of nationwide polls of attitudes toward police officers reveal that although attitudes concerning the ability of the police to combat crime are generally positive, respect for, confidence in, and ratings of the police vary with the ethnic background and political party affiliation of the respondents. Responses to questions concerning unfair treatment or brutality by

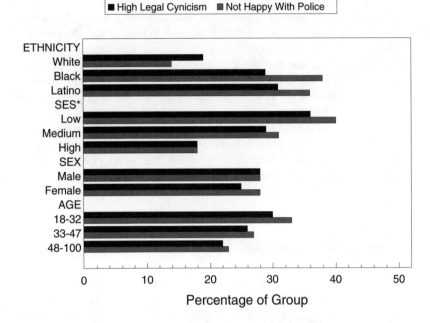

Figure 5.4. Percentage of People in Various Demographic Groups Showing High Legal Cynicism and Low Satisfaction With Police

SOURCE: Based on data from Sampson and Bartusch (1998).
NOTE: SES = socioeconomic status.

police also vary with the ethnicity and politics of the respondents. In general, the attitudes of Whites and Republicans regarding the police are more positive than those of non-Whites, Democrats, and Independents (Gallup, 2000, pp. 163-164).

Another finding of Sampson and Bartusch's (1998) survey was that higher percentages of Blacks and Latinos than Whites, particularly those of lower SES, viewed legal norms as not binding and were generally cynical about the law (see Figure 5.4). These percentages were also inversely related to age. Furthermore, compared with the attitudes of Whites and people of lower SES, Blacks, Latinos, and people of lower SES were much less satisfied with the police.

In summary, participants in the Sampson and Bartusch (1998) study who lived in neighborhoods characterized by poverty and instability were more tolerant of deviant behavior other than teen fighting. But when compared with Whites, minority group members who lived in these neighborhoods were, even after taking poverty and instability into account, less tolerant of deviance. Once economic disadvantage was taken into account, the views of Blacks were actually quite similar to those of Whites. Thus, the results of this study suggest that a major reason why a larger percentage of Blacks are cynical about the law and dissatisfied with the police is because they are more likely to reside in disadvantaged neighborhoods. At least in this study, racial differences in the attitudes disappeared when the neighborhood context was considered.

Sampson and Bartusch (1998) concluded that if there is a system of attitudes and values that tolerates social deviance and is cynical about the law and its agents, it is not directly related to race. Rather than race, the crucial factor influencing attitudes and beliefs concerning crime and the law appears to be neighborhood context.

Recommended Readings

Bolig, E. E., Borkowski, J., & Brandenberger, J. (1999). Poverty and health across the life span. In T. L. Whitman, T. V. Merluzzi, & R. D. White (Eds.), *Life-span perspectives on health and illness* (pp. 67-84). Mahwah, NJ: Lawrence Erlbaum.

Diener, E., & Oishi, S. (2000). Money and happiness: Income and subjective well-being across nations. In E. Diener & E. M. Suh (Eds.), *Culture and subjective well-being* (pp. 185-218). Cambridge, MA: MIT Press.

Flanagan, T. J. (1996). Public opinion on crime and justice: History, development, and trends. In T. J. Flanagan & D. R. Longmire (Eds.), *Americans view crime and justice: A national public opinion survey* (pp. 1-15). Thousand Oaks, CA: Sage.

Henderson, G., & Bryan, W. V. (1997). *Psychosocial aspects of disability* (2nd ed.). Springfield, IL: Charles C Thomas.

Pruitt, D. G. (1998). Social conflict. In D. T. Gilbert, S. T. Fiske, & G. Lindzey (Eds.), *The handbook of social psychology* (4th ed., Vol. 2, pp. 470-503). New York: McGraw-Hill/Oxford.

Rank, M. R. (2000). Poverty and economic hardship in families. In D. H. Demo, K. R. Allen, & M. A. Fine (Eds.), *Handbook of family diversity* (pp. 293-316). New York: Oxford University Press.

Salovey, P., Rothman, A. J., & Rodin, J. (1998). Health behavior. In D. T. Gilbert, S. T. Fiske, & G. Lindzey (Eds.), *The handbook of social psychology* (4th ed., Vol. 2, pp. 633-693). New York: McGraw-Hill/Oxford.

Tangri, S. S., & Browne, J. M. (1999). Climbing out of the pit: From the Black middle class to homeless and (almost) back again. In M. Romero & A. J.

Stewart (Eds.), *Women's untold stories: Breaking silence, talking back, voicing complexity* (pp. 125-141). Florence, KY: Taylor & Francis/ Routledge.

Note

1. The percentage of the U.S. population without health insurance was 15.5% in 1999, but this figure represented a decrease from 16.3% in 1998, the first decline since 1987 (U.S. Census Bureau, 1999a).

Appendix 5.1

Representative Questionnaires and Scales Concerning Attitudes and Opinions Toward Selected Personal and Social Problems

AIDS Information and Opinion Survey (Rhodes & Wolitslci, 1989). Designed to measure attitudes toward and knowledge about AIDS. Uses a Likert-type agree-disagree scale for the attitude survey and 5-point true-false scales for the knowledge portion. English and Spanish versions. Mean score norms available.

AIDS Knowledge, Attitudes, and Practice Scale (Flaskerud & Nyamathi, 1989). Consists of 16 items measuring women's (a) knowledge about AIDS, including knowledge of symptoms, transmission, prevention, and community resources; (b) attitudes about AIDS, including attitudes toward sexuality, drug use, and fears; and (c) practices, including the individuals' current sexual and drug use practices. May be administered in English or Spanish.

Attitudes Toward AIDS Scale (Goh, 1993). Includes a Knowledge scale consisting of 25 true-false items and an Attitudes scale consisting of 25 items in 5-point, Likert-type rating format (*strongly agree, agree, neutral, disagree, strongly disagree*). The Knowledge scale is designed to measure a person's understanding of the state of knowledge about HIV/AIDS prevalence, medical facts, modes of transmission, misconceptions, and prevention. The Attitudes items are designed to assess affective responses to items concerned with AIDS as a disease, HIV/AIDS-infected persons, and AIDS-related issues.

Attitudes Toward AIDS Scale—High School Version (Goh, 1994). This scale was developed using the original (Goh, 1993) measure designed to assess HIV/AIDS-related attitudes among college students as a model in structure and methodology. The scale consists of 20 items, each measured on a 3-point scale in Likert format (1 = *least desirable attitudes*, 2 = *neutral attitudes*, 3 = *most desirable attitudes*). Total scores range from 20 to 60.

Attitudes Toward Disabled Persons Scale (H. E. Yuker & J. R. Block; Center for the Study of Attitudes Toward Persons with Disabilities, Hofstra University). Measures attitudes of students and adults toward disabled persons. For more detailed description, see Antonek and Livneh (1988).

Attitudes Toward Guns and Violence Questionnaire (AGVQ; J. P. Shapiro; Western Psychological Services). For ages 6 to 29, 26 items. Total score plus Aggressive Response to Shame, Comfort with Aggression, Excitement, and Power/Safety.

Attitudes Toward Rape Victims Scale (Ward, 1988). This instrument was designed as a specific assessment of attitudes toward rape victims. On a 5-point, Likert-type scale, respondents indicate how strongly they agree or disagree with 8 positive and 17 negative statements about victims of rape. The statements encompass issues of blame, denigration, credibility, responsibility, deservingness, and trivialization.

Attitudes Toward Wife Abuse Scale (Briere, 1987). Consists of eight items pertaining to violence against wives. Half of the items accept wife abuse and half oppose it. Based on a 7-point, Likert-type rating scale, the response options range from *strongly agree* to *strongly disagree*. This self-administered inventory can be completed in less than 5 minutes and is appropriate for high school students and older. Reliability and validity data are available.

Attitudes Towards Dating Violence Scales (Price & Byers, 1999). This instrument consists of three Attitudes Towards Male Dating Violence Scales (AMDV) and three Attitudes Towards Female Dating Violence Scales (AFDV). These scales measure attitudes toward the use of psychological, physical, and sexual dating violence, respectively, by boys and by girls.

Attitudes Towards Violence Scale (Funk, Elliott, Urman, Flores, & Mock, 1999). A 15-item, Likert-type scale (1 = *strongly disagree* to 5 = *strongly agree*) concerning possible responses to violence. The items were based on existing information concerning factors contributing to juvenile violence.

Community Service Attitudes Inventory (Collins, Stemmel, King, & Gwen, 1991). A 25-item rating scale designed to assess attitudes of family caregivers of individuals with Alzheimer's disease toward community services developed to help them. On a 4-point, Likert-type scale, family members indicate the reasons why they do or do not make use of community services. The instrument has five subscales: Concern for Opinions of Others, Confidence in Service System, Preference for Informal Care, Belief in Caregiver Independence, and Acceptance of Government Services.

Disability Rights Attitude Scale (Herandez, Keys, Balcazar, & Drum, 1998). Designed to assess attitudes toward the Americans With Disabilities Act (ADA), a law that protects the civil rights of individuals with disabilities. Thirty-four Likert-type, 6-point items.

HIV Prevention Attitude Scale (Torabi & Yarber, 1992). Developed to measure teenagers' attitudes toward prevention of the spread of the HIV virus. Each of the two alternate forms of the scale contains 15 Likert-type items.

Public Attitudes Toward Homelessness Scale (Guzewicz & Verdi, 1992). A brief scale designed to assist researchers in identifying the public attitudes toward homeless people that might be key factors to finding solutions to the problem of homelessness. On a 4-point, Likert-type scale, respondents indicate how strongly they agree or disagree with five statements about homeless people.

Violence Attitudes Scale (Revised) (VAS–R; Jackson, Brown, Davis, & Pitman, 1999). This scale evaluates the manner in which individuals attribute blame for violence.

6

Natural and Unnatural Death

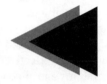

The focus of this chapter—death and dying—has not always been a popular topic among scholars and researchers, but in the past half-century or so it has become of greater interest and more subject to scientific examination and reflection. Of particular significance in this context is the question of preserving life versus permitting or assisting death: Under what circumstances is it best for an individual to be permitted or encouraged to continue living rather than dying? The answers to this question vary with the particular person and the circumstances, and in any case the answers are not likely to be greeted with pleasure or approval by everyone. Efforts to resolve such matters of life and death must be attentive to personal and social attitudes regarding acceptable behavior; moral, religious, and political beliefs and practices; and the goal of preserving a tranquil, productive, and mutually supportive society.

Attitudes Toward Death

Although elephants and certain other animals allegedly bury their dead, human beings are presumably the only living creatures who realize that they will eventually die. How do they cope with this knowledge and how does it shape their attitudes, beliefs, and actions? Do they simply refuse to think about it, actively or passively avoiding or denying it? Do they become resigned, or lapse into a state of depression and despair? There is, of course, a limit to the effectiveness of the delusion that one is immortal. Personal vulnerability and impending annihilation become all too apparent as people age and experience the increasing incidence of accidents, illnesses, and the deaths of friends, relatives, and idols.

Like attitudes toward many other objects and events, rather than being either this or that, attitudes toward death are on a negative to positive continuum. At one end of the continuum is the perception of death as humanity's worst enemy, a horrible Grim Reaper who, despite one's fear and inadequacy, must be confronted aggressively with whatever measures are required and available. This extreme negative viewpoint has been expressed by those who characterize death as a foe that can be avoided for a while if one is alert, capable, and persistent, but a foe that is ultimately victorious. Still, the biblical query "O Death where is your victory? O Death where is your sting?" (1 Corinthians 15:55) provides hope that the state of death need not be permanent if one believes in an afterlife.

People at the more positive end of the attitude-toward-death continuum view death as the passage to a more pleasant state of existence and may even welcome it. A person with this attitude can approach the grave, as in William Cullen Bryant's "Thanatopsis," "like one who wraps the drapery of his couch about him and lies down to pleasant dreams." Finally, those who are somewhere in the middle of the attitude-toward-death continuum, who are perhaps more characteristic of the population at large, have a feeling of mystery or bewilderment in the face of death and view it as a place beyond human experience that is of uncertain character and cannot be described in words.

Individual Differences

As with the causes and rate of death, attitudes toward death vary with a host of demographic variables, including gender, ethnicity, culture, nationality, educational level, occupation, personal adjustment, and religion. Women tend to score higher than men on measures of death anxiety and to view death as a compassionate mother, an understanding doctor, or a gentle comforter rather than an evil antagonist, a grinning butcher, or a hangman (Back, 1971; Kastenbaum, 2000). Research findings also indicate that negative attitudes or fears do not invariably increase with age; fear of death tends to be more intense in middle age than in young adulthood or old age (Bengtson, Cuellar, & Ragan, 1977; Gesser, Wong, & Reker, 1987-1988; Kalish & Reynolds, 1976/1981).

People with higher than average education express less negative attitudes and are more likely to talk about death than those with less education (Keith, 1979). Related to educational level are high self-esteem, goal attainment, and financial stability—all three of which are associated with a greater acceptance of death. Personality and mental disorders are also correlated with attitudes toward death: more negative attitudes are expressed by people with psychoneurotic, defensive, or depressive symptoms (Conte, Weiner, & Plutchik, 1982; Gilliland & Templer, 1985-1986; Howells & Field, 1982). With respect to religious faith, both strong believers and confirmed atheists tend to be less apprehensive about death than people who are inconsistent or uncertain in their religious beliefs (Aday, 1984-1985; McMordie, 1981).

Historical Changes

In addition to demographic factors, attitudes toward death have varied with historical era. From his studies of documents and artifacts from the European Middle Ages of a thousand years ago up through the 20th century, Philippe Ariès (1981) concluded that attitudes toward death are related to awareness of self or sense of individuality. According to Ariès, there have been five major shifts in attitudes toward death since the Middle Ages. During the *tame death* period of the Middle Ages, death was accepted and expected as a terrible but necessary human misfortune; the dead were thought to be merely sleeping until the Second Coming of Christ. During the *death of the self* period of the 14th and 15th centuries, individuality was minimized. It was believed that without a last confession, at the moment of death the immortal soul of the person would be seized by a devil instead of an angel. Thus, dying in one's sleep or otherwise without confessing one's sins was to be avoided at all costs. During the *remote death* period of the 17th and18th centuries, death was viewed as a sorrowful but remote event; human mortality was accepted, but thoughts of it still made people anxious. Romantic or macabre eroticism was intermingled with sex in art and literature. During the *death of the other* period of the early to mid-19th century, the view of death as ugly and the belief in a literal hell began to diminish. Death was seen as a beautiful event leading to a happy reunion in paradise. The personal self survived death and roamed the Earth with other disembodied spirits. In the *denial of death* period of the late 19th century to the present time, death became less visible. Dying people were hidden away in hospitals, children were spared the unpleasantness of viewing and knowing about death and dying, and public mourning was eliminated. Death was more likely to be seen as an accident or a medical failure, and the best way to die was in one's sleep. In an addendum to these five periods, Aries concluded that denial and externalization of death diminished somewhat during the 20th century. Death was beginning to be seen as a part of what it means to be human, and it is inhuman for people to die alone, connected to medical apparatus, and without having a chance to make their peace and say goodbye to others.

Stages in Dying

Another temporal factor that is related to attitude toward death is what has been called stages of dying. According to Elisabeth Kübler-Ross (1975), most dying patients pass through a series of psychological stages in their attitude, or acceptance, of imminent death. In Stage 1 (*denial*), patients reject the reality of impending death. This denial provides patients with time to direct their energies toward coping with the new reality. In Stage 2 (*anger*), patients resent the interruption of their personal hopes and plans. The expression of anger in this stage allows patients to move to the next stage. In Stage 3 (*bargaining*), patients try to avoid the reality of death by entering into an agreement with God, doctors, family members, or anyone with seeming influence. Because the bargaining process is ultimately unsuccessful, patients gradually come to understand the reality of the situation. In Stage 4 (*preparatory depression*), patients mourn for what has been and will be lost with dying. Successful resolution of this crisis leads patients to move toward self-understanding and contact with other people. At Stage 5 (*acceptance*), patients are calmer, more confident, and realistic, expressing less fear and anger.

Kübler-Ross's theory has been criticized for the assumption of a series of fixed stages through which dying patients invariably pass (e.g., Corr, 1993; Doka, 1995; Kastenbaum, 1991). In actuality, not all dying patients go through the exact sequence listed above. They usually progress from an initial stage of shock to one of acceptance, but there is considerable movement back and forth between denial and acceptance. Some patients never reach a stage or state of acceptance: some die angry at everyone and everything, whereas others die depressed. In all fairness, Kübler-Ross cautioned that the five stages should not be interpreted as a fixed, unvarying, unidirectional sequence, but rather as a useful device for understanding how dying people feel and think. Alternative models of the dying process have also been proposed (e.g., Pattison, 1977; Shneidman, 1980, 1987; Weisman & Kastenbaum, 1968).

Assessing Attitudes Toward Death

A variety of methods have been used to assess attitudes toward death: behavioral observations, interviews, projective techniques, diaries, physiological reactions, perceptual responses to death words or images, questionnaires, inventories, and scales. Appendix 6.1 is a descriptive list of representative paper-and-pencil instruments designed to measure attitudes toward death in general or toward specific forms of death (abortion, euthanasia, suicide, capital punishment, or euthanasia). A typical inventory designed to assess attitudes toward death in general, the Lester Attitude Toward Death Scale, is displayed in Form 6.1. Also administered in a number of research studies on death and dying are the Death Attitude Profile, the Death Attitude Profile–Revised, and the Multidimensional Measurement of Death Attitudes. In addition to the attitude instruments listed in Appendix 6.1, numerous measures of death anxiety are available (see Aiken, 2001b, pp. 343-345).

Abortion and the Right to Life

The personal and social problem of women giving birth to more children than they, their families, and society can care for has been a topic of continuing concern for many generations. Due to the efforts of Margaret Sanger and other proponents of birth control, notable sociological and medical advances in this area were made during the 20th century. Progress in birth control was not made without intense religious, political, and social opposition, particularly from the Roman Catholic Church, but it did occur throughout the world. The results of numerous public opinion polls conducted over the past several decades have shown that a large majority of people in the United States and many other countries believe that birth control information should be available to anyone who wants it. Whether and how this information is acted on varies, however, with the particular country and culture.

FORM 6.1   The Lester Attitude Toward Death Scale

Directions: Circle A or D for each of the following statements. If you agree with the statement, circle A. If you disagree, circle D. Try to circle a reply for each statement. Consider the death in each statement to mean your death at the present time.

1.   A   D   What we call death is only the birth of the soul into a new and delightful life.

2.   A   D   One should not grieve over the dead, because they are eternally happy in heaven.

3.   A   D   Death comes to comfort us.

4.   A   D   Death will be one of the most interesting experiences of my life.

5.   A   D   A peaceful death is a fitting end to a successful life.

6.   A   D   I don't want to die right now, but I'm glad that I will die someday.

7.   A   D   Death is better than a painful life.

8.   A   D   I would be willing to die to save my best friend.

9.   A   D   Death makes all people equal.

10.   A   D   Death is a great mystery.

11.   A   D   Death is neither good nor bad since there's no consciousness in it.

12.   A   D   You can't take it with you when you die.

13.   A   D   I would feel better about death if I knew what it was going to be like.

14.   A   D   It is a pity when a talented person dies, even if he or she has stopped creating.

15.   A   D   Death is an unwanted sleep.

16.   A   D   Death is to be feared for it brings grief.

17.   A   D   I am afraid to die because there may be a future punishment.

18.   A   D   Nothing can be so bad that a sane person would commit suicide.

19.   A   D   Death is the last and worst insult to humanity.

20.   A   D   I would avoid death at all costs.

21.   A   D   Death is the worst thing that could possibly happen to me.

SOURCE: Reprinted with permission from "The Lester Attitude Toward Death Scale," by D. Lester, 1991, *Omega, 23*(1), 67-75. Copyright © 1991 Baywood Publishing Company, Inc.
NOTE: Item scoring weights: 1(1.29), 2(2.00), 3(2.81), 4(3.25), 5(3.75), 6(4.12), 7(4.59), 8(5.00), 9(5.11), 10(5.58), 11(6.18), 12(6.85), 13(7.17), 14(7.42), 15(7.92), 16(8.15), 17(9.42), 18(9.80), 19(10.19), 20(10.42), 21(10.86).

Among the various methods of birth control that are currently practiced, only abstinence, which includes several forms of the rhythm method, is acceptable to highly conservative organizations. However, a variety of other contraceptive methods provide women with an opportunity to choose if and when they have children. The most popular of these are the hormonal methods, followed by barrier techniques. Despite the wide availability and use of contraceptive methods of birth control, unplanned and unwanted pregnancies still occur in large numbers. Consequently, the method of last resort in fertility control—abortion—is the choice of millions of women throughout the world.

Definitions and Statistics

By definition, a voluntary *abortion* is any procedure that results in the death of an unborn child. An abortion may be *spontaneous*, as in a *miscarriage*, or *induced* by an external agent. Every year a million or more pregnant women in the United States end their pregnancies by means of abortion. The number of abortions per 1,000 live births plus abortions, or the *abortion ratio*, is lower for White Americans than for all other ethnic groups combined. The ratio is lower for women aged 25 to 39 than for any other age group, and substantially lower for married than for unmarried women. In 1996, the abortion ratio for all women in the United States aged 15 to 44 was 351 (259 for Whites and 701 for Blacks). The abortion ratio also varies with geographical area, being significantly higher in the District of Columbia and lower in Wyoming than in other states (U.S. Census Bureau, 1999c).

Inducing Abortion

Either chemical or surgical procedures may be used to induce an abortion, but it becomes increasingly more hazardous to the health of the mother after the start of the third trimester. Chemical procedures (e.g., the "morning-after pill" and RU-486) may be employed up to about 7 weeks gestation. Surgical procedures—scraping the fetus from the uterus or aspirating it by means of a special suction pump—may be used during the first 12 weeks, and especially during the last 5 weeks of that interval. Although the maternal mortality rate in first-trimester abortions is even lower than that for childbirth, later abortions cause a dramatic increase in the rate. The traditional abortion procedure after the first trimester consists of injecting a hormone-like substance or a saline solution into the fluid surrounding the fetus. If this procedure fails, a *hysterotomy*, which is essentially a cesarean section, may be performed.

Usually restricted to emergencies late in gestation and used infrequently is *partial birth abortion*. In this procedure, the fetus is partially delivered to the vagina and then killed before completing delivery. Partial birth abortion has been the subject of heated political debate, but efforts to enact federal legislation banning it have so far been unsuccessful.

The Great Debate

The political debate over partial birth abortion is just one aspect of the continuing controversy over abortion. Organized Christianity, and the Catholic Church in particular, has historically opposed induced abortion, taking its position from the Sixth Commandment ("Thou shalt not kill."). Buddhism, Hinduism, and Judaism have also opposed abortion. Compared with Roman Catholicism, Protestantism and Judaism have been less vehement in their opposition to abortion. Most Protestant and Jewish groups have viewed abortion as acceptable if needed to save the life or preserve the health of the mother. On the other hand, the position of the Roman Catholic Church, which is based on the 16th-century doctrine that "ensoulment" occurs at the moment of conception, is that abortion is unjustified even when the mother's life is in danger.

Public opposition to abortion is not restricted to the religious community; many professional and lay groups argue that an unborn child is actually a human being and therefore abortion is murder. Antiabortionists (pro-lifers) maintain that this is certainly true of the fetus (third month to term) and, according to some opponents of abortion, even of the embryo and the fertilized egg. Abortion is seen as a violation of the fetus's right to life and (it is believed by some) may even lead to the acceptance of infanticide and a disregard for human life in general. The pro-choice argument, on the other hand, is that the fetus is part of a woman's body and that she has a legal right to control her own body. Pro-choicers also maintain that making abortion illegal would lead to unsafe practices and have a disproportionate effect on poor people who cannot afford to travel to places where abortion is legal.

The pro-choice interpretation of a pregnant woman's right to have an abortion characterized U.S. Supreme Court decisions during the 1970s, particularly the decision in the case of *Roe v. Wade* (1973). This ruling stated that (a) states cannot prohibit abortion during the first 3 months of pregnancy, but beyond that period they may regulate abortion in ways that reasonably relate to maternal health, and (b) states may prohibit abortion in the final 10 weeks of pregnancy except when the mother's life is at stake. In justifying its decision, the Court stipulated that an unborn child is not a person within the meaning and protection of the term *person* in the Fourteenth Amendment of the U.S. Constitution and that a woman's right to privacy implies that a decision to have an abortion during the first 3 months of pregnancy should be left to her and her doctor. However, a number of court rulings during the 1980s and 1990s (e.g., *Webster v. Reproductive Health Service,* 1989, *Ohio v. Akron Center for Reproductive Health,* 1990, *Planned*

Parenthood of Southeastern Pennsylvania v. Casey, 1992) were interpreted by pro-choice advocates as legal efforts to slowly rescind the decision in *Roe v. Wade* by limiting access to abortion.

Organized opposition to induced abortion is not as strong in most other countries as in the United States. For example, abortions by qualified physicians are performed with virtually no restrictions in Eastern Europe, Russia, Japan, and China. In Russia and Romania, where contraceptives are in short supply, in certain years more than 60% of pregnancies have ended in abortion. It is noteworthy that abortion is also legal in heavily Roman Catholic Italy. In the United States, it is legal in many states to abort for reasons of the mother's health, because of a suspected serious birth defect in the fetus, or when pregnancy is caused by rape or incest. Most of the abortions that take place in this country every year are, however, prompted by reasons other than health or unlawful sexual intercourse.

Public Opinions Regarding Abortion

As seen from statistics based on the General Social Surveys data regarding attitudes toward abortion (Table 6.1), a substantial majority of Americans agree that abortion is justifiable under certain circumstances. Approximately four-fifths of the respondents agreed that a pregnant woman should be able to obtain a legal abortion if her health is seriously endangered by the pregnancy, if she became pregnant as a result of rape, or if there is a strong chance of serious defect in the baby. Less than half of the respondents approved of an abortion for the other four reasons listed in the table.

The results of a 1999 Gallup poll (Gallup, 2000, pp. 185-188) indicated that the American public is fairly evenly divided on the issue of abortion; 48% of the sample identified themselves as "pro-choice," and 42% as "pro-life." The pro-lifers were, however, more intense in their feelings; two thirds of the pro-lifers felt very strongly about their position, compared with only one half of pro-choicers. The survey also showed that abortion was not a key electoral issue for most Americans. Overall, 39% of the respondents said that abortion should be legal in all or most circumstances, and 58% said they would restrict it to only a few or no circumstances. Despite the belief that men often encourage women to have abortions in order to avoid their obligations or responsibilities, the survey found few gender differences in either opinions or reported voting behavior with respect to abortion. Approximately the same percentages of men and women viewed themselves as pro-choice or pro-life, but larger numbers of both genders preferred the pro-choice label. With respect to their views regarding the legality of abortion, 41% of women and 35% of men said that abortion should be legal under all or most circumstances. In addition, the attitudes of women respondents toward abortion were somewhat more intense than those of men.

TABLE 6.1 Percentage of Agreement With Various Reasons for a Pregnant Woman to Obtain a Legal Abortion

Reason for Abortion	Percentage Agreement
1. The woman's own health is seriously endangered by the pregnancy.	88
2. The woman became pregnant as a result of rape.	80
3. There is a strong chance of serious defect in the baby.	78
4. The woman is married and does not want any more children.	44
5. The family has a very low income and cannot afford any more children.	44
6. The woman is not married and does not want to marry the man.	43
7. The woman wants it for any reason.	42

SOURCE: Based on General Social Surveys data from the World Wide Web: www.icpsr. umich.edu/GSS/.

As expected, attitudes toward abortion were also related to political party, with Democrats and Independents being much more likely than Republicans to consider themselves pro-choice. Among respondents who said that religion is very important in their lives, more than 50% identified themselves as pro-life.

Euthanasia and Suicide

Euthanasia ("good death"), or mercy killing, is the act of painlessly causing or allowing a person who is suffering from an unbearably painful incurable disease or condition to die. Euthanasia may be active, passive, voluntary, or involuntary. In *active euthanasia*, measures are taken that will terminate a person's life and end his or her suffering. In *passive euthanasia*, a terminally ill person is permitted to die without the application of lifesaving measures. Euthanasia is *voluntary* when it occurs with the patient's permission, and *involuntary* when it is against the person's will. In law, involuntary euthanasia is considered tantamount to murder.

Most of the debate surrounding euthanasia is concerned with active euthanasia, which has been practiced throughout history on certain groups of people: infants, the elderly, the chronically ill, physically deformed or mentally ill persons, and even members of socially unpopular ethnic or religious groups. Euthanasia has sometimes been associated with *genocide*, as seen in the extermination of millions of European Jews by the Nazis during World War II. However, genocide, which is both active and involuntary, is generally viewed as mass murder.

Religion and Law

Christianity, Islam, and Judaism have traditionally opposed both active euthanasia and suicide. Hinduism and Buddhism discourage the use of medical intervention to end life, but Buddhists tend to be less strict than Hindus with regard to the issue. Different Protestant Christian denominations hold different positions regarding euthanasia and passive euthanasia in particular. Roman Catholic opposition to euthanasia stems from the Sixth Commandment ("Thou shalt not kill.") and St. Augustine's maxim that the Scriptures do not authorize the destruction of innocent human life. Current teaching of the Roman Catholic Church stems from St. Thomas Aquinas's assertion that "suicide contradicts the natural inclination of the human being to preserve and perpetuate his life . . . and is contrary to love for the living God." However, as seen in the *double-effect principle*, Roman Catholic theologians have expressed a greater interest in saving souls than in preserving life. According to this principle, an action that has the primary effect of relieving human suffering may be considered justifiable even when it shortens human life (Wasmuth, 2000). The administration of narcotics to relieve pain in terminally ill patients can also lead to respiratory depression and thus hasten death, but Roman Catholicism considers it permissible because it is consistent with the double-effect principle.

Modern Catholic theologians have also considered the question of passive euthanasia; for example, when should a dying patient's respirator be turned off or all lifesaving medical measures be terminated? Addressing this question in 1957, Pope Pius XII concluded that there is no moral obligation to keep the respirator on in such circumstances (Address of Pope Pius XII, 1957). This decision was applied in the case of Karen Ann Quinlan, a patient in an irreversible coma during the 1970s. When the respirator was turned off, however, Karen continued to breathe. Because her parents declined to have the feeding tube removed as well, she continued to live longer than expected.

In the case of Nancy Cruzan, a 25-year-old woman who went into an irreversible coma after an automobile accident in 1983, the Missouri state court rejected the request to have the feeding tube removed after concluding that there was no clear and convincing evidence that the patient would not wish to continue her vegetative existence. This decision was appealed to the U.S. Supreme Court by Nancy's father, but the court ruled that the parents of a comatose woman do not have an automatic right under the U.S. Constitution to insist that the hospital stop feeding her (*Cruzan et al. v. Director, Missouri Department of Health et al.*, 1990). Artificial feeding was eventually discontinued in December 1990 after a Missouri circuit court ruled that "clear and convincing" evidence now existed that Nancy would not wish to continue existing in a persistent vegetative state. Nancy's gravestone bore the inscription (Information Plus, 1998, p. 121):

NANCY BETH CRUZAN

MOST LOVED

DAUGHTER—SISTER—AUNT

BORN JULY 20, 1957

DEPARTED JAN 11, 1983

AT PEACE DEC 26, 1990

Surveys of Attitudes Toward Euthanasia

Attitudes and opinions toward euthanasia may be assessed by interviews, questionnaires, and attitude scales (e.g., Euthanasia Attitudes Scale, Suicide Opinion Questionnaire). Pollsters have periodically sampled the attitudes of the general public in the United States and other countries, and many less professional polls have been conducted on samples of college students. The findings of these polls show that the percentage of Americans approving of euthanasia varies with the circumstances. For example, in the General Social Survey of 1996 (Web site www.icpsr.umich.edu/GSS), 61% of the respondents agreed that a person with an incurable disease has the right to end his or her own life. However, only 17% of the respondents agreed that a person has that right if he or she is tired of living and ready to die, only 9% if he or she has gone bankrupt, and only 5% if he or she has dishonored the family. Attitudes also vary with the method employed; for example, life-support withdrawal is more acceptable than lethal injection (Achille & Ogloff, 1997). Differences in the attitudes of various demographic groups have also been examined. For example, greater support for euthanasia is found among younger than older adults, among Protestants than Catholics, among liberals than conservatives, among Whites than Blacks, among highly educated than less educated people, and among less religious than more religious people (Caddell & Newton, 1995; Csikai, 1999; MacDonald, 1998).

Physician-Assisted Suicide

In response to the growing interest in physician-assisted suicide and cases pitting the "right to live" against the "right to die," the U.S. Supreme Court ruled in 1997 that state bans on physician-assisted suicide did not violate the U.S. Constitution (*Washington et al. v. Harold Glucksberg et al.*, 1997). This action by the Court provided support for the statutes of three dozen states prohibiting physician- or doctor-assisted suicide. Physician-assisted suicide is criminalized through the common law in eight of the remaining states and the District of Columbia, in five states the law is unclear regarding its legality, and in one state (Oregon) physician-assisted suicide is legal. The Oregon law, approved in 1994, permits physicians to write prescriptions for lethal drugs for adults with a diagnosed terminal illness and a prognosis of 6 months or less to live.

Even more pro-euthanasia than the Oregon law is the situation in the Netherlands, where a procedure established by the Dutch medical profession is followed in helping persons terminate their lives through lethal injection. Since 1993, physicians in the Netherlands have not been prosecuted for giving lethal drugs to patients to help them commit suicide. Until fairly recently, however, it remained a crime that carried a prison sentence of up to 12 years. Under legislation passed in 2000-2001 (Dahlburg, 2000; Williams, 2001):

1. The physician must ascertain that a person requesting assistance in committing suicide is suffering from an "unbearable" and irremediable physical or mental pain from an incurable condition.

2. The patient also needs to obtain a second opinion.

3. The diagnosis must be certified by a regional commission on which several doctors sit.

4. The patient must make the request when of sound mind and do so voluntarily, independently, and repeatedly.

5. The patient can make an advance request in writing, allowing the physician to exercise a directive as to what should be done when the patient becomes too physically or mentally ill to make the decision.

6. The physician must know the patient well.

7. The consent of at least one parent is required for patients up to 16 years old.

Despite the legal sanctions in the United States against physician-assisted suicide, a small percentage of doctors and nurses, often at the family's request, have assisted terminally ill patients in ending their lives (Emanuel, Daniels, Fairclough, & Claridge, 1998; Meier et al., 1998; see also Humphry, 1991).

The most famous and controversial character in this drama has been Dr. Jack Kevorkian, who has assisted some 130 terminally ill patients to commit suicide. The last of these deaths resulted in Dr. Kevorkian being convicted of second-degree murder and receiving a 25-year sentence.

The National Right to Life Committee (NRLC) is opposed to euthanasia of any kind, arguing that the desire of terminally ill patients to end their own lives is a subconscious cry for help. These individuals, and suicidal people in general, are viewed as mentally ill or depressed, for which the NRLC considers the proper response to be treatment rather than euthanasia.

Be that as it may, public opinion polls indicate that a majority of Americans approve of physician-assisted suicide. As shown in the findings of a 1999 Gallup poll illustrated in Figure 6.1, more than 60% of a representative sample of Americans agreed that "when a person has a disease that cannot be cured and is living in severe pain, doctors should be allowed by law to assist the patient to commit suicide if the patient requests it." The percentage of respondents agreeing with this statement was higher for males than females, higher for Whites than for non-Whites and Blacks, higher for those with some college or college graduates than for those with no college or postgraduates, higher for those living in the East or West than in the Midwest or South, and higher for those younger than age 65 than for those age 65 and older. When asked, however, whether they would consider committing suicide if they personally had a disease that could not be cured and were living in severe pain, only 40% of the respondents said yes. Variations by sex, ethnicity, education, region, and age in the percentage answering yes to this question were similar to those depicted in Figure 6.1 for responses to the first question.

Regarding the attitudes of physicians to physician-assisted suicide, the results of a survey conducted by Meier et al. (1998) of 1,902 physicians in 10 medical specialties are instructive. Partial results of this survey are listed in Table 6.2. As illustrated by the percentages in the last column of the table, as a group physicians are quite conservative in their practices and prospects with respect to physician-assisted suicide. In general, making euthanasia legal would reportedly triple the number of physicians who would be willing to write a prescription for a lethal dose of medication. Although the percentage of physicians indicating that they would actually give a lethal injection if it were legal to do so is significantly less than the percentage of those who would write a prescription for one if it were legal, both percentages are approximately three times as great as under current legal constraints. Also of interest is the finding that the percentage of physicians who reported that they had received a request for assistance with suicide is slightly higher than the percentage of those who had received a request for a lethal injection. Furthermore, the percentage of those who had reportedly written a prescription

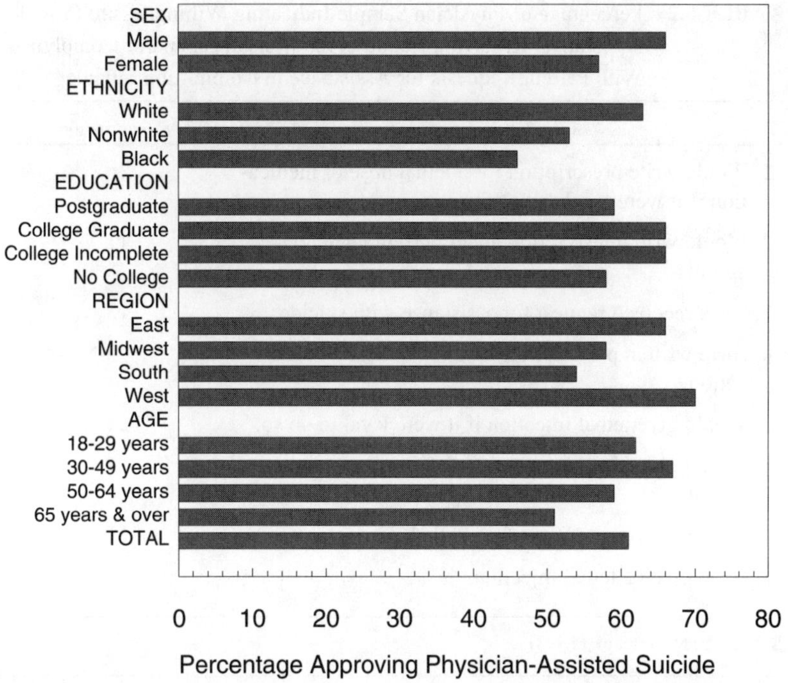

Figure 6.1. Percentage of Respondents in Various Demographic Groups Answering Yes to Question in 1999 CNN/USA Gallup Poll Survey Concerning Physician-Assisted Suicide

NOTE: The question was, "When a person has a disease that cannot be cured and is living in severe pain, do you think doctors should be allowed by law to assist the patient to commit suicide if the patient requests it?" (Gallup, 2000, pp. 161-163).

for a lethal dose of medication is lower than those who had actually given a lethal injection.

Capital Punishment

Another controversial topic concerned with actively taking the life of a person is capital punishment, also referred to as the death penalty. The death penalty has been applied to hundreds of different crimes since ancient times. Even as late as 1819, British law designated 223 capital crimes

TABLE 6.2 Percentage of Physician Sample Indicating Willingness to Provide Assistance, Receiving Requests for Assistance, and/or Complying With Patient Requests for Assistance in Committing Suicide

	Percentage
1. Would write prescription for a lethal dose of medication if it were legal to do so.	36
2. Would write prescription under current legal constraints.	11
3. Have received request for assistance with suicide.	13
4. Have written prescription for a lethal dose of medication.	3
5. Would give lethal injection if it were legal to do so.	24
6. Would give lethal injection under current legal constraints.	7
7. Have received a request for a lethal injection.	11
8. Have given a lethal injection.	5

SOURCE: Meier et al. (1998).

(Radzinowicz, 1948). The colony of Massachusetts listed 13 crimes as capital in 1636: adultery, assault in sudden anger, blasphemy, buggery, idolatry, manstealing, murder, perjury in a capital trial, rape, rebellion, sodomy, statutory rape, and witchcraft (Haskins, 1956). There was no uniform system of criminal justice in the American colonies, and whether an offense was considered a capital crime depended not only on the nature of the offense but also on the locality in which it occurred.

Death Penalty Statistics

The total number of crimes warranting the death penalty has declined in modern America, but during the 20th century people were executed in this country for armed robbery, arson, kidnapping, murder, rape, treason, and military desertion. Most of these executions were for the crime of murder; the crime of rape was second.

Figure 6.2 is a plot of the number of legal executions carried out by the states and the federal government of the United States from 1930 to 2000. A consequence of a 1972 ruling by the U.S. Supreme Court (*Furman v. Geor-*

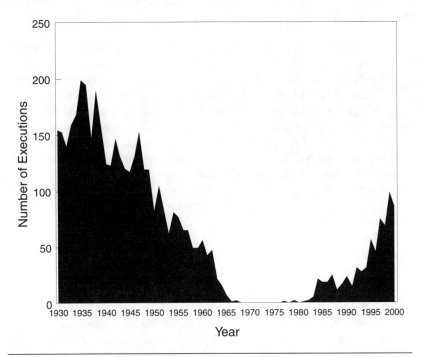

Figure 6.2. Number of Executions by Year From 1930 to 2000

SOURCE: Based on data from U.S. Department of Justice, Bureau of Justice Statistics (2000).

gia) and related cases was that all executions in this country were suspended from 1968 through 1976. Following additional court decisions in 1976 (*Gregg v. Georgia, Jurek v. Texas, Profitt v. Florida*), executions were resumed in 1977. Among the 98 persons executed in the United States in the year 2000, 61 were White, 33 were Black, 2 were American Indian, 2 were Asian, and none were women. In that same year, 3,577 inmates of U.S. prisons were under sentence of death for capital crimes. Among the 3,527 males in this group, 1,948 were White, 1,514 were Black, 28 were American Indian, 24 were Asian, and 13 were of other races.

Over half of all homicide victims in the United States are people of color, but nearly 90% of those who are executed are convicted for killing Whites. The fact that capital defendants who kill White victims are more likely to receive the death penalty than those who kill Black victims has been cited in support of the allegation that capital punishment is racist (National Coalition to Abolish the Death Penalty, 1999a).

Methods of Execution

Historically, people who were convicted of capital crimes were subjected to a variety of execution methods, many of which were cruel and inhuman. Hanging was the most common method of execution in England during colonial times; the axe was reserved for treason, burning at the stake for witchcraft, and disemboweling and quartering for counterfeiting. At the beginning of the 21st century, lethal injection was the predominant method of execution in 34 of the United States. The laws of 11 states authorized electrocution for capital crimes; the laws of 4 states, lethal gas; the laws of 3 states, hanging; and the laws of 3 states, firing squad. The laws of 16 states authorize lethal injection and an alternative method. Lethal injection and electrocution have been the most common methods since 1976, accounting for more than 70% of all executions in this country. Federal executions are carried out according to the preferred method of the state in which they are performed.

Pros and Cons of the Death Penalty

Many prominent Americans have expressed their attitudes—pro and con—toward the death penalty, both orally and in writing. The debate has centered on four purported benefits of capital punishment: deterrence, retribution, economy, and protection (Caldwell, 2000). The first of these, *deterrence*, is also the most common, alleging that the fear of the death penalty keeps people from committing capital crimes. Although the matter is debatable, there appears to be no real evidence that murderers, who tend to act impulsively, are deterred by the threat of the legal consequences of their acts. In a survey of criminologists, who should know the research literature on the subject, 84% rejected the notion that the death penalty acts as a deterrent to murder (Radelet & Akers, 1996). Additional indirect evidence against the deterrence argument is seen in the fact that enactment of the death penalty appears to have no significant effect on the murder rate. Furthermore, in the United States the average murder rate is higher in those states with capital punishment than in those without it (National Coalition to Abolish the Death Penalty, 1999b). In general, it is the swiftness with which punishment is administered rather than the threat of it that deters crime. Unfortunately, the U.S. judicial system is not known for its swiftness in punishing capital crimes.

With respect to the second argument for capital punishment, *retribution*, it is maintained that capital punishment serves as an expression of community outrage and society's moral right to retribution. This "an eye for an eye" (or more accurately, "a life for a life") principle of Mosaic law may be a justification for the death penalty, but it is at odds with the teachings of many religions (National Interreligious Task Force on Criminal Justice, n.d.). However, Christians who approve of capital punishment interpret the scriptural prohibition against killing as applying only to the actions of individuals acting on their own.

Even if one argues for capital punishment on the grounds of social retribution, it is crucial for the punishment to be imposed without regard to race, sex, social status, or special influence. Unfortunately, American justice has never been applied very consistently or without regard to personal characteristics or social standing.

The third argument for capital punishment—*economy*—states that it is cheaper to execute a person than to keep him or her in an institution for a long period of time. The counterargument is that the increasing cost and time for appeals have resulted in capital punishment becoming more and more expensive. Furthermore, simple incarceration for life or for a long period of time would provide a convicted person with the opportunity for self-support and some form of restitution to the relatives of the victim (Caldwell, 2000).

The fourth, or *protection*, argument for the death penalty is that it protects society from dangerous criminals by keeping them from repeating their crimes and passing on their undesirable characteristics to others. However, institutional rehabilitation programs, coupled with probation and parole, can limit the risk of sending dangerous criminals back into the community. With respect to the "contagion" part of the protection argument, few convicted murderers have hereditary defects in cognitive, affective, or physical characteristics that can be passed on to their progeny. Furthermore, only a small minority of people who commit crimes suffer from mental disorders that may have a genetic component.

Perhaps more pernicious than all four of the above arguments for capital punishment is the belief that by executing a fellow human being one is doing something constructive about crime. In reality, sanctioning official killing as a response to private killing may only make matters worse by brutalizing society.

Research on Attitudes Toward Capital Punishment

Attitudes toward capital punishment may be assessed in various ways: from letters, articles, and other writings of persons, usually professional writers or scholars, who have thought about the pros and cons of the issue; from public opinion polls in which large samples of the public are interviewed; and by means of ad hoc questionnaires or formal attitude scales (see Attitude Toward Capital Punishment in Appendix 6.1).

Attitude toward capital punishment is positively correlated with attitude toward war, in that people who approve of the violence expressed in capital punishment also tend to approve of the violence expressed in war. Research findings show that a greater percentage of women than men disapprove of both capital punishment and war (e.g., Levy, 1995). The negativity and lack of enthusiasm that women typically manifest toward capital punishment is also seen in their attitudes toward armed conflict (Bendyna, Finucane, Kirby, O'Donnell, & Wilcox, 1996; Hull, Hurd, & Margolis, 1993; Lester, 1994).

Despite rather heated opposition to capital punishment, public sentiment in favor of the death penalty in this country remains high. In a 1999 Gallup poll, 71% of a national sample of Americans indicated that they were in favor of the death penalty for a person convicted of murder, 22% were opposed to it, and 7% had no opinion (Gallup, 2000). But when the interviewers asked whether the penalty for murder should be execution or life in prison with no possibility of parole, 56% of the sample supported the death penalty and 38% indicated a preference for life imprisonment without parole. The percentage supporting the death penalty is even less when the circumstances surrounding the crime are considered (Sandys & McGarrell, 1995). Be that as it may, public support for capital punishment in the United States has been fairly high during the past several decades, peaking at 80% in 1994.

The criticism that capital punishment unfairly targets minorities and poor people is generally acknowledged as true by the American public. When asked whether a poor person is more likely than a person of average or above-average income to receive the death penalty for the same crime, 65% of the respondents in a 1999 Gallup poll agreed and 32% disagreed. A smaller percentage of Whites (22%) than minorities (41%) agreed that the death penalty is imposed too often, and a greater percentage of Whites (66%) than non-Whites (52%) said that capital punishment is not used often enough (Gallup, 2000).

Another nationwide poll (Louis Harris & Associates, 1997) found that the death penalty was approved of by a greater percentage of men than women, adults older than age 70 than adults younger than 70, people living in the West and South than in the East and Midwest, and Republicans than Democrats.

Attitudes toward capital punishment are also related to personality characteristics. For example, Valliant and Oliver (1997) found that university students with either autocratic-submissive or autocratic-aggressive leadership styles had significantly harsher attitudes toward capital punishment than those with a laissez-faire leadership style. Studies have also demonstrated that attitudes toward capital punishment can be changed. For example, Howells, Flanagan, and Hagan (1995) found that adults who viewed a videotape of two executions became less supportive of capital punishment, when compared with the changes in attitudes observed in a control group who viewed a nature film.

Recommended Readings

Aiken, L. R. (2001). *Dying, death, and bereavement* (4th ed., pp. 194-210). Mahwah, NJ: Lawrence Erlbaum.

Ariès, P. (1974). *Western attitudes toward death: From the Middle Ages to the present.* Baltimore: Johns Hopkins University Press.

Battin, M. P., Rhodes, R., & Silvers, A. (Eds.). (1998). *Physician assisted suicide: Expanding the debate.* New York: Routledge.

Critchlow, D. T. (1999). *Intended consequences: Birth control, abortion, and the federal government in modern America.* New York: Oxford University Press.

Irving, J. (1999). *The cider house rules: A novel.* New York: Modern Library.

Neimeyer, R. A., & Fortner, B. (1997). Death attitudes in contemporary perspective. In S. Strack et al. (Eds.), *Death and the quest for meaning: Essays in honor of Herman Feifel* (pp. 3-29). Northvale, NJ: Jason Aronson.

Torr, J. D., & Egendorf, L. K. (2000). *Problems of death: Opposing viewpoints.* San Diego, CA: Greenhaven.

Williams, M. E. (Ed.). (2000). *Capital punishment.* San Diego, CA: Greenhaven.

Zucker, M. B. (Ed.). (1999). *The right to die debate: A documentary history.* Westport, CT: Greenwood.

Appendix 6.1

Instruments for Assessing Attitudes Toward Death-Related Subjects

---

Alpha-Omega Completed Sentence Form (R. Klein et al.; ERIC, ED 167 218). Fifty items, higher education; developed to identify and measure individuals' adaptational approaches to information concerning their own death or the possible death of a significant other.

Attitude Toward Capital Punishment (S. Salbod & J. J. Mitchell; ETS Test Collection Library). Twenty-six items, approximately 10 minutes testing time. An attitude measure used to assess public's attitude toward the death penalty or capital punishment.

Death Attitude Profile (Gesser, Wong, & Reker, 1987-1988). Twenty-one items; adults; designed to measure attitudes about death according to five different factors: fear of the state of death; fear of the process of dying; approach-oriented death acceptance, where death is viewed as an entrance to a happy afterlife; escape-oriented death acceptance, where death is viewed as an escape form pain and suffering; and neutral acceptance, where death is viewed as a reality; 5-point response scale.

Death Attitude Profile–Revised (Wong, Reker, & Gesser, 1994). Thirty-two items; 7-point scale; adults; five subscales: Fear of Death/Dying (having negative thoughts and feelings about death as a state and dying as process), Approach Acceptance (viewing death as a passage to a satisfying afterlife), Escape Acceptance (seeing death as an alternative to a painful existence), Neutral Acceptance (understanding death as a reality that is to be neither feared nor welcomed), and Death Avoidance (a defensive attempt to keep thoughts of death out of one's consciousness.

Death Depression Scale (Templer, LaVoie, Chalgujian, & Thomas-Dobson, 1990). Seventeen true-false or Likert-type items, adolescents and adults; designed to assess depression associated with the topic of death; found to have six factors associated with death: despair, loneliness, dread, sadness, depression, and finality.

Euthanasia Attitudes Scale (Holloway et al., 1994-1995). Thirty-item Likert-type scale measures attitudes toward euthanasia. Assesses five factors: general orientation toward euthanasia, patients' rights issues, role of life-sustaining technology, professionals' role, and ethics and values. Acceptable internal consistency and test-retest reliability coefficients and discriminant validity data reported.

Klug Death Acceptance Scale (Klug & Sinha, 1987-1988). Sixteen true-false items; adults; measures death acceptance by assessing two components: confrontation of death and integration of death.

Lester Attitude Toward Death Scale (Lester, 1991). Twenty-one equal-interval scale items; designed to assess an adult's attitude toward death.

Multidimensional Measurement of Death Attitudes (Nelson, 1978). Fifteen items; higher education; designed to assess three factors of attitudes toward death: death avoidance, disengagement from death, and death fear.

Omega Scale (I. M. Staik; ERIC, ED 292 829). Twenty-five Likert-type items, adults; developed to assess the attitudes of college students toward their own deaths, burial practices, traditional versus nontraditional funeral options, and preferences as to the disposition of their bodies after death; factors include nontraditional secular funeral, personal funeral arrangement, traditional funeral, and preferred disposition of the body.

Revised Twenty Statement Test (Durlak, Horn, & Kass, 1990). To the question "What does your own death mean to you?" respondents give 20 open-ended responses, which are then coded into seven mutually exclusive content and three summary-affective categories.

Suicide Opinion Questionnaire (Domino, MacGregor, & Hannah, 1988-1989). 107 items, 100 attitudinal and 7 demographic 5-point Likert-type scale (*strongly agree* to *strongly disagree*) items; scored on eight scales: Mental Illness, Cry for Help, Right to Die, Religion, Impulsivity, Normality, Aggression, and Moral Evil.

7

Schools, Subjects, and Students

Evaluating Schools and Students
Phi Delta Kappa/Gallup Polls Regarding
  Public Schools
Other Research on Attitudes Toward Schools

Attitudes Toward Mathematics
Demographic Differences
Modifying Attitudes and Achievement in Mathematics

Computers and Technology
Attitudes Toward Computers
Teachers and Technology

Attitudes Toward Science
Demographic Differences
Public Attitudes Toward Science

Attitudes Toward Other School Subjects
Reading, Writing, and Foreign Languages
Social Studies, Physical Education, and Music

Next to sleeping, most people spend the greatest part of their lives in school or on the job. Those attending school are more likely to be children and adolescents, and those on the job are more likely to be adults, but modern living often involves a mixture of education and work for people of all ages. Beginning in adolescence, the work role typically alternates with school attendance and studying. Adolescents and young adults, in particular, may work so they can afford to stay in school, or they may stay in or return to school or college to obtain a better job or to improve their chances of promotion.

Support for the strongly held viewpoint that it is wise to get as much education as one can is provided by Figure 7.1. As shown in this figure, average income is higher for men than for women and higher for Whites than for Blacks and Hispanics. Average annual earnings also increase almost linearly with level of education.

Although income is the best measure of socioeconomic status, level of education is a close second. The relationship between education and material wealth is so well established that a large percentage of college freshmen report that their main goal in attending college is to ensure a bright financial future for themselves (see Weiss, 2001).

It is true that more Americans than ever before are graduating from high school and college and thereby are able to obtain high-paying jobs. Nevertheless, there are still glaring educational differences between Whites and Blacks or Hispanics and between native and foreign-born citizens (Newburger & Curry, 2000). There has also been an erosion of standards in recent years such that many high school and even college graduates are deficient in basic skills and are inadequately prepared to assume their assigned responsibilities in the world of work. Despite the fact that over four-fifths of American adults have completed high school and over one-quarter have earned a bachelor's degree or higher, many of these graduates still cannot read and write well or are deficient in their knowledge of common school subjects (science, mathematics, literature, history, geography, etc.). They may also lack important technical skills that are needed to function effectively in today's jobs and in other activities. The results of tests administered in dozens of nations throughout the world show that American schoolchildren have serious educational deficiencies in comparison with students in many other countries (National Center for Education Statistics, 2001). These facts have been known for many years, but efforts to improve the educational status of American children and adults in comparison with people in many other countries have not been very successful.

Evaluating Schools and Students

The results of surveys conducted by the National Opinion Research Center of the University of Chicago between 1976 and 1998 indicated that confidence in education and in the nation's educational leaders declined markedly during the latter part of the 20th century.[1] This loss of confidence in American education appears to be justified by the relatively poor perfor-

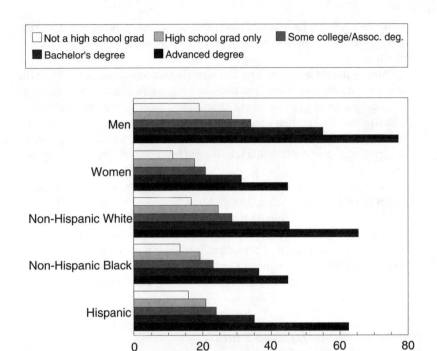

Figure 7.1. Average Annual Income of Year-Round, Full-Time U.S. Workers by Sex, Ethnicity, and Highest Educational Attainment

SOURCE: Based on data from Newburger and Curry (2000).

mance of American schoolchildren on traditional measures of achievement. But perhaps schools and teachers are being asked to do too much, and perhaps blaming the educational establishment for what are consequences of deeper social problems is merely another version of blaming the messenger who brings bad news.

Much of the formal evaluation of students that occurs in schools and colleges throughout the United States involves the administration of standardized and teacher-made tests of cognitive abilities and achievements. These tests are designed to evaluate the extent to which students have attained specific educational objectives. Although cognitive objectives are generally viewed as the most important goals of formal education, they are not the only goals. Depending on the nature of the school and the teachers, affective, social, psychomotor, and other objectives are also of concern. Many of these goals are not formally assessed, and those that are usually rely on more subjective procedures than those used in the assessment of cognitive outcomes of education.

Among the methods employed in assessing student attainment of specific affective objectives, in addition to evaluating teachers, administrators, and schools as a whole, are measures of attitudes, values, opinions, and beliefs (see Appendix 7.1). Many of these same types of instruments, and especially opinion questionnaires, are administered to students, teachers, and parents to identify problems within the schools and to suggest remedies or improvements.

Of all the factors that influence student learning, one of the most important is the classroom teacher. The abilities, attitudes, and personality of the teacher can have a profound effect on the extent to which students benefit from school experiences. For this reason, it is essential for teachers, as well as students, to be evaluated periodically on their performance. This is usually accomplished by having students, peers, and supervisors rate teachers on both classroom and extra-classroom behaviors and attitudes that have a bearing on teaching effectiveness.

Phi Delta Kappa/Gallup Polls
Regarding Public Schools

One public opinion poll concerning education and the schools that has been conducted on a national level each year for the past three decades is the annual Phi Delta Kappa/Gallup Poll of the Public's Attitudes Toward the Public Schools (Rose & Gallup, 2000, 2001). Some of the results of the polls that were conducted from 1992 to 2001 are shown in Figure 7.2. This figure is a graph of the percentage of people in the national sample who cited what they considered to be the major problems facing the local public schools. Five major problems identified in the 2000 and 2001 polls, in order of the percentage of people who cited them, were lack of financial support/funding/money, lack of discipline/more control, fighting/violence/gangs, overcrowded schools, and use of drugs/dope. Note that the percentage of respondents who cited each of these five problems varied over the 10-year period from 1992 through 2001.

Teachers do not always see "eye to eye" with other people regarding the issues and problems facing the public schools. The teachers who responded to the questions in the Sixth Phi Delta Kappa Poll of Teachers' Attitudes Toward the Public Schools (Langdon & Vesper, 2000) viewed these schools in a more positive light than the general public. When asked about their own school, the schools in their local communities, or the schools across the country, the teachers gave those schools higher grades than those given by the public.

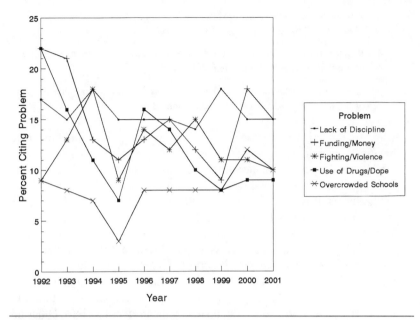

Figure 7.2. Items Most Frequently Cited by the General Public as Major Problems Facing Local Public Schools: 1992-2001

SOURCE: From "The Annual Gallup Poll of the Public's Attitudes" (various years).

Both the teachers and the general public surveyed in the sixth Phi Delta Kappa poll agreed that in selecting a school the quality of the teaching staff is foremost, followed closely by discipline and curriculum. Regarding the role that the reputation of the school should play in whether or not it is selected, a larger majority of the general public (80%) than the teachers (59%) said that this is an important consideration. Another difference between the teachers and the general public was in responding to the question of whether children should be exposed to a less diverse student body: 12% of the teachers and 45% of the public thought it was a fairly important consideration. Other differences between the responses of the teachers and those of the general public concerned the following:

1. How safe the public schools are: 43% of the teachers and 24% of the public said the public schools are very safe and orderly.

2. What it takes to keep teachers on the job: 53% of the teachers and 90% of the public favored tying teachers' pay to their performance.

3. Whether students' test scores should be a factor in determining teachers' salaries: 3% of the teachers and 47% of the public favored this option.

4. Whether the public schools should place major emphasis on academics: 48% of the teachers and 39% of the public agreed.

5. Whether the best way to use federal money is for class-size reduction: 70% of the teachers and 50% of the public agreed.

In addition, a larger percentage of teachers than the general public agreed that greater parent involvement was one thing they would stress to improve public schools and that finances/funding is the main obstacle to improving the schools in their community.

Significant differences between the attitudes of teachers and those of the general public were also found in the Fifth Phi Delta Kappa Poll of Teachers' Attitudes Toward the Public Schools (Langdon, 1999). For example, a majority (56%) of all teachers who were questioned said that children get a better education today than they themselves received, but a larger percentage of teachers in inner-city schools (35%) than of those in urban (25%), suburban (19%), small-town (21%), and rural (21%) schools stated that children today get a poorer education than they themselves received. Other interesting findings of the fifth Phi Delta Kappa poll were the following:

1. The great majority of teachers (78%) opposed allowing students and parents to choose a private school to attend at public expense.

2. Only a small percentage of teachers favored paying higher salaries to teachers of science, math, technical subjects, and vocational subjects for which teacher shortages are known to exist.

3. A majority of teachers agreed with the majority of the public that prayers should be allowed in the public schools.

4. The top four subjects that teachers would require college-bound high school students to take are English, mathematics, science, and history/U.S. government; for students not planning to attend college, the top four subjects that teachers would require are English, mathematics, history/U.S. government, and industrial arts/homemaking.

Other Research on Attitudes Toward Schools

Many other surveys and research studies of the school-related attitudes and opinions of students, teachers, and parents have been conducted. Among the findings of such studies are that overall attitudes toward schools are more positive for girls than for boys, for academically gifted than for average or below-average students, for students of higher socioeconomic status (SES) than for those lower in SES, for students with higher grades than for other students, for Whites and Asian Americans than for Hispanics and Blacks, and for teachers than for the general public. Research on attitudes toward more specific aspects of school and education, as abstracted in PsycINFO, includes students' attitudes toward ethnic minorities, bullying, alcohol and drug use, sex education, individuals with disabilities, smoking, rape, and specific subjects (mathematics, science, foreign languages, etc.). Among the investigations of teachers' attitudes are those concerned with mainstreaming, health education, substance abuse, sex education, AIDS and AIDS education, contraception, and bullying. Fewer studies have been conducted on parents' attitudes, but examples are attitudes toward at-risk students, corporal punishment, and disabled students. Rather than providing brief synopses of these studies, more detailed summaries will be given of attitudes toward selected school subjects. Special emphasis is given to mathematics, science, and computers. These are more technical, precise subjects in which there are demonstrably correct answers to assigned problems, and consequently achievement in these three subjects can be evaluated more objectively than in many other school subjects.

Attitudes Toward Mathematics

Positive feelings toward mathematics are related to success in that subject, but in no way do they guarantee it. Good numerical, problem-solving, spatial, and other cognitive abilities, together with good study habits, ample time for studying, and effective teaching, also play important roles in determining achievement in mathematics. Actually, the relationship between attitudes and achievement in mathematics, as in many other school subjects, is reciprocal: positive attitudes toward the subject motivate students to spend more time studying and thinking about it, and the resulting high grades and other rewards make them feel good about the subject and interested in pursuing it further.

Hundreds of research investigations, the majority of which are based on small samples that were probably unrepresentative of the population to which the findings were to be generalized, have been conducted over the past several decades. A large percentage of these studies were done by graduate students in mathematics education with little training in measurement or research methods who were fulfilling a thesis or dissertation requirement for a graduate degree. Even so, as a group these teacher trainees were certainly more knowledgeable in mathematics and less afraid of it than the elementary school teachers who are required to teach math as well as other subjects in the lower grades.

Demographic Differences

Because of its correlational nature, much of the research on attitudes and achievement in mathematics has been concerned with identifying demographic, and particularly gender, differences in these variables. The findings of research on gender differences underscore the common observation that at the high school level and beyond, females in almost all countries that have been studied do not perform as well in mathematics as males and have less positive attitudes toward the subject (Collis, 1987; Etsey & Snetzler, 1998; Kwiatkowski, Dammer, Mills, & Jih, 1993; Mullis & Martin, 1998; Pedro, Wolleat, Fennema, & Becker, 1981; Randel, Stevenson, & Witruk, 2000; Terwilliger & Titus, 1989).

Another demographic variable of interest with respect to mathematics achievement and attitudes is nationality. As an illustration, consider the findings of the Third International Mathematics and Science Study (Beaton et al., 1997). Measures of attitude and achievement in mathematics are typically positively correlated, but the correlation is usually not very high. Likewise, perception of one's performance in mathematics is often not closely related to how well one actually performs in the subject. Self-appraisals of ability depend on how well one does relative to other people and praise received from other people, as well as personal and social expectations and mores. An illustration of the less-than-perfect positive relationship between perceived ability and actual ability is given by the cross-national data depicted in Figure 7.3. The right-hand panel of the figure is a plot, in order from highest to lowest, of the mean scores on a mathematics achievement test taken by a sample of eighth-grade students in each of 25 countries represented. In addition to obtaining their scores on a mathematics achievement test, the sample of eighth graders in each country was asked to indicate on a 4-point scale (*strongly disagree, disagree, agree, strongly agree*) their degree of agreement with the statement that they usually did well in mathematics. The left-hand panel of Figure 7.3 is a plot of the percentage of the sample of tested students in each country who answered "strongly agree." Note that unlike the corresponding mathematics achievement test scores in the right-hand panel, the "strongly agree" percentages in the left-hand panel are not in order of magnitude. In fact, there is a negative relationship between the numbers in the left- and right-hand panels ($r = -.69$). Thus, the "strongly agree" percentages are inversely related to the mean mathematics test scores. This result, which might not have been expected, may be interpreted as due to cultural differences in the perception or expression of personal achievement. Observe that the four Asian countries (Korea, Singapore, Japan, Hong Kong) with the highest mean mathematics test scores had the smallest "strongly agree" percentages of all 25 countries. How should these differences be interpreted: that the Asian students were more humble, hon-

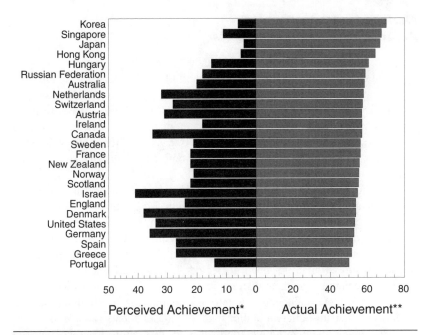

Figure 7.3. Eighth-Grade Students' Perceptions Concerning Their Achievement and Their Mean Scores on Mathematics Test

SOURCE: Based on data from Beaton et al. (1997).
*Percentage who strongly agree that they usually do well in math.
**Mean score of group on mathematics achievement test.

est, "soul-searching," or deferent to authority, or less boastful and deceitful, than the European and American students?

Consistent with the findings described in the preceding paragraph are those obtained in a subsequent study of the attitudes, beliefs, and mathematics achievement of large samples of German and Japanese 11th-grade students (Randel et al., 2000). The German students in this study scored significantly lower than the Japanese students on a test of basic concepts and operations in high school mathematics. However, the German students were less critical of themselves and their academic ability, held lower standards for their performance, and were less likely to attribute excellence in performance in mathematics to studying. In discussing these findings, the authors attributed the poorer math performance of the German students, as with that observed in studies of American students, to the similar beliefs held by German and American students, as contrasted with the beliefs of Japanese and other Asian students.

Modifying Attitudes and Achievement in Mathematics

Not all researchers have been satisfied with an experiential or psychosocial explanation of achievement and attitudinal differences in mathematics, and the results of a number of investigations point to the importance of genetic factors in mathematical abilities (see Geary, 1993). Most efforts to change attitudes and performance in mathematics have, however, focused on environment rather than heredity. No one gets to choose his or her own grandparents, but most people exercise some choice in what they experience.

Stimulated to some extent by political and social concerns associated with gender and ethnic inequality of opportunity, the treatment of math anxiety and attitude has received a great deal of attention during the past two or three decades. These efforts have been concerned mainly with modifying the anxieties or attitudes of college-age and adult learners, but the feelings of schoolchildren have not been neglected. Tobias and Donady (1977) employed techniques such as systematic desensitization, immersion, and psychological support. Other researchers also conducted workshops and special classes for math-deficient and/or math-anxious students (e.g., Ben-Jacob, 1986), using nonquantitative approaches to instruction (Katz & Tomazic, 1988), cooperative learning (Sherman & Christian, 1999), metacognitive strategies (Maqsud, 1998), and even humor (Berk & Nanda, 1998).

Educational arrangements, such as providing single-sex classrooms for mathematics instruction, have also been found to have a positive impact on the attitudes of girls in particular (Walter, 1997).

The results of research studies demonstrate that it is possible to modify attitudes toward mathematics by emphasizing appropriate instructional procedures, materials, and teaching, but the question of the permanence of such changes persists when no follow-up observations are made. Furthermore, even after years of attempting to produce permanent improvements in the interests and attitudes of girls and women in mathematics and math-related subjects and careers, differences between males and females in this area appear to be as large as ever. Despite periodic changes in the way mathematics is taught, from "back to basics" to "modern math," from making math more meaningful, engaging, and practical to creating the ability to solve abstract problems, these problems continue.

Computers and Technology

When digital computers first became available in the late 1950s and 1960s, their use in education was limited to a great extent to administration and research, and by small numbers of students in mathematics, business, and the physical sciences. Only a handful of precollege students had any exposure to computers at that time, but the situation was about to change. With the advent of microcomputers in the mid-1970s, computer usage both in and outside of academic contexts became more widespread. Not only older adolescents and young adults but children of all ages became exposed to computers at home, in schools, in video game parlors, and elsewhere. In addition to playing games, these computers could be used for a variety of purposes—word processing, spreadsheet computations, graphics, and so on—by persons with little technical know-how and interest. By the end of the 1980s, students were carrying their own microcomputers to school, on vacations or other trips, and wherever they might prove useful. Approximately 8% of American adults had computers in their homes in 1983, a number that had increased to 54% by 1999. From 1997 to 1999, the percentage of American homes with more than one computer rose from 12% to 17%, and the number of homes with e-mail addresses rose from 18% to 32% (National Science Foundation [NSF], 2000). With the rapid expansion of the Internet and the World Wide Web during the late 1980s and 1990s, it became obvious that the technological revolution was knocking at the door of the educational establishment. The use of computers was no longer confined to prepackaged software that had to be loaded and unloaded by the operator. By means of information and procedures that became immediately available from electronic learning sites throughout the world, opportunities for new experiences and activities were at the fingertips of an Internet browser, and the term *distance learning* was added to the educational glossary.

Attitudes Toward Computers

Because computers are no longer precisely what they were in previous decades, attitudes and beliefs pertaining to these devices have changed. Computers are now seen and used almost everywhere, and exposure to them in homes and schools has made them more familiar and increased the degree of comfort in using them. Nevertheless, negative attitudes and anxiety ("computerphobia," "cyberphobia," or "technophobia") continue to exist. A larger percentage of its victims are female than male (Brosnan & Lee, 1998; Shashaani, 1994, 1997), persons without home computers (Sexton, King, Aldridge, & Goodstadt-Killoran, 1999), and other people having little experience with computers (Czaja & Sharit, 1998; Leutner & Weinsier, 1994). Older adults, who tend to be less experienced with computers than younger adults (Baldi, 1997), generally feel less comfortable, efficacious, and in control when attempting to make use of them. Certain studies have also found that younger pupils, both male and female, have greater experience with and more positive attitudes toward computers than older pupils (Comber, Colley, Hargreaves, & Dorn, 1997).

Attitudes toward computers generally become more positive, and confidence in using them increases, with positive experiences, especially when bolstered by peer support (Corston & Colman, 1996; Crombie & Armstrong, 1999) and expert instruction (Czaja & Sharit, 1998; Torkzadeh, Pflughoeft, & Hall, 1999). Parents whose own attitudes toward computers are favorable also contribute to similar attitudes in their children (DeSantis & Youniss, 1991).

The results of a number of investigations have shown that attitudes toward computers are generally positive but vary to some extent with country and culture (e.g., Brosnan & Lee, 1998). For example, in a comparison of attitude differences in Japanese and Swedish ninth graders, Makrakis (1992) found that the Japanese students were less anxious about computers, more aware of the usefulness of computing skills, and more interested in learning about them.

Despite the expanded uses and usage of computers, they are still associated more with mathematics and science than with other school subjects and are seen as demanding higher cognitive abilities to operate. Consistent with this perception is Subhi's (1999) finding that the best predictors of attitudes toward computers are mathematical ability and IQ. Other studies have found that attitudes toward computers are significant predictors of their usage (e.g., Al-Khaldi & Al-Jabri, 1998).

Teachers and Technology

It is commonly recognized that teachers are at the center of the educational enterprise. Consequently, for students to obtain the maximum benefit from the power of the Internet, teachers must be knowledgeable in its uses as an instructional tool. Unfortunately, many teachers, and particularly those who were educated in the B.C. (before computers) era, view modern information technology as too complex and as inappropriate to their teaching. These teachers may maintain that they grew up without computers, managed to get through school and college without them, and can continue to perform their jobs very well without them. A national survey found that approximately two thirds of all teachers never used a computer before they were introduced to one in the classroom and that approximately the same number feel that they are not adequately prepared to use technology in their teaching (Web-Based Education Commission, 2000).

Survey findings reveal that although the great majority of teachers, and particularly those under age 35, have some knowledge of the Internet, they still cannot apply their computer skills to classroom instruction. Younger teachers possess more computer-based skills, but, like their older colleagues, they often do not know how to apply those skills to teaching.

Presumably, the problem of teachers' inadequate technological knowledge and skills could be remedied by training, but current expenditures for teacher training in technology are only a fraction of what is needed. Over three fourths of public school teachers received some technology-related professional development in 1998-1999, but the training was often too little, too basic, and too general to help them acquire the needed expertise in teaching with technology (Web-Based Education Commission, 2000). What teachers require, more than a brief course in basic computer operations, is guidance in using the best tools in the best ways to support the best kinds of instruction. Furthermore, they need time to learn, practice, and plan ways to use computers and the Internet.

Attitudes Toward Science

Like mathematics, science is a heterogeneous field that is related, in both content and methodology, to many other areas of knowledge. The instrumentation, procedures, and findings of research in the physical and biological sciences have contributed not only to engineering, architecture, medicine, business, and other applied fields but to the social sciences, the humanities, and other disciplines as well.

When interpreting the results of research on attitudes toward science, it is important to examine the instruments and procedures that were used to assess these attitudes. The statements on different attitude questionnaires, inventories, or scales may be concerned with the emotional, motivational, cognitive, or behavioral aspects of attitudes. For example, a questionnaire constructed by the author was designed as a set of separate scales for assessing four kinds of attitudes toward science or mathematics: fear, enjoyment, motivation, and value or importance. It is easy enough to imagine what sorts of statements would be appropriate to measure the emotional (fear, anxiety, enjoyment, etc.) component of attitudes toward science. Changing "mathematics" to "science" in Form 2.2 from Chapter 2 yields a set of items for assessing the affective or emotional component of attitude toward science.

Table 7.1 is a list of eight statements concerned with the cognitive component of attitudes toward science and technology. Compare these statements with the seven statements in Table 7.2. The statements in Table 7.1 are attitude items, whereas those in Table 7.2 are more like achievement test items. Answers to several of these achievement items, however, also reflect attitudes toward science. The numbers in the two right-hand columns of Tables 7.1 and

TABLE 7.1 Attitudes Toward Science and Technology

	Percentage	
	Agree	Disagree
1. Scientific invention is largely responsible for our standard of living in the United States.	62	3
2. Overall, science and technology have caused more good than harm.	44	10
3. On balance, computers and factory automation will create more jobs than they will eliminate.	26	22
4. One trouble with science is that it makes our way of life change too fast.	24	31
5. New inventions will always be found to counteract any harmful consequences of technological development.	25	20
6. In this complicated world of ours, the only way we can know what is going on is to rely on leaders and experts who can be trusted.	28	28
7. Scientific researchers are dedicated people who work for the good of humanity.	43	9
8. Because of their knowledge, scientific researchers have a power that makes them dangerous.	26	30

SOURCE: Miller and Pifer (1993). Reprinted with permission of Northern Illinois University.

7.2 are the percentages of 1,650 high school seniors who (in 1993) agreed or disagreed with the respective statements.

Demographic Differences

The findings of research on demographic (gender, age, SES, race/ethnicity, culture, etc.) variables related to attitudes toward science are similar to those obtained in research on attitudes toward mathematics. At all grade levels and ages, males typically have more positive attitudes and higher science achievement test scores than females (Francis & Greer, 1999; Greenfield, 1996; Jones, Howe, & Rua, 2000; Lips, 1992; Mullis & Martin, 1998; Weinburgh, 1995).

TABLE 7.2   Understanding of Scientific Concepts

	Percentage	
	Agree	*Disagree*
1. Human beings, as we know them today, developed from earlier species of animals.	33	24
2. Smoking causes serious health problems.	75	3
3. In the entire universe, it is likely that there are thousands of planets like our own on which life could have developed.	44	8
4. The continents on which we live have been moving their locations for millions of years and will continue to move in the future.	57	4
5. Some numbers are especially lucky for me.	26	37
6. A scientific theory is a scientist's best understanding of how something works.	61	7
7. All scientific theories change from time to time as scientists improve their understanding.	64	4

SOURCE: Miller and Pifer (1993). Reprinted with permission of Northern Illinois University.

As is the case with mathematics, students tend to like science in the elementary grades. But by the time they reach junior high school, their attitudes toward science have, on the whole, become more negative. Contributing to this increased negativity of attitudes is the fact that the subject matter of science courses becomes more abstract and complex in secondary school. In addition, students are held more accountable for activities in which the outcomes are not specified beforehand (Piburn & Baker, 1993).

Recognizing the importance of science in certain careers, for health and well-being, for public awareness and action, and as a prerequisite for advanced courses in science and courses in other areas, teachers of science are concerned with applying creative instructional approaches to encourage students to do well in the subject and develop positive attitudes toward it. Among the many methods that have been employed by science teachers to attain these goals are (a) using female role models in teaching female students (Harvey & Stables, 1986; Smith & Erb, 1986); (b) planning special units and field trips in space science, environmental science, human heredity, or other interesting and motivating topics (e.g., Sorge, Newsom, & Hagerty, 2000); (c) designing cooperative learning exercises (Johnson,

Johnson, Scott, & Ramolae, 1985); (d) conducting lessons and assigning homework involving practical work (Parkinson, Hendley, Tanner, & Stables, 1998); and (e) showing television programs on contemporary scientific topics (Ormerod, Rutherford, & Wood, 1989).

Teachers and schools cannot, of course, be held completely responsible for fostering positive science attitudes. The home environment and parental involvement in particular have both direct and indirect effects on attitudes mediated through science activities and visits to libraries, museums, and other repositories of scientific information (George & Kaplan, 1998).

Public Attitudes Toward Science

The results of a 1999 survey by the NSF (2000) indicate that the attitudes of most Americans toward science and technology are highly positive and that those attitudes have improved in recent years. According to the 1999 NSF survey, attitudes toward science and technology expressed by North Americans and Europeans are more favorable than those of the Japanese. University-educated citizens have the most positive attitudes, whereas the adults who did not complete high school have the least favorable attitudes and the most reservations concerning science.

Ninety percent of the respondents in the NSF (2000) survey agreed that science and technology are making our lives healthier, easier, and more comfortable. Eighty-three percent of the respondents agreed that most scientists want to work on things that will make life easier for the average person. Seventy-three percent agreed that with the application of science and technology, work will become more interesting. And 84% of the respondents agreed that because of science and technology, there will be more opportunities for the next generation.

Nearly half the respondents in a 1996 NSF survey (Roper Center for Public Opinion Research, 1996) said that their reaction to science and technology was "satisfaction or hope," 36% said that it was "excitement or wonder," and only 6% said it was "fear or alarm." Over 50% of the respondents said that new developments in science and technology will have a positive impact on the overall standard of living in the United States, whereas one fifth felt that the impact would be negative. Finally, 80% of the respondents agreed that a top national priority should be to encourage the brightest young people to go into scientific careers.

Despite mainly positive signs, a sizable percentage of the American public has reservations about science. For example, half the respondents in the 1999 NSF survey agreed that "we depend too much on science and not enough on faith." And approximately 40% agreed that "science makes our way of life change too fast" (NSF, 2000).

An indirect indicator that many people lack an appreciation of science and an adequate knowledge of science and the scientific method is the sizable percentage of Americans who profess beliefs in astrology, extrasensory perception (ESP), UFOs, alien abduction, haunted houses, and other paranormal phenomena (see Figure 7.4). However, fairly small percentages of Americans consider themselves to be superstitious about such things as a black cat crossing their path, walking under a ladder, the number 13, or breaking a mirror. Also of interest are that a larger percentage of women than men and a larger percentage of non-high school than high school graduates believe in astrology (Harris Poll, 1998).

Attitudes Toward Other School Subjects

Of all school subjects, the largest number of research papers have been published in the areas of mathematics and science education. To facilitate that research, more paper-and-pencil instruments have been designed to measure attitudes toward these two subjects than any other. Although not as frequently as in the subjects of science and mathematics, attitudes toward reading, writing, foreign languages, social studies, music, and physical education have also been measured and investigated. As with science and mathematics, many of these studies were concerned with the development of particular attitude instruments and with determining their psychometric qualities. Other studies focused on demographic or other group differences in attitudes, correlates of attitudes, and methods of modifying attitudes.

Reading, Writing, and Foreign Languages

Surveying the research papers on attitudes toward reading, we find that a distinction is made between recreational and academic reading, that girls in the elementary grades have more favorable attitudes than boys (McKenna, Kear, & Ellsworth, 1995), that reading activity at home has a positive effect on reading attitudes and achievement (Rowe, 1991), and that adults who have more education and are employed in higher-status jobs have more positive attitudes toward reading (Smith, 1990).

The development of basic skills in both reading and writing is a critical task in the elementary grades. Students who fall behind in these core subjects, and especially reading, experience difficulty with other subjects as well and may never fully recover from their deficiency. An inability to read well handicaps students in almost every school and college subject, even in quantitative subjects. Though perhaps not as critical as reading to the acquisition of knowledge, an inability to express oneself adequately in writing

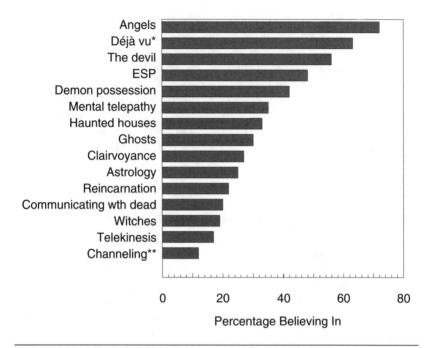

Figure 7.4. Percentage of National Sample in 1996 Gallup Poll Who Believed in the Respective Paranormal Object or Event

SOURCE: Based on data from Gallup (1997).
NOTES: *The feeling you have been somewhere or done something before.
**Allowing a "spirit being" to assume control of a human body during a trance.

may obscure a person's real knowledge of a subject whenever he or she is required to demonstrate that knowledge on an essay test or term paper.

Reading, writing, spelling, and speaking are, of course, interdependent, and a person who is good in one of these subjects is usually good in the other three as well. The interdependency of reading and writing is inherent in the advice that if one wants to write well, one should read works by good writers and imitate them. The interdependency between reading and speaking is seen in the observation that poor public speakers are typically poor readers and poor writers.

As with reading, gender, grade level, and attitude toward writing are good predictors of writing achievement (Knudson, 1995). In turn, attitude toward writing is related to both gender and grade level. The results of research conducted with elementary and secondary school children show that girls usually have more positive writing attitudes than boys (Knudson, 1993a, 1993b). Attitude toward writing also varies with grade level, but not always in the direction that one might expect. For example, a study of elementary school children conducted by Knudson (1992) found that third graders had significantly more positive attitudes toward writing than fifth graders. This finding may, of course, be attributable to the fact that because of more extensive experience, fifth graders are more aware of their performance limitations and more self-critical than third graders. Certainly, teachers' criteria and evaluations of writing quality become more stringent as one moves up the grade ladder.

As teachers of college freshman English composition would probably admit, writing ability can be improved but it is rarely easy. Various experimental procedures have been used to improve writing, including practice in writing collaboratively or interactively (Louth, McAllister, & McAllister, 1993), by using word processors (Seawel et al., 1994), and by special types of workshops (Lenski & Pardieck, 1999). Unfortunately, the reluctance of some college teachers to assign and correct written work limits the opportunities of many students to practice and improve their writing skills.

Both reading and writing become more specialized in secondary school and college. Oral reading in English is less common in the higher grades, but both oral and silent reading enter the picture again when students take foreign language courses. Two reasons commonly cited by undergraduate students for taking a foreign language course in college are "greater understanding of culture" and "for business" (Roberts, 1992). Attitudes toward foreign languages, like attitudes toward reading and writing, are generally more positive in females than in males (Wright, 1999).

Social Studies, Physical Education, and Music

There is relatively little published research on attitudes toward social studies, but an article by McGowan, Sutton, and Smith (1990) provides an interesting discussion of the effects of teaching style on modifying attitudes toward the subject. Some insight into the attitudes of the general public and college faculty toward the social sciences of psychology and sociology were obtained in a study by Janda, England, Lovejoy, and Drury (1998). Both psychology and sociology were rated by a large percentage of samples of the general public and college faculty as having made less important contributions to society and as requiring less expertise than biology, chemistry, physics, and medicine.

Two remaining subjects to be discussed—music and physical education—are similar in that they involve perceptual-motor skills and make use of performance tests in evaluating student achievement. Because performance in music and physical education can be greatly affected by physical handicaps, many of the attitude studies pertaining to these subjects have been concerned with disabled or handicapped students. Some investigations have compared the attitudes of teachers of music or physical education toward students with physical or mental handicaps (e.g., Rizzo & Vispoel, 1991; Sideridis & Chandler, 1996; Zanandrea & Rizzo, 1998), whereas others have been concerned with the effects of instruction in music (Wilson & McCrary, 1996) or physical education (Moode & Finkenberg, 1994). In general, the attitudes of physical education and music teachers toward teaching handicapped students are not greatly different from their attitudes toward teaching nonhandicapped students. However, teachers' attitudes vary to some extent with the nature of the handicap and the amount of effort and time required.

A variety of studies have also examined differences between the attitudes toward music or physical education of different gender, ethnic, or cultural groups (Birtwistle & Brodie, 1991; Faulkner & Reeves, 2000; Tannehill et al., 1994; Tannehill & Zakrajsek, 1993). The attitudes of most students toward sports and other physical education activities are quite positive, which is not surprising considering the current societal emphasis on fitness and athletics. Physical activity has beneficial effects not only on one's physical condition but also on the self-concept and emotional health of the individual. Listening to and performing music are also valuable activities that contribute to individual health and a sense of well-being.

Recommended Readings

Aiken, L. R. (1999). *Human differences* (pp. 110-139). Mahwah, NJ: Lawrence Erlbaum.

Burns, M. (1998). *Math: Facing an American phobia*. Sausalito, CA: Math Solutions.

Dole, J. A., & Sinatra, G. M. (1994). Social psychology research on beliefs and attitudes: Implications for research on learning from text. In R. Garner & P. A. Alexander (Eds.), *Belief about text and instruction with text* (pp. 245-264). Hillsdale, NJ: Lawrence Erlbaum.

Kottkamp, R. B. (1990). Teacher attitudes about work. In P. Reyes (Ed.), *Teachers and their workplace: Commitment, performance, and productivity* (pp. 86-114). Thousand Oaks, CA: Sage.

Langdon, C. A., & Vesper, N. (2000, April). The sixth Phi Delta Kappa poll of teachers' attitudes toward the public schools. *Phi Delta Kappan, 81*, 607-611.

National Center for Education Statistics. (2001, January). *Digest of education statistics 2000* (pp. 445-470). Washington, DC: U.S. Department of Education.

Randel, B., Stevenson, H. W., & Witruk, E. (2000). Attitudes, beliefs, and mathematics achievement of German and Japanese high school students. *International Journal of Behavioral Development, 24*(2), 190-198. Retrieved from the World Wide Web: www.ed.gov.

Rose, L. C., & Gallup, A. M. (2001, September). The 33rd annual Phi Delta Kappa/Gallup poll of the public's attitudes toward the public schools. *Phi Delta Kappan, 83,* 41-58.

Note

1. As determined from responses to variable CONEDUC of the General Social Surveys (see Web site www.icpsr.umich.edu/GSS).

Appendix 7.1

Representative Measures of Attitudes and Opinions Concerned With Schools and School Subjects

Arlin-Hills Attitude Surveys (M. Arlin & D. Hills; Psychologists and Educators, Inc.). Measures the attitudes of students in Grades K-12.

Attitude Toward Mainstreaming Scale (J. D. Berryman, W. R. Neal, Jr., & C. Berryman; University of Georgia). Developed to measure teachers' attitudes toward the integration of handicapped students into the regular classroom. Four scores: Learning Capability, General Mainstreaming, Traditional Learning Disabilities, and Total.

Attitudes Toward Mathematics and Its Teaching Scale (Ludlow & Bell, 1996). This scale was designed to measure the attitudes and experiences associated with mathematics and its teaching. It consists of 29 items and uses a 6-point, Likert-type scale. The scale has been used with prospective elementary teachers.

Indiana Mathematical Belief Scales (Kloosterman & Stage, 1992). This scale was developed to measure secondary school and college students' beliefs about mathematics as a subject and about how mathematics is learned. It is used to determine the beliefs that motivate students to study mathematics and to learn and solve mathematical problems. It consists of six subscales: I Can Solve Time-Consuming Mathematics Problems; There Are Word Problems That Cannot Be Solved With Simple, Step-by-Step Procedures; Understanding Concepts Is Important in Mathematics; Word Problems Are Important in Mathematics; Effort Can Increase Mathematical Ability; and Mathematics Is Useful in Daily Life. Respondents indicate, on a 5-point, Likert-type scale, how strongly they agree or disagree with each statement.

Mathematics Attitude Inventory (R. S. Sandman; Psychological Foundations of Education). This inventory was designed to measure the attitudes toward mathematics of secondary school students (Grades 7-12). It is scored on six variables: Perception of the Mathematics Teacher, Anxiety Toward Mathematics, Value of Mathematics in Society, Self-Concept in Mathematics, Enjoyment of Mathematics, and Motivation in Mathematics.

Mathematics Self-Efficacy Scale (N. E. Betz & G. Hackett; Mind Garden, Inc.). This scale is intended to measure beliefs of college freshmen regarding their abilities to perform various math-related tasks and behaviors. Each of the two forms (A and B) of the scale yields three scores: Mathematics Task Self-Efficacy, Math-Related School Subjects Self-Efficacy, and Total Mathematics Self-Efficacy.

Scientific Orientation Test (G. R. Meyer; GRM Educational Consultancy). This instrument was designed to measure a range of affective outcomes for students of science or science-related subjects in school years 5-12. There are four scores: Interest in Science, Scientific Attitude, Attitude to School Science, and Total.

Study Attitudes and Methods Survey (W. B. Michael, J. J. Michael, & W. S. Zimmerman; EdITS). This survey form was developed to assess dimensions of a motivational, noncognitive nature that are related to school achievement and that contribute to student performance beyond what is measured by traditional ability tests.

Survey of Study Habits and Attitudes (W. F. Brown & W. H. Holtzman; Psychological Corporation). This survey instrument measures study methods, motivation for studying, and certain attitudes toward scholastic activities that are important in the classroom.

Teacher Opinion Inventory, Revised Edition (National Study of School Evaluation). This inventory was designed to assess teachers' opinions concerning many facets of the school, to compile teachers' recommendations for improvement, and to provide data to guide the school professional staff in decision making regarding program development. It is appropriate for administration to elementary and secondary school teachers and is scored on seven subscales.

8

Work, Leisure, and Retirement

Work is an outlet for one's energies and creativity and gives meaning to personal existence. Work helps to organize one's life and time and provides a sense of pride and social acceptance. People are often identified by the kind of work they do, and their status, social relationships, self-concept, and even their reason for living are all connected to their work. Sexual, avocational, cultural, and even family interests may be perceived as less important than the job. This is particularly true of men, who have traditionally been perceived as the family breadwinners (Jena, 1999). Because work is so important to human existence, it is hardly surprising when a person says that he or she would continue working at something even if no pay was forthcoming or if he or she became so rich that working was no longer necessary. For example, 69% of the respondents in a survey conducted in 1998 by the National Opinion Research Center of the University of Chicago said they would continue to work if they had enough money to live as comfortably as they would like for the rest of their lives.[1]

Be that as it may, perhaps only a minority of people would subscribe to the notion that the major purpose of life is to engage in productive work. Work means more than money, but most people today probably view work more as a means than an end in itself. Rather than working just for the joy of it or because they feel that it is their duty, people work to obtain material necessities and advantages for themselves and their families. Many workers, particularly those who are young and have more opportunities, do not stay on a particular job for very long; they move to where they can obtain better rewards for plying their trade or other skills (Bianco, 1997).

Often as great in importance as the job is the time spent away from its demands, relaxing or otherwise engaging in activities unrelated to work. Such leisure time is, of course, not necessarily wasted or valueless simply because no productive work is accomplished. Leisure may be even more critical to health and happiness than many other things that a person does. Wherever it takes place—inside or outside the home, and whether the time is spent alone or with other people—the expenditure of leisure or recreational time is recognized as being an important contributor to one's physical and mental fitness and happiness. Leisure can and should continue throughout life, even after a worker decides to "hang up the tools and time card" or it is decided for him or her that it is time to retire.

Job Satisfaction and Work Experiences

The modern view of workers is that they are not mere automata who perform physical labor for reasonable monetary rewards, but complex creatures with psychological and social needs who expect more from a job than a periodic paycheck and a farewell handshake at the end of a career. Concepts such as job satisfaction, *job involvement, organizational commitment,* and work attitudes and values are part of the terminology of organizational psychology. These concepts are indicative of the fact that their jobs mean more to most workers than the performance of arduous chores. People need to be accepted, be appreciated, and feel that they are part of an organized, productive group of individuals who respect each other and feel that what they are doing is personally meaningful and socially useful.

One of the most frequently studied variables in organizational behavior research is job satisfaction. As defined by Locke (1976), *job satisfaction* is "a pleasurable or positive emotional state resulting from the appraisal of one's job or job experiences" (p. 1300). This definition emphasizes the affective, or emotional, component of job satisfaction, but in many of the thousands of studies dealing with the topic the cognitive component has been featured. In any event, job satisfaction consists of a combination of attitudes toward one's work, workplace, and fellow workers. Job satisfaction is also associated with job involvement behavior and job commitment attitudes (Keller, 1997).

When questioned by survey researchers, a large majority of workers (85%) say they are satisfied with their jobs.[2] However, the level of job satisfaction varies with the characteristics of the workers, the nature of the work performed, the physical and psychological environments in which it takes place, status of the job, and the rewards provided for the work.

Equity Theory

Rather than being directly associated with the absolute amount of salary or other material benefits received by a worker, the perceived *value* of these rewards is a relative matter. It depends on whether the rewards are considered equitable, that is, commensurate with job level and with the rewards received by others who perform similar tasks. According to *equity theory*, in a given situation people form an implicit ratio of their inputs (e.g., intellectual abilities, psychomotor skills, personality traits, seniority, experience) to the outcomes or benefits received (e.g., money, promotions, praise) in that situation. If the ratio of a person's inputs to outcomes equals that of other people, the situation is perceived by the person as equitable and does not create tension; if the ratio of inputs to outcomes is unequal to that of other people, the individual develops tension and becomes motivated to reduce it.

Theory and research concerning the concept of *equity*, as it applies to fairness or impartiality in organizational contexts, was pioneered by Adams (1965) and, more formally, by Walster, Walster, and Berscheid (1978). Research stemming from equity theory has continued and has provided some interesting results. Examples are research on the relationship of equity to workplace status (Greenberg, 1988) and the moderating effect of equity sensitivity (how sensitive people are to overreward and underreward situations) on the relationship between *self-efficacy* (task-specific self-confidence) and workplace attitudes (O'Neill & Mone, 1998). Another illustration is a study by Griffeth, Vecchio, and Logan (1989) concerned with the effects of inducing interpersonal attraction in employees by providing them with information that the attitudes of coworkers were highly similar to their own attitudes. The results confirmed previous findings that under such circumstances participants alter the quantity and quality of their performance to achieve equity.

Other Theories of Job Satisfaction

Equity theory is, of course, not the only formulation concerned with job performance and satisfaction. A number of other theories of what job satisfaction consists of and how it functions have been proposed. Among these are Herzberg's (1966) two-factor theory, Locke's (1976) value-percept theory, Hulin's (1991; Hulin, Roznowski, & Hachiya, 1985) integrative model, and Hackman and Oldham's (1976) job characteristics model.

A common distinction in research and theory on job satisfaction is concerned with the relative importance of extrinsic factors such as pay, company policies, and working conditions and intrinsic factors such as responsibilities, achievements, and the work itself. Herzberg (1966) labeled these two sets of factors *hygiene* and *motivator* factors and maintained that the former influences the extent of the worker's dissatisfaction (but not satisfaction) with the job, whereas the latter affects the degree of the worker's satisfaction (but not dissatisfaction) with the job. Herzberg's two-factor, *motivator-hygiene theory* has stimulated a great deal of research, but the results have not been generally supportive of the theory, which has other problems as well.

According to Locke (1976, p. 1300), the amount of job satisfaction experienced by a person depends on whether his or her values are realized by the job. Locke's *value-percept theory* conceptualizes job satisfaction (S) in terms of the formula $S = (V_c - P) \times V_i$, where V_c is the amount of a particular value that the individual desires, P is the perceived amount of the value that the job provides, and V_i is the importance of the value to the individual. Research stemming from this formulation has been mainly supportive of Locke's theory (e.g., Rice, Gentile, & McFarlin, 1991).

Hulin's *integrative model* views job satisfaction as a comparative function of the balance between role inputs and role outputs. *Role inputs* are what the person puts into the work role (e.g., training, experience, time), and *role outputs* are what the person receives from the work role (pay, status, working conditions, intrinsic factors). The higher the role outputs received relative to the role inputs invested, the greater the person's role (job) satisfaction. The *opportunity costs* of the individual also affect his or her degree of job satisfaction. For example, in an open labor market, where there are many applicants for few jobs, work inputs will be perceived as less valuable and the opportunity cost of the work will decline. In this situation, the perceived value of work inputs will be lower relative to outputs, and so job satisfaction will increase. In a tight labor market, where there are few applicants for many jobs, the opportunity cost of the work will increase. Consequently, the perceived value of work inputs will be greater relative to outputs, and so job satisfaction will decrease. Also incorporated within the integrative model is the notion that an individual's past experience with particular work outcomes influences how he or she perceives current outcomes. Persons who have received fewer, or less valued, outcomes in the past will perceive those same outcomes as greater relative to inputs and thereby experience greater job satisfaction. Despite the impressiveness of Hulin's model, it has not been adequately tested.

According to the *job characteristics model* (Hackman & Oldham, 1976), the major factor contributing to job satisfaction is job enrichment. This model focuses on five characteristics presumed to be important in making a job challenging and fulfilling: *task identity* (the extent to which the work can be seen by the person from beginning to end), *task significance* (the extent to which the person views the work as important), *skill variety* (the extent to which the job requires the performance of multiple tasks), *autonomy* (the extent to which the worker has control over the job), and *feedback* (the extent to which the worker receives feedback from the work itself). The job characteristics model holds that enriching a job by providing for these five core characteristics in performance of the job will make it more motivating and satisfying than jobs in which these characteristics are not provided.

All of the above models or theories of job satisfaction have their supporters and critics, and they should all be viewed more as proposals than as finished explanations. Research based on these and other theories has, for the most part, confirmed that job satisfaction is related to the intrinsic characteristics of jobs. Although the correlations between job characteristics and job satisfaction have not been found to be very high, Judge (2000) concluded that the data indicate that intrinsic job characteristics are the most reliable situational predictors of job satisfaction.

Job Satisfaction Versus Life Satisfaction

In the process of getting along and getting through life, people do not usually respond uniquely to every situation they encounter. To be sure, individuals with different personalities may respond differently to the same situation, but, because time is short and the ability to discriminate is limited, a certain amount of response generalization occurs from one situation to another. Because of their natural endowments and experiences, some people are more likely to make negative appraisals of situations and generalize those to other situations, whereas other people—optimists if you will—are more likely to appraise their experiences more positively and generalize those appraisals to their subsequent encounters.

The generalized expression of experience and personality in various domains may also be seen in the significant relationships between job satisfaction and life satisfaction. This result is consistent with the so-called *spillover theory:* "Positive or negative feelings in one life area may reach out and carry over (spillover) into other facets of life" (Wiener, Vardi, & Muczyk (1981, p. 51). For example, experiences on the job may spill over into encounters outside the work situation and influence one's responses to them. One alternative to spillover theory is *compensation theory:* People try to compensate for job dissatisfaction by seeking satisfaction in their lives outside the work situation, and consequently a negative or contrasting relationship exists between life and job satisfaction. Another alternative is *segmentation theory:* The degrees of satisfaction experienced on and off the job have little to do with each other, and consequently there is no relationship between job and life satisfaction. Empirical tests comparing predictions from spillover theory with predictions from compensation and segmentation theories have typically shown spillover theory to be most accurate. However, individuals differ in the extent to which their behavior appears to confirm a particular theory. Furthermore, certain circumstances seem to favor one theory over another. There have been situations, for example, those involving undesirable jobs, in which compensation theory has won out. The Quality of Employment Survey, concerned with similarities and differences between job and life satisfaction, was conducted by Judge and Watanabe (1994) in two waves from 804 respondents. An analysis of the results showed that 68% of the workers could be classified in terms of their job and nonjob behaviors as confirming spillover theory, whereas the behavior of another 20% confirmed segmentation theory and 12%, compensation theory.

Factors Affecting Job Satisfaction

A number of factors can affect job satisfaction. Some are characteristics of the job, others are characteristics of the physical or social situation in which the job takes place, and still others are characteristics of the individuals who perform the job. These factors do not act alone or independently, but rather interactively. The same combination of job and situational determinants, for example, may have different effects on different people.

Job status. The degree of satisfaction experienced on a job varies with the status, power, financial compensation, and other rewards or indicators of successful performance. As shown in Table 8.1, grouping occupations according to the type of work performed also classifies them by monetary reward (median income). Income is, however, not the only factor in defining occupational prestige: required education and training, working conditions, and other variables also contribute to the status of a given occupation in the

TABLE 8.1 Median Weekly Earnings of Full-Time Wage and Salary Workers by Occupational Group and Sex, 2000

Occupational Group	*Median Weekly Earnings ($)*		
	Males	*Females*	*Combined*
Executive, administrators, and managerial	1,014	686	840
Professional specialty	977	725	832
Technicians and related support	761	541	648
Precision production, craft, and repair	628	445	613
Sales occupations	684	407	550
Transportation and material moving	558	407	540
Machine operators, assemblers, and inspectors	495	355	436
Handlers, equipment cleaners, helpers, and laborers	394	320	378
Service occupations	414	316	355
Farming, forestry, and fishing	347	294	334

SOURCE: Unpublished data, Bureau of Labor Statistics, 2000.

eyes of the general public. Socioeconomic status, as measured by a combination of income and education, is even more significantly related to job satisfaction than either of these variables by itself (Fotinatos-Ventouratos & Cooper, 1998). Furthermore, both status and seniority—how long an individual has been on a particular job—can influence the extent to which a person is satisfied with his or her work (Burke, 1996; Guppy & Rick, 1996). In most cases, the higher a worker's status and the greater his or her seniority, the higher his or her degree of satisfaction with the job.

Chronological age. Age, gender, ethnicity, and other demographic variables may also be related to the level of job satisfaction in a particular organization. Some studies have found that both younger and older workers express greater job satisfaction than middle-aged workers (Birdi, Warr, & Oswald, 1995; Clark, Oswald, & Warr, 1996; Warr, 1992)—a so-called U-shaped function. Other studies have found a moderately positive linear relationship between age and job satisfaction or some other functional relationship, depending on the status of the job (professional, etc.; Bernal, Snyder, & McDaniel, 1998; Zeitz, 1990). In general, although the level of job satisfaction is relatively high among younger workers, they have a greater degree of absenteeism, more disabling injuries, a higher accident rate, and less commitment to the organization than older workers (Human Capital Initiative, 1993).

Various factors contribute to the lower level of job satisfaction and occupational well-being observed in many middle-aged workers. Realizing that their careers and chances for advancement are limited, and being bored with their circumstances and having concerns about the future, middle-aged workers tend to be under greater stress with respect to their jobs than either younger or older workers (see Hunter, 2000).

It would seem that boredom and limited opportunities for advancement would cause older adults to be even more dissatisfied than middle-aged adults with their jobs, but this does not appear to be the case. In general, older workers express less job dissatisfaction than their younger coworkers (Doering, Rhodes, & Schuster, 1983; Waldman & Avolio, 1986) and are reportedly more contented and enthusiastic about their jobs (Warr, 1992). In addition, compared with both younger and middle-aged workers, older workers express a greater degree of commitment to the organization in which they are employed (Mathieu & Zajac, 1990).

Gender. A common observation is that work is less central in the lives of women than in the lives of men. Traditionally, women were expected to attend to the three "Ks" of the feminine role—*Kinder, Küche, und Kirche* (children, kitchen, and church)—and let the husband or a male relative be the breadwinner of the family. From this traditional viewpoint, women are dependent creatures who, even if they go to college, aim more for the "MRS." than the BS and are happiest remaining at home in a perpetual state of pregnancy. Potential rebellion against this image (and perhaps her rural origin as well) is seen in the remark of a 40-year-old alumna of a women's college who declared that "this institution is doing nothing but turning out brood sows!"

The number of women who are gainfully employed has increased dramatically since World War II, but a large percentage of women workers are still part-timers who view their main multiple roles of wife and mother as being outside the job situation. The question of job satisfaction is reportedly not as important to women in part-time and lower-level jobs as to those with full-time or higher-level jobs. And even when they express dissatisfaction with the work situation, women tend to emphasize different things—for example, cleanliness, comfort, and congeniality—than men workers.

According to Ross and Wright (1998), women typically have low personal control, as represented by their disproportionate representation in homemaking and part-time work. Because it is often less enjoyable and more isolated, part-time work causes women workers to have a low sense of control. A large number of the jobs held by women are fairly uninteresting and provide little opportunity to advance to more engaging work that allows employees to exercise their abilities and advance in the world of work.

Women who work full-time are still seen less often in high-status positions than men workers, and many women in such positions eventually "bump up" against the glass ceiling and encounter other forms of gender discrimination. On full-time jobs that involve more worker control and on which women are treated equally by coworkers and management, sex differences in job satisfaction are reportedly nonexistent (e.g., Weeks & Nantel, 1995).

Ethnicity. The overall results of nationwide opinion polls conducted between 1972 and 1996 indicated that, on the whole, African Americans are less satisfied with their jobs than European Americans. This ethnic difference in job satisfaction has been observed in both men and women across all levels of education, ages, and occupations (Weaver, 1998). The lower job satisfaction of African Americans has been attributed to the relative disadvantage experienced by this ethnic group in most work organizations (Tuch & Martin, 1991). Similar findings have been reported in research on other ethnic groups. For example, in a research study comparing Hispanics and non-Hispanic Whites in south Florida, it was found that Hispanics were less satisfied with their pay, supervision, and coworkers (Chusmir & Koberg, 1990).

Dispositional factors. The nature of a particular job and where it is performed are obviously related to satisfaction or dissatisfaction with the job. However, level of satisfaction goes beyond the particular occupation and the context in which it takes place. As demonstrated by the findings depicted in Figure 8.1, both job satisfaction and job involvement are highly consistent over time and across different jobs. This figure is based on the results of a study by Steel and Rentsch (1997) of the relationship between two measures of job satisfaction (and job involvement) made 10 years apart on the same individuals employed in similar or different jobs. Statistically significant positive correlations were obtained between the measures of job satisfaction at Time 1 and Time 2 (10 years apart), whether the jobs being performed at the two different times were similar or different. The same was true on the measure of job involvement. For both job satisfaction and job involvement, the correlation was higher when the jobs performed at Times 1 and 2 were similar than when they were different.

How can the individual consistency in job satisfaction and job involvement represented by the above findings be explained? One possibility is that level of job satisfaction is as much, if not more, a reflection of temperament

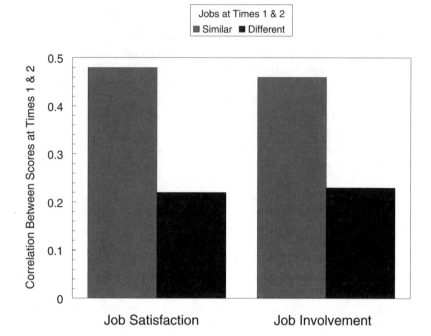

Figure 8.1. Correlations Between Two Measures of Job Satisfaction and Job Involvement for Different or Similar Kinds of Work Obtained 10 Years Apart

SOURCE: Based on data from Steel and Rentsch (1997).

or personality, which is fairly consistent after childhood, than of the particular job situation. For example, research by Judge and his coworkers (Judge, Bono, & Locke, 2000; Judge, Locke, Durham, & Kluger, 1998) showed that job satisfaction, and life satisfaction in general, is related to core self-evaluations—a broad personality dimension composed of self-esteem, generalized self-efficacy, internal locus of control, and neuroticism. And in a study conducted by Staw, Bell, and Clausen (1986), it was found that affective temperament assessed in childhood was significantly correlated with measures of job satisfaction in the same persons obtained 40 years later.

Personality is, of course, not entirely shaped by environment; heredity also plays a role in determining temperament and personality. In this regard, there is evidence that a large percentage of the variance in job satisfaction among individuals is explicable in terms of genetic factors (Arvey, Carter, & Buerkley, 1991; Keller, Bouchard, Arvey, Segal, & Dawis, 1992).

Alienation and Burnout

The detection of job satisfaction or dissatisfaction obviously does not rely exclusively on the administration of questionnaires or other psychometric research procedures. It requires no great stretch of one's observational powers to realize when a person is dissatisfied with his or her work: most people will complain, show less enthusiasm for the job, increase their rate of absenteeism, and in other ways show displeasure for their employment situation.

Dull, uninteresting work can lead to *alienation*, a feeling of personal disconnectedness or self-removal from the job. This is particularly likely when workers feel that their efforts are meaningless and unappreciated and they fail to see the connection between their work and the final product. Because worker alienation is costly to an organization, management has been alerted to the need to prevent it and cope with it. Involving employees in the decision-making processes of an organization, making work schedules flexible (*flextime*), and instituting worker development and enhancement programs are procedures that employers have instituted to avoid alienation among workers (Roth, 1991).

Unlike the alienated worker, who perceives his or her job as boring and unrewarding, the burned-out worker finds it too involving and demanding. *Burnout*, a condition precipitated by the stress of overwork, is characterized by a cluster of physical, psychological, and behavioral symptoms. These include emotional exhaustion, negative attitudes, headache, backache, reduced productivity, feelings of depersonalization, and social withdrawal. An employee who is suffering from burnout can no longer keep up with the pace and pressure—often self-imposed—of an occupation, and eventually his or her energy and motivation become severely depleted. Burnout is not limited to the job; it carries over into the family situation. In general, burnout and other signs of stress on the job are more likely to affect family life than stress in the family is to affect performance at work. In addition, burnout is more common among married women workers, who are subject to a greater amount of both work and nonwork stress than their husbands. Working women are more likely to show *multiple-role strains*, in that stress arising from the demands of the role of worker interferes with the effective performance of the roles of wife and mother (Repetti, Matthews, & Waldron, 1989).

Some of the same techniques for dealing with alienation can be used with burnout. Workers should be made to feel that they are an important part of the organization by involving them in decisions. Communication and helpfulness on the part of management should be improved, and a sense of camaraderie and teamwork should be promoted. Workers who suffer from burnout should also be encouraged to lower their expectations of what they can realistically expect to accomplish and to obtain assistance in their efforts to deal with constraints on the job and elsewhere.

Accidents and Personality

Accident rate at work is another indicator of possible dissatisfaction with one's job. At one time a great deal of attention was focused on the so-called *accident-prone personality.* It was maintained that people with this type of personality are, because of temperament or habit pattern, more likely to have accidents. The observation that in job situations a small number of employees seemed to have a large percentage of the accidents appeared to give credence to this notion, but later research failed to demonstrate that accident proneness is a consistent personality trait. This does not mean, of course, that temporary emotional states such as anger or depression cannot increase the likelihood of an accident. Any emotional or cognitive state that distracts a person or induces him or her to take unwarranted risks can increase the chances of accidents and consequent injuries.

The results of a number of investigations have offered some support for a connection between specific personality characteristics and accidents. For example, Shaw and Sichel (1971) found that accident repeaters were less emotionally stable, were more hostile toward authority, were higher in anxiety, had more problems getting along with other people, and had less stable work histories than nonrepeaters. Another investigator (McGuire, 1976) found that excessively ambitious people who harbored revengeful attitudes had a higher than average rate of accidents. And Niemcryk, Jenkins, Rose, and Hurst (1987) found that air traffic controllers who displayed *Type A* behavior were more likely than those showing *Type B* behavior to experience injuries on the job.

With regard to traffic accidents, for example, research findings indicate that drivers with higher levels of arousal take more risks, are more likely to engage in thrill- and adventure-seeking behavior, and are less inhibited in socially stimulating situations than drivers with lower levels of arousal (Trimpop & Kircaldy, 1997). The results of other studies indicate that an aggressive-competitive personality (Magnavita et al., 1997), alcoholism, a personality disorder of some kind (McDonald & Davey, 1996), or a low level of conscientiousness (Arthur & Graziano, 1996) are more common among people who have a greater number of automobile accidents. Also related to accident rate is the attitude of the driver, particularly toward driving violations (Baum, 2000; West & Hall, 1997). But perhaps even more important than personality characteristics or attitudes as a causal factor in accidents is the age of the driver (Assum, 1997). Many of the psychosocial risk factors associated with accidents seem to accumulate in younger drivers, causing them to have an excessively high accident rate.

Assessment in Organizational Contexts

Evaluations of people, products, and organizations in their entirety are common in business and industry. Potential employees are evaluated to determine whether they possess the characteristics and abilities that make them likely to succeed on particular jobs, and employees are periodically evaluated on their job performance to determine if they should be separated, transferred, promoted, and/or paid a different wage. Products, whether objects, processes, proposals, or whatever, may be evaluated on their usefulness, profitability, and other features. Finally, a business/industrial organization may be evaluated in its entirety to determine if it is a healthy, productive, and profitable place in which to work. Measures of attitudes, values, and beliefs may be employed in any or all of these types of evaluation. Measures of cognitive and perceptual-motor abilities may also be used in personnel selection and placement as well as performance appraisal.

Personnel Selection and Placement

Today's personnel psychologists are interested not only in an employee's work efficiency but also in his or her job satisfaction and attitudes. Personnel selection is concerned with selecting, from a group of applicants, those who can best perform certain tasks. The most scientific approach to personnel selection, but by no means the only approach, is to administer psychological tests and other empirically evaluated instruments and procedures to screen, select, classify, and place employees. Along with cognitive instruments, standardized measures of attitudes and values such as those listed in Appendix 8.1 may also be administered to applicants. Initial screening of the applicant pool is usually followed by classification, or assignment of those who have been selected to one of several occupational categories. Classification decisions may involve grouping the applicants on the basis of their scores on more than one psychometric instrument, including tests of ability and measures of personality, attitudes, work habits, and the like. Screening and classification may then be followed by assigning (placing) those who have been selected to a particular level of a certain job or program.

Performance Appraisal

The task of evaluating the performance of employees usually falls squarely on the shoulders of supervisors. *Performance appraisals* serve a number of functions: providing information for personnel decisions, feedback to employees on how well they are doing, planning training and employee counseling programs, and other matters pertaining to the operation and development of an organization. The results of performance appraisals also serve as criteria for determining the validity of employee selection and placement procedures and as predictors of employee performance. Performance appraisals also provide information for making decisions regarding promotions, job transfers, pay increases, training, disciplining, and other personnel matters.

Both objective and subjective procedures may be used to evaluate employees. Among the most common objective measures of job performance are direct indices of productivity, such as volume or dollar amount of sales, quantity and quality of goods produced, number of errors made, and less direct indicators such as absences, accidents, tardiness, turnover, and arguments. Because such behavioral measures are not available for evaluating performance on all jobs, subjective criteria are often used. The accuracy with which employees can be evaluated or rated on "quality," "initiative," "adaptability," and other subjective variables is, because of the absence of absolute standards, almost impossible to determine. The process can be made more reliable, however, by using a number of raters and training them thoroughly. Depending on the particular type and level of a job, employees may be rated by many different people in an organization—by coworkers, immediate supervisors, middle- and upper-level managers, and even themselves. The most common, and usually the most valid source, is the person's immediate supervisor. This is the person who is responsible for direct oversight of the employee's work and hence has the best opportunity to observe and evaluate him or her.

Consumer Behavior

Applications of psychology to advertising and selling were among the first practical uses of the fledgling science in business and industry (Scott, 1908). Subsequently, psychological models of advertising that characterized consumers as attending to, comprehending, and yielding to advertising claims made use of theory and research on attitude change (see Alwitt & Mitchell, 1985; Maloney, 1994). Research on communication and persuasion, and the distinction made by the elaboration likelihood model (ELM) between central and peripheral processing, which is discussed in some detail in Chapter 3, contributed to marketing psychology and the new field of consumer behavior.

Careful attention to the perceptual and general motivational features of advertisements can improve their effectiveness, but so can evaluating potential consumers of the organization's products or services. In evaluating consumer behavior for marketing (advertising and selling) purposes, not only demographic features of the target population but also the personal characteristics of individuals within that population may be taken into account.

Consumer psychology is concerned with identifying attitudes, interests, opinions, values, personality traits, and lifestyles that are associated with preferences for and the purchase of certain products and services. Checklists, rating scales, and attitude inventories may all be used to evaluate consumers' reactions to selected products and services, and whether or not they actually purchase them. Many different measures of attitudes and other instruments designed for marketing purposes are described by Bruner and Hensel (1996).

A number of different types of questionnaires, inventories, and scales have been used in attempting to describe the characteristic patterns of temperament, cognition, and behavior that differentiate among diverse human components of the marketplace. *Psychographic* research on these patterns may contribute to the segmentation of a particular market according to the personality characteristics and behaviors of consumers (see Gilbert & Warren, 1995; Shim & Bickle, 1994). Effective market segmentation may then lead to the preparation of advertising copy, packaging, and promotional materials that appeal to and motivate the identified market segments.

Two of the most popular psychographic approaches are AIO (activities, interests, and opinions) inventories and VALS (values and lifestyles) (see Kahle & Chiagouris, 1997).

An *AIO inventory* is a list of statements concerning activities, interests, and opinions designed for administration to a selected sample of people with the directions to indicate their agreement or disagreement with each statement. An analysis of their responses, in combination with demographic information on the sample, will, it is hoped, identify a set of lifestyle groups that will respond differently to different types of advertising and sales approaches.

Somewhat more complex and a priori is the *VALS™* psychographics approach, which is based on the dimensional concepts of self-orientation and resources. Consumers are considered to be motivated by one of three *self-orientations:* principle, status, and action (see Figure 8.2). The choices of *principle-oriented consumers* are guided by abstract, idealized criteria, rather than by feelings, events, or the behaviors or opinions of other people. *Status-oriented consumers* are interested in products and services that indicate success to their peers, and *action-oriented consumers* are motivated toward social or physical activity, variety, and risk taking.

The *resources dimension* of the VALS system refers to the psychological, physical, demographic, and material means and capacities available to consumers. Resources, which include education, income, self-confidence, health, eagerness to buy, and energy level, are on a continuum from minimal to abundant. Resources generally increase from adolescence to middle age, but decrease in old age. They also decrease with depression, financial reverses, and physical or psychological impairment.

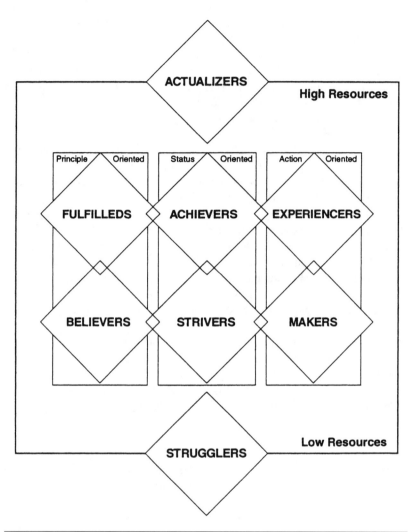

Figure 8.2. VALS^{TM} Network

As illustrated in Figure 8.2, the three self-orientations and the minimal to abundant resources dimension of the VALS model define eight segments of adult behavior and decision making. These eight segments represent approximately equal numbers of people, and each segment is a viable marketing target.

At the top of the hierarchy are *Actualizers*, who have high self-esteem and abundant resources. The high levels of resources available to Actualizers allow them to express a blend of the most positive aspects of the principle, status, and action orientations. The two primarily principle orientation segments are *Fulfilleds*, who have more abundant resources, and *Believers*. The two primarily status-oriented segments are *Achievers*, who have more resources, and *Strivers*. The two primarily action-oriented segments are *Experiencers*, who have more abundant resources, and *Makers*. At the bottom of the VALS hierarchy are the *Strugglers*—those whose lives are constricted and difficult and who are therefore cautious customers.

Leisure

Perhaps with the exception of workaholics, even prior to retirement people do not spend all of their time working. Most people have at least some time left for leisure after their gainful employment, domestic duties, and personal care have been taken care of. In contrast to the extrinsic rewards, accomplishment, learning, and altruism provided by work, the satisfactions provided by leisure include enjoyment, companionship, novelty, relaxation, aesthetic appreciation, and intimacy (Tinsley, Hinson, Tinsley, & Holt, 1993). Increasing recognition of the value of leisure and the increased time and wherewithal for its pursuit have led to an increase in research on this topic in recent years. To facilitate that research and make it more objective, a number of questionnaires, inventories, and scales have been devised. One such instrument, as described in Appendix 8.1, is the Leisure Search Inventory (LSI). The LSI has been administered both for research and for measuring a person's leisure interests for purposes of career guidance and employment counseling.

Participating in leisure activities is desirable for a number of reasons. In addition to being a means of expressing personal interests and associating with people whose interests are similar to their own, leisure may help people cope with stress, improve their physical and mental functioning, and generally contribute to positive feelings about themselves. Regular physical exercise, for example, enhances one's sense of well-being, feelings of self-efficacy and control, ability to cope with psychologically stressful situations, and general psychological health (King, Taylor, Haskell, & DeBusk, 1989; Ransford & Bartolomeo, 1996). Leisure activities also have significant effects on anxiety, depression, and other symptoms of psychological disorder (Kerr & Van Den Wollenberg, 1997; McNeil, LeBlanc, & Joyner, 1991;

Petruzello, Landers, Hatfield, Kubitz, & Salazar, 1991; Yeung, 1996). In addition to feeling physically healthier, people who have more positive attitudes toward and engage in leisure activities report experiencing higher levels of positive affect, less general psychological distress, and lower levels of anxiety, depression, and hostility (Cassidy, 1996).

The extent to which recreation and other leisure activities are pursued varies with age, health, interests, abilities, financial resources, transportation, sociocultural factors, and personality. Because of their personality traits, energy level, concern with keeping fit and healthy, or simply desiring an interesting and meaningful lifestyle, many people spend as much time as they can in leisure activities. Young adults tend to participate in more leisure activities of a physical nature and for longer periods of time than middle-aged and older adults. Middle-aged and older adults, on the other hand, are more likely to participate in relatively passive leisure pursuits. For example, Bammell and Bammell (1985) found that the rate of participation in active sports declines to an estimated 10% among Americans over age 65. The feeling that they will not be welcome and will not succeed in their attempts to do well causes many middle-aged and older adults to avoid the playing field. Age differences in leisure activities are, however, as much a reflection of generational differences as of aging per se. Participation in leisure activities is fairly consistent across the life span, in that children who take part in many activities tend to continue doing so in adulthood and old age (Cutler & Hendricks, 1990).

Leisure activities and avocations pursued in early and middle adulthood provide a greater number of role options and hence increase the likelihood of successful adjustment in later life. Such activities need not be limited to the traditional pastimes of fishing, gardening, shuffleboard, pool, and golf. Some older adults engage in more strenuous sports activities, such as tennis or skiing. For the majority of older adults, however, daily walks (with or without dog) constitute the best kind of physical exercise. Perhaps even more popular as leisure activities than physical activities are social interactions. In general, women are more socially active than men, but the differences are not great.

An obvious conclusion to be drawn from personal observation as well as research findings is that the leisure activities of the older generation differ in many respects from those of younger people. The differences, however, are undoubtedly due as much to upbringing and cultural contrasts between generations as to chronological age. Because the prior experiences of tomorrow's older population will have been different from those of today's, one might expect their behavior to be different too. Rather than playing checkers or shuffleboard and puttering around in the garden or garage, the next generation of older adults may spend more of their leisure time swimming, playing musical instruments, visiting museums, and in other ways continuing to engage in the interests favored by young and middle-aged adults of today.

Retirement

Rather than being a privilege accorded to a select few, as it once was, retirement is now viewed as a right earned by the worker for contributing to the growth and prosperity of society. In addition to being a status and an event, retirement is a process involving the withdrawal from a job and assuming the role of a retiree.

Although the expected role for older Americans today involves retirement rather than work, many professions and organizations have never established fixed retirement ages. On the other hand, firefighters, law enforcement officers, members of the armed forces, and other high-risk occupations have typically faced early retirement. Some organizations have instituted the practice of gradually reducing employee workload during the later years of employment. Be that as it may, age 65 has served for years as a kind of benchmark or point of passage between middle and old age and from the status of worker to that of retiree.

Reasons for Retiring

Various reasons are given for retiring. The expressed reason is, of course, not necessarily the real reason for retiring. It may be more socially acceptable to say that one retired for "health reasons" than because of dissatisfaction with the job, inability to get along with coworkers, or just plain wanting to retire. This kind of rationalization is less common and less expected now, when retirement is considered the right or appropriate thing to do, than it was in previous years.

Whatever the reason for deciding to retire may be, a sizable majority of retirees claim to be satisfied with retirement living (Vinick & Ekerdt, 1989). Understandably, attitudes toward retirement are positively related to the retiree's financial situation. Some retirees miss their jobs, but what they report missing most of all is "the money" (Atchley, 1987).

Planning and Preparing for Retirement

Retirement, like any relatively abrupt change in life, would seem to require some kind of preparation and planning to facilitate adjustment to the new roles associated with it. Planning for retirement presumably leads to more realistic expectations and greater preparedness in terms of finances, attitudes, and constructive use of one's time. Some informal planning and preparation almost always occurs, but it is usually on a hit-or-miss basis and does not cover all matters that should be of concern to preretirees. For this reason, coupled with enactment of the Employees Retirement Income Security Act (ERISA) and the Age Discrimination in Employment Act (ADEA), many business and industrial organizations in the United States have instituted formal retirement programs covering a variety of subjects but mainly finances and attitudes. However, only a minority of preretirees participate in these programs, and those who do are typically not representative of retirees in general. A typical participant in a retirement program is a married man with a family, whose health is good, whose income is moderate, and whose occupational level is somewhat higher than average (Campione, 1988). Retirees who are in poor health and have low incomes are unlikely to have participated in formal retirement counseling or planning sessions.

The majority of retirement planning programs are unsystematic and of limited scope, explaining only the company's pension plan and the retirement options to employees. A relatively small percentage of companies have comprehensive programs that go beyond financial planning. Certain larger business and industrial firms have developed their own comprehensive programs, whereas others have adopted the retirement planning programs of the American Management Association, the American Association of Retired Persons, or the National Council on the Aging. Because retirement affects not only the retiree but the entire family, spouses and other family members may also be encouraged to participate in the programs.

Depending on the objectives of the program designers, a retirement planning program may involve literature handouts; lectures on rights and benefits; media presentations; and in-depth seminars, workshops, and counseling sessions held after work hours. Depending on how ambitious they are, retirement planning workshops or educational programs include not only financial matters (providing for adequate income, how to develop a realistic budget for the retirement years, Social Security, pensions, etc.) and health-related concerns (Medicare and Medicaid, health insurance issues, physical changes with aging, etc.) but also legal issues (wills, trusts, rights of senior citizens, etc.), leisure activities (travel, hobbies, organizational memberships, educational opportunities), avocational and new vocational pursuits (e.g., voluntary services, part-time employment), and physical and mental health needs. Some workshops also cover such matters as sexual behavior, adjusting to changing morals and values, and more mundane affairs such as planning and preparing meals. Even the most comprehensive planning programs emphasize the practical aspects of retirement, but more subtle psychosocial matters may also be discussed. Included among these are stresses within the family and the loss of a sense of being important to others.

Adjusting to Retirement

The traditional picture of retirement as a stressful event and an indication that society considers the individual as worn out and useless, ready to be put "on the shelf" or "out to pasture," has never been totally accurate and is particularly not so today. Understandably, adjustment to retirement is affected by the retiree's financial status, health, social support network, and the activities in which he or she engages. Though retirement can be a stressful time for persons with low financial resources, poor health, and little conception of how they wish to spend the rest of their lives, for most older adults it is an active, rewarding time with positive social psychological consequences. For example, there is no evidence that retirement is associated with a drop in self-esteem, increased depression, or other negative consequences (Reitzes, Mutran, & Fernandez, 1996). When anxiety and depression occur immediately after retirement, they are usually mild and short-lived (Palmore, Burchett, Fillenbaum, George, & Wallman, 1985). Furthermore, there is certainly no evidence that postretirement depression increases the risk of suicide (Stenback, 1980).

As with many other life changes, reactions to retirement are highly individual, varying with the preretirement personality and behavior of the person and the social context in which retirement takes place. In general, people who were satisfied and happy before retirement remain so afterward (Palmore et al., 1985). According to Atchley (1999), retirement is simply another event in the continuing, lifelong adaptation, adjustment, and development of adulthood, an event to which the individual responds with mechanisms and mannerisms that have been used throughout life. In general, new retirees adjust similarly to the manner in which they adjusted to changes in their preretirement lives. Those who were flexible and able to cope effectively with changes in status and roles as preretirees are likely to do so as retirees. On the other hand, those who in young adulthood and middle age were rigid and found it difficult to adjust to change are likely to respond in the same way in retirement (Atchley, 1989).

Recommended Readings

Brown, M. T., Fukunaga, C., Umemoto, D., & Wicker, L. (1996). Annual review, 1990-1996: Social class, work, and retirement behavior. *Journal of Vocational Behavior, 49*(2), 159-189.

Cotton, J. L. (1993). *Employee involvement: Methods for improving performance and work attitudes.* Thousand Oaks, CA: Sage.

George, J. M., & Jones, G. R. (1997). Experiencing work: Values, attitudes, and moods. *Human Relations, 50*(4), 393-415.

Kahle, L. R., & Chiagouris, L. (Eds.). (1997). *Advertising and consumer psychology*. Mahwah, NJ: Lawrence Erlbaum.

Lease, S. H. (1998). Annual review, 1993-1997: Work attitudes and outcomes. *Journal of Vocational Behavior, 53*(2), 154-183.

Schaie, K. W., & Schooler, C. (Eds.). (1998). *Impact of work on older adults*. New York: Springer.

Spector, P. E. (1997). *Job satisfaction: Application, assessment, causes, and consequences: Advanced topics in organizational behavior*. Thousand Oaks, CA: Sage.

Tang, T. L.-P., & Gilbert, P. R. (1995). Attitudes toward money as related to intrinsic and extrinsic job satisfaction, stress and work-related attitudes. *Personality and Individual Differences, 19*(3), 327-332.

West, R., & Hall, J. (1997). The role of personality and attitudes in traffic accident risk. *Applied Psychology: An International Review, 46*(3), 253-264.

Notes

1. As determined from responses to variable RICHWORK of the General Social Surveys (see Web site www.icpsr.umich.edu/GSS).

2. As determined from responses to variable JOBSAT of the General Social Surveys (see Web site www.icpsr.umich.edu/GSS).

Appendix 8.1

Inventories, Questionnaires, and Scales for Use in Job-Related Contexts

Career Attitudes and Strategies Inventory (J. L. Holland & G. D. Gottfredson; Psychological Assessment Resources). Assesses career attitudes and obstacles in employed and unemployed adults.

Career Orientation Placement and Evaluation (L. F. Knapp & R. R. Knapp; EdITS). Designed to measure those personal values that have been observed to be related to the type of work one chooses and the satisfactions derived from the work one does.

Easy.Gen Employee Attitude Survey Generator (Wonderlic Personnel Test, Inc.). Computer software for designing attitude questions and selecting questions from a database of 515 questions covering 41 topics; also administers attitude questionnaires by computer or paper-and-pencil and produces graphs and reports of results.

Educational Leadership Practices Inventory (C. W. Nelson & J. J. Valenti; Management Research Associates). Measures ideal and actual attitudes for individual and group teacher styles; for teachers and administrators; two scores—ideal and actual.

Inventory of Retirement Activities (IRA; E. N. Chapman; Career Research and Testing). This inventory is designed to help retirees improve their retirement hours by estimating the amount of time available for activities. The results will give retirees a clear idea of their true interests, help them clarify options available to them, and permit better leisure planning. There are no wrong or right answers, only individual preferences. Individuals rate each statement choosing from 1 (indicating not wanting to participate) to 10 (indicating looking forward with great enthusiasm to participating). The inventory consists of three parts. Part 1 covers ranking your activity preferences. Part 2 covers constructing and interpreting your personal profile. Part 3 covers comparing your profile with others.

Job Descriptive Index (1997 Revision) and the Job in General Scales (P. C. Smith et al., Bowling Green State University, Department of Psychology). Designed as measures of job satisfaction to be useful for diverse organizations and employee groups. Six scores: Work on Present Job, Pay, Opportunities for Promotion, Supervision, People on Your Present Job, and Job in General.

Job Satisfaction (V. R. Wood et al.; see Bearden & Netemeyer, 1999). This scale characterizes job satisfaction as satisfaction with (a) information, (b) variety and freedom, (c) ability to complete tasks, and (d) pay and security. The scale consists of 14 items scored on a 7-point, Likert-type scale (*strongly disagree* to *strongly agree*). Item scores are summed within dimensions to form dimension scores, or scores on all 14 items can be summed to form an overall index of job satisfaction.

Job Values Inventory (JVI; L. E. Tagliaferri; Talico Inc.). This inventory is designed to achieve a good person-job match by assessing the extent to which a person is motivated by the factors of achievement, challenge, leadership, and affiliation. Individuals can then relate their career values and motives to the values and motive requirements of various jobs within their organization. It is based on David C. McClelland's research that divides people into three types based on their job-related motivation or motives.

Leisure Search Inventory (LSI; J. J. Liptak; JIST Works). This scale is designed to measure a person's leisure interests in order to help him or her turn these interests into career or employment opportunities. It is intended for use in career guidance or employment counseling for students in junior high school or above.

Minnesota Importance Questionnaire (MIQ; J. B. Rounds, Jr. et al.; Vocational Psychology Research). Designed to measure 20 psychological needs and six underlying values that have been found to be relevant to work adjustment, specifically to satisfaction with work; ages 16 and above; 21 scores.

Minnesota Satisfaction Questionnaire (MSQ; D. J. Weiss et al.; Vocational Psychology Research). Designed to measure an employee's satisfaction with his or her job; business and industry; 21 scores (long form), 3 scores (short form).

Retirement Anxiety Scale (Hayslip, Beyerlein, & Nichols, 1997). This scale was designed to measure the concerns, feelings, and emotions about issues related to retirement among university faculty members who are anticipating retirement. The 14 items on the scale cover four factors that contribute to anxiety about retirement: Lack of Personal Well-Being, Avoidance of Loss of Productivity, Loss of Social Relationships, and Loss of Marital Support. Respondents indicate how strongly they agree or disagree with each of the items.

Social Components of Retirement Anxiety Scale (SCRAS; Fletcher & Hansson, 1991). This instrument is designed to measure retirement anxiety based on the changes in interpersonal relationships created by retirement. On a 5-point, Likert-type scale, respondents indicate how strongly they agree or disagree with statements regarding anxiety about retirement due to four factors: Social Integration and Identity, Social Adjustment/Hardiness, Anticipated Social Exclusion, and Lost Friendships. Items reflect interpersonal relationships with family, coworkers, nonwork relationships, and community involvement. The scale strongly predicts fear of retirement and negative attitudes toward retirement.

The Values Scale (2nd ed.; D. E. Super & D. D. Nevill; Consulting Psychologists Press). Measures extrinsic and intrinsic values related to career development and most personally satisfying career.

Work Attitudes Questionnaire (M. S. Doty & N. E. Betz; Marathon Consulting & Press). Designed to differentiate the "workaholic" or Type A personality from the highly committed worker; managers; three scores (Work Commitment, Psychological Health, Total).

Work Locus of Control Scale (WLCS; Spector, 1988). This scale was developed to measure the degree of control that people believe they have in work settings. On a 6-point, Likert-type scale, respondents indicate how strongly they agree or disagree with 16 statements concerning attitudes pertaining to factors that may cause employees to be successful at work. Scores on the WLCS correlate significantly with measurements of employee job satisfaction, commitment, intention, autonomy, influence, role stress, consideration, and initiating structuring. May be used to predict work behavior.

Work Values Inventory (D. E. Super; Riverside Publishing Company). Measures the relative importance of work values in Grades 7-12; provides guidance counselors, teachers, and administrators with profiles of student values for counseling them in occupational choices and course selections.

9

Politics, Religion, and Morality

Politics and Government
Demographic Differences in Voting Behavior
Attitudes Toward Public Officials
Liberals and Conservatives
Political Leaders

Religious Beliefs
Varieties of Religious Faith
Religious Development
Correlates of Religious Beliefs
The Protestant Ethic

Moral Values and Behavior
Psychoanalytic Theory of Moral Development
Piaget's and Kohlberg's Stages of Moral Development
Criticisms of Kohlberg's Stage Theory
Social Learning Theory
Bystander Intervention
Altruism and Its Components

Of all the arguments in which human beings have engaged over the millennia, perhaps the most difficult to resolve have been those concerned with politics and religion. Such debates have sometimes contributed to the unity and regulation of a society and the nature of its relationships with other societies and cultures, but the political and religious disagreements represented by them have seldom been easy to resolve. Despite what the proponents of one side, one position or another, may have claimed, the arguments have not been based entirely on fact and reason. On many occasions, the irrational has become so dominant and the differences so irreconcilable that the result has been physical aggression, grudges, long-lasting feuds, and even armed conflict. However heated political or religious controversies may be, the only rational alternative to prolonged discord is for the disputants to continue talking and attempting to resolve their differences. Meanwhile, philosophers and scientists sit on the sidelines and try to understand the nature of politics and religion, why human differences with regard to these matters are so extensive, and what else might be done to keep the debate from getting out of hand.

In this last chapter, we will take a brief look at the topics of political opinions, religious beliefs, and moral values. Morality forms a part of discussions of politics and religion, but the development and functioning of moral values is also a topic in its own right. Because a thorough discussion of any one of the three topics featured in this chapter might very well be extended to cover an entire chapter or even a book, only a few points will be considered under each topic. It is hoped this will be sufficient to whet the reader's appetite for more comprehensive treatments and direct him or her to places where such information can be obtained.

In addition to the citations within the text and the recommended readings at the end of the chapter, descriptions of a number of questionnaires, inventories, and scales designed for use in research and practice concerned with political, religious, and moral beliefs and values and ethics in business and other contexts are given in Appendix 9.1. For a more comprehensive treatment of measures of political attitudes, the reader is referred to the volume by Robinson, Shaver, and Wrightsman (1999). A great deal of information pertaining to people's attitudes, beliefs, and values on political, religious, and moral concerns has also been obtained by informal listening and reading or by interviews rather than carefully designed questionnaires and scales.

Conclusions drawn from polls of *political attitudes* and opinions are, of course, no better than the design of the questionnaires and other instruments and procedures used to evaluate them. Details concerning the design, construction, administration, scoring, and evaluation of questionnaires are given in chapters and books devoted exclusively to these topics (e.g., Aiken, 1997).

Politics and Government

Politics, defined as the science or art of government, was, like religion, traditionally viewed as a topic that could become quite heated and consequently, in the interest of social harmony, to be avoided whenever possible. At the very least, politics was considered to be a subject suitable for men's ears alone, perhaps to be pursued by them during an after-dinner smoke while members of the fairer sex retired to a separate room for friendlier conversation. Politics was often viewed in such a negative light that "playing politics" was a phrase imbued with connotations such as "opportunistic, exploitative, devious, and manipulative."

Compared with people in other developed countries, Americans appear to be less preoccupied with politics. Voter turnout in this country, which is often less than 50%, is typically around 20 to 30 percentage points lower than in European countries. Consistent with the low level of concern that most Americans have with politics, the political decisions made by the vast majority of people in this country appear to be based more on simple heuristics and group attachment than on thoughtful reflection on what is best for one's self-interest (Kinder, 1998). It might seem as if the wide differences in education and income in the United States would be reflected in the political opinions of the citizenry. Income and education are, however, not associated as closely with political opinions as in other countries. These and other variables, such as self-interest, certainly influence the political decision making of Americans, but these decisions are typically based more on membership in and identification with specific religious, ethnic, racial, regional, or gender groups.

Demographic Differences in Voting Behavior

Some information on demographic differences in political interests and behavior can be obtained from voter registration and voting records (see Figure 9.1). Data from the 1998 congressional elections indicate that the following groups are more likely to vote:

1. Whites, women, older people, and married people

2. People with more education, higher incomes, and employment

3. Homeowners and longtime residents

4. People living in the West who register to vote

These demographic variables are, of course, not independent. For example, race differences in voting participation diminish when other characteristics (e.g., age, educational attainment, family income, and tenure) are taken into account (Day & Gaither, 2000).

As shown in Figure 9.1, the percentage of Americans who actually vote is substantially lower than the percentage who register to vote. When ques-

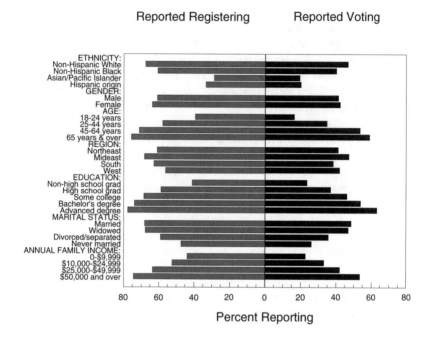

Figure 9.1. Percentage of Americans in Various Demographic Groups Who Reported Registering to Vote and Actually Voted in the Congressional Election of November 1998

SOURCE: Based on data from Day and Gaither (2000).

tioned about this discrepancy, a large percentage of respondents stated that they did not vote because they were too busy or had conflicting work or school schedules. Others indicated that they did not vote because they were not interested or felt their vote would not make a difference. Still others reported that they did not vote because they were ill, disabled, had a family emergency, or were out of town. Among the other reasons for not voting were dislike of the candidates or campaign issues, forgetting to vote, confusion or uncertainty about registration, and transportation problems (Day & Gaither, 2000).

The percentages of people who register to vote and actually vote are not the only political variables associated with demographic differences. For example, attitudes expressed toward political issues such as abortion, euthanasia, gay rights, school prayer, gender discrimination, capital punishment, racial equality, and affirmative action are all related to age, gender, ethnicity, socioeconomic status, and geographical region (Gault & Sabini, 2000; Lottes & Kuriloff, 1992; Pratto, Stallworth, & Sidanius, 1997).

Attitudes Toward Public Officials

As demonstrated by the results of public opinion polls, the general public often holds government officials and other career politicians in lower regard than members of professions such as medicine or teaching. For example, Figure 9.2 is an illustration of the partial results of a Gallup poll conducted on a national sample of Americans in 1999. The poll question was, "Please tell me how you would rate the honesty and ethical standards of people in these different fields—very high, high, average, low, or very low." As illustrated in the figure, a large percentage of respondents rated nurses and other health professionals high or very high in honesty and ethical standards. In contrast, less than a quarter of the respondents rated state governors, U.S. senators, and U.S. congressmen in the high or very high categories. Comparing these results with those obtained in polls going back to the 1970s, Gallup (2000) nevertheless concluded that Americans continue to express high levels of confidence in government and public officeholders.

Holbrook, Bizer, and Krosnick (2000) list the following as characteristics of the candidate for whom people are more likely to vote:

1. The candidate with whom they most agree on policy issues they care most about (Krosnick, 1988)

2. The candidate who most closely shares their ideology (Knight, 1985)

3. The candidate of the incumbent party if they believe that the incumbent has performed well in handling national problems (Fiorina, 1981)

4. The candidate who is perceived to possess more competence, integrity, leadership strength, and empathy (Kinder, 1986)

5. The candidate who evokes more positive emotions from voters (Abelson, Kinder, Peters, & Fiske, 1982)

As noted by Knight (1985), voters' characteristics are also important in determining for whom they will vote. Policy issues and ideological agreement are given more weight by people with greater political knowledge, whereas people with less knowledge of politics are more likely to base their vote on the candidate's party, personality, and past performance.

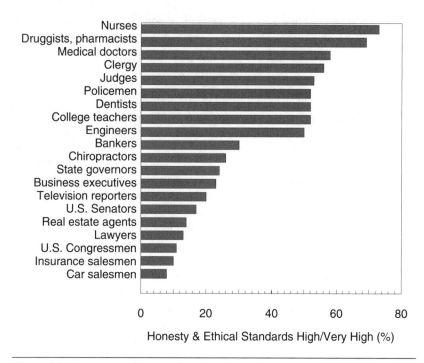

Figure 9.2. Percentage of Respondents in 1999 Gallup Poll Who Rated Various Occupational Groups as Having High or Very High Honesty and Ethical Standards

SOURCE: Based on data from Gallup (2000).

Liberals and Conservatives

In general, people support political parties that express attitudes similar to their own on the ideological dimensions of individual equality and liberalism versus conservatism. The meanings of *liberalism* and *conservatism* have undergone something of a switch during the past century or so. The term *liberal* is now often used pejoratively by Republicans in referring to members of the Democrat party, whereas the term *conservative* is used proudly by Republicans but by their opponents as a designation for "wooden soldiers of the status quo." Traditionally, a political liberal was a person who subscribed to the notion of minimal government intervention in the lives of people. A conservative, on the other hand, was a person who believed in strong government control. In modern American politics, however, liberals are more likely to support government regulation, protection, and entitlements, whereas conservatives campaign for less government (Barzun, 2000).

The perception of younger adults as more politically liberal and of older adults as more politically conservative is to some extent an accurate one. Older adults tend to have more conservative political views and are more likely than younger and middle-aged adults to support Republican candidates and issues. As a group, older adults are typically more conservative on domestic economic and social issues and more "hawkish" on foreign policy. But when their own rights and benefits, such as Social Security and Medicare, are at stake, normally conservative older Americans typically adopt a more liberal position.

Despite the association of later life with a conservative political philosophy, polling data demonstrate that a greater percentage of older than younger adults identify themselves as Democrats (Stanley & Niemi, 1990). Many of today's young adults are far to the right, whereas many older adults are just as far to the left in a political sense. The relationship between political conservatism and chronological age appears to be largely a generational or cohort effect, in that as people grow older they tend to retain the political orientation of their youth.

A classic illustration of the consistency of political attitudes and behaviors is a follow-up study of Bennington College women graduates conducted by Theodore Newcomb and his colleagues (Alwin, Cohen, & Newcomb, 1991; Newcomb, 1943). As shown in Figure 9.3, unlike women of comparable age, education, and socioeconomic status, a sizable majority of the Bennington College graduates voted for the more liberal candidate for president during the elections from 1952 through 1984. These were the same women whose liberal attitudes had been forged as students at Bennington College in the 1930s. As was the case of many other college students, the passage through college had a liberalizing effect on the attitudes of these women: they tended to be more liberal as juniors and seniors than they were as freshmen and sophomores (Newcomb, 1943). After graduation, the attitudes of the majority remained consistent and continued to influence their actions over a period of 50 years or more. Even in later life, these women maintained their interest in political and other matters associated with governmental affairs.

The liberal-conservative political dimension has also been found to be related to gender and childhood experiences. For example, males are more supportive of conservative ideology, whereas females are more supportive of social programs and equal rights characterized as liberal (Pratto et al., 1997). Gender may also interact with childhood experiences in its effects on political ideology. Milburn, Conrad, Sala, and Carberry (1995) found, for example, that males with high punishment backgrounds were more conservative than males with low punishment backgrounds, but that females with high punishment backgrounds were more liberal than those with low punishment backgrounds. As indicated in a study by Lottes and Kuriloff (1994),

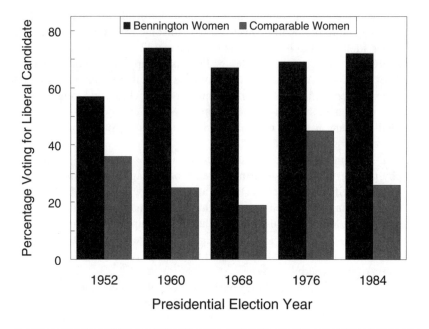

Figure 9.3. Comparisons of the Presidential Election Voting Preferences of Bennington College Graduates With Those of Comparable Women From 1952 to 1984

SOURCE: Based on data from Alwin, Cohen, and Newcomb (1991) and the Institute for Social Research, National Election Studies (1952-1984).

the passage through college is also associated with changes in liberalism-conservatism. These researchers found that seniors scored higher on measures of liberalism, social conscience, homosexuality tolerance, and feminist attitudes, but lower on male-dominant attitudes, than they did as freshmen.

Political Leaders

Psychobiographical studies of many famous people, including political leaders such as Adolf Hitler (Binion, 1976; Langer, 1972), Mohandas Gandhi (Erikson, 1969), and a number of American presidents (Brodie, 1983; Freud & Bullitt, 1967; Glad, 1980; Kearns, 1976), have been conducted for both theoretical and practical reasons. The practical reasons have centered on providing opposition leaders (or others who are forced to contend with certain political figures) with insights into the personality and behavior of those leaders and some means of predicting what they are likely to do under particular circumstances.

Most psychobiographies have been written by historians or psychoanalysts, but psychologists with a dispositional perspective have also analyzed the personalities of political leaders. Among the most famous of these are studies of the *authoritarian personality* conducted with a paper-and-pencil inventory known as the F (fascism) Scale (Adorno, Frenkel-Brunswik, Levinson, & Sanford, 1950; see Chapter 4). In contrast to those who process information in a more sophisticated manner, high scorers on the F Scale tend to think in rigid, simplistic terms.

The personality trait of *authoritarianism* is related to political conservatism. The attitudes of authoritarians toward homosexuals (Haddock, Zanna, & Esses, 1993), African Americans (Duckitt & Farre, 1994), and environmentalism (Schultz & Stone, 1994) are generally negative, but their attitudes toward more severe solutions to social problems are generally positive (Peterson, Doty, & Winter, 1993). Leak and Randall (1995) also found that authoritarians were more likely to vote for a bill to decrease benefits to immigrants as well as being orthodox in their religious behavior (Leak & Randall, 1995).

Political psychologists have analyzed the roles of concepts such as the power motive, the achievement motive, and the affiliation motive in shaping the actions of political leaders. Measures of dominance, extraversion, flexibility, intelligence, morality, idealism, and Machiavellianism have also been found to be related to political behavior (Simonton, 1990). Other variables that have been examined by researchers in an effort to account for the behavior of political leaders are birth order, situational factors, and the interaction between individual characteristics and situational factors. How valid the resulting conclusions are and whether they should be used for practical purposes, however, remain open questions.

Religious Beliefs

To *believe* in something is to have confidence, without absolute proof, that it exists or is true. People believe in many things, taking them for granted without firsthand experience or demonstration that they are so. Many believe in a certain thing because someone has told them that it is true and that their existence, peace of mind, or acceptability to other people depends on their believing. Like all people, scientists take certain things for granted without formal proof, but they feel more comfortable when the objective truth or exactness of something has been demonstrated by controlled observation or experiment.

Of all the things in which people believe, religious beliefs or faiths are among the most influential. These beliefs are concerned with the origin, nature, and final state of the universe and the place of human beings in that universe. Particularly important to the world's religions are the nature and power of a supreme being (or beings), what such a god or gods expect of humans and how they can be influenced, and the existence and nature of an afterlife. All societies and cultures have had religious beliefs and practices of some kind, varying from mythology and totemism to more modern religions such as Christianity and Islam.

Varieties of Religious Faith

In all countries on all continents and Oceania, there are adherents to a variety of religions. In addition to followers of the four major religions—Christianity, Islam, Hinduism, and Buddhism—there are Sikhs, Spiritists, Jews, Baha'is, Chinese folk religionists, ethnic religionists, new religionists, and millions of nonreligious people and atheists. The dominant religion on all continents except Asia is Christianity, which is particularly dominant in Northern and Latin America. The largest number of Christians are Roman Catholics, who are especially numerous in Latin America and Europe (U.S. Census Bureau, 1999c). After Roman Catholics, the largest numbers of affiliated Christians are Protestants, Orthodox, Anglicans, or "other Christians." In addition, 100 million people who identify themselves as "Christians" are not affiliated with any denomination.

Despite the reputation of the United States as a materialistic, self-preoccupied nation, the results of public opinion polls conducted in this country indicate that it is one of the most religious countries in the entire world. The vast majority of Americans profess a belief in God and are members of a church, synagogue, mosque, or other religious organization. The religiosity of Americans is expressed not only in their professed spiritual beliefs but also in many other characteristics of their appearance and behavior. Older Americans attend religious services more often than younger and middle-aged adults, women attend more often than men, non-Whites more often than Whites, Protestants more often than Catholics, and Republicans more often than Democrats. Attendance is also more common among less educated than more highly educated Americans, among those with lower incomes, and among residents of southern and eastern states than western and midwestern states (Newport & Saad, 1997).

Approximately 87% of Americans say they are Christians; 58% are Protestant, 27% Roman Catholic, 1% Mormon, and 1% Eastern Orthodox.

Among non-Christian Americans, the largest percentage are Jews, followed by Muslims, Buddhists, Hindus, Sikhs, or those with no religious preference at all. Among Protestants, 19% say they are Baptists, 9% Methodists, 6% Lutherans, 5% Presbyterians, 3% Church of Christ members, and 2% Episcopalians (Newport & Saad, 1997). Due in some measure to the growth of evangelical Christian and many non-Christian religions in the past three decades, the memberships of traditional, more doctrinaire denominations (e.g., Presbyterian, Episcopal, Congregational) have declined in recent years. Many young adults, in particular, have joined nondenominational megachurches or become involved in hybrid combinations of two or more religions (Rourke, 1998). Another sign of the expanding cultural diversity of the United States is the increase in religious intolerance, as seen in discrimination and religiously motivated hate crimes. The political influence of the religious Right with respect to issues such as abortion, censorship, and family values in general has also tended to polarize the nation and prompted the question of whether cultural diversity will ever result in unified pluralism.

The United States prides itself on being a religious nation, and belief in a hereafter is held quite strongly by many Americans. Approximately two thirds of the respondents in a nationwide poll conducted in 1998 by the National Opinion Research Center stated that they believed in life after death (see Web site www.icpsr.umich.edu/GSS). However, the exact percentages of believers varied somewhat with gender, race, age, and education. A slightly greater percentage of women than men, of Whites than Blacks, of those under 70 than those aged 70 and older, and those with a high school education or more said that they believe in life after death.

Compared with nonchurchgoers or sporadic attenders, those who attend church regularly report experiencing greater life satisfaction and better adjustment. According to Crandall (1980), this is so because a philosophy of life and a set of beliefs, attitudes, and values accompanying a commitment to a religious faith help people to remain interested in the world and to continue trying to understand it. In addition, church provides people with a sense of social and community integration that contributes to their feelings of personal well-being and greater life satisfaction (Markides, 1983; Ortega, Crutchfield, & Rushing, 1983). As illustrated in Figure 9.4, both the percentage of Americans who consider religion to be very important in their own lives and who attend religious services every week or almost every week increase with chronological age.

Religious Development

Human beings are not born with a ready-made knowledge of religious precepts. Religious beliefs are acquired, along with morals and ethics, as a

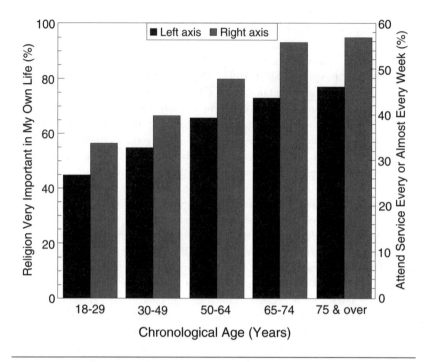

Figure 9.4. Percentage of Respondents in 1999 Gallup Poll Who Indicated That Religion Is Very Important in "My Own Life" (dark bars and left vertical axis) and That They Attended Religious Service at Least Once a Week or Almost Every Week (light bars and right vertical axis)

SOURCE: Based on data from Gallup (2000).

consequence of being brought up around religious people. With development, the simple, magical concepts of the child give way to more intricate mythologies, supernatural concepts, and moral values. Instruction and training cause these belief systems to become more abstract, conventional, and internalized. Adherence to these religious precepts and beliefs may serve to control feelings of insecurity and fear, but they may also be a source of guilt and anxiety (see Pressman, Lyons, Larson, & Gartner, 1992).

By the time they are adolescents or adults, there are noticeable individual differences among people in the extent to which they are concerned with religion. As a group, females are more religious than males, Blacks are more religious than Whites, and people of lower socioeconomic status (working class) are more religious than those of higher socioeconomic status (middle or upper class) (Francis & Wilcox, 1996).

Correlates of Religious Beliefs

Perceptions and attitudes concerning various issues are affected by religious beliefs. For example, Greeley (1993) found that low levels of concern for the environment are correlated with biblical literalism and with confidence in the existence of God. On the other hand, support for environmental spending is positively correlated with a gracious image of God and with being Catholic. Attitudes toward female sexuality, male dominance, homosexuality, and feminist attitudes also vary significantly with biblical literalism and religious conservatism. Liberals have less traditional views than conservatives, and Jews have less traditional views than Protestant Christians on all of the above (Lottes & Kuriloff, 1992). Attitudes toward sexual behavior, and particularly sexual behavior in marriage and deviant sexual behavior, are greatly influenced by religious beliefs. In general, highly religious people are more tolerant of premarital sexuality than of extramarital sexuality or homosexuality (Cochran & Beeghley, 1991; Davidson, 2000). It has also been found that, compared with their nonliteral counterparts (e.g., Catholic, Episcopal), persons affiliated with religious denominations that emphasize a literal belief in the Bible (e.g., Baptist, Nazarene) prefer the use of corporal punishment over alternative methods of discipline (Wiehe, 1990).

It has been alleged that the following four beliefs of certain right-wing denominations may serve as a justification for spouse abuse: (a) God intends that men dominate and women submit, (b) woman is morally inferior to man and cannot trust her own judgment, (c) suffering is a Christian virtue and women in particular have been designated to be "suffering servants," and (d) Christians must quickly forgive and be reconciled with those who sin against them (Heggen, 1996).

The influence of religion in the modern world is not nearly as great as it was in previous times. Prior to the modern era, and even now in certain theocratic societies in the Middle East, priests and other religious representatives dominated the child-rearing, educational, economic, political, and many other personal, social, and civil activities of the nation. Many laws—ancient and modern—bear the stamp of religion. For example, a listing of the 13 capital crimes in Massachusetts in 1636 (adultery, assault in sudden anger, blasphemy, buggery, idolatry, manstealing, murder, perjury in a capital trial, rape, rebellion, sodomy, statutory rape, and witchcraft) underscores the influence of both sex and religion on legal punishment (Haskins, 1956). Violators of such laws, and particularly for crimes involving religion in some form, were severely punished.[1]

The Protestant Ethic

Medieval theology emphasized the importance of good works in attaining salvation, but the Calvinist doctrine of predestination maintained that whether a given person ends up in heaven or hell is predetermined and that there is absolutely nothing that a person can do to change his or her fate. Stemming from this Calvinistic credo is the *doctrine of assurance*—that a person can never be certain of being chosen for salvation, but can only hope that he or she will be saved by God's grace. However, Protestants of various denominations came to believe that avoiding temptation, being pious, participating in the punishment of sinners and the destruction of evil, and even working hard (the so-called *Protestant ethic*) could improve one's chances of going to heaven rather than hell. Sixteenth-century Calvinism, which became less harsh in modern Presbyterianism, was quite stern in its judgment of disease and suffering as punishments for sin. However, Calvinism also had a practical side. Calvin did not consider one type of work as necessarily superior to another, but he did believe that making a reasonable profit and accumulating wealth are indicative of God's favor. According to Max Weber (1930), this notion inspired the "capitalist spirit," and hence modern capitalism.

Barker and Carman (2000) note that the individualistic theology of religious fundamentalists, evangelicals, and charismatics also supports individualistic economic policies. To test this hypothesis, these authors performed a series of data analyses, using probit analysis, structural equation modeling, and other statistical methods. The findings provided substantial support for Max Weber's thesis, and in particular the influence of religious beliefs on core political values.

Moral Values and Behavior

The moral attitudes or values of a society, as embodied in its mores, consist of standards of right and wrong conduct with regard to sexual behavior, property, and other significant social activities. *Moral* and *ethical* have similar meanings and, though not synonymous with religion, form a part of religious teaching in most cultures. *Moral* is also different from *legal*, but the fundamental moral and legal principles or rules are greatly influenced by the religious teachings of a particular group and usually accepted without question by members of that group. The notions of personal responsibility for one's actions and that violators of the legal, moral, or religious codes should be punished form a part of those codes.

Despite the age-old adage that "the punishment should fit the crime," what is accepted as "fitting" has varied extensively with time and place. As illustrated by the fact more than 70% of the sample of respondents either agreed somewhat or strongly agreed with Statements 2 and 4 in Table 9.1,

TABLE 9.1 Percentage of Sample Agreeing or Disagreeing With Each of Four Statements Concerning Moral Beliefs

	Response Category				
	DK	*SD*	*DS*	*AS*	*SA*
1. Those who violate God's rules must be punished.	5.9	10.0	24.6	37.4	22.0
2. Right and wrong are not usually a simple matter of black and white; there are many shades of gray.	2.9	6.9	7.8	42.4	40.0
3. Immoral actions by one person can corrupt society in general.	3.3	18.3	27.8	32.5	19.1
4. Morality is a personal matter, and society should not force everyone to follow one standard.	3.9	7.7	17.6	39.0	31.8

SOURCE: General Social Survey, National Opinion Research Center (Web site www.icpsr. umich.edu/GSS).
NOTE: DK = don't know, SD = strongly disagree, DS = disagree somewhat, AS = agree somewhat, SA = strongly agree.

most Americans recognize that morality is to some extent relative and personal. As shown by the responses to Statements 1 and 3 in Table 9.1, however, a sizable percentage of Americans recognize that people who commit immoral acts can have a corrupting influence on society and should be punished.

Many of the moral principles and prohibitions of Western countries were derived from the Ten Commandments and related ethico-religious codes and were subsequently interpreted and elaborated on in the process of formulating and codifying the laws of these countries. Western nations, of course, have no monopoly on moral values, and the nature of these values differs to some extent from culture to culture. Nevertheless, there are many cross-cultural similarities as well as differences in values. Starting with the premise that diversity and universality of moral values can coexist in the human community, Kinnier, Kernes, and Dautheribes (2000) searched through well-known religious texts and documents, as well as publications of selected intercultural secular organizations such as the United Nations, to determine the extent of cross-cultural similarity in values. Their analyses yielded the four major categories and more specific moral values listed in Table 9.2.

TABLE 9.2 Universal Moral Values

---

1. Commitment to something greater than oneself.
   To recognize the existence of and be committed to a Supreme Being,
       higher principle, transcendent purpose or meaning to one's existence
   To seek the Truth (or truths)
   To seek Justice

2. Self-respect, but with humility, self-discipline, and acceptance of personal
   responsibility.
   To respect and care for oneself
   To not exalt oneself or overindulge—to show humility and avoid
       gluttony, greed, or other forms of selfishness or self-centeredness
   To act in accordance with one's conscience and to accept responsibility
       for one's behavior

3. Respect and caring for others (i.e., the Golden Rule).
   To recognize the connectedness between all people
   To serve humankind and to be helpful to individuals
   To be caring, respectful, compassionate, tolerant, and forgiving of others
   To not hurt others (e.g., do not murder, abuse, steal from, cheat, or lie to
       others)

4. Caring for other living things and the environment.

SOURCE: Reprinted with permission from Kinnier, R. T., Kernes, J. L., & Dautheribes, T. M. (2000). A short list of universal moral values. *Counseling & Values, 45,* 4-16. © ACA. No further reproduction is authorized without written permission of the American Counseling Association.

Psychoanalytic Theory of Moral Development

Learning rules of right conduct and adhering to them is an important developmental task that faces all children in a given culture. Despite Jean-Jacques Rousseau's belief that children are born in a state of goodness, they are not born moral. So those who manage to become moral creatures must acquire this characteristic somewhere along the way. To Sigmund Freud (1930), acquisition of a sense of right and wrong, or morality, occurred with the development of a superego, that portion of the personality consisting in large measure of the internalization of parental prohibitions and sanctions. Conflict between the superego and the id was said to result in *moral anxiety*, a feeling of apprehensiveness at having violated, or having been tempted to violate, the moral code. Freud maintained that the superego, which is composed of the conscience and the ego ideal, is essentially in place by the end of the preschool period of development. Through the process of socialization and *identification* with parents and other significant adults, a child's conscience—the basis of his or her moral choices—has presumably developed by that time. Freud maintained that resolution of the Oedipus complex through fear of castration and resulting identification with the father creates a deeper reservoir of fear and guilt in boys, and hence a stronger conscience, than in girls.

Piaget's and Kohlberg's Stages of Moral Development

Whereas Freud and other psychoanalysts emphasized the development of moral feelings or emotions, Jean Piaget and Lawrence Kohlberg took a more cognitive approach in theorizing about morality. Piaget saw the maturation of moral judgment as occurring in a series of stages roughly paralleling the preoperational, concrete operational, and formal operational periods of cognitive development. To Piaget, the first stage in the development of moral judgment is that of *moral realism*. During this stage, which lasts until age 7 or 8, the child believes in rigid rules and unquestioned reliance on authority. Between the ages of 7 and 11, adherence to a belief in moral realism gives way to a second stage (*morality of cooperation*). At this stage, the child comes to believe in equal treatment or reciprocity ("taking turns") as a basis for deciding what is fair. The highest stage (*moral relativism*) of moral judgment comes into play at around age 11 or 12. Now the child realizes that the particular situation or circumstances leading to a given action, including the intentions of the perpetrator, affect whether that action should be judged good or bad.

In a related stage theory of moral development, Kohlberg (1969, 1976) maintained that the development of personal moral judgment progresses through three ascending levels consisting of two stages each. At the lowest level (Level I, or *preconventional morality*), moral judgments are based on doing what is right to avoid punishment (Stage 1), or doing what is right because it is fair (Stage 2). At an intermediate level (Level II, or *conventional morality*), moral judgments are based either on doing what is right because parents, teachers, or peers expect it ("good boy/good girl" morality, Stage 3), or on doing what is right because it is one's duty to obey the law (Stage 4). In the first stage of the highest level (Level III, or *postconventional morality*), moral judgments are based on doing what is right because it contributes to the welfare and security of people ("the good of all," Stage 5), or on doing what is right because of a self-accepted set of moral principles and a conscience that directs judgment and behavior (Stage 6).

To assess the stage of moral judgment attained by a particular child, Kohlberg developed the Moral Judgment Scale. Administration of this scale consists of presenting nine hypothetical moral dilemmas to a person and eliciting a judgment and reasons for the judgment pertaining to the dilemma. Scoring responses to the dilemmas posed by the Moral Judgment Scale is an elaborate process of making subjective evaluations of the person's responses in terms of the six stages. Unfortunately, the scoring of responses to the items on the scale is not very reliable.

Criticisms of Kohlberg's Stage Theory

Kohlberg's theory of a universally fixed sequence of six stages of moral development has not received extensive research support, although certain investigations (e.g., Nisan & Kohlberg, 1982) have found a sequence of moral judgment stages similar to those postulated by Kohlberg. In addition, it should be emphasized that moral judgment, which is highly dependent on the level of cognitive development (Mischel & Mischel, 1976), is not the same as moral behavior or moral feelings. Many children and adults can logically determine and easily verbalize the difference between right and wrong, and yet, often with no expressed feelings of guilt or remorse, violate those very principles in their behavior. They may behave quite morally on most occasions, but, acting from a need for excitement, material gain, or social approval, engage in flagrant rule breaking when encouraged and supported by their peers.

Kohlberg's theory of moral development was based on an all-male sample, and it has been alleged that as such it may reflect only a male orientation toward morality. Gilligan (1982), in particular, took exception to generalizing the theory to women; she maintained that it neglected morality based on responsibility and caring. She contended that men and women follow different patterns of moral development, a contention that has, however, not been strongly supported by research. However, Gilligan's claim that moral dilemmas of the sort posed by Kohlberg can be approached from a perspective of care rather than, as alleged by Kohlberg, one of justice, has received more research support. The distinction made by Gilligan between justice and care would appear to be valid, but the nature and significance of the distinction is unclear (Batson, 1998).

Kohlberg's theory has also been criticized from the standpoint of political behavior. Emler, Renwick, and Malone (1983) argued that the kind of moral reasoning used by a person in judging an issue depends on the person's political ideology rather than his or her level of cognitive development. People who share liberal ideologies, which usually oppose the status quo, are more apt to use general moral principles (i.e., Kohlberg's postconventional stage) than rules or conventions in describing their political beliefs. On the other hand, people who share right-wing ideologies, which support tradition and the maintenance of the status quo, argue for the upholding of law and order in society (Kohlberg's conventional stage).

Social Learning Theory

Unlike theories that presuppose a general trait of morality, social learning theorists consider moral behavior, like other kinds of behavior, as resulting from the punishment of behavior that deviates from social standards and rewarding behavior that conforms to those standards (Aronfreed, 1964). Social leaning theorists also view moral behavior as highly situation specific. Whether a person lies, cheats, steals, or in other ways behaves immorally is said to depend on the situation or circumstances. A classic study demonstrating the situational specificity of moral behavior was the Character Education Inquiry of Hartshorne and May (1928). In this series of investigations, children were surreptitiously provided with an opportunity to demonstrate their honesty, altruism, and other character traits. For example, to test for honesty, the investigators placed the children in a situation in which they could steal some coins and in another situation in which they could copy test answers, seemingly without being detected. Not all of the children were equally honest or dishonest in all the situations. Older children, less intelligent children, children of lower socioeconomic status, and more emotionally unstable children tended to be less honest in the contrived situations. But the most widely cited finding of these studies was that honesty and other character traits varied as much with the situation as with the individual. In other words, whether a child was honest, altruistic, or engaged in other kinds of behavior depended on the situation in which the child was observed. Subsequent reanalyses of the Hartshorne and May data (Burton, 1963; Epstein, 1979) yielded more transsituational consistency in behavior than was originally reported, but a great deal of situational specificity of behavior remained. Thus, the findings of the Hartshorne and May studies appear to be more explicable in terms of social learning theory, which emphasizes the role of situations in determining behavior, than by trait or stage theories of moral behavior. Social learning theorists also stress the role of observation and modeling in the acquisition of moral behavior (Bandura & McDonald, 1963).

Bystander Intervention

Evidence for situational specificity has also been found in research on other kinds of *prosocial behaviors*. An illustration is the *bystander intervention effect*, that is, whether or not a person elects to come to the aid of someone who has been or is being attacked or has had an accident of some kind. Fear may, of course, keep an individual from helping a person who is being attacked, but it is rarely the most important factor. In their studies of this phenomenon, Latane and Darley (1970) found that whether or not an observer decides to help a victim is significantly affected by the actions of other spectators at the scene. When many people are present, responsibility becomes so diffuse that a given individual is less likely to intervene. Unless a particular person is focused on by the victim or other bystanders to provide help, that person may assume it is not his or her responsibility. Darley and Latane found that the personality and demographic characteristics of bystanders were not very predictive of whether they tried to assist an accident victim, but personal factors such as whether the bystander was in a hurry, was feeling guilty, was in a good mood, or was from a small town or rural area were related to intervention. Bystanders are also more likely to render assistance if the victim is similar to them in some way, appears to need and desire help, and if someone else is being helpful (e.g., Carlson, Charlin, & Miller, 1988; Latane & Dabbs, 1975).

Altruism and Its Components

Altruism, an unselfish concern for or devotion to the welfare of others, is an aspect of generosity and cooperativeness, a willingness to contribute and work with other people to achieve a common goal (see Form 9.1[2]). It might be expected that a person who is altruistic would be more inclined to come to the aid of a suffering fellow human, and this has generally been found to be the case (see Oliner & Oliner, 1988).

When a national sample of Americans was asked the question "Would you say that most of the time people try to be helpful, or that they are mostly just looking out for themselves?" 43% of the respondents answered, "try to be helpful" and 49% answered, "mostly just looking out for themselves." As shown in Figure 9.5, these percentages varied with gender, race, age, and education.

Charles Darwin, the father of the theory of evolution, maintained that humans constituted the only "moral" species because only they are aware of their past and have the ability to anticipate a future (Rushton, 1989). It can be argued from a sociobiological perspective that, even though self-sacrifice may not contribute to the survival of the individual, much "moral" or "altruistic" behavior has survival value for humanity as a species and hence is perpetuated by evolution (Hamilton, 1964; Liebert, 1979). Critics of the sociobiological perspective that altruism is transmitted genetically argue that cultural concepts such as norms and religion are necessary to explain why people sometimes help not only their close relatives but also those who are unrelated to them (Kitcher, 1985). Sociobiologists such as Wilson (1978) counter that culture can affect behavior within limits, but those limits are set by biology. Although there is no conclusive evidence of a gene for altruism, studies of identical and nonidentical twins have suggested that inherited factors play a role in personal distress and sympathetic concern—two

---

FORM 9.1   Altruism Questionnaire

Directions: For each of the statements listed below, write the appropriate letter on the line to indicate your degree of agreement or disagreement with the statement. SA = strongly agree, A = agree, U = undecided, D = disagree, SD = strongly disagree

_____ 1. I want to live a life that is filled with caring for other people and service to them.

_____ 2. Admittedly I'm a rather self-centered person, but that's only natural.

_____ 3. I have a great deal of respect for people who devote their lives to helping those who are less fortunate than they.

_____ 4. In this life people should look after their own affairs first and be concerned with helping others only after taking care of their own needs.

_____ 5. Most of the time people resent it when someone tries to help them, so it's usually not worth the trouble.

_____ 6. There is nothing finer and nobler than a person who goes out of the way to render assistance to another human being.

_____ 7. People should be more concerned with the feelings and welfare of others than with how everything affects them personally.

_____ 8. Enlightened self-interest is a very realistic and appropriate philosophy of life.

_____ 9. I am willing to devote my life to helping people who are less fortunate than I.

_____ 10. Like most people, I'm primarily interested in my own life and how things affect me personally.

_____ 11. I would sacrifice my life for a friend or relative whom I loved or respected.

_____ 12. Intelligent people stick to their own affairs and let others take care of themselves.

_____ 13. It is usually wise not to become involved or interfere when someone whom you don't know has a problem or is in trouble.

_____ 14. I am quite willing to give money and time to charitable causes or organizations that provide help to needy people.

_____ 15. I wouldn't donate one of my kidneys or any other duplicate internal organ of my own body to someone while I'm still alive.

_____ 16. If given half a chance, anyone can be generous and considerate to other people.

NOTE: Score responses to Items 1, 3, 6, 7, 9, 11, 14, and 16 as SA = 4, A = 3, U = 2, D = 1, SD = 0. Score responses to Items 2, 4, 5, 8, 10, 12, 13, and 15 as SA = 0, A = 1, U = 2, D = 3, and SD = 4. Then add the scoring weights. Possible scores range from 0 to 64, with higher scores representing more altruism values.

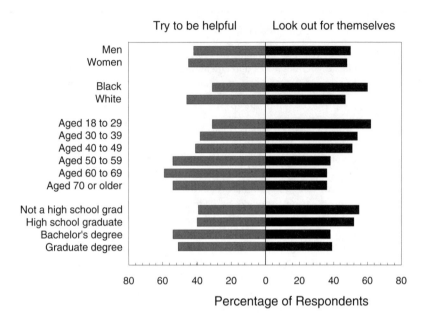

Figure 9.5. Percentage of Sample of Americans in Various Demographic Groups Who Indicated That Most of the Time People Try to Be Helpful or Look Out for Themselves

SOURCE: Based on data from the General Social Survey, National Opinion Research Center, University of Chicago.

affective aspects of empathy, which, in turn, is an aspect of altruism (Davis, Luce, & Kraus, 1994).

Positively reinforcing helpfulness toward others (Schroeder, Penner, Dovidio, & Piliavin, 1995) and modeling altruistic behavior should increase altruistic behavior in children. The fact that prosocial behavior such as altruism, generosity, and cooperativeness can be taught by example and differential reward in families and schools has been documented by a number of studies (e.g., Knight & Kagan, 1977; Oliner & Oliner, 1988; Rushton, 1976). Oliner and Oliner (1988) found, for example, that rescuers of other people in crisis situations were three times more likely than idle bystanders to report that their parents had taught them to care for others.

In general, altruistic, generous, and cooperative parents, teachers, and peers tend to ensure that children will develop similar prosocial behaviors. All of these behaviors depend to some extent on *empathy*, the ability to experience vicariously the feelings, thoughts, and attitudes of another person. For example, an empathic person can become embarrassed simply by watching people in embarrassing situations (Miller, 1999). Empathy seems to vary with the degree of similarity (in age, sex, ethnicity, etc.) between two people, as well as one's ability to observe carefully and listen attentively to the other person. Understandably, the concern and perspective taking that make up empathy are negatively related to aggression (Richardson, 1999).

In addition to empathy, four other variables were designated by Oliner and Oliner (1988) as being key components of the *altruistic personality*. One of these components is *belief in a just world*, that is, perception of the world as a fair and predictable place in which good behavior is rewarded and bad behavior is punished. Another component of the altruistic personality is *social responsibility*—the belief that every person should do his or her best to help people who are in need. *Internal locus of control*, or believing that one can, through his or her behavior, affect the occurrence of good and bad outcomes, is another component of the altruistic personality. The last component of the altruistic personality is *low egocentrism*, that is, having a low level of self-absorption and competitiveness.

Altruism requires being able to separate oneself from self-preoccupation and to take the place and share the feelings of another person.

Recommended Readings

Batson, C. D. (1998). Altruism and prosocial behavior. In D. T. Gilbert, S. T. Fiske, & G. Lindzey (Eds.), *The handbook of social psychology* (4th ed., Vol. 2, pp. 282-316). New York: McGraw-Hill/Oxford.

Bergin, A. E., & Richards, P. S. (2000). Religious experience. In A. E. Kazdin (Ed.), *Encyclopedia of psychology* (Vol. 7, pp. 49-62). Oxford, UK: Oxford University Press.

Catellani, P. (1996). Political psychology. In G. R. Semin & K. Fiedler (Eds.), *Applied social psychology* (pp. 282-311). Thousand Oaks, CA: Sage.

Coles, R. (1997). *The moral intelligence of children.* New York: Random House.

Eysenck, H. J. (1999). *The psychology of politics.* New Brunswick, NJ: Transaction Publishing.

Hill, P. C. (1997). Toward an attitude process model of religious experience. In B. Spilka & D. N. McIntosh (Eds.), *The psychology of religion: Theoretical approaches* (pp. 184-193). Boulder, CO: Westview.

Hunt, M. O. (2000). Status, religion, and the "belief in a just world": Comparing African Americans, Latinos, and Whites. *Social Science Quarterly, 81*, 325-343.

Kinder, D. R. (1998). Opinion and action in the realm of politics. In D. T. Gilbert, S. T. Fiske, & G. Lindzey (Eds.), *The handbook of social psychology* (4th ed., Vol. 2, pp. 778-867). New York: McGraw-Hill/Oxford.

Tetlock, P. E. (1998). Social psychology and world politics. In D. T. Gilbert, S. T. Fiske, & G. Lindzey (Eds.), *The handbook of social psychology* (4th ed., Vol. 2, pp. 868-912). New York: McGraw-Hill/Oxford.

Notes

1. A more current example of the influence of religion on jurisprudence is the continuing existence in the United Kingdom of laws against blasphemy.

2. A useful student project is to make copies of this scale, administer it to various groups of people, and score the results. Compare the scores of people of different ages, genders, educational levels, religions, ethnicities, and nationalities, and interpret any differences that you find.

Appendix 9.1

Measures of Religious Beliefs, Moral Values, and Ethics

Corporate Ethics Scale (CEP; S. D. Hunt et al.; see Bearden, Netemeyer, & Mobley, 1993). This scale defines corporate ethics in terms of three broad-based perceptions: (a) the extent to which employees perceive that managers are acting ethically in their organization, (b) the extent to which employees perceive that managers are concerned about the issues of ethics in their organization, and (c) the extent to which employees perceive that ethical (unethical) behavior is rewarded (punished) in their organization. The CEP is a five-item scale on which item scores are averaged to form an overall index of corporate ethics. All items are scored on 7-point scales ranging from *strongly disagree* to *strongly agree*, so the index range is 1 to 7. The scale is considered unidimensional.

Individual Beliefs About Organizational Ethics Scale (Froelich & Kotte, 1991). This scale is designed to assess employees' attitudes concerning ethical behavior in business situations. On a 7-point, Likert-type scale, employees indicate how strongly they agree or disagree with statements concerning ethical dilemmas in the workplace. Statements reflect the extent to which individuals believe the company should be supported in the face of an ethical conflict and the extent to which employees should lie to protect the company.

Moral Attitudes Index (Woodrum & Ventis, 1992). This scale uses five items concerning abortion, pornography, prayer, homosexuality, and sexual relationships to measure moral attitudes. The items are rated on a 5-point, Likert-type scale.

Moral Judgment Interview and Scoring System (L. Kohlberg; Cambridge University Press). Three *parallel forms* of this interview are composed of three hypothetical moral dilemmas followed by 9 to 12 questions. These questions were designed to elicit the respondents' justification for their judgment in each case, elaborations on their reasons for choosing, and clarifications of their moral judgment. The dilemmas focus on preserving life versus upholding the law, leniency versus punishment for someone who has broken the law out of conscience, and obeying one's parent versus upholding an agreement.

OD Values-Clarification Instrument (S. H. DeVogel; Pfeiffer & Company). This instrument provides a framework within which organization development consultants can recognize the values that they use in solving ethical dilemmas. The resulting information can help consultants in their own individual decision making and identify colleagues with similar values, thereby forming support networks. The ethical principles measured are client autonomy, client freedom, collaboration, objectivity and independence, anonymity, truthfulness, professional development, social justice, and recognition of limits.

Scale for Improving Evaluations of Business Ethics (R. E. Reidenbach & D. P. Robin; Bearden et al., 1993). The scale is composed of eight semantic differential items distributed across three factors: (a) moral equity, (b) relativism, and (c) contractualism. The items are based on five major moral issues: justice, relativism, utilitarianism, egoism, and deontology. Each item is operationalized using a 7-point bipolar scale. Item scores can be summed within factors to form factor indexes, or overall for an overall measure of ethics.

Visions of Morality Scale (Shelton & McAdams, 1990). This self-evaluation instrument was designed to measure the everyday morality of high school seniors. It consists of descriptions of 45 everyday situations in which students may find themselves. On a 7-point, Likert-type scale, respondents indicate how likely it would be that they would respond as the situation states.

Students' empathy and prosocial inclinations across three levels of morality—private, interpersonal, and social—are measured. The instrument may be used as an alternative to Kohlberg's structural-development approach to measuring individuals' morality.

Appendix A

Suppliers of Psychosocial Assessment Instruments

Behaviordyne, Inc., 94 San Antonio Road, P.O. Box 10944, Palo Alto, CA 94303-0997; tel: 415-857-0111; fax: 415-853-9361

Bowling Green State University, Department of Psychology, Bowling Green, OH 43403; tel: 419-372-8247; fax: 419-372-6013; e-mail: jdiebgnet.bgsu.edu; Web URL: www.bgsu.edu/departments/psych/JDI

Cambridge University Press, 110 Midland Avenue, Port Chester, NY 10573-4930; tel: 800-872-7423; fax: 914-927-4712

Career Research and Testing, Inc., P.O. Box 611930, San Jose, CA 95161-1930; tel: 408-441-9100; fax: 408-441-9101; e-mail: tests@ careertrainer.com; Web URL: www.careertrainer.com

Center for the Study of Attitudes Toward Persons With Disabilities, Hofstra University; Hofstra University, Hempstead, NY 11549-1000; tel: 516-463-6600

Consulting Psychologists Press, Inc. (CPP), 3803 East Bayshore Road, P.O. Box 10096, Palo Alto, CA 94303; tel: 800-624-1765; fax: 650-969-8608; Web URL: www.cpp-db.com

CTB/McGraw-Hill, 20 Ryan Ranch Road, Monterey, CA 93940-5703; tel: 800-538-9547; fax: 800-282-0266; Web URL: www.ctb.com

EdITS/Educational and Industrial Testing Service, P.O. Box 7234, San Diego, CA 92167; tel: 800-416-1666; fax: 619-226-1666; e-mail: edits @k-online.com; Web URL: www.edits.net

Educational Testing Service (ETS) Test Collection Library, Rosedale and Carter Roads, Princeton, NJ 98541; tel: 609-734-5689

ERIC Document Reproduction Service, 7420 Fullerton Road, Suite 110, Springfield, VA 22153-28522

GRM Educational Consultancy, P.O. Box 154, Beecroft, NSW 2119; Australia; tel: 61-2-9484-1598; fax: 61-2-9875-3638

Harcourt Educational Measurement, 555 Academic Court, San Antonio, TX 78204-2498; tel: 800-211-8378; Web URL: www.HEMWEB.com

JIST Works, Inc., 720 Park Avenue, Indianapolis, IN 46202-3431; tel: 800-648-5478; fax: 800-547-8329; e-mail: jistworks@aol.com; Web URL: www.jist.com

Management Research Institute, Inc., 11304 Spur Wheel Lane, Potomac, MD 20853; tel: 301-299-9200; fax: 301-299-9227; e-mail: mrieaf@aol. com

Marathon Consulting and Press, 797 South Ashburton Road, Columbus, OH 43227-1027

Mind Garden, Inc., 1690 Woodside Road, Suite 202, Redwood City, CA 94061; tel: 650-261-3500; fax: 650-261-3505; e-mail: info@mindgarden. com

National Study of School Evaluation, 1699 E. Woodfield Road, #406, Schaumburg, IL 60173; tel: 847-995-9080; fax: 847-995-9088; Web URL: www.nsse.org

NCS Assessments, P.O. Box 1416, Minneapolis, MN 55440; tel: 800-627-7271; Web URL: assessments.ncspearson.com

NCS London House, 9701 West Higgins Road, Rosemont, IL 60018-4720; tel: 800-221-8378; Web URL: londonhouse.ncspearson.com

Organizational Tests Ltd, P.O. Box 324, Fredericton, N.B. E3B 4Y9 Canada; tel: 506-452-7194; fax: 506-452-2931

Pfeiffer & Company International Publishers, 2780 Circleport Drive, Erlanger, KY 41018; tel: 800-274-4434; 606-647-3030; fax: 800-569-0443

Psychological Assessment Resources, Inc., P.O. Box 998, Odessa, FL 33556-9908; tel: 800-331-8378 or 800-383-6595; fax: 800-727-9329; Web URL: www.parinc.com

Psychological Corporation, 555 Academic Court, San Antonio, TX 78204-2498; tel: 800-211-8378; fax: 800-232-1223; e-mail: customer_service@HBTOC.com; Web URL: www.HBEM.com

Psychological Foundations of Education, University of Minnesota, 178 Pillsbury Drive, SE, 315 Burton Hall, Minneapolis, MN 55455

Psychologists and Educators, Inc., Sales Division, P.O. Box 513, Chesterfield, MO 63006; tel: 314-536-2366; fax: 314-434-2331

Riverside Publishing Company, 425 Spring Lake Drive, Itasca, IL 60143-2079; tel: 800-323-9540; fax: 630-467-7192; Web URL: www.riverpub.com

Sigma Assessment Systems, Inc., 511 Fort Street, Suite 435, P.O. Box 610984, Port Huron, MI 48061-0984; tel: 800-265-1285; fax: 800-361-9411; e-mail: SIGMA@sigmaassessmentsystems.com; Web URL: www.sigmaassessmentsystems.com

Talico Inc., 2320 S. Third Street, Suite 5, Jacksonville, FL 32250-4057

University of Georgia, College of Education, Division for the Education of Exceptional Children, Aderhold Hall, Athens, GA 30602

Vocational Psychology Research, N657 Elliott Hall, University of Minnesota–Twin Cities, 75 East River Road, Minneapolis, MN 55455-0344; tel: 612-625-1367; fax: 612-626-0345; e-mail: vpr@tc.umn.edu

Western Psychological Services, 12031 Wilshire Blvd., Los Angeles, CA 90025-1251; tel: 310-478-2061; fax: 310-478-7838

Wonderlic Personnel Test, Inc., 1795 N. Butterfield Road, Libertyville, IL 60048-1238; tel: 800-323-3742; fax: 847-680-9492; e-mail: testingservices@wonderlic.com; Web URL: www.wonderlic.com

Appendix B

Recommendations for Constructing and Administering Questionnaires

Constructing Questionnaires

1. Questions of the same type or that deal with the same topic should be grouped together. Grouping according to form and content may not be strictly realizable, but it should be approximated as closely as possible.

2. The general directions for a questionnaire should be clear but brief, including, in relatively simple language, a statement of the purpose of the questionnaire, how responses should be indicated, approximately how long it should take to complete, and what the respondent should do with it.

3. Short questions are preferable to long ones, but enough information should be included in a question to make the form and nature of the requested response clear.

4. The most important questions should not be placed at the end of the questionnaire. Boredom, fatigue, and time pressure increase the likelihood that questions near the end will not be answered as conscientiously as those toward the beginning of the questionnaire.

5. The terms used and the items in which they appear should not be overly technical, too general, ambiguous, or unclear. If there is more than one way to say something, always choose the simplest way.

6. Emotionally loaded words, loaded questions, leading questions, double questions, and hypothetical questions should be avoided. Because of prior associations, *emotionally loaded words* elicit emotional reaction in the respondent and bias the respondent's answer. *Loaded questions*, including *leading questions* such as "Isn't it reasonable to suppose that . . . ?" or "Don't you believe, like so many other Americans, that . . . ?" are phrased in such a way that the respondent is more likely to give a desired answer. *Double questions* are those that contain more than one query (e.g., "Do you go to the movies every week, and do you enjoy it?"). *Hypothetical* ("What if?") *questions*, such as "What if you lost your job . . . ?" are typically too speculative to provide useful information.

7. *Nonspecific adjectives or adverbs* (e.g., *many* or *sometimes*), words having more than one meaning, double negatives, and slang and colloquialisms should be avoided. These kinds of terms tend to make questions more ambiguous or less clear.

8. Multiple questions should be used to assess attitudes, beliefs, opinions, interests, aspirations, expectations, and other affective variables. A sum of scored responses on several nonfactual items of these kinds is usually necessary to obtain a reliable measure.

9. A logical, conversational sequence should be followed in presenting questions. The questionnaire should not "jump around," in content or style. It should begin with a few simple, interesting, and nonthreatening questions and proceed in a logical order from there to more complex questions and from more general to more specific topics. When uninteresting and difficult questions are included, they should be placed nearer the end of the questionnaire.

10. The questions should be sensitive to the feelings and values of the particular individuals to whom the questionnaire is administered. Strong emotions and defensiveness, rather than accurate answers, are likely reactions to insensitive questioning.

11. Questions concerning socioeconomic and other demographic data should be placed near the end of the questionnaire. When such questions are placed near the beginning of a questionnaire, they may appear to be inconsistent with the stated purpose of the questionnaire that is expressed in the title and the general directions.

12. The length of a mailed questionnaire should be such that no more than 30 minutes is required to finish it, and only half that amount of time in a telephone interview. A statement concerning how long it will take to

complete the questionnaire should be included in the general directions. It may also be helpful to have respondents indicate their starting and stopping times on the questionnaire.

13. The respondent should be thanked for his or her cooperation, either personally or in printed form, at the end of the questionnaire.

Administering Questionnaires

1. Different fonts or underlining should be used to distinguish between what the questioner actually says and what he or she reads silently.

2. *Skip patterns*, indicating which questions can be skipped by respondents who answer a previous question in a certain way, should be clearly marked.

3. Sufficient space should be left for the interviewer (questioner) to record additional observations and information.

4. The number of response options for an item should be sufficiently small so the respondent can keep all of them in mind.

5. The interviewer should be careful not to overreact to the respondent's answers so the latter will be more concerned with giving accurate answers to questions than with pleasing the interviewer.

6. The interviewer should avoid asking intimidating questions that lead to under- or overreporting of certain behaviors.

Mailed Questionnaires

1. An identification number should be placed on the questionnaire, except in the case of anonymous administration.

2. The questionnaire should be attractive, interesting, and arranged in booklet form.

3. The title should be placed at the beginning of the questionnaire, but words such as *questionnaire* and *opinionnaire* should be avoided.

4. Instructions, both general and for each part, should be underlined or printed in boldface type.

5. The pages of the questionnaire should not be overcrowded and should be numbered or otherwise identified.

6. Each question should be typed in its entirety on one side of a page and should not be overly long (more than 20 words or so).

7. Important questions should not be placed at the end of the questionnaire.

8. The questions should be directly related to the variables and hypotheses that the questionnaire is designed to investigate. Questions of peripheral interest that are not directly related to the purposes and hypotheses of the study should not be included.

9. *Over, continued on back*, or a similar word or phrase should appear at the bottom of the first side of a page that is printed on both sides.

10. Open-ended questions should be placed near the end of the questionnaire, rather than at the beginning.

11. Responses should be marked close to the questions to which they refer. If a separate response sheet is used, it should be coordinated with the questionnaire and easy to follow.

12. The questionnaire should be printed in an attractive format and on good-quality paper.

13. Even when a return envelope is included with a mailed questionnaire, the name and address of the person to whom the completed questionnaire should be returned should be listed at the bottom or top of the form.

SOURCE: Adapted from Aiken (1997).

Glossary

Accident proneness   Now largely discredited theory of a particular personality type associated with a greater tendency to have accidents.

Acquiescence response set (style)   Tendency of a person to answer affirmatively ("yes" or "true") to personality test items and in other alternative-response situations.

Affirmative action   Actions by governmental or other organizations designed to reduce inequality of opportunities among ethnic, gender, age, or other appropriate social groups.

Ageism   Social stereotyping of and/or discrimination against older people.

Aggregation   Combining or averaging measures of personality across situations to enhance **reliability.**

Alienation   Feelings of indifference, unconnectedness, or dislike toward another person, group, or situation.

Alternate-forms reliability   An index of reliability (**coefficient of equivalence**) determined by correlating the scores made by a group of people on one form of a test with their scores on another form of the test.

Altruism   Unselfish concern or devotion to the welfare of other people at the cost of some sacrifice to oneself. Voluntary actions designed to help other people without expecting to receive a tangible reward or benefit.

Ambiguity index Measure of the ambiguity (semi-interquartile range) of an attitude statement as perceived by a group of judges in L. L. Thurstone's **equal-appearing intervals** technique of attitude scale construction.

Assessment Appraising the presence or magnitude of one or more personal characteristics. Assessing human behavior and mental processes includes such procedures as observations, interviews, rating scales, checklists, inventories, **projective techniques**, and tests.

Attitude A relatively stable, learned tendency to respond positively or negatively to a given person, situation, or object. Attitudes consist of cognitive, affective, and behavioral components. Examples of attitudes are political preferences, prejudices, scientific views, religious beliefs, and other complex response predispositions.

Attitude accessibility Degree of readiness to be activated at a particular time of a person's evaluation of an attitude object.

Attitude object A particular entity (e.g., social policy, social group, individual person, behaviors) toward which the evaluative responses characteristic of an attitude are expressed.

Attitude representation theory Theory of attitude formation and consistency that is based on (a) a representation postulate that views responses to attitude-relevant objects as being produced by subjective representations of the objects and direct perceptions of the attitude objects in the immediate environment, and (b) a matching postulate that describes the consistency or stability of attitude-relevant responses as depending on the degree of the match between the subjective representations of the attitude object and perceptions of it at different times and in different situations.

Attitude scale A paper-and-pencil instrument consisting of a series of statements concerning an institution, situation, person, or event. The examinee responds to each statement by endorsing it or indicating his or her degree of agreement or disagreement with the statement.

Attitude-to-behavior process model An explanatory model of the influence of attitudes on behavior that stresses the roles of attitudes and stored knowledge of behavior that is appropriate in a particular situation on how a person defines the situation, such definition, in turn, guiding the person's behavior in that situation.

Attribution Process of interpreting a person's behavior as caused by forces within (internal attribution or disposition) or outside (external attribution or situation) the person.

Attribution theory The theory based on the viewpoint that people attempt to explain and understand the behavior of others by attributing the causes of that behavior to characteristics of the person or factors in the environment; the expectancies and behaviors of the individual are influenced by those causal attributions.

Augmentation (principle of) Tendency to attribute greater importance to a cause of behavior when it occurs in the presence of other causes that serve to inhibit it. See **discounting.**

Authoritarian personality Tendency to view the world in terms of a strict social hierarchy in which someone higher up in the hierarchy demands cooperation and deference from those below him or her.

Axiology A branch of philosophy that deals with values, such as those of ethics, aesthetics, or religion.

Balance theory T. M. Newcomb and F. Heider's theory that people organize their attitudes and attractions in a symmetrical way: a state of *balance* exists, and consequently a pleasant emotional state occurs when two people like each other and have similar opinions on a topic, whereas a state of *imbalance* occurs, and hence an unpleasant emotional state, when two people like each other but have dissimilar opinions about a topic.

Behavior modification Psychotherapeutic procedures based on learning theory and research and designed to change inappropriate behavior to more personally and/or socially acceptable behavior. Examples of such procedures are systematic desensitization, counterconditioning, extinction, and implosion.

Belief Confidence in the truth or existence of something not immediately susceptible to rigorous proof.

Bias A preformed negative opinion or attitude toward a group of persons based on their race, religion, disability, sexual orientation, or ethnicity/national origin.

Bias crime A criminal offense committed against a person or property that is motivated, in whole or in part, by the offender's bias against a race, religion, disability, sexual orientation, or ethnicity/national origin. Also known as *hate crime.*

Burnout Emotional and behavioral impairment resulting from high levels of stress in occupational situations and precipitated by overwork; characterized by emotional exhaustion, lessened productivity, and feelings of depersonalization.

Bystander intervention effect   Whether or not a person chooses to come to the aid of someone who has had an accident or is being attacked.

Causal attributions   Beliefs concerning the reasons—ability, effort, difficulty of the task, or luck—for one's success or failure in a particular situation.

Central route to persuasion   Thinking carefully about a communication and consequently being convinced by the soundness of its arguments. See **peripheral route to persuasion.**

Checklist   List of words, phrases, or statements descriptive of personal characteristics; respondents endorse (check) those items that are characteristic of themselves (*self-ratings*) or other people (*other ratings*).

Classical conditioning   Simple form of learning in which a formerly neutral (conditioned) stimulus that is paired with a stimulus (unconditioned stimulus) that evokes a response comes to evoke the response by itself.

Coefficient alpha   An internal-consistency reliability coefficient, appropriate for tests consisting of a series of dichotomous or multipoint items; the split-half reliability averaged across random divisions of the items into subsets of equal size.

Coefficient of equivalence   A reliability coefficient (correlation) obtained by administering two different forms of a test to the same people. See **alternate-forms reliability.**

Coefficient of internal consistency   Reliability coefficient based on estimates of the internal consistency of a test. Examples are split-half and alpha coefficients.

Coefficient of stability   A reliability coefficient (correlation) obtained by administering a test to the same group of people on two different occasions.

Cognitive capacity hypothesis   Hypothesis of attitude formation and change that maintains that it is not so much perceptions of danger in the world but rather the capacity of the individual to process the information while remaining free from distractions generated by his or her current affective state that determines the level of cognitive processing given to an incoming message.

Cognitive dissonance   Unharmonious internal state that occurs when a person observes an inconsistency between two or more of his or her attitudes or between the person's attitude(s) and behavior(s).

Cognitive therapy   Psychotherapeutic process in which a person's faulty cognitions or beliefs are changed to more realistic ones.

Common in-group identity model Recategorization model of how inter-group bias and conflict can be reduced by processes that enable members of different groups to perceive themselves as belonging to the same group.

Comparable worth Principle that jobs having comparable value to an organization deserve comparable pay.

Compatibility (principle of) Attitudes and behavior are more highly correlated when they are measured at the same level of generality or specificity.

Concurrent validity The extent to which scores obtained by a group of people on a particular psychometric instrument are related to their simultaneously determined scores on another measure (criterion) of the same characteristic that the instrument is supposed to measure.

Conditioning See **classical conditioning** and **operant conditioning.**

Construct validity The extent to which scores on a psychometric instrument designed to measure a certain psychological construct are related to scores on other psychometric instruments or to patterns of behavior in ways that are consistent with a theory concerning the operation of the particular construct.

Consumer psychology A field of psychology concerned with the identification or segmentation of markets based on the psychological characteristics of consumers; designing, advertising, and selling products and services with respect to consumer characteristics.

Contact hypothesis The hypothesis that increasing the amount of personal contact between members of different social groups is effective in reducing intergroup prejudice. The hypothesis appears to be confirmed only when the intergroup contact occurs under favorable circumstances. See **extended contact hypothesis.**

Content validity The extent to which a group of people who are experts in the material with which a test deals agree that the test or other psychometric instrument measures what it was designed to measure.

Correlation coefficient A numerical index of the degree of relationship between two variables. Correlation coefficients usually range from -1.00 (perfect negative relationship), through .00 (total absence of a relationship) to $+1.00$ (perfect positive relationship). Two common types of correlation coefficients are the product-moment coefficient and the point-biserial coefficient.

Covert measures of attitudes Measures of attitudes that are disguised in order to control for the effects of self-presentation and social desirability motives on responses.

Criterion-related validity   The extent to which an assessment instrument measures what it was designed to measure, as indicated by the correlation of scores on the instrument with scores on some criterion measure.

Cross-categorization models   Models of intergroup conflict reduction based on the idea that most people have multiple social identities that cut across different social dimensions.

Cumulative scale   Attitude scale, such as E. S. Bogardus's Social Distance Scale or L. Guttman's scalogram measures, on which items are arranged in a hierarchy so that endorsing a particular item implies endorsement of all items below it on the hierarchy.

Developmental method   Research method in which changes in behavior over time are observed and measured by following up the same group of people over a lengthy time period, by comparing groups of people of different ages at a given point in time (cross-sectional method), or variations on these procedures.

Discounting (principle of)   Principle that when a response can be explained in a number of ways, the plausibility of any one cause is weakened (discounted). See **augmentation**.

Discrimination (social discrimination)   Unfairly penalizing people who are members of particular groups regardless of the cause of their characteristics or behavior.

Distinct social identity model   "Subcategorization" model of intergroup contact based on the notion that positive intergroup experiences occur by structuring the social situation so members of both groups play distinct but complementary roles.

Doctrine of assurance   Early Protestant religious doctrine, related to the doctrine of predestination, that one can never be assured of salvation, regardless of one's "good works."

Double-effect principle   Principle espoused by the Roman Catholic Church that an action having the primary effect of relieving human suffering may be justified even when it shortens human life.

Dual-process models   Models of attitude change, such as the elaboration likelihood model and the heuristic-systematic model, that emphasize the importance of two cognitive processes, one more superficial than the other, in changing attitudes.

Elaboration likelihood model (ELM)   Theory that persuasion occurs in one of two separate ways: by systematic processing of information via the central route, or by heuristic processing via the peripheral route. See **systematic processing** and **heuristic processing.**

Empathy Experiencing vicariously the thoughts, feelings, and attitudes of another person.

Equal-appearing intervals (method of) Method of attitude scaling devised by L. L. Thurstone in which a large sample of "judges" sort attitude statements into 11 piles. The scale value of a statement is computed as the median, and the ambiguity index as the semi-interquartile range, of the distribution of ratings given by the judges to the statement.

Equity theory The theory that if the ratio of a person's inputs (abilities, efforts, etc.) to the person's outcomes (e.g., money, promotions, praise) is equal to that of other people, the situation is perceived as equitable and does not create tension; if the ratio of inputs to outcomes is not equal to that of other people, tension is created in the person and he or she becomes motivated to reduce it.

Ethnocentrism Belief in the superiority of one's own ethnic group or culture as compared with other ethnic groups or cultures.

Euthanasia Actively or passively contributing to the death of a human being or animal suffering from a terminal illness or injury; also known as "mercy killing."

Expectancy J. B. Rotter's term for the subjective probability that a given behavior will be instrumental in obtaining a certain reinforcement.

Expectancy-value (E-V) scaling Multidimensional attitude-scaling technique in which the respondent begins by assigning an approval rating to each of a set of value (V) dimensions. Next the respondent indicates his or her expectancy (E) of the extent to which each of the value dimensions applies to a particular issue. The expectancy and value dimensions are then combined as the respondent's E-V score.

Experiment Systematic scientific procedure for determining the cause of a relationship between two variables (independent and dependent) by manipulating the independent variable while controlling for the effects of extraneous variables, and then measuring the resulting changes in the dependent variable.

Experimental method Scientific method of determining cause and effect by manipulating independent variables while controlling for extraneous variables, and measuring (observing) changes in dependent variables.

Extended contact hypothesis   Hypothesis that prejudice against another group (out-group) may be reduced by knowing that members of one's own group have formed close relationships with members of the out-group.

Faceism   Depiction of females in newspapers, magazines, and art portrayals with a predominance of the body, and males with a predominance of the head and face.

Facet analysis   A complex, a priori, multidimensional paradigm for item construction and analysis that may be applied to an attitude, an object, or a situation.

Factor analysis   A mathematical procedure for analyzing a matrix of correlations among measurements made on a set of variables to determine what factors (constructs) are sufficient to explain the intercorrelations among the variables.

Fundamental attribution error (correspondence bias)   Tendency to attribute the behavior of other people to dispositional factors (internal attributions) rather than situational influences (external attributions).

Galvanic skin response (GSR)   Change in skin resistance produced by an arousing stimulus.

Gender identity   An individual's view of himself or herself with respect to gender; the introspective part of gender role.

Gender role   A culture-specific pattern of behavior that is considered appropriate to a particular gender.

Gender schema   Internalized beliefs about what men and women are and how they are supposed to behave.

Glass ceiling   A subtle barrier to the advancement of women; the level to which they can rise but which they cannot surpass in an organization.

Hate crime   See **bias crime**.

Heritability coefficient (h^2)   Ratio of the test score variance attributable to heredity to the variance attributable to both heredity and environment.

Heuristic processing   Type of information processing that occurs when the receiver develops judgments about a message based on mental shortcuts, rules of thumb, or heuristics, such as cues external to the message itself. Examples of such heuristics are perceived source credibility, use of emotional appeals, attractiveness, status, and expertise of the source. Also known as **peripheral route to persuasion**.

Heuristic-systematic model (HSM) Extension of the **elaboration likelihood model (ELM)** of attitude formation and change. Rather than being limited to either central or peripheral processing at any given time, as in ELM, in HSM messages are viewed as being processed simultaneously using both heuristic and systematic processes.

Identification Taking on the personal characteristics of another person, as when a developing child identifies with a significant other person. Also, in psychoanalytic theory, an ego-defense mechanism for coping with anxiety.

Identity The gradual emergence and continual change in an individual's sense of self.

Implicit attitudes Attitudes that are activated (by particular objects, events, persons, or situations) and influence behaviors without conscious awareness of those attitudes.

Inoculation theory Theory that resistance to arguments and to attitude change can be built up by exposing the person to weaker versions of the arguments so he or she can develop counterarguments to ward off future attacks on his or her attitudes.

Instrumental values Values concerned with modes of conduct. M. Rokeach subdivided instrumental values into moral values and competence values.

Integrative model C. L. Hulin's model that views job satisfaction as a comparative function of the balance between role inputs and role outputs.

Internal consistency The extent to which all items on a test measure the same variable or construct. The reliability of a test computed by the Spearman-Brown, Kuder-Richardson, or Cronbach coefficient alpha formulas is a measure of the test's internal consistency.

Interpersonal attraction Positive attitude, or degree of liking, of another person.

Interval scale A measurement scale on which equality of numerical differences implies equality of differences in the attribute or characteristic being measured. The scale of temperature (Celsius, Fahrenheit) and, presumably, standard score scales (z, T, etc.), are examples of interval scales.

Interview A systematic procedure for obtaining information from a person by asking questions and, in general, verbally interacting with the interviewee.

Inventory A set of questions or statements to which a person responds (e.g., by indicating agreement or disagreement); designed to provide a measure of personality, interest, attitude, or behavior.

Item   One of the units, questions, or tasks of which a psychometric instrument is composed.

Item analysis   A general term for procedures designed to assess the utility or validity of a set of test items.

Jigsaw classroom   Cooperative group learning procedure for reducing intergroup prejudice. A small amount of information is given to group members, who are then required to teach it to the other group members.

Job characteristics model   J. R. Hackman and G. R. Oldham's model that job satisfaction is based on job enrichment. The model delineates five job characteristics—task identity, task significance, skill variety, autonomy, and feedback—that are important in making a job challenging and fulfilling.

Job involvement   The extent to which a worker becomes interested and personally connected to a job; the job becomes a part of the worker's sense of self.

Job satisfaction   A pleasurable or positive emotional state resulting from the appraisal of one's job or job experiences (Locke, 1976, p. 1300).

Just-world belief   The belief that the world is a just place and that people generally get what they deserve and deserve what they get.

Latent structure analysis   Statistical procedure for designing multidimensional psychometric scales; the basic postulate of latent structure and latent class analysis is that the observed relationships among a set of attitude statements or other psychometric items can be accounted for by a set of latent (unobserved) variables.

Likert scale   An attitude scale on which respondents indicate their degree of agreement or disagreement with a particular proposition concerning some object, person, or situation.

Locus of control   J. B. Rotter's term for a cognitive-perceptual style characterized by the typical direction (internal or "self" vs. external or "other") from which individuals perceive themselves as being controlled.

Machiavellianism   Personality trait in which the individual is concerned with manipulating other people or using them for his or her own benefit.

Magnitude estimation   Attitude-scaling procedure based on a psychophysical method for scaling stimuli according to their perceived intensity. The respondent assigns a numerical rating to each of a set of objects or events. The ratings are then plotted against a measure of the actual values of the objects or events.

Measurement The assignment of numbers to events. Measurements may be made on scales ranging in their refinement or accuracy from nominal through ordinal and interval to ratio scales.

Modeling Learning social and cognitive behaviors by observing and imitating the behaviors of other people.

Moderator variable Demographic or personality variable (e.g., age, sex, cognitive style, compulsivity) affecting the correlation between two other variables (e.g., aptitude and achievement).

Motivator-hygiene theory F. Herzberg's theory of job satisfaction that extrinsic (hygiene) factors such as pay, company policies, and working conditions influence a worker's level of dissatisfaction (but not satisfaction) with the job, whereas intrinsic (motivator) factors such as responsibilities, achievements, and the work itself influence worker satisfaction (but not dissatisfaction) with the job.

Multidimensional scaling Multivariate statistical procedure(s) (facet analysis, latent class analysis, latent structure analysis, latent partition analysis, repertory grid technique) used in constructing multidimensional scales of attitudes and other psychometric constructs.

Nonverbal behavior Any behavior in which the respondent does not make word sounds or signs. Nonverbal behavior serving a communicative function includes movements of large (*macrokinesics*) and small (*microkinesics*) external body parts, interpersonal distance or territoriality (*proximics*), tone and rate of voice sounds (*paralinguistics*), and communications imparted by culturally prescribed matters relating to time, dress, memberships, and the like (*culturics*).

Norms A list of scores on a psychometric instrument and the corresponding percentile ranks, standard scores, or other transformed scores of a group on which the instrument has been standardized.

Operant conditioning Learning that occurs when positive or negative consequences follow a response.

Opinion A verbalized judgment concerning a specific occurrence or situation. The meaning of *opinion* is similar to that of *attitude*, but the former term has the connotation of being more specific and based on more thought than the latter term. In addition, a person is aware of his or her opinions, but not necessarily aware of his or her attitudes.

Opinion polling Questioning a sample of a target population on the population's opinions concerning particular persons, issues, or events.

Organizational commitment Attitudes of loyalty or belongingness toward an organization or place of work.

Paired comparisons (method of) Method of attitude scale construction in which every item is compared with every other item with regard to its magnitude on an attitudinal dimension.

Parallel forms Two tests, or other psychometric instruments, that are equivalent in the sense that they contain the same kinds of items of equal difficulty and are highly correlated. The scores made on one form of the test are very close to those made by the same persons on the other form.

Parallel-forms reliability An index of reliability determined by correlating the scores of individuals on parallel forms of a test or other psychometric instrument.

Performance appraisal The periodic formal evaluation of an employee's on-the-job performance.

Peripheral route to persuasion Type of persuasion that depends on heuristics such as the expertise of the persuader and the arguments presented by him or her rather than by the content of those arguments. This type of persuasion does not involve as much thinking as the **central route to persuasion.**

Personal orientations Similar to interests and values, personal orientations cut across a wide range of personality variables, including cognitive and perceptual styles and the concept of lifestyle, and direct behavior in a variety of situations. Examples of personal orientations are gender role and self-actualization.

Personal values Self-centered terminal values, including end states such as peace of mind and salvation (M. Rokeach).

Personality The sum total of all the qualities, traits, and behaviors that characterize the thoughts, feelings, and behaviors of a person and by which, together with his or her physical attributes, the person is recognized as unique.

Personality assessment Description and analysis of personality by means of various techniques, including observing and interviewing, and administering checklists, rating scales, personality inventories, and projective techniques.

Personalization model Type of social categorization (or decategorization) model that contact with individual members of an out-group tends to break down the personalized categorization of those individuals and, by extension, the group as a whole.

Political attitudes   Attitudes having implications for governmental policy or relations between social groups.

Predictive validity   Extent to which scores on a test or other psychometric instrument are predictive of performance on some criterion measured at a later time; usually expressed as a correlation between the predictor variable and the criterion measure.

Prejudice   Unreasonable attitudes, opinions, or feelings regarding a particular racial, religious, or national group.

Priming   Prior exposure to a particular stimulus, usually below the level of conscious awareness, that increases the accessibility or retrievability of information from memory; a technique employed in the study of implicit attitudes.

Principle of compatibility   Principle that attitudes are better predictors of behavior when both are measured at the same level of generality and specificity.

Projective technique   A relatively unstructured personality assessment technique in which the examinee responds to materials such as inkblots, ambiguous pictures, incomplete sentences, and other materials by telling what he or she perceives, making up stories, or constructing and arranging sentences and objects. Theoretically, because the material is fairly unstructured, whatever structure the examinee imposes on it represents a projection of his or her own personality characteristics (needs, conflicts, sources of anxiety, etc.).

Propaganda   Information, ideas, or rumors disseminated to help or hurt a person, group, institution, organization, or nation.

Prosocial behavior   Behaviors that benefit other people but provide no clear benefit to the individual who carries out the action and may even involve risk for him or her.

Prototype/willingness model   Theory that attitudes influence behavior by means of their effects on behavioral intentions and willingness to engage in certain actions (behavioral willingness).

Psychographics   Assessment of the relationships of consumer behavior to personality characteristics and lifestyles.

Pupillometrics   Measuring pupillary diameter as an indicator of pleasure or interest in a specific stimulus.

Q-sort   Assessment procedure that centers on sorting cards or other materials containing self-descriptive statements into categories on some continuum and correlating the responses of different individuals or the same individuals at different times.

Racism The belief that certain racial groups are inferior to others and should therefore be treated as such.

Rating scale A list of words or statements concerning traits or characteristics, sometimes in the form of a continuous line divided into sections corresponding to degrees of the characteristic, on which the rater indicates judgments of either his or her own behavior and traits or the behavior and traits of another person (ratee).

Realistic conflict theory Viewpoint that social prejudice can result from direct competition between different social groups over resources that are scarce and valuable.

Reasonable woman standard A legal standard, enunciated in *Ellison v. Brady* (1991), stating that even if a male perpetrator of an action allegedly involving sexual harassment does not see it as offensive, it is considered in law as being so if a "reasonable woman" considers it as such.

Reinforcement Application (*positive reinforcement*) or removal (*negative reinforcement*) of a stimulus that affects the probability of a response.

Reliability The extent to which a test or other psychometric instrument measures anything consistently. A reliable test is relatively free from errors of measurement, so the examinees' obtained test scores are close in numerical value to their true test scores.

Reliability coefficient A numerical index, between .00 and 1.00, of the reliability of a psychometric instrument. Methods for determining reliability include test-retest, parallel-forms, and internal consistency.

Reproducibility coefficient Index of the degree to which a set of attitude statements approximates a true Guttman (cumulative) scale; the proportion of actual responses falling in a perfect pattern of a true Guttman scale.

Response sets (styles) Tendencies for individuals to respond in relatively fixed or stereotyped ways in situations where there are two or more response choices, such as on personality inventories. Tendencies to guess, to answer true (acquiescence), and to give socially desirable answers are some of the response sets that have been investigated.

Reverse discrimination Treating members of minority groups more favorably than members of the majority (dominant) group in educational, occupational, and other organizations or situations.

Scalogram analysis Method of attitude scaling pioneered by Louis Guttman. The attitude statements are arranged in a hierarchy in such a way that endorsing a statement at any point on the hierarchy implies endorsement of all statements below it. The extent to which this occurs is indicated by a **reproducibility coefficient.**

Scapegoating Mistreatment of people of other groups (out-groups) by members of an in-group due to frustration of the needs and wants of in-group members.

Segmentation theory Theory that the degrees of satisfaction experienced on and off the job have little to do with each other and that there is no relationship between job satisfaction and life satisfaction.

Self-actualization Process by which a person attempts to develop his or her abilities to the fullest, thereby becoming the kind of person he or she would ideally like to be.

Self-efficacy A person's judgment concerning his or her ability to accomplish a particular task in a certain situation successfully; a central construct of social cognitive theory.

Self-esteem Degree of positivity or negativity felt by a person toward his or her self.

Self-monitoring The extent to which a person is sensitive to, or monitors, his or her own behavior according to environmental cues. High self-monitors are more sensitive to what is situationally appropriate and act accordingly. Low self-monitors are less sensitive to external cues and act more in response to their own internal attitudes and feelings.

Self-report inventory A paper-and-pencil measure of personality traits or interests, composed of a series of items that the respondent indicates as characteristic (true) or not characteristic (not true) of himself or herself.

Semantic differential A rating scale, introduced by C. E. Osgood, for evaluating the connotative meanings that selected concepts have for a person. Each concept is rated on a 7-point, bipolar adjectival scale.

Sentence completion test A projective test of personality consisting of a series of incomplete sentences that the examinee is instructed to complete.

Sexism The belief that the two sexes are fundamentally different in their abilities and that each is more suited for certain jobs or areas of concentration.

Sleeper effect An increase over time in the effect of a communication.

Social categorization theory Theoretical framework of how social contact may change attitudes between groups. The model emphasizes the role of cognitive representation of the contact situation in determining the outcomes of group interactions. See **common in-group identity model, distinct social identity model**, and **personalization model.**

Social comparison Determining whether one's view of social reality is correct or incorrect by comparing oneself with other people.

Social desirability response set Response set or style affecting scores on personality inventories. Refers to the tendency to respond to assessment materials in a more socially desirable way rather than in a way that is truly characteristic or descriptive of one's personality.

Social distances method Cumulative attitude-scaling procedure, originated by E. S. Bogardus, that has as its object the determination of the closest distance to a person of another racial or nationality group at which a respondent feels comfortable.

Social learning theory Conceptualizations of learning that occur by imitation or interactions with other people.

Social values Socially centered terminal values, including end states such as equality and world peace (M. Rokeach).

Sociometric technique Technique for determining and describing the pattern of acceptances and rejections among a group of people.

Somatoform disorders Psychiatric disorders involving physical symptoms with no apparent physiological basis; includes somatization disorder, conversion disorder, pain disorder, hypochondriasis, and body dysmorphic disorder.

Spillover theory Theory that positive or negative feelings in one area of life may reach out and carry over (spill over) into other areas of life.

Split-half coefficient An estimate of reliability determined by applying the Spearman-Brown formula for $m = 2$ to the correlation between two halves of the same test, such as the odd-numbered items and the even-numbered items.

Standard scores A group of scores, such as z scores, T scores, or stanine scores, having a desired mean and standard deviation. Standard scores are computed by transforming raw scores to z scores, multiplying the z scores by the desired standard deviation, and then adding the desired mean to the product.

Standardization   Administering a carefully constructed test or other psychometric instrument to a large, representative sample of people under standard conditions for the purpose of determining norms.

Stereotype   Generalizations concerning the attributes and behaviors of people who belong to certain groups.

Subjective norm   A person's perception that most people who are important to him or her think that the person should or should not engage in a specific action.

Successive categories (method of)   Technique of attitude scale construction, devised by L. L. Thurstone, that, unlike the method of equal-appearing intervals, does not assume equal intervals among adjacent attitude statements.

Summated ratings (method of)   Technique of attitude scale construction devised by R. Likert. Raters check the numerical values on a 5-point scale corresponding to the degree of positivity or negativity of each of a large number of attitude statements concerned with the topic in question. Twenty or so statements are selected by certain statistical criteria to make up the final attitude scale.

Survey   Popular descriptive research method in which people respond to certain questions or directions orally or in writing. Data are collected on large numbers of people by means of questionnaires, interviews, inventories, and scales to assess the incidence, distribution, and interrelationships of selected variables.

Systematic processing   Method of processing information that relies on a critical examination of the content and ideas of a message; central route to persuasion.

Terminal values   Values concerned with end states. M. Rokeach subdivided terminal values into personal values and social values.

Theory   A set of assumptions or propositions set forth to explain available information and to predict new facts with respect to some phenomenon. Theories are typically conjectural rather than established fact and are usually fairly broad in scope.

Theory of planned behavior   I. Ajzen's revised theory of attitudes that the perceived ease of performing a particular behavior is, when combined with the person's attitude and the subjective norms regarding its performance, predictive of the person's intention to perform the behavior and, subsequently, the behavior itself.

Theory of reasoned action (TORA) I. Ajzen's theory of attitudes that the tendency to engage in a specific behavior is determined by the person's intention to do so, which itself is determined by a combination of the person's attitude toward the behavior and the subjective norm regarding its performance.

Tokenism Positive actions on a small scale to reduce discrimination that serve as an excuse for avoiding more meaningful actions.

Tolerance A fair, objective, and permissive attitude toward people whose opinions, practices, race, religion, nationality, and so on are different from one's own; absence of bigotry.

Type A personality Personality pattern characterized by a combination of behaviors, including aggressiveness, competitiveness, hostility, quick actions, and constant striving; associated with a high incidence of coronary heart disease.

Type B personality Personality pattern characterized by a relaxed, easygoing, patient, noncompetitive lifestyle; associated with a low incidence of coronary heart disease.

Ultimate attribution error The tendency of people who hold strong stereotypes to attribute negative behaviors by minority group members to dispositional characteristics and to attribute positive behavior on their part to situational factors.

Unimodel Model that combines the two modes of persuasion included in the elaboration likelihood model and the heuristic-systematic model into a single process.

Unobtrusive observation Observation made without the knowledge or awareness of the person who is observed.

Validity The extent to which a psychometric instrument measures what it was designed to measure. Validity can be assessed in several ways: by analysis of the instrument's content (**content validity**), by relating scores on the test to a criterion (**predictive** and **concurrent validity**), and by a more thorough study of the extent to which the test is a measure of a certain psychological construct (**construct validity**).

Validity coefficient The correlation between scores on a measure of a predictor variable and scores on a measure of a criterion variable.

Value The worth, merit, or importance attaching to something.

Value-percept theory E. A. Locke's theory that conceptualizes job satisfaction in terms of the amount of a particular value that a worker desires, the perceived amount of the value that the job provides, and the importance of the value to the worker.

Word association technique   A list of words read aloud to a person who has been instructed to respond with the first word that comes to mind.

References

Abelson, R. P., Kinder, D. R., Peters, M. D., & Fiske, S. T. (1982). Affective and semantic components in political person perception. *Journal of Personality and Social Psychology, 42*, 619-630.

Achille, M. A., & Ogloff, J. R. P. (1997). When is a request for assisted suicide legitimate? Factors influencing public attitudes toward euthanasia. *Canadian Journal of Behavioural Science, 29*, 19-27.

Adams, J. S. (1965). Inequity in social exchange. In H. L. Tosi & W. C. Hammer (Eds.), *Organizational behavior and management: A contingency approach* (3rd ed., pp. 209-225). New York: John Wiley.

Adams, P. F., & Marano, M. A. (1995). Current estimates from the National Health Interview Survey, 1994. *Vital and Health Statistics, 10*(193). Hyattsville, MD: National Center for Health Statistics.

Aday, R. H. (1984-1985). Belief in afterlife and death anxiety: Correlates and comparisons. *Omega, 15*, 67-75.

Address of Pope Pius XII to an International Congress of Anesthesiologists, AASXXXXXIX. (1957, November 24). (Trans. from the original French, *The Pope Speaks*, Spring 1958, Vol. 4, No. 4, pp. 393-398.)

Adorno, T. W., Frenkel-Brunswik, E., Levinson, D. J., & Sanford, R. N. (1950). *The authoritarian personality*. New York: Harper.

Affleck, G., Tennen, H., Croog, S., & Levine, S. (1987). Causal attribution, perceived beliefs, and morbidity after a heart attack: An 8-year study. *Journal of Consulting and Clinical Psychology, 55*, 29-35.

Aiken, L. R. (1983). Number of response categories and statistics on a teacher rating scale. *Educational and Psychological Measurement, 43*, 397-401.

Aiken, L. R. (1992). Some measures of interpersonal attraction and group cohesiveness. *Educational and Psychological Measurement, 52*, 63-67.

Aiken, L. R. (1996). *Rating scales & checklists: Evaluating behavior, personality, and attitudes.* New York: John Wiley.

Aiken, L. R. (1997). *Questionnaires & inventories: Surveying opinions and assessing personality.* New York: John Wiley.

Aiken, L. R. (1998). *Tests & examinations: Measuring abilities and performance.* New York: John Wiley.

Aiken, L. R. (2001a). *Aging and later life: Growing old in modern society.* Springfield, IL: Charles C Thomas.

Aiken, L. R. (2001b). *Dying, death, and bereavement* (4th ed.). Mahwah, NJ: Lawrence Erlbaum.

Ajzen, I. (1988). *Attitudes, personality, and behavior.* Chicago: Dorsey.

Ajzen, I. (1991). The theory of planned behavior. *Organizational Behavior and Human Decision Processes, 50*, 179-211.

Ajzen, I., & Fishbein, M. (1977). Attitude-behavior relations: A theoretical analysis and review of empirical research. *Psychological Bulletin, 84*, 888-918.

Al-Khaldi, M. A., & Al-Jabri, I. M. (1998). The relationship of attitudes to computer utilization: New evidence from a developing nation. *Computers in Human Behavior, 14*, 23-42.

Allport, G. W. (1935). Attitudes. In C. Murchison (Ed.), *Handbook of social psychology* (pp. 798-1124). Worcester, MA: Clark University Press.

Allport, G. W. (1944). *The ABC's of scapegoating.* Chicago: Central Y.M.C.A. College.

Allport, G. W. (1954). *The nature of prejudice.* Cambridge, MA: Addison-Wesley.

Allport, G. W., & Vernon, P. E. (1931). A test for personal values. *Journal of Abnormal & Social Psychology, 26*, 231-248.

Alwin, D. F., Cohen, R. L., & Newcomb, T. M. (1991). *Political attitudes over the life span: The Bennington women after fifty years.* Madison: University of Wisconsin Press.

Alwin, D. F., & Krosnick, J. A. (1991). The reliability of survey attitude measurement. *Sociological Methods & Research, 20*, 139-181.

Alwitt, L. F., & Mitchell, A. A. (1985). Concluding remarks. In L. F. Alwitt & A. A. Mitchell (Eds.), *Psychological processes and advertising effects: Theory, research, and application* (pp. 273-293). Mahwah, NJ: Lawrence Erlbaum.

Amato, P. R., & Booth, A. (1991). The consequences of divorce for attitudes toward divorce and gender roles. *Journal of Family Issues, 12*, 306-322.

Amato, P. R., & Rogers, S. J. (1999). Do attitudes toward divorce affect marital quality? *Journal of Family Issues, 29*, 69-86.

Anderson, K. B., Cooper, H., & Okamura, L. (1997). Individual differences and attitudes toward rape: A meta-analytic review. *Personality and Social Psychology Bulletin, 23*, 295-315.

Andrich, D. (1978a). A binomial latent trait model for the study of Likert-style attitude questionnaires. *British Journal of Mathematical & Statistical Psychology, 31*, 84-98.

Andrich, D. (1978b). A rating formulation for ordered response categories. *Psychometrika, 43*, 561-573.

Andrich, D. (1978c). Scaling attitude items constructed and scored in the Likert tradition. *Educational and Psychological Measurement, 38*, 665-680.

Anisfield, M., Munoz, S. R., & Lambert, W. E. (1963). The structure and dynamics of the ethnic attitudes of Jewish adolescents. *Journal of Abnormal & Social Psychology, 66*, 31-36.

The annual Gallup poll of the public's attitudes toward the public schools. (Various years). *Phi Delta Kappan.*

Antonek, R. F., & Livneh, H. (1988). *The measurement of attitudes toward people with disabilities: Methods, psychometrics and scales.* Springfield, IL: Charles C Thomas.

Aries, P. (1981). *The hour of our death* (H. Weaver, Trans.). New York: Knopf.

Aronfreed, J. (1964). The origin of self-criticism. *Psychological Review, 71*, 193-218.

Aronson, E., Blaney, N., Stephan, C., Sikes, J., & Snapp, M. (1978). *The jig-saw classroom.* London: Sage.

Arthur, W., Jr., & Graziano, W. G. (1996). The five-factor model, conscientiousness, and driving accident involvement. *Journal of Personality, 64*, 593-618.

Arvey, R. D., Bouchard, T. J., Segal, N. L., & Abraham, L. M. (1989). Job satisfaction: Environmental and genetic components. *Journal of Applied Psychology, 74*, 187-192.

Arvey, R. D., Carter, G. W., & Buerkley, D. K. (1991). Job satisfaction: Dispositional and situational influences. *International Review of Industrial and Organizational Psychology, 6*, 359-383.

Ashmore, R. D., Del Boca, F. K., & Bilder, S. M. (1995). Gender Attitude Inventory. *Sex Roles, 32*, 753-785.

Assum, T. (1997). Attitudes and road accident risk. *Accident Analysis & Prevention, 29*, 153-159.

Atchley, R. C. (1987). *Aging: Continuity and change* (2nd ed.). Belmont, CA: Wadsworth.

Atchley, R. C. (1989). A continuity theory of normal aging. *The Gerontologist, 29*, 183-190.

Atchley, R. C. (1999). *Continuity and adaptation in aging.* Baltimore: Johns Hopkins University Press.

Attitude. (1997). In *The new encyclopedia Britannica* (Vol. 1, pp. 687-688). Chicago: Encyclopedia Britannica.

Back, K. W. (1971). Metaphors as a test of personal philosophy of aging. *Sociological Forces, 5*, 1-8.

Baldi, R. A. (1997). Training older adults to use the computer: Issues related to the workplace, attitudes, and training. *Educational Gerontology, 23*, 453-465.

Bammell, L. L. B., & Bammell, G. (1985). Leisure and recreation. In J. E. Birren & E. W. Schaie (Eds.), *Handbook of the psychology of aging* (pp. 848-863). New York: Van Nostrand Reinhold.

Bandura, A. (1969). *Principles of behavior modification.* New York: Holt, Rinehart & Winston.

Bandura, A. (1977). *Social learning theory.* Englewood Cliffs, NJ: Prentice Hall.

Bandura, A., & McDonald, F. J. (1963). Influence of social reinforcement and the behavior of models in shaping children's moral judgments. *Journal of Abnormal & Social Psychology, 67*, 274-281.

Barker, D. C., & Carman, C. J. (2000). The spirit of capitalism? Religious doctrine, values, and economic attitude constructs. *Political Behavior, 22,* 1-27.

Baron, R. A., & Byrne, D. (2000). *Social psychology* (9th ed.). Boston: Allyn & Bacon.

Barone, M. J., Miniard, P. W., & Romeo, J. B. (2000). The influence of positive mood on brand extension evaluations. *Journal of Consumer Research, 26,* 386-400.

Barzun, J. (2000). *From dawn to decadence: 1500 to the present.* New York: HarperCollins.

Bass, A. R., & Rosen, H. (1969). Some potential moderator variables in attitude research. *Educational and Psychological Measurement, 29,* 331-348.

Bassili, J. N., & Reil, J. (1981). On the dominance of the old-age stereotype. *Journal of Gerontology, 36,* 682-688.

Bates, A. S., Fitzgerald, J. F., & Wolinsky, F. D. (1994). The Parent Health Belief Scales: Replication in an urban clinic population. *Medical Care, 32,* 958-964.

Batson, C. D. (1998). Altruism and prosocial behavior. In D. T. Gilbert, S. T. Fiske, & G. Lindzey (Eds.), *The handbook of social psychology* (4th ed., Vol. 2, pp. 282-316). New York: McGraw-Hill/Oxford.

Baum, S. (2000). Drink driving as a social problem: Comparing the attitudes and knowledge of drink driving offenders and the general community. *Accident Analysis & Prevention, 32,* 689-694.

Bearden, W. O., & Netemeyer, R. G. (1999). *Handbook of marketing scales: Multi-item measures for marketing and consumer behavior research* (2nd ed.). Thousand Oaks, CA: Sage.

Bearden, W. O., Netemeyer, R. G., & Mobley, M. F. (1993). *Handbook of marketing scales: Multi-item measures for marketing and consumer behavior research.* Newbury Park, CA: Sage.

Beaton, A. E., Martin, M. O., Mullis, I. V. S., Gonzalez, E. J., Smith, T. A., & Kelly, D. L. (1997). *Mathematics achievement in the middle school years: IEA's Third International Mathematics and Science Study.* Chestnut Hill, MA: Boston College.

Beattie, J. R., Anderson, R. J., & Antonak, R. F. (1997). Modifying attitudes of prospective educators toward students with disabilities and their integration into regular classrooms. *Journal of Psychology, 131,* 245-259.

Bell, J. (1992). In search of a discourse on aging: The elderly on television. *The Gerontologist, 32,* 305-311.

Bem, D. J. (1972). Self-perception theory. In L. Berkowitz (Ed.), *Advances in experimental social psychology* (Vol. 6, pp. 1-62). New York: Academic Press.

Bem, S. L. (1974). The measurement of psychological androgyny. *Journal of Consulting and Clinical Psychology, 42,* 165-172.

Bendyna, M. E., Finucane, T., Kirby, L., O'Donnell, J. P., & Wilcox, C. (1996). Gender differences in public attitudes toward the Gulf War: A test of competing hypotheses. *Social Science Journal, 33,* 1-22.

Bengtson, V. L., Cuellar, J. B., & Ragan, P. K. (1977). Stratum contrasts and similarities in attitudes toward death. *Journal of Gerontology, 32,* 76-88.

Ben-Jacob, M. G. (1986). A workshop for students who are math deficient or math anxious. *College Student Journal, 20,* 194-201.

Benson, P. L., & Vincent, S. (1980). Development and validation of the Sexist Attitudes Toward Women Scale (SATWS). *Psychology of Women Quarterly, 5,* 276-291.

Berk, R. A., & Nanda, J. P. (1998). Effects of jocular instructional methods on attitudes, anxiety, and achievement in statistics courses. *Humor: International Journal of Humor Research, 11*, 383-409.

Bernal, D., Snyder, D., & McDaniel, M. (1998). The age and job satisfaction relationship: Does its shape and strength still evade us? *Journals of Gerontology: Series B. Psychological Sciences & Social Sciences, 53B*(5), 287-293.

Bianco, E. (1997, February 18). More Americans hold down 2 jobs to keep cash flow up. *Los Angeles Times*, p. A5.

Binion, R. (1976). *Hitler among the Germans*. New York: Elsevier.

Birdi, K., Warr, P., & Oswald, A. (1995). Age differences in three components of employee well-being. *Applied Psychology: An International Review, 44*, 345-373.

Birtwistle, G. E., & Brodie, D. A. (1991). Children's attitudes towards activity and perceptions of physical education. *Health Education Research, 6*, 465-478.

Black, L. E., & Sprenkle, D. H. (1991). Gender differences in college students' attitudes toward divorce and their willingness to marry. *Journal of Divorce & Remarriage, 14*(3-4), 47-60.

Bogardus, E. S. (1925). Measuring social distances. *Journal of Applied Sociology, 9*, 299-308.

Bogardus, E. S. (1928). *Immigration and race attitudes*. Boston: D. C. Heath.

Bornstein, R. F. (1989). Subliminal techniques as propaganda tools: Review and critique. *Journal of Mind & Behavior, 10*, 231-262.

Bouchard, T. J., Jr. (1994). Genes, environment, and personality, *Science, 264*, 1700-1701.

Bouchard, T. J., Jr., Lykken, D. T., McGue, M., Segal, N. L., & Tellegen, A. (1990). Sources of human psychological differences: The Minnesota Study of Twins Reared Apart. *Science, 250*, 223-228.

Bourne, L. E., Jr., & Ekstrand, B. R. (1979). *Psychology: Its principles and meanings*. New York: Holt, Rinehart & Winston.

Brady, E. C., Chrisler, J. C., Hosdale, D. C., Osowiecki, D. M., & Veal, T. A. (1991). Date rape: Expectations, avoidance strategies, and attitudes toward victims. *Journal of Social Psychology, 131*, 427-429.

Brannon, L., & Feist, J. (1997). *Health psychology: An introduction to behavior and health* (3rd ed.). Pacific Grove, CA: Brooks/Cole.

Brewer, M. B. (2000). Reducing prejudice through cross-categorization: Effects of multiple social identities. In S. Oskamp (Ed.), *Reducing prejudice and discrimination* (pp. 165-183). Mahwah, NJ: Lawrence Erlbaum.

Brewer, M. B., & Miller, N. (1984). Beyond the contact hypothesis: Theoretical perspectives on desegregation. In N. Miller & M. B. Brewer (Eds.), *Groups in contact: The psychology of desegregation* (pp. 281-302). New York: Academic Press.

Brewer, M. B., & Miller, N. (1988). Contact and cooperation: When do they work? In P. A. Katz & D. A. Taylor (Eds.), *Eliminating racism: Profiles in controversy* (pp. 315-326). New York: Plenum.

Briere, J. (1987). Attitudes toward wife abuse. *Journal of Research in Personality, 21*, 61-69.

Brigham, J. C. (1974). Views of Black and White children concerning the distribution of personality characteristics. *Journal of Personality, 42*, 145-158.

Britt, T. W., Boniecki, K. A., Vescio, T. K., Biernat, M., & Brown, L. M. (1996). Inter-group anxiety: A person × situation approach. *Personality and Social Psychology Bulletin, 22,* 1177-1188.

Brodie, F. M. (1983). *Richard Nixon: The shaping of his character.* Cambridge, MA: Harvard University Press.

Brosnan, M., & Lee, W. (1998). A cross-cultural comparison of gender differences in computer attitudes and anxieties: The United Kingdom and Hong Kong. *Computers in Human Behavior, 14,* 559-577.

Brown, R. (1986). *Social psychology* (2nd ed.). New York: Free Press.

Brown v. Board of Education of Topeka, 347 U.S. 483 (1954).

Bruner, G. C., II, & Hensel, P. J. (1996). *Marketing scales handbook: A compilation of multi-item measures.* Chicago: American Marketing Association.

Bruvold, W. H. (1975). Judgmental bias in the rating of attitude statements. *Educational and Psychological Measurement, 35,* 605-611.

Bureau of Justice Statistics. (2001, January). *Criminal victimization in the United States, 1999.* Washington, DC: Author.

Bureau of Labor Statistics. (2001, January). Employment situation summary. *The Employment Situation News Release.* Washington, DC: Author. Retrieved from www.bls.gov/news.release/empsit.nr0.htm

Burke, R. J. (1996). Sources of job satisfaction among employees of a professional services firm. *Psychological Reports, 78,* 1231-1234.

Burton, R. V. (1963). Generality of honesty reconsidered. *Psychological Review, 70,* 481-499.

Buss, A. H., & Plomin, R. (1984). *Temperament: Early developing personality traits.* Mahwah, NJ: Lawrence Erlbaum.

Butler, R. N. (1974). Successful aging. *Mental Health, 58*(3), 7-12.

Cacioppo, J. T., Petty, R. E., Losch, M. E., & Crites, S. L. (1994). Psychophysiological approaches to attitudes: Detecting affective dispositions when people won't say, can't say, or don't even know. In S. Shavitt & T. C. Brock (Eds.), *Persuasion: Psychological insights and perspectives* (pp. 43-69). Needham Heights, MA: Allyn & Bacon.

Cacioppo, J. T., Petty, R. E., Losch, M. E., & Kim, H. S. (1986). Electromyographic activity over facial muscle regions can differentiate the valence and intensity of affective reactions. *Journal of Personality and Social Psychology, 50,* 260-268.

Caddell, D. P., & Newton, R. R. (1995). Euthanasia: American attitudes toward the physician's role. *Social Science & Medicine, 40,* 1671-1681.

Caldwell, R. G. (2000). Capital punishment. In *Encyclopedia Americana* (Vol. 5, pp. 596-599). Danbury, CT: Grolier.

Callahan, T. J. (1994). Managers' beliefs about and attitudes toward the Americans With Disabilities Act of 1990. *Applied H.R.M. Research, 5*(1), 28-43.

Campione, W. A. (1988). Predicting participation in retirement preparation programs. *Journal of Gerontology, 43,* 591-595.

Carlson, B. E. (1991). Outcomes of physical abuse and observation of marital violence among adolescents in placement. *Journal of Interpersonal Violence, 6,* 526-534.

Carlson, M., Charlin, V., & Miller, N. (1988). Positive mood and helping behavior: A test of six hypotheses. *Journal of Personality and Social Psychology, 55,* 211-229.

Carver, T. N. (2000). Value. In *Encyclopedia Americana* (Vol. 27, p. 867). Danbury, CT: Grolier.

Cassidy, T. (1996). All work and no play: A focus on leisure time as a means for promoting health. *Counseling Psychology Quarterly, 9*, 77-90.

Castro, J. G., & Jordan, J. E. (1977). Facet theory attitude research. *Educational Researcher, 6*, 7-11.

Cattell, R. B. (1965). *The scientific analysis of personality.* New York: Penguin.

Chaiken, S., Liberman, A., & Eagly, A. H. (1989). Heuristic and systematic processing within and beyond persuasion context. In J. S. Uleman & J. A. Bargh (Eds.), *Unintended thought* (pp. 212-222). New York: Guilford.

Ching, C. L., & Burke, S. (1999). An assessment of college students' attitudes and empathy toward rape. *College Student Journal, 33*, 573-583.

Christie, R., & Garcia, J. (1951). Subcultural variation in authoritarian personality. *Journal of Abnormal & Social Psychology, 46*, 457-469.

Christie, R., & Jahoda, M. (Eds.). (1954). *Studies in the scope and method of "The authoritarian personality."* New York: Free Press.

Chusmir, L. H., & Koberg, C. S. (1990). Ethnic differences in the relationship between job satisfaction and sex-role conflict among Hispanic and non-Hispanic White individuals. *Psychological Reports, 66*, 567-578.

Clark, A., Oswald, A., & Warr, P. (1996). Is job satisfaction U-shaped in age? *Journal of Occupational and Organizational Psychology, 69*, 57-81.

Clydesdale, T. T. (1999). Toward understanding the role of Bible beliefs and higher education in American attitudes toward eradicating poverty, 1964-1996. *Journal for the Scientific Study of Religion, 38*, 103-118.

Cochran, J. K., & Beeghley, L. (1991). The influence of religion on attitudes toward nonmarital sexuality: A preliminary assessment of reference group theory. *Journal for the Scientific Study of Religion, 30*, 45-62.

Cognitive dissonance. (2001). In B. R. Strickland (Ed.), *The Gale encyclopedia of psychology* (2nd ed., pp. 132-133). Detroit, MI: Gale.

Collins, C., Stemmel, M., King, S., & Gwen, C. C. (1991). Community Service Attitudes Inventory. *The Gerontologist, 31*, 756-761.

Collins, J. G., & LeClere, F. B. (1997). *Health and selected socioeconomic characteristics of the family: United States, 1988-90.* (PHS) 97-1523. GPO stock number 017-022-01361-4. Washington, DC: National Center for Health Statistics.

Collis, B. A. (1987). Sex differences in the association between secondary school students' attitudes toward mathematics and toward computers. *Journal for Research in Mathematics Education, 18*, 394-402.

Comber, C., Colley, A., Hargreaves, D. J., & Dorn, L. (1997). The effects of age, gender and computer experience upon computer attitudes. *Educational Research, 39*, 123-133.

Conte, H. R., Weiner, M. B., & Plutchik, R. (1982). Measuring death anxiety: Conceptual, psychometric, and factor-analytic aspects. *Journal of Personality and Social Psychology, 43*, 775-785.

Converse, P. E., Dotson, J. D., Hoag, W. J., & McGee, W. H., III. (1980). *American social attitudes data sourcebook, 1947-78.* Cambridge, MA: Harvard University Press.

Cooney, T. M., & Uhlenberg, P. (1990). The role of divorce in men's relations with their adult children after mid-life. *Journal of Marriage and the Family, 53*, 677-688.

Cooper, J., & Fazio, R. H. (1984). A new look at dissonance theory. In L. Berkowitz (Ed.), *Advances in experimental social psychology* (Vol. 17, pp. 229-266). New York: Academic Press.

Cooper, J., Zanna, M. P., & Taves, P. A. (1978). Arousal as a necessary condition for attitude change following induced compliance. *Journal of Personality and Social Psychology, 36*, 1101-1106.

Cooper, J. B., & Pollock, D. (1959). The identification of prejudicial attitudes by the galvanic skin response. *Journal of Social Psychology, 50*, 241-245.

Corey, S. M. (1937). Professed attitudes and actual behavior. *Journal of Educational Psychology, 28*, 271-280.

Corr, C. A. (1993). Coping with dying: Lessons that we should and should not learn from the work of Elisabeth Kuebler-Ross. *Death Studies, 17*, 69-83.

Corston, R., & Colman, A. M. (1996). Gender and social facilitation effects on computer competence and attitudes toward computers. *Journal of Educational Computing Research, 14*, 171-183.

Covey, H. C. (1988). Historical terminology used to represent older people. *The Gerontologist, 28*, 291-297.

Crandall, J. E. (1980). Adler's concept of social interest: Theory, measurement, and applications for adjustment. *Journal of Personality and Social Psychology, 39*, 481-495.

Crane, M. (1996). The situation of older homeless people. *Reviews of Clinical Gerontology, 6*, 389-398.

Crano, W. D. (1995). Attitude strength and vested interest. In R. E. Petty & J. A. Krosnick (Eds.), *Attitude strength: Antecedents and consequences* (Vol. 4, pp. 131-157). Mahwah, NJ: Lawrence Erlbaum.

Crano, W. D. (1997). Vested interest, symbolic politics, and attitude-behavior consistency. *Journal of Personality and Social Psychology, 72*, 485-491.

Crelia, R. A., & Tesser, A. (1996). Attitude heritability and attitude reinforcement: A replication. *Personality and Individual Differences, 21*, 803-808.

Crombie, G., & Armstrong, P. I. (1999). Effects of classroom gender composition on adolescents' computer-related attitudes and future intentions. *Journal of Educational Computing Research, 20*, 317-327.

Cruzan et al. v. Director, Missouri Department of Health et al., 497 U.S. 261 (1990).

Csikai, E. L. (1999). The role of values and experience in determining social workers' attitudes toward euthanasia and assisted suicide. *Social Work in Health Care, 30*(1), 75-95.

Cutler, S. J., & Hendricks, J. (1990). Leisure and time use across the life course. In R. H. Binstock & L. K. George (Eds.), *Handbook of aging and the social sciences* (3rd ed., pp. 169-185). New York: Academic Press.

Czaja, S. J., & Sharit, J. (1998). Age differences in attitudes toward computers. *Journals of Gerontology: Series B. Psychological Sciences & Social Sciences, 53B*, 329-340.

Dahlburg, J.-T. (2000, November 29). Dutch take step to make assisted suicide legal. *Los Angeles Times*, p. A4.

Darrow, A.-A., & Johnson, C. M. (1994). Junior and senior high school music students' attitudes toward individuals with a disability. *Journal of Music Therapy, 31,* 266-279.

Davidson, M. G. (2000). Religion and spirituality. In R. M. Perez, K. A. DeBord, & K. J. Bieschke (Eds.), *Handbook of counseling and psychotherapy with lesbian, gay, and bisexual clients* (pp. 409-433). Washington, DC: American Psychological Association.

Davis, J. A., & Smith, T. W. (1994). *General Social Surveys, 1972-1994.* Chicago: National Opinion Research Center.

Davis, M. H., Luce, C., & Kraus, L. A. (1994). The heritability of characteristics associated with dispositional empathy. *Journal of Personality, 62,* 369-391.

Day, J. C., & Gaither, A. L. (2000, August). *Voting and registration in the election of November 1998. Current Population Reports,* P20-523RV. Washington, DC: U.S. Census Bureau.

Derogatis, L., Abeloff, M., & Melisaratos, N. (1979). Psychological coping mechanisms and survival time in metastatic breast cancer. *Journal of the American Medical Association, 112,* 45-56.

DeSantis, J. P., & Youniss, J. (1991). Family contributions to adolescents' attitudes toward new technology. *Journal of Adolescent Research, 6,* 410-422.

Deschamps, J.-C., & Brown, R. J. (1983). Superordinate goals and intergroup conflict. *British Journal of Social Psychology, 22,* 189-195.

Devine, P. G. (1989). Stereotypes and prejudice: Their automatic and controlled components. *Journal of Personality and Social Psychology, 56,* 5-18.

Devine, P. G., Evett, S. R., & Vasquez-Suson, K. A. (1995). Exploring the interpersonal dynamics of intergroup contact. In R. Sorrentino & E. T. Higgins (Eds.), *Handbook of motivation and cognition: The interpersonal context* (Vol. 3). New York: Guilford.

Diamond, K., le Furgy, W., & Blass, S. (1993). Attitudes of preschool children toward their peers with disabilities: A year-long investigation in integrated classrooms. *Journal of Genetic Psychology, 154,* 215-221.

Doering, M., Rhodes, S. R., & Schuster, M. (1983). *The aging worker: Research and recommendations.* Beverly Hills, CA: Sage.

Doise, W. (1978). *Groups and individuals: Explanations in social psychology.* Cambridge, UK: Cambridge University Press.

Doka, K. J. (1995). Coping with life-threatening illness: A task model. *Omega, 32,* 111-122.

Domino, G., MacGregor, J. C., & Hannah, M. T. (1988-1989). Collegiate attitudes toward suicide: New Zealand and United States. *Omega, 19,* 351-364.

D'Onofrio, B. M., Eaves, L. J., Murrelle, L., Maes, H. H., & Spilka, B. (1999). Understanding biological and social influences on religious affiliation, attitudes and behaviors: A behavior genetic perspective. *Journal of Personality, 67,* 953-984.

Doyle, A., Beaudet, J., & Aboud, F. (1988). Developmental patterns in the flexibility of children's ethnic attitudes. *Journal of Cross-Cultural Psychology, 19,* 3-18.

Duckitt, J., & Farre, B. (1994). Right-wing authoritarianism and political intolerance among Whites in the future majority-rule South Africa. *Journal of Social Psychology, 134,* 735-741.

Dunton, B. C., & Fazio, R. H. (1997). An individual difference measure of motivation to control prejudiced reactions. *Personality and Social Psychology Bulletin, 23,* 316-326.

Durlak, J. A., Horn, W., & Kass, R. A. (1990). A self-administering assessment of personal meanings of death: Report on the revised Twenty Statements Test. *Omega, 21,* 301-309.

Duryea, E. J. (1983). Utilizing tenets of inoculation theory to develop and evaluate a preventive alcohol education intervention. *Journal of School Health, 53,* 250-256.

Eagly, A. H. (2000). The processing of nested persuasive messages. *Psychological Inquiry, 10,* 123-127.

Eagly, A. H., & Chaiken, S. L. (Eds.). (1993). *The psychology of attitudes.* Fort Worth, TX: Harcourt Brace Jovanovich.

Eagly, A. H., & Chaiken, S. L. (1998). Attitude structure and function. In D. T. Gilbert, S. T. Fiske, & G. Lindzey (Eds.), *The handbook of social psychology* (4th ed., Vol. 1, pp. 269-322). New York: McGraw-Hill/Oxford.

Ellison v. Brady, 924 F.2d 872 (1991).

Emanuel, E. J., Daniels, E. R., Fairclough, D. L., & Claridge, B. R. (1998). The practice of euthanasia and physician assisted suicide in the United States. *Journal of the American Medical Association, 280,* 507-513.

Emler, N., Renwick, S., & Malone, B. (1983). The relationship between moral reasoning and political orientation. *Journal of Personality and Social Psychology, 45,* 1073-1080.

Epstein, S. (1979). The stability of behavior: I. On predicting most of the people much of the time. *Journal of Personality and Social Psychology, 37,* 1097-1126.

Erikson, E. H. (1969). *Gandhi's truth: On the origins of militant nonviolence.* New York: Norton.

Etsey, Y. K., & Snetzler, S. (1998, April). *A meta-analysis of gender differences in student attitudes toward mathematics.* Paper presented at the annual meeting of the American Educational Research Association, San Diego, CA. (ERIC Document Reproduction Service No. ED 435 543)

Faulkner, G. E. J., & Reeves, C. (2000). Primary school student teachers' physical self-perceptions and attitudes toward teaching physical education. *Journal of Teaching in Physical Education, 19,* 311-324.

Fazio, R. H. (1989). On the power and functionality of attitudes: The role of attitude accessibility. In A. R. Pratkanis, S. J. Breckler, & A. G. Greenwald (Eds.), *Attitude structure and function* (pp. 153-179). Mahwah, NJ: Lawrence Erlbaum.

Fazio, R. H. (1990). Multiple processes by which attitudes guide behavior: The MODE model as an integrative framework. In M. P. Zanna (Ed.), *Advances in experimental social psychology* (Vol. 23, pp. 75-109). New York: Academic Press.

Fazio, R. H., Chen, J., McDonel, E. C., & Sherman, S. J. (1982). Attitude accessibility, attitude-behavior consistency, and the strength of the object-evaluation association. *Journal of Experimental Social Psychology, 18,* 339-357.

Fazio, R. H., Jackson, J. R., Dunton, B. C., & Williams, C. J. (1995). Variability in automatic activation as an unobtrusive measure of racial attitudes: A bona fide pipeline? *Journal of Personality and Social Psychology, 69,* 1013-1027.

Fazio, R. H., & Roskos-Ewoldsen, D. R. (1994). Acting as we feel: When and how attitudes guide behavior. In S. Shavitt & T. C. Brock (Eds.), *Persuasion* (pp. 71-93). Boston: Allyn & Bacon.

Fazio, R. H., & Zanna, M. P. (1978). On the predictive validity of attitudes: The roles of direct experience and confidence. *Journal of Personality, 46*, 228-243.

Fazio, R. H., & Zanna, M. P. (1981). Direct experience and attitude-behavior consistency. In L. Berkowitz (Ed.), *Advances in experimental social psychology* (Vol. 14, pp. 161-202). San Diego, CA: Academic Press.

Fein, S., Hilton, J. L., & Miller, D. T. (1990). Suspicion of ulterior motivation and the correspondence bias. *Journal of Personality and Social Psychology, 58*, 753-764.

Festinger, L. (1957). *A theory of cognitive dissonance.* Stanford, CA: Stanford University Press.

Festinger, L. (1964). *Conflict, decision, and dissonance.* Stanford, CA: Stanford University Press.

Finegan, J. E., & Seligman, C. (1993). Values modification through self-confrontation. *Canadian Journal of Behavioural Science, 25*, 421-445.

Fiorina, M. P. (1981). *Retrospective voting in American national elections.* New Haven, CT: Yale University Press.

Fischer, G. J., & Chen, J. (1994). The Attitudes Toward Forcible Date Rape (FDR) scale: Development of a measurement model. *Journal of Psychopathology & Behavioral Assessment, 16*, 13-51.

Fishbein, M., & Ajzen, I. (1975). *Belief, attitude, intention, and behavior: An introduction to theory and research.* Reading, MA: Addison-Wesley.

Fishbein, M., & Middlestadt, S. E. (1997). A striking lack of evidence for nonbelief-based attitude formation and change: A response to five commentaries. *Journal of Consumer Psychology, 6*, 107-115.

Fitzgerald, L. F., & Ormerod, A. J. (1991). Perceptions of sexual harassment: The influence of gender and academic context. *Psychology of Women Quarterly, 15*, 281-294.

Flaskerud, J. H., & Nyamathi, A. M. (1989). AIDS Knowledge, Attitudes, and Practice Scale. *Research in Nursing and Health, 12*, 339-346.

Fletcher, W. L., & Hansson, R. O. (1991). Assessing the social components of retirement anxiety. *Psychology and Aging, 6*, 76-85.

Fotinatos-Ventouratos, R., & Cooper, C. L. (1998). Social class differences and occupation stress. *International Journal of Stress Management, 5*, 211-222.

Fox, R. (1992). Prejudice and the unfinished mind: A new look at an old failing. *Psychological Inquiry, 3*, 137-152.

Fraboni, M., Saltstone, R., & Hughes, S. (1990). The Fraboni Scale of Ageism (FSA): An attempt at a more precise measure of ageism. *Canadian Journal on Aging, 9*, 56-66.

Francis, L. J., & Greer, J. E. (1999). Attitude toward science among secondary school pupils in Northern Ireland: Relationship with sex, age and religion. *Research in Science & Technological Education, 17*, 67-74.

Francis, L. J., & Wilcox, C. (1996). Religion and gender orientation. *Personality and Individual Differences, 20*, 119-121.

Freud, S. (1930). *Civilization and its discontents* (J. Riviere, Trans.). London: Hogarth.

Freud, S., & Bullitt, W. C. (1967). *Thomas Woodrow Wilson.* Boston: Houghton Mifflin.

Friedman, H. S. (Ed.). (1990). *Personality and disease.* New York: John Wiley.

Friedman, H. S. (1992). Understanding hostility, coping, and health. In H. S. Friedman (Ed.), *Hostility, coping and health* (pp. 3-9). Washington, DC: American Psychological Association.

Friedman, H. S., & Booth-Kewley, S. (1987). Personality, Type A behavior, and coronary heart disease: The role of emotional expression. *Journal of Personality and Social Psychology, 53,* 783-792.

Froelich, K. S., & Kotte, J. L. (1991). Measuring individual beliefs about organizational ethics. *Educational and Psychological Measurement, 51,* 377-383.

Funk, J. B., Elliott, R., Urman, M. L., Flores, G. T., & Mock, R. M. (1999). The Attitudes Towards Violence Scale: A measure for adolescents. *Journal of Interpersonal Violence, 14,* 1123-1136.

Furman v. Georgia, 408 U.S. 238 (1972).

Gaertner, S., & Bickman, L. (1971). A nonreactive indicator of racial discrimination: The wrong number technique. *Journal of Personality and Social Psychology, 20,* 218-222.

Gaertner, S. L., Dovidio, J. F., & Bachman, B. A. (1996). Revisiting the contact hypothesis: The induction of a common ingroup identity. *International Journal of Intercultural Relations, 20,* 271-290.

Gaertner, S. L., Dovidio, J. F., Banker, B. S., Houlette, M., Johnson, K. M., & McGlynn, E. A. (2000). Reducing intergroup conflict: From superordinate goals to decategorization, recategorization, and mutual differentiation. *Group Dynamics, 4,* 98-114.

Gaertner, S. L., Rust, M. C., Dovidio, J. F., Bachman, B. A., & Anastasio, P. A. (1994). The contact hypothesis: The role of a common ingroup identity on reducing intergroup bias. *Small Group Research, 25,* 224-249.

Gagné, R. M., & Briggs, L. J. (1974). *Principles of instructional design.* New York: Holt, Rinehart & Winston.

Gallup, G. (1936). Measuring public opinion. *Vital Speeches of the Day, 2,* 370-372.

Gallup, G., Jr. (1997). *The Gallup poll: Public opinion 1996.* Wilmington, DE: Scholarly Resources.

Gallup, G., Jr. (2000). *The Gallup poll: Public opinion 1999.* Wilmington, DE: Scholarly Resources.

Gardner, P. L. (1975). Attitude measurement: A critique of some recent research. *Educational Research, 17,* 101-109.

Garske, G. G. (1996). The relationship of self-esteem to attitudes of personal attendants toward persons with disabilities. *Journal of Applied Rehabilitation Counseling, 27*(1), 3-6.

Gault, B. A., & Sabini, J. (2000). The roles of empathy, anger, and gender in predicting attitudes toward punitive, reparative, and preventative public policies. *Cognition & Emotion, 14,* 495-520.

Geary, D. C. (1993). Mathematical disabilities: Cognitive, neuropsychological, and genetic components. *Psychological Bulletin, 114,* 345-362.

George, J. M., & Jones, G. R. (1997). Experiencing work: Values, attitudes, and moods. *Human Relations, 50,* 393-415.

George, R., & Kaplan, D. (1998). A structural model of parent and teacher influences on science attitudes of eighth graders: Evidence from NELS:88. *Science Education, 82,* 93-109.

Gesser, G., Wong, P. T. P., & Reker, G. T. (1987-1988). Death attitudes across the life-span: The development and validation of the Death Attitude Profile (DAP). *Omega, 18,* 113-128.

Gibbons, F. X., Gerrard, M., Blanton, H., & Russell, D. W. (1998). Reasoned action and social reaction: Willingness and intention as independent predictors of health risk. *Journal of Personality and Social Psychology, 74,* 1164-1180.

Gibbons, F. X., Gerrard, M., & McCoy, S. B. (1995). Prototype perception predicts (lack of) pregnancy prevention. *Personality and Social Psychology Bulletin, 21,* 85-93.

Gilbert, D. T. (1989). Thinking lightly about others: Automatic components of the social inference process. In J. S. Uleman & J. A. Bargh (Eds.), *Unintended thought* (pp. 189-211). New York: Guilford.

Gilbert, F. W., & Warren, W. E. (1995). Psychographic constructs and demographic segments. *Psychology & Marketing, 12,* 223-237.

Gilchrest, E., Bannister, J., Ditton, J., & Farrall, S. (1998). Women and the "fear of crime": Challenging the accepted stereotype. *British Journal of Criminology, 38,* 283-298.

Gilligan, C. (1982). *In a different voice: Psychology theory and women's development.* Cambridge, MA: Harvard University Press.

Gilliland, J. C., & Templer, D. L. (1985-1986). Relationship of Death Anxiety Scale factors to subjective states. *Omega, 16,* 155-167.

Glad, B. (1980). *Jimmy Carter: In search of the great White House.* New York: Norton.

Glennon, F., & Joseph, S. (1993). Just world beliefs, self-esteem, and attitudes towards homosexuals with AIDS. *Psychological Reports, 72,* 584-586.

Glick, P., & Fiske, S. T. (1996). The Ambivalent Sexism Inventory: Differentiating hostile and benevolent sexism. *Journal of Personality and Social Psychology, 70,* 491-512.

Godfrey, S., Richman, C. L., & Withers, T. N. (2000). Reliability and validity of a new scale to measure prejudice: The GRISMS. *Current Psychology: Developmental, Learning, Personality, Social, 19,* 3-20.

Goh, S. (1993). The development and reliability of the Attitudes Toward AIDS Scale. *College Student Journal, 27,* 208-214.

Goh, D. S. (1994). Internal consistence and stability of the Attitudes Toward AIDS Scale—High School Version. *Psychological Reports, 74,* 329-330.

Gonzales, M. H., Davis, J. M., Loney, G. L., KuKens, C. K., & Junghans, C. M. (1983). Interactional approach to interpersonal attraction. *Journal of Personality and Social Psychology, 44,* 1192-1197.

Goodstadt, M. S., & Magid, S. (1977). When Thurstone and Likert agree: A confounding of methodologies. *Educational and Psychological Measurement, 37,* 811-818.

Graves, E. J., & Gillum, B. S. (1996). 1994 summary: National Hospital Discharge Survey. *Advance Data From Vital and Health Statistics,* No. 278. Hyattsville, MD: National Center for Health Statistics.

Greeley, A. (1993). Religion and attitudes toward the environment. *Journal for the Scientific Study of Religion, 32*, 19-28.

Greenberg, J. (1988). Equity and workplace status: A field experiment. *Journal of Applied Psychology, 73*, 606-613.

Greene, M. G., Hoffman, S., Charon, R., & Adelman, R. (1987). Psychosocial concerns in the medical encounter: A comparison of the interactions of doctors with their young and old patients. *The Gerontologist, 27*, 164-168.

Greenfield, S., Blanco, D. M., Elashoff, R. M., & Ganz, P. A. (1987). Patterns of care related to age of breast cancer patients. *Journal of the American Medical Association, 257*, 2766-2770.

Greenfield, T. A. (1996). Gender, ethnicity, science achievement and attitudes. *Journal of Research in Science Teaching, 33*, 901-933.

Greenwald, A. G. (1968). Cognitive learning, cognitive response to persuasion, and attitude change. In A. G. Greenwald, T. C. Brock, & T. M. Ostrom (Eds.), *Psychological foundations of attitudes* (pp. 147-170). San Diego, CA: Academic Press.

Greenwald, A. G., & Banaji, M. R. (1995). Implicit social cognition: Attitudes, self-esteem, and stereotypes. *Psychological Review, 102*, 4-27.

Greenwald, A. G., & Farnham, S. D. (2000). Using the Implicit Association Test to measure self-esteem and self-concept. *Journal of Personality and Social Psychology, 79*, 1022-1038.

Greenwald, A. G., McGhee, D. E., & Schwartz, J. L. K. (1998). Measuring individual differences in implicit cognition: The Implicit Association Test. *Journal of Personality and Social Psychology, 74*, 1464-1480.

Greer, S. (1991). Psychological response to cancer and survival. *Psychological Medicine, 21*, 43-49.

Gregg v. Georgia, 428 U.S. 153 (1976).

Gregory, W. E. (1957). The orthodoxy of the authoritarian personality. *Journal of Social Psychology, 45*, 217-232.

Grice, J. W., & Harris, R. J. (1998). A comparison of regression and loading weights for the computation of factor scores. *Multivariate Behavioral Research, 33*, 221-247.

Griffeth, R. W., & Rogers, R. W. (1976). Effects of fear-arousing components of driver education on students' safety attitudes and simulator performance. *Journal of Educational Psychology, 68*, 501-506.

Griffeth, R. W., Vecchio, R. P., & Logan, J. W. (1989). Equity theory and interpersonal attraction. *Journal of Applied Psychology, 74*, 394-401.

Griffin, E., & Sparks, G. G. (1990). Friends forever: A longitudinal exploration of intimacy in same-sex friends and platonic pairs. *Journal of Social & Personal Relationships, 7*, 29-46.

Guppy, A., & Rick, J. (1996). The influences of gender and grade on perceived work stress and job satisfaction in white collar employees. *Work & Stress, 10*, 154-164.

Guttman, L. (1944). A basis for scaling quantitative data. *American Sociological Review, 9*, 139-150.

Guttman, L. (1947). The Cornell technique for scale and intensity analysis. *Educational and Psychological Measurement, 7*, 247-280.

Guttman, L. (1968). A general nonmetric technique for finding the smallest coordinate space for a configuration of points. *Psychometrika, 33*, 469-506.

Guttman, L. (1982). Facet theory, smallest space analysis, and factor analysis. *Perceptual & Motor Skills, 54,* 491-493.

Guzewicz, T. D., & Verdi, W. M. (1992). Public Attitudes Toward Homelessness Scale. *Journal of Social Distress and the Homeless, 1*(1), 67-79.

Hackman, J. R., & Oldham, G. R. (1976). Motivation through the design of work: Test of a theory. *Organizational Behavior and Human Performance, 16,* 250-279.

Haddock, G., Zanna, M. P., & Esses, V. M. (1993). Assessing the structure of prejudicial attitudes: The case of attitudes toward homosexuals. *Journal of Personality and Social Psychology, 65,* 1105-1118.

Hamburger, Y. (1994). The contact hypothesis reconsidered: Effects of the atypical outgroup member on the outgroup stereotype. *Basic and Applied Social Psychology, 15,* 339-358.

Hamersma, R. J., Paige, J., & Jordan, J. E. (1973). Construction of a Guttman facet designed cross-cultural attitude-behavior scale toward racial ethnic interaction. *Educational and Psychological Measurement, 33,* 565-576.

Hamilton, W. D. (1964). The genetical theory of social behavior (1 & 2). *Journal of Theoretical Biology, 7,* 1-16; 17-32.

Harris, L., & Associates. (1981). *Aging in the '80s: America in transition.* Washington, DC: National Council on Aging.

Harris Poll. (1998). *Large majority of people believe they will go to heaven: Only one in fifty thinks they will go to hell: Many Christians and non-Christians believe in astrology, ghosts, and reincarnation* (No. 41). New York: Louis Harris & Associates, Inc.

Harris, R. J. (2001). *Primer of multivariate statistics* (3rd ed.). Mahwah, NJ: Lawrence Erlbaum.

Hartman, S. E. (1999). Another view of the Paranormal Belief Scale. *Journal of Parapsychology, 63,* 131-141.

Hartmann, G. W. (1939). Value as the unifying concept in the social sciences. *Journal of Social Psychology, 10,* 563-575.

Hartshorne, H., & May, M. A. (1928). *Studies in the nature of character: Vol. 1. Studies in deceit.* New York: Macmillan.

Harvey, T. J., & Stables, A. (1986). Gender differences in attitudes to science for third year pupils: An argument for single-sex teaching groups in mixed schools. *Research in Science & Technological Education, 4,* 163-170.

Haskins, G. (1956). The capital lawes of New England. *Harvard Law School Bulletin,* pp. 7, 10.

Hatch, R. L., Burg, M. A., Naberhaus, D. S., & Hellmich, L. K. (1998). The Spiritual Involvement and Beliefs Scale: Development and testing of a new instrument. *Journal of Family Practice, 46,* 476-486.

Haug, M. (Ed.). (1981). *Elderly patients and their doctors.* New York: Springer.

Haugtvedt, C. P. (1997). Beyond fact or artifact: An assessment of Fishbein and Middlestadt's perspectives on attitude change processes. *Journal of Consumer Psychology, 6,* 99-106.

Hayslip, B., Jr., Beyerlein, M., & Nichols, J. A. (1997). Assessing anxiety about retirement: The case of academicians. *International Journal of Aging and Human Development, 44,* 15-36.

Heggen, C. H. (1996). Religious beliefs and abuse. In C. C. Kroeger & J. R. Beck (Eds.), *Women, abuse, and the Bible: How scripture can be used to hurt or to heal* (pp. 15-27). Grand Rapids, MI: Baker.

Heider, F. (1958). *The psychology of interpersonal relationships.* New York: John Wiley.

Hendricks, J., & Leedham, C. A. (1980). Creating psychological and societal perspectives in old age. In P. S. Fry (Ed.), *Psychological perspectives on helplessness and control in the elderly* (pp. 369-394). Amsterdam: Elsevier North-Holland.

Heppner, M. J., Good, G. E., Hillenbrand-Gunn, T. L., Hawkins, A. K., Hacquard, L. L., Nichols, R. K., DeBord, K. A., & Brock, K. J. (1995). Examining sex differences in altering attitudes about rape: A test of the elaboration likelihood model. *Journal of Counseling & Development, 73,* 640-647.

Herek, G. M. (1994). Assessing attitudes toward lesbians and gay men: A review of empirical research with the ATLG scale. In B. Greene & G. M. Herek (Eds.), *Lesbian and gay psychology: Theory, research, and clinical application* (pp. 206-228). Thousand Oaks, CA: Sage.

Hershberger, S. I., Lichtenstein, P., & Knox, S. S. (1994). Genetic and environmental influences on perceptions of organizational climate. *Journal of Applied Psychology, 79,* 24-33.

Hernandez, B., Keys, C., Balcazar, F., & Drum, C. (1998). Construction and validation of the Disability Rights Attitude Scale: Assessing attitudes toward the Americans With Disabilities Act (ADA). *Rehabilitation Psychology, 43,* 203-218.

Herzberg, F. (1966). *Work and the nature of man.* Cleveland, OH: World.

Hess, E. H. (1965). Attitude and pupil size. *Scientific American, 212,* 46-54.

Hewstone, M., & Brown, R. (1986). Contact is not enough: An intergroup perspective on the "contact hypothesis." In M. Hewstone & R. Brown (Eds.), *Contact and conflict in intergroup encounters* (pp. 1-44). Cambridge, MA: Basil Blackwell.

Holbrook, A. L., Bizer, G. Y., & Krosnick, J. A. (2000). Political behavior. In A. E. Kazdin (Ed.), *Encyclopedia of psychology* (Vol. 6, pp. 226-230). Oxford, UK: Oxford University Press.

Holloway, H. D., Hayslip, B., Murdock, M. E., Maloy, R., Servanty, H. L., Henard, K., Lopez, L., Lysaght, R., Moreno, G., Moroney, T., Smith, D., & White, S. (1994-1995). Measuring attitudes toward euthanasia. *Omega, 30,* 53-65.

Hoover, D. W. (1993). Community studies. In M. K. Clayton, E. J. Gorn, & P. W. Williams (Eds.), *Encyclopedia of American social history* (Vol. 1, pp. 1297-305). New York: Scribner's.

Hovland, C. I., & Janis, I. L. (Eds.). (1959). *Personality and persuasibility.* New Haven, CT: Yale University Press.

Hovland, C. I., Janis, I. L., & Kelley, H. H. (1953). *Communication and persuasion: Psychological studies of opinion change.* New Haven, CT: Yale University Press.

Hovland, C. I., & Rosenberg, W. J. (1960). *Attitude organization and change.* New Haven, CT: Yale University Press.

Hovland, C. I., & Sears, R. R. (1940). Minor studies in aggression: 6. Correlation of lynchings with economic indices. *Journal of Psychology, 9,* 301-310.

Howells, G. N., Flanagan, K. A., & Hagan, V. (1995). Does viewing a televised execution affect attitudes toward capital punishment? *Criminal Justice and Behavior, 22*, 411-424.

Howells, K., & Field, D. (1982). Fear of death and dying among medical students. *Social Science and Medicine, 16*, 1421-1424.

Hulin, C. L. (1991). Adaptation, persistence, and commitment in organizations. In M. D. Dunnette & L. M. Hough (Eds.), *Handbook of industrial and organizational psychology* (Vol. 2, pp. 445-505). Palo Alto, CA: Consulting Psychologists Press.

Hulin, C. L., Roznowski, M., & Hachiya, D. (1985). Alternative opportunities and withdrawal decisions: Empirical and theoretical discrepancies and an integration. *Psychological Bulletin, 97*, 233-250.

Hull, G., Hurd, T. L., & Margolis, D. N. (1993). Gender differences in students' attitudes towards the Persian Gulf War. *College Student Journal, 27*, 480-489.

Human Capital Initiative. (1993). *Vitality for life: Psychological research for productive aging*. Washington, DC: American Psychological Association.

Humphry, D. (1991). *Final exit: Self-deliverance and assisted suicide for the dying*. Eugene, OR: Hemlock Society.

Hunt, R. A. (1993). "A cross-cultural comparison of religious belief: Canadian and Spanish students' responses to the Hunt Scale": Response. *International Journal for the Psychology of Religion, 3*, 201-204.

Hunter, M. (2000). *The changing nature of work*. Washington, DC: American Association of Retired Persons. Retrieved November 1, 2001 from the World Wide Web: www.aarp.org/mmaturity/may_jun99/

Huth, M. J., & Wright, T. (Eds.). (1997). *International critical perspectives on homelessness*. Westport, CT: Praeger.

Information Plus. (1998). *Death & dying: Who decides?* Wylie, TX: Author.

Jackson, T. L., Brown, J. M., Davis, J., & Pitman, L. J. (1999). The Violence Attitudes Scale (Revised) (VAS-R). In L. VandeCreek & T. L. Jackson (Eds.), *Innovations in clinical practice: A source book* (Vol. 17, pp. 307-315). Sarasota, FL: Professional Resource Press.

Janda, L. H., England, K., Lovejoy, D., & Drury, K. (1998). Attitudes toward psychology relative to other disciplines. *Professional Psychology: Research & Practice, 29*, 140-143.

Janis, I. L., & Feshbach, S. (1953). Effects of fear-arousing communications. *Journal of Abnormal & Social Psychology, 48*, 78-92.

Janoff-Bulman, R. (1979). Characterological versus behavioral self-blame: Inquiries into depression and rape. *Journal of Personality and Social Psychology, 37*, 1798-1809.

Jena, S. P. K. (1999). Job, life satisfaction and occupational stress of women. *Social Science International, 15*(1), 75-80.

Johnson, B. T., & Eagly, A. H. (1989). The effects of involvement on persuasion. *Psychological Bulletin, 106*, 290-314.

Johnson, R. T., Johnson, D. W., Scott, L. E., & Ramolae, B. A. (1985). Effects of single-sex and mixed-sex cooperative interaction on science achievement and attitudes and cross-handicap and cross-sex relationships. *Journal of Research in Science Teaching, 22*, 207-220.

Jones, E. E. (1979). The rocky road from acts to dispositions. *American Psychologist, 34*, 107-117.

Jones, E. E., & Nisbett, R. E. (1972). The actor and the observer: Divergent perceptions of the cause of behavior. In E. E. Jones, D. E. Karouse, H. H. Kelley, R. E. Nisbett, S. Valins, & B. Weiner (Eds.), *Attribution: Perceiving the causes of behavior.* Morristown, NJ: Learning Press.

Jones, M. G., Howe, A., & Rua, M. J. (2000). Gender differences in students' experiences, interests, and attitudes toward science and scientists. *Science Education, 84*, 180-192.

Judge, T. A. (2000). Job satisfaction. In A. E. Kazdin (Ed.), *Encyclopedia of psychology* (Vol. 4, pp. 399-403). Oxford, UK: Oxford University Press.

Judge, T. A., Bono, J. E., & Locke, E. A. (2000). Personality and job satisfaction: The mediating role of job characteristics. *Journal of Applied Psychology, 85*, 237-249.

Judge, T. A., Locke, E. A., Durham, C. C., & Kluger, A. N. (1998). Dispositional effects on job and life satisfaction: The role of core evaluations. *Journal of Applied Psychology, 83*, 17-34.

Judge, T. A., & Watanabe, S. (1994). Individual differences in the nature of the relationship between job and life satisfaction. *Journal of Occupational and Organizational Psychology, 67*, 101-107.

Jurek v. Texas, 428 U.S. 262 (1976).

Kahle, L. R., & Chiagouris, L. (1997). *Values, lifestyles, and psychographics: Advertising and consumer psychology.* Mahwah, NJ: Lawrence Erlbaum.

Kalish, R. A., & Reynolds, D. K. (1981). *Death and ethnicity: A psychocultural study.* Farmingdale, NY: Baywood. (Originally published by University of Southern California Press, 1976)

Kastenbaum, R. J. (1991). *Death, society, and human experience* (4th ed.). Columbus, OH: Merrill.

Kastenbaum, R. J. (2000). Death and dying. In A. E. Kazdin (Ed.), *Encyclopedia of psychology* (Vol. 2, pp. 444-450). Oxford, UK: Oxford University Press.

Katz, B. M., & Tomazic, T. J. (1988). Changing students' attitudes toward statistics through a nonquantitative approach. *Psychological Reports, 62*, 658.

Katz, D. (1960). The functional approach to the study of attitudes. *Public Opinion Quarterly, 24*, 163-204.

Katz, D., & Braly, K. (1933). Racial stereotypes of one hundred college students. *Journal of Abnormal & Social Psychology, 28*, 280-290.

Katz, D., & Braly, K. W. (1935). Racial prejudice and racial stereotypes. *Journal of Abnormal & Social Psychology, 30*, 175-193.

Kearns, D. (1976). *Lyndon Johnson and the American dream.* New York: Wilson.

Keith, P. M. (1979). Life changes and perceptions of life and death among older men and women. *Journal of Gerontology, 34*, 870-878.

Keller, L. M., Bouchard, T. J., Arvey, R. D., Segal, N., & Dawis, R. V. (1992). Work values: Genetic and environmental influences. *Journal of Applied Psychology, 77*, 79-88.

Keller, P. A., & Block, L. G. (1999). The effect of affect-based dissonance versus cognition-based dissonance on motivated reasoning and health-related persuasion. *Journal of Experimental Psychology: Applied, 5*, 302-313.

Keller, R. T. (1997). Job involvement and organizational commitment as longitudinal predictors of job performance: A study of scientists and engineers. *Journal of Applied Psychology, 82,* 539-545.

Kerlinger, F. N. (1972). A Q validation of the structure of social attitudes. *Educational and Psychological Measurement, 32,* 987-995.

Kerr, J. H., & Van Den Wollenberg, A. E. (1997). High and low intensity exercise and psychological mood stats. *Psychology & Health, 12,* 603-618.

Kerr, P. S., & Holden, R. R. (1996). Development of the Gender Role Beliefs Scale (GRBS). *Journal of Social Behavior & Personality, 11*(5), 3-16.

Kim, J., Lim, H.-S., & Bhargava, M. (1998). The role of affect in attitude formation: A classical conditioning approach. *Journal of the Academy of Marketing Science, 26,* 143-152.

Kim, K. K., Horan, M. L., Gendler, P., & Patel, M. K. (1991). Development and evaluation of the Osteoporosis Health Belief Scale. *Research in Nursing & Health, 14,* 155-163.

Kinder, D. R. (1986). Presidential character revisited. In R. R. Lau & D. O. Sears (Eds.), *Political cognition* (pp. 233-255). Mahwah, NJ: Lawrence Erlbaum.

Kinder, D. R. (1998). Opinion and action in the realm of politics. In D. T. Gilbert, S. T. Fiske, & G. Lindzey (Eds.), *The handbook of social psychology* (4th ed., Vol. 2, pp. 778-867). New York: McGraw-Hill/Oxford.

King, A. C., Taylor, G. B., Haskell, W. L., & DeBusk, R. F. (1989). Influence of regular aerobic exercise on psychological health: A randomized, controlled trial of healthy, middle-aged adults. *Health Psychology, 8,* 305-324.

King, G. W. (1975). Analysis of attitudinal and normative variables as predictors of intentions and behavior. *Speech Monographs, 42,* 237-244.

Kinnier, R. T., Kernes, J. L., & Dautheribes, T. M. (2000). A short list of universal moral values. *Counseling & Values, 45,* 4-16.

Kitcher, P. (1985). *Vaulting ambition.* Cambridge, MA: MIT Press.

Kite, M. E., Deaux, K., & Miele, M. (1991). Stereotypes of young and old: Does age outweigh gender? *Psychology and Aging, 6,* 19-27.

Kloosterman, P., & Stage, F. K. (1992). Indiana Mathematical Belief Scales. *School Science and Mathematics, 92,* 109-115.

Klug, L., & Sinha, A. (1987-1988). Death acceptance: A two-component formulation and scale. *Omega, 18,* 229-235.

Klump, K. L., McGue, M., & Iacono, W. G. (2000). Age differences in genetic and environmental influences on eating attitudes and behaviors in preadolescent and adolescent female twins. *Journal of Abnormal Psychology, 109,* 239-251.

Knight, G. P., & Kagan, S. (1977). Development of prosocial and competitive behaviors in Anglo-American and Mexican-American children. *Child Development, 48,* 1385-1394.

Knight, K. (1985). Ideology in the 1985 election: Ideological sophistication does matter. *Journal of Politics, 47,* 828-853.

Knudson, R. E. (1992). Development and application of a writing attitude survey for Grades 1 to 2. *Psychological Reports, 70,* 711-720.

Knudson, R. E. (1993a). Development of a writing attitude survey for Grades 9 to 12: Effects of gender, grade, and ethnicity. *Psychological Reports, 73,* 587-594.

Knudson, R. E. (1993b). Effects of ethnicity in attitudes toward writing. *Psychological Reports, 72*, 39-45.

Knudson, R. E. (1995). Writing experiences, attitudes, and achievement of first to sixth graders. *Journal of Educational Research, 89*, 90-97.

Kohlberg, L. (1969). *Stages in the development of moral thought and action*. New York: Holt.

Kohlberg, L. (1976). Moral stages and moralization: The cognitive-developmental approach. In T. Lickona (Ed.), *Moral development and behavior: Theory, research and social issues* (pp. 31-53). New York: Holt, Rinehart & Winston.

Korman, A. K. (1974). Disguised measure of civil rights attitudes. *Journal of Applied Psychology, 59*, 239-240.

Kraus, S. J. (1995). Attitudes and the prediction of behavior: A meta-analysis of the empirical literature. *Personality and Social Psychology Bulletin, 21*, 58-75.

Krebs, D., & Schmidt, P. (1993). *New directions in attitude measurement*. Berlin: Walter de Gruyter.

Kristiansen, C. M., & Giulietti, R. (1990). Perceptions of wife abuse: Effects of gender, attitudes toward women, and just-world beliefs among college students. *Psychology of Women Quarterly, 14*, 177-189.

Krosnick, J. A. (1988). The role of attitude importance in social evaluation: A study of political preferences, presidential candidate evaluations, and voting behavior. *Journal of Personality and Social Psychology, 55*, 196-210.

Krosnick, J. A., Betz, A. L., Jussim, L. J., & Lynn, A. R. (1992). Subliminal conditioning of attitudes. *Personality and Social Psychology Bulletin, 18*, 152-162.

Kübler-Ross, E. (Ed.). (1975). *Death: The final stage of growth*. Englewood Cliffs, NJ: Prentice Hall.

Kuh, G. D. (1976). Persistence of the impact of college on attitudes and values. *Journal of College Student Personnel, 17*, 116-122.

Kulik, L. (1999). Gendered personality disposition and gender role attitudes among Israeli students. *Journal of Social Psychology, 139*, 736-747.

Kulik, L. (2000). Jobless men and women: A comparative analysis of job search intensity, attitudes toward unemployment and related responses. *Journal of Occupational and Organizational Psychology, 73*, 487-500.

Kunin, T. (1998). The construction of a new type of attitude measure. *Personnel Psychology, 51*, 823-824.

Kwiatkowski, E., Dammer, R., Mills, J. K., & Jih, C. (1993). Gender differences in attitudes toward mathematics among undergraduate college students: The role of environmental variables. *Perceptual & Motor Skills, 77*, 79-82.

Langdon, C. A. (1999, April). The fifth Phi Delta Kappa poll of teachers' attitudes toward the public schools. *Phi Delta Kappan, 80*, 611-618.

Langdon, C. A., & Vesper, N. (2000, April). The sixth Phi Delta Kappa poll of teachers' attitudes toward the public schools. *Phi Delta Kappan, 81*, 607-611.

Lange, R., Irwin, H. J., & Houran, J. (2000). Top-down purification of Tobacyk's revised Paranormal Belief Scale. *Personality and Individual Differences, 29*, 131-156.

Langer, W. C. (1972). *The mind of Adolf Hitler*. New York: Basic Books.

LaPiere, R. T. (1934). Attitudes versus actions. *Social Forces, 13*, 230-237.

Latane, B., & Dabbs, J. M., Jr. (1975). Sex, group size and helping in three cities. *Sociometry, 38*, 180-194.

Latane, B., & Darley, J. (1970). Social determinants of bystander intervention in emergencies. In J. Macaully & L. Berkowitz (Eds.), *Altruism and helping behavior.* New York: Academic Press.

Lavine, H. (1999). Types of evidence and routes to persuasion: The unimodel versus dual-process models. *Psychological Inquiry, 19*, 141-144.

Lawrence, T. R., & De Cicco, P. (1997). The factor structure of the Paranormal Belief Scale: More evidence in support of the Oblique Five. *Journal of Parapsychology, 61*, 243-251.

Leak, G. K., & Randall, B. A. (1995). Clarification of the link between right-wing authoritarianism and religiousness: The role of religious maturity. *Journal for the Scientific Study of Religion, 34*, 245-252.

Lease, S. H. (1998). Annual review, 1993-1997: Work attitudes and outcomes. *Journal of Vocational Behavior, 53*, 154-183.

Lee, T. M. C., & Rodda, M. (1994). Modification of attitudes toward people with disabilities. *Canadian Journal of Rehabilitation, 7*, 229-238.

Lenski, S. D., & Pardieck, S. (1999). Improving preservice teachers' attitudes toward writing. In J. A. R. Dugan, P. E. Linder, W. M. Linek, & E. G. Sturdevant (Eds.), *Advancing the world of literacy: Moving into the 21st century: The twenty-first yearbook of the College Reading Association* (pp. 269-281). Carrollton, GA: College Reading Association.

Lester, D. (1991). The Lester Attitude Toward Death Scale. *Omega, 23*(1), 67-75.

Lester, D. (1994). The Collett-Lester Fear of Death Scale. In R. A. Neimeyer (Ed.), *Death anxiety handbook: Research, instrumentation, and application* (pp. 45-60). Washington, DC: Taylor & Francis.

Leutner, D., & Weinsier, P. D. (1994). Attitudes towards computers and information technology at three universities in Germany, Belgium, and the U.S. *Computers in Human Behavior, 10*, 569-591.

Levy, J. M., Jessop, D. J., Rimmerman, A., & Levy, P. H. (1993). Attitudes of executives in Fortune 500 corporations toward the employability of persons with severe disabilities: Industrial and service corporations. *Journal of Applied Rehabilitation Counseling, 24*(2), 19-31.

Levy, S. G. (1995). Attitudes toward the conflict of war. *Peace & Conflict: Journal of Peace Psychology, 1*, 179-197.

Levy, S. M., Lee, J., Bagley, C., & Lippman, M. (1988). Survival hazard analysis in first recurrent breast cancer patients. Seven-year follow-up. *Psychosomatic Medicine, 50*, 520-528.

Levy, S. M., & Roberts, D. C. (1992). Clinical significance of psychoneuroimmunology: Prediction of cancer outcomes. In N. Schneiderman, P. McCabe, & A. Baum (Eds.), *Stress and disease processes* (pp. 165-174). Mahwah, NJ: Lawrence Erlbaum.

Lewis, C. A., & Maltby, J. (1994). Religious attitudes and obsessional personality traits among UK adults. *Psychological Reports, 75*, 353-354.

Liberman, A., & Chaiken, S. (1992). Defensive processing of personally relevant health messages. *Personality and Social Psychology Bulletin, 18*, 669-679.

Liebert, R. M. (1979). Moral development: A theoretical and empirical analysis. In G. J. Whitehurst & B. Zimmerman (Eds.), *The functions of language and cognition* (pp. 229-264). New York: John Wiley.

Likert, R. (1932). A technique for the measurement of attitudes. *Archives of Psychology*, No. 140.

Lindzey, G., & Rogolsky, S. (1950). Prejudice and identification of minority group membership. *Journal of Abnormal & Social Psychology, 45*, 37-53.

Lips, H. M. (1992). Gender- and science-related attitudes as predictors of college students' academic choices. *Journal of Vocational Behavior, 40*, 62-81.

Locke, E. A. (1976). The nature and causes of job satisfaction. In M. D. Dunnette (Ed.), *Handbook of industrial and organizational psychology* (pp. 1297-1343). Chicago: Rand McNally.

Locke, L. M., & Richman, C. L. (1999). Attitudes toward domestic violence: Race and gender issues. *Sex Roles, 40*, 227-247.

Lord, C. G., & Lepper, M. R. (1999). Attitude representation theory. In M. P. Zanna (Ed.), *Advances in social psychology* (pp. 265-343). San Diego, CA: Academic Press.

Lottes, I. L., & Kuriloff, P. J. (1992). The effects of gender, race, religion, and political orientation on the sex role attitudes of college freshmen. *Adolescence, 27*, 675-688.

Lottes, I. L., & Kuriloff, P. J. (1994). The impact of college experience on political and social attitudes. *Sex Roles, 31*, 31-54.

Louis Harris & Associates, Inc. (1997, June 11). *The Harris poll*. Los Angeles: Creators Syndicate.

Louth, R., McAllister, C., & McAllister, H. A. (1993). The effects of collaborative writing techniques on freshman writing and attitudes. *Journal of Experimental Education, 61*, 215-224.

Ludlow, L. H., & Bell, K. N. (1996). Psychometric characteristics of the Attitudes Toward Mathematics and Its Teaching (ATMAT) scale. *Educational and Psychological Measurement, 56*, 864-880.

Lugaila, T. A. (1998, October 29). Marital status and living arrangements: March 1998 (Update). *Current Population Reports,* P20-514. Washington, DC: U.S. Census Bureau.

MacDonald, W. L. (1998). The difference between Blacks' and Whites' attitudes toward voluntary euthanasia. *Journal for the Scientific Study of Religion, 37*, 411-426.

MacRae, C. N., Bodenhausen, G. V., Milne, A. B., & Jetten, J. (1994). Out of mind but back in sight: Stereotypes on the rebound. *Journal of Personality and Social Psychology, 67*, 808-817.

Magnavita, N., Narda, R., Sani, L., Carbone, A., DeLorenzo, G., & Sacco, A. (1997). Type A behaviour pattern and traffic accidents. *British Journal of Medical Psychology, 70*, 103-107.

Makrakis, V. (1992). Cross-cultural comparison of gender differences in attitude toward computers in Japan and Sweden. *Scandinavian Journal of Educational Research, 36*, 275-287.

Mallinckrodt, B., & Fretz, B. R. (1988). Social support and the impact of job loss on older professionals. *Journal of Counseling Psychology, 35*, 281-286.

Maloney, J. C. (1994). The first 90 years of advertising research. In E. M. Clark, T. C. Brock, & D. W. Stewart (Eds.), *Attention, attitudes, and affect in response to advertising* (pp. 13-54). Mahwah, NJ: Lawrence Erlbaum.

Maltby, J. (1997). Obsessional personality traits: The association with attitudes toward Christianity and religious Puritanism. *Journal of Psychology, 131*, 675-677.

Manstead, A. S. R., & van der Pligt, J. (1999). One process or two? Quantitative and qualitative distinctions in models of persuasion. *Psychological Inquiry, 19*, 144-149.

Maqsud, M. (1998). Effects of metacognitive instruction on mathematics achievement and attitude towards mathematics of low mathematics achievers. *Educational Research, 40*, 237-243.

Maras, P., & Brown, R. (1996). Effects of contact on children's attitudes toward disability: A longitudinal study. *Journal of Applied Social Psychology, 26*, 2113-2134.

Markides, K. S. (1983). Age, religiosity, and adjustment: A longitudinal analysis. *Journal of Gerontology, 38*, 621-625.

Martin, E., & McDuffee, D. (1981). *A sourcebook of Harris national surveys: Repeated questions, 1963-76*. Chapel Hill: University of North Carolina, Institute for Research in Social Science.

Martinez, D. J. G. (1998). The Prejudice Perception Assessment Scale: Measuring stigma vulnerability among African American students at predominantly Euro-American universities. *Journal of Black Psychology, 24*, 305-321.

Masters, J. R. (1974). Relationship between number of response categories and reliability of Likert-type questionnaires. *Journal of Educational Measurement, 11*, 49-53.

Matarazzo, J. D. (1980). Behavioral health and behavioral medicine: Frontiers for a new health psychology. *American Psychologist, 35*, 807-817.

Mathieu, J. E., & Zajac, D. M. (1990). A review and meta-analysis of the antecedents, correlates, and consequences of organizational commitment. *Psychological Bulletin, 108*, 171-194.

McClure, J. (1998). Discounting causes of behavior: Are two reasons better than one? *Journal of Personality and Social Psychology, 73*, 7-20.

McConahay, J. B. (1986). Modern racism, ambivalence and the modern racism scale. In J. F. Dovidio & S. L. Gaertner (Eds.), *Prejudice, discrimination, and racism* (pp. 91-125). Orlando, FL: Academic Press.

McDonald, A. S., & Davey, G. C. L. (1996). Psychiatric disorders and accidental injury. *Clinical Psychology Review, 16*, 105-127.

McFadyen, R. G. (1998). Attitudes toward the unemployed. *Human Relations, 51*, 179-199.

McGowan, T. M., Sutton, A. M., & Smith, P. G. (1990). Instructional elements influencing elementary student attitudes toward social studies. *Theory & Research in Social Education 18*, 37-52.

McGuire, F. L. (1976). Personality factors in highway accidents. *Human Factors, 18*, 433-442.

McGuire, W. J. (1968). Personality and attitude change: An information-processing theory. In A. G. Greenwald, T. C. Brock, & T. M. Ostrom (Eds.), *Psychological foundations of attitudes* (pp. 171-196). San Diego, CA: Academic Press.

McGuire, W. J. (1985). Attitudes and attitude change. In G. Lindzey & E. Aronson (Eds.), *Handbook of social psychology* (Vol. 1, pp. 233-346). New York: Random House.

McKenna, M. C., Kear, D. J., & Ellsworth, R. A. (1995). Children's attitudes toward reading: A national survey. *Reading Research Quarterly, 30,* 934-956.

McMordie, W. R. (1981). Religiosity and fear of death: Strength of belief system. *Psychological Reports, 49,* 921-922.

McNeil, J. K., LeBlanc, E. M., & Joyner, M. (1991). The effects of exercise on depressive symptoms in the moderately depressed elderly. *Psychology and Aging, 6,* 487-488.

Meichenbaum, D. H. (1977). *Cognitive-behavior modification: An integrative approach.* New York: Plenum.

Meichenbaum, D. H. (1985). *Stress-inoculation training.* New York: Pergamon.

Meier, D. E., Emmons, G.-A., Wallenstein, S., Quill, T., Morrison, R. S., & Cassel, C. K. (1998). A national survey of physician-assisted suicide and euthanasia in the United States. *New England Journal of Medicine, 338,* 1193-1201.

Milburn, M. A., Conrad, S. D., Sala, F., & Carberry, S. (1995). Childhood punishment, denial, and political attitudes. *Political Psychology, 16,* 447-478.

Millar, M. G., & Millar, K. U. (1990). Attitude change as a function of attitude type and argument type. *Journal of Personality and Social Psychology, 59,* 217-228.

Miller, J. D., & Pifer, L. K. (1993). *Longitudinal study of American youth.* De Kalb: Northern Illinois University, Social Science Research Institute.

Miller, N. E., & Bugelski, R. (1948). Minor studies of aggression: 2. The influence of frustration imposed by the in-group on attitudes expressed toward out-groups. *Journal of Psychology, 25,* 437-452.

Miller, R. S. (1999). Emotion. In V. J. Derlega, B. A. Winstead, & W. H. Jones (Eds.), *Personality: Contemporary theory and research* (2nd ed., pp. 405-431). Chicago: Nelson-Hall.

Mischel, W., & Mischel, H. N. (1976). A cognitive social learning approach to morality and self-regulation. In T. Lickona (Ed.), *Moral development and behavior: Theory, research and social issues* (pp. 81-107). New York: Holt.

Monteith, M. J. (1993). Self-regulation of prejudiced responses: Implications for progress in prejudice-reduction efforts. *Journal of Personality and Social Psychology, 65,* 469-485.

Monteith, M. J. (2000). Prejudice. In A. E. Kazdin (Ed.), *Encyclopedia of psychology* (Vol. 6, pp. 278-281). Oxford, UK: Oxford University Press.

Moode, F. M., & Finkenberg, M. E. (1994). Participation in a wellness course and attitude toward physical education. *Perceptual & Motor Skills, 79,* 767-770.

Moskowitz, J. M., Malvin, J. H., Schaeffer, G. A., & Schaps, E. (1985). Evaluation of jigsaw, a cooperative learning technique. *Contemporary Educational Psychology, 10,* 104-112.

Moyer, R. H. (1977). Environmental attitude assessment: Another approach. *Science Education, 61,* 347-356.

Mueller, D. J. (1986). *Measuring social attitudes: A handbook for researchers and practitioners.* New York: Teachers College Press.

Mullis, I. V. S., & Martin, M. O. (1998). *Mathematics and science achievement in the final year of secondary school: IEA's Third International Mathematics and Science Study.* Chestnut Hill, MA: Boston College.

Murrell, A. J. (2000). Discrimination. In A. E. Kazdin (Ed.), *Encyclopedia of psychology* (Vol. 3, pp. 49-54). Oxford, UK: Oxford University Press.

Myers, D. G. (1990). *Social psychology* (3rd ed.). New York: McGraw-Hill.

National Center for Education Statistics. (2001). *Digest of education statistics 2000.* Washington, DC: U.S. Department of Education.

National Center for Health Statistics. (1991). *Health, United States, 1990.* Hyattsville, MD: U.S. Department of Health and Human Services.

National Center for Health Statistics. (1995). *Health, United States, 1994.* Hyattsville, MD: Public Health Service.

National Center on Elder Abuse. (1998, September). *The National Elder Abuse Incidence Study: Final report.* Retrieved November 1, 2001, from the World Wide Web: www.aoa.gov/abuse/report

National Coalition to Abolish the Death Penalty. (1999a). *Fact Sheet #2: Executing minorities: An American tradition.* Washington, DC: Author. Retrieved November 1, 2001, from the World Wide Web: www.ncadp.org/html/fact2.html

National Coalition to Abolish the Death Penalty. (1999b). *Fact Sheet #5: Deterrence: Fact or fiction.* Washington, DC: Author. Retrieved November 1, 2001, from the World Wide Web: www.ncadp.org/html/fact5.html

National Council on the Aging. (2000). *Facts about older Americans.* Washington, DC: Author.

National Crime Prevention Council. (1995). *Preventing violence against women, not just a women's issue.* Washington, DC: Author.

National Interreligious Task Force on Criminal Justice. (n.d.). *Capital punishment: What the religious community says.* New York: Author.

National Science Foundation. (2000). *Science and technology: Public attitudes and public understanding: Public attitudes toward science and technology.* Washington, DC: Government Printing Office. Retrieved November 1, 2001, from the World Wide Web: www.nsf.gov/search97cgi/vtopic

Nelson, L. D. (1978). The multidimensional measurement of death attitudes: Construction and validation of a three-factor instrument. *Psychological Record, 28,* 525-533.

Nesdale, D., & Durkin, K. (1998). Stereotypes and attitudes: Implicit and explicit processes. In K. Kirsner, C. Speelman, M. Maybery, A. O'Brien-Malone, M. Anderson, & C. MacLeod (Eds.), *Implicit and explicit mental processes* (pp. 219-232). Mahwah, NJ: Lawrence Erlbaum.

Neville, H. A., Lilly, R. L., Duran, G., Lee, R. M., & Browne, L. (2000). Construction and initial validation of the Color-Blind Racial Attitudes Scale (CoBRAS). *Journal of Counseling Psychology, 47,* 59-70.

Newburger, E. C., & Curry, A. (2000, August). *Educational attainment in the United States, March 1999. Current Population Reports,* P20-528. Washington, DC: U.S. Census Bureau.

Newcomb, T. M. (1943). *Personality and social change.* New York: Dryden.

Newcomb, T. M., Koenig, K. E., Flacks, R., & Warwick, D. P. (1967). *Persistence and change: Bennington College and its students after twenty-five years.* New York: John Wiley.

Newell, R., & Shrubb, S. (1994). Attitude change and behaviour therapy in body dysmorphic disorder: Two case reports. *Behavioural & Cognitive Psychotherapy, 22,* 163-169.

Newport, E., & Saad, L. (1997, March). Religious faith is widespread but many skip church. *The Gallup Poll Monthly,* pp. 20-29.

Niemcryk, S. J., Jenkins, C. D., Rose, R. M., & Hurst, M. W. (1987). The prospective impact of psychosocial variables on rates of illness and injury in professional employees. *Journal of Occupational Medicine, 29,* 645-652.

Nisan, M., & Kohlberg, L. (1982). Universality and variation in moral judgment: A longitudinal and cross-sectional study in Turkey. *Child Development, 53,* 865-876.

Norušis, M. J. (1992). *SPSS/PC+ professional statistics, version 5.0.* Chicago: SPSS.

Ohio v. Akron Center for Reproductive Health, 497 U.S. 502 (1990).

O'Leary, A. (1990). Stress, emotion, and human immune function. *Psychological Bulletin, 108,* 363-382.

Oliner, S. P., & Oliner, P. M. (1988). *The altruistic personality: Rescuers of Jews in Nazi Europe.* New York: Free Press.

Olson, J. M., Vernon, P. A., Harris, J. A., & Jang, K. L. (2001). The heritability of attitudes: A study of twins. *Journal of Personality and Social Psychology, 80,* 845-860.

O'Neill, B. S., & Mone, M. A. (1998). Investigating equity sensitivity as a moderator of relations between self-efficacy and workplace attitudes. *Journal of Applied Psychology, 83,* 805-816.

Ormerod, M. B., Rutherford, M., & Wood, C. (1989). Relationships between attitudes to science and television viewing among pupils aged 10 to 13+. *Research in Science & Technological Education, 7,* 75-84.

Orpinas, P., Murray, N., & Kelder, S. (1999). Parental influences on students' aggressive behaviors and weapon carrying. *Health Education & Behavior, 26,* 774-787.

Ortega, S. T., Crutchfield, R. D., & Rushing, W. A. (1983). Race differences in elderly personal well-being. Friendship, family and church. *Research on Aging, 5,* 101-118.

Osgood, C. E., Suci, G. J., & Tannenbaum, P. H. (1957). *The measurement of meaning.* Urbana: University of Illinois Press.

Ostrom, T. M. (1994). Attitude theory. In R. J. Corsini (Ed.), *Encyclopedia of psychology* (2nd ed., Vol. 1, pp. 116-118). New York: John Wiley.

Ostrom, T. M., Bond, C. F., Jr., Krosnick, J. A., & Sedikides, C. (1994). Attitude scales: How we measure the unmeasureable. In S. Shavitt & T. C. Brock (Eds.), *Persuasion: Psychological insights and perspectives* (pp. 15-42). Boston: Allyn & Bacon.

Page, M. M. (1969). Social psychology of a classical conditioning of attitudes experiment. *Journal of Personality and Social Psychology, 11,* 177-186.

Palmore, E. (1990). *Ageism: Negative and positive.* New York: Springer.

Palmore, E., Burchett, B., Fillenbaum, G. G., George, L. K., & Wallman, L. M. (1985). *Retirement: Causes and consequences.* New York: Springer.

Parkinson, J., Hendley, D., Tanner, H., & Stables, A. (1998). Pupils' attitudes to science in key stage 3 of the national curriculum: A study of pupils in south Wales. *Research in Science & Technological Education, 16,* 165-176.

Pat-Horenczyk, R. (1998). Changes in attitudes toward insomnia following cognitive intervention as part of a withdrawal treatment from hypnotics. *Behavioural & Cognitive Psychotherapy, 26,* 345-357.

Pattison, E. M. (1977). Death throughout the life cycle. In E. M. Pattison (Ed.), *The experience of dying* (pp. 18-27). Englewood Cliffs, NJ: Prentice Hall.

Pedro, J. D., Wolleat, P., Fennema, E., & Becker, A. D. (1981). Election of high school mathematics by females and males: Attributions and attitudes. *American Educational Research Journal, 18,* 207-218.

Pellegrini, R. J., Queirolo, S. S., Monarrez, V. E., & Valenzuela, D. M. (1997). Political identification and perceptions of homelessness: Attributed causality and attitudes on public policy. *Psychological Reports, 80,* 1139-1148.

Perry, A. R., & Baldwin, D. A. (2000). Further evidence of associations of type A personality scores and driving-related attitudes and behaviors. *Perceptual & Motor Skills, 91,* 147-154.

Peterson, B. E., Doty, R. M., & Winter, D. G. (1993). Authoritarianism and attitudes toward contemporary social issues. *Personality and Social Psychology Bulletin, 19,* 174-184.

Peterson, R. C., & Thurstone, L. L. (1933). *Motion pictures and the social attitudes of children.* New York: Macmillan.

Petkova, K. G., Ajzen, I., & Driver, B. L. (1995). Salience of anti-abortion beliefs and commitment to an attitudinal position: On the strength, structure, and predictive validity of anti-abortion attitudes. *Journal of Applied Social Psychology, 25,* 463-483.

Petruzello, S. J., Landers, D. M., Hatfield, B. D., Kubitz, K. A., & Salazar, W. (1991). A meta-analysis on the anxiety-reducing effects of acute and chronic exercise. *Sports Medicine, 11,* 143-182.

Pettigrew, T. F. (1958). Personality and socio-cultural factors in intergroup attitudes: A cross-national comparison. *Journal of Conflict Resolution, 2,* 29-42.

Pettigrew, T. F. (1979). The ultimate attribution error: Extending Allport's cognitive analysis of prejudice. *Personality and Social Psychology Bulletin, 5,* 461-476.

Pettingale, K. W., Morris, T., Greer, S., & Haybittle, J. L. (1985). Mental attitudes to cancer: An additional prognostic factor. *Lancet, 1,* 750.

Petty, R. E., & Cacioppo, J. T. (1986). *Communication and persuasion: Central and peripheral routes to attitude change.* New York: Springer-Verlag.

Petty, R. E., Wegener, D. T., & Fabrigar, L. R. (1997). Attitudes and attitude change. *Annual Review of Psychology, 48,* 609-647.

Petty, R. E., Wells, G. L., & Brock, T. C. (1976). Distraction can enhance or reduce yielding to propaganda: Thought disruption versus effort justification. *Journal of Personality and Social Psychology, 34,* 874-884.

Petty, R. E., Wheeler, S. C., & Bizer, G. Y. (1999). Is there one persuasion process or more? Lumping versus splitting in attitude change theories. *Psychological Inquiry, 10,* 156-163.

Phelan, J. C., Link, B. G., Moore, R. E., & Stueve, A. (1997). The stigma of homelessness: the impact of the label "homeless" on attitudes toward poor persons. *Social Psychology Quarterly, 60,* 323-337.

Phillips, S. T., & Ziller, R. C. (1997). Toward a theory and measure of the nature of nonprejudice. *Journal of Personality and Social Psychology, 72,* 420-434.

Piburn, M. D., & Baker, D. R. (1993). If I were the teacher . . . Qualitative study of attitude toward science. *Science Education, 77,* 393-406.

Planned Parenthood of Southeastern Pennsylvania v. Casey, 112 S. Ct. 2791 (1992).

Poetker, J. S. (1977). Techniques for assessing attitudes and values. *Clearing House, 51,* 172-175.

Pratto, F., Stallworth, L. M., & Sidanius, J. (1997). The gender gap: Differences in political attitudes and social dominance orientation. *British Journal of Social Psychology, 36,* 49-68.

Pressman, P., Lyons, J. S., Larson, D. B., & Gartner, J. (1992). Religion, anxiety, and fear of death. In J. F. Schumaker (Ed.), *Religion and mental health* (pp. 98-109). New York: Oxford University Press.

Price, E. L., & Byers, E. S. (1999). The Attitudes Towards Dating Violence Scales: Development and initial validation. *Journal of Family Violence, 14,* 351-375.

Procter, M. (1993). Measuring attitudes. In N. Gilbert (Ed.), *Researching social life* (pp. 116-134). London: Sage.

Profitt v. Florida, 428 U.S. 242 (1976).

Prothro, E. T., & Miles, O. K. (1953). Social distance in the deep South as measured by a revised Bogardus scale. *Journal of Social Psychology, 37,* 171-174.

Public opinion. (1997). In *The new encyclopedia Britannica* (Vol. 26, pp. 310-316). Chicago: Encyclopedia Britannica.

Radecki, S. E., Kane, R. L., Solomon, D. H., Mendenhall, R. C., & Beck, J. C. (1988). Do physicians spend less time with older patients? *Journal of the American Geriatrics Society, 36,* 713-718.

Radelet, M. L., & Akers, R. L. (1996). Deterrence and the death penalty: The view of experts. *Journal of Criminal Law & Criminology, 87,* 1-16.

Radzinowicz, L. (1948). *A history of English criminal law.* London: Pilgrim Trust.

Raja, S., & Stokes, J. P. (1998). Assessing attitudes toward lesbians and gay men: The Modern Homophobia Scale. *Journal of Gay, Lesbian, & Bisexual Identity, 3,* 113-134.

Randel, B., Stevenson, H. W., & Witruk, E. (2000). Attitudes, beliefs, and mathematics achievement of German and Japanese high school students. *International Journal of Behavioral Development, 24,* 190-198.

Ransford, H. E., & Bartolomeo, P. J. (1996). Aerobic exercise, subjective health and psychological well-being within age and gender subgroups. *Social Science & Medicine, 43,* 1555-1559.

Reitzes, D. C., Mutran, E. J., & Fernandez, M. E. (1996). Does retirement hurt well-being? Factors influencing self-esteem and depression among retirees and workers. *The Gerontologist, 36,* 649-656.

Remmers, H. H. (1960). *Manual for the Purdue Master Attitude Scales.* Lafayette, IN: Purdue Research Foundation.

Repetti, R. L., Matthews, K. A., & Waldron, I. (1989). Employment and women's health: Effects of paid employment on women's mental and physical health. *American Psychologist, 44,* 1394-1401.

Rhodes, F., & Wolitslci, R. J. (1989). AIDS Information and Opinion Survey. *Journal of American College Health, 37,* 266-271.

Rhodes, S. R. (1983). Age-related differences in work attitudes and behavior: A review and conceptual analysis. *Psychological Bulletin, 93*, 328-367.

Rice, R. W., Gentile, D. A., & McFarlin, D. B. (1991). Facet importance and job satisfaction. *Journal of Applied Psychology, 76*, 31-39.

Richardson, D. R. (1999). Aggression. In V. J. Derlega, B. A. Winstead, & W. H. Jones (Eds.), *Personality: Contemporary theory and research* (2nd ed., pp. 458-488). Chicago: Nelson-Hall.

Rizzo, T. L., & Vispoel, W. P. (1991). Physical educators' attributes and attitudes toward teaching students with handicaps. *Adapted Physical Activity Quarterly, 8*(1), 4-11.

Roberts, C. M., & Smith, P. R. (1999). Attitudes and behaviour of children toward peers with disabilities. *International Journal of Disability, Development & Education, 46*(1), 35-50.

Roberts, J. S., Laughlin, J. E., & Wedell, D. H. (1999). Validity issues in the Likert and Thurstone approaches to attitude measurement. *Educational and Psychological Measurement, 59*, 211-233.

Roberts, L. P. (1992). Attitudes of entering university freshmen toward foreign language study: A descriptive analysis. *Modern Language Journal, 76*, 275-283.

Robinson, J. P., Athanasiou, R., & Head, K. B. (1974). *Measurement of occupational attitudes and occupational characteristics*. Ann Arbor: University of Michigan, Institute for Social Research.

Robinson, J. P., Shaver, P. R., & Wrightsman, L. S. (1991). *Measures of personality and social psychological attitudes*. San Diego, CA: Academic Press.

Robinson, J. P., Shaver, P. R., & Wrightsman, L. S. (1999). *Measures of political attitudes*. San Diego, CA: Academic Press.

Roe v. Wade, 410 U.S. 113 (1973).

Rogers, S. J., & Amato, P. R. (2000). Have changes in gender relations affected marital quality? *Social Forces, 79*, 731-752.

Rokeach, M. (1960). *The open and closed mind: Investigations into the nature of belief systems and personality systems*. New York: Basic Books.

Rokeach, M. (1968). *Beliefs, attitudes, and values: A theory of organization and change*. San Francisco: Jossey-Bass.

Rokeach, M. (1973). *The nature of human values*. New York: Free Press.

Rombough, S., & Ventimiglia, J. C. (1981). Sexism: A tri-dimensional phenomenon. *Sex Roles, 7*, 747-755.

Roper Center for Public Opinion Research. (1996, July 25). *American views of science and technology. A survey commissioned by the National Science & Technology Medals Foundation*. Washington, DC: Government Printing Office.

Rose, L. C., & Gallup, A. M. (2000, September). The 32nd annual Phi Delta Kappa/Gallup poll of the public's attitudes toward the public schools. *Phi Delta Kappan, 82*, 41-58.

Rose, L. C., & Gallup, A. M. (2001, September). The 33rd annual Phi Delta Kappa/Gallup poll of the public's attitudes toward the public schools. *Phi Delta Kappan, 83*, 41-58.

Rosenbaum, M. E. (1986). The repulsion hypothesis: On the nondevelopment of relationships. *Journal of Personality and Social Psychology, 51*, 1156-1166.

Rosenberg, M. J., Hovland, C. I., McGuire, W. J., Abelson, R. P., & Brehm, J. W. (1960). *Attitude organization and change: An analysis of consistency among attitude components.* New Haven, CT: Yale University Press.

Ross, C. E., & Wright, M. P. (1998). Women's work, men's work, and the sense of control. *Work and Occupations, 25,* 333-355.

Ross, L. (1977). The intuitive psychologist and his shortcomings. Distortions in the attribution process. In L. Berkowitz (Ed.), *Advances in experimental social psychology* (Vol. 10, pp. 174-221). New York: Academic Press.

Roth, W. F. (1991). *Work and rewards: Redefining our work-life reality.* New York: Praeger.

Rothman, A. J., Salovey, P., Antone, C., Keough, K., & Martin, C. D. (1993). The influence of message framing on intentions to perform health behaviors. *Journal of Experimental Social Psychology, 29,* 408-433.

Rotter, J. B. (1954). *Social learning and clinical psychology.* Englewood Cliffs, NJ: Prentice Hall.

Rourke, M. (1998, June 21). Redefining religion in America. *Los Angeles Times,* pp. A1, A30-A31.

Rowe, K. J. (1991). The influence of reading activity at home on students' attitudes toward reading, classroom attentiveness and reading achievement: An application of structural equation modeling. *British Journal of Educational Psychology, 61,* 19-35.

Rudman, L. A., Greenwald, A. G., Mellott, D. S., & Schwartz, J. L. K. (1999). Measuring the automatic components of prejudice: Flexibility and generality of the Implicit Association Test. *Social Cognition, 17,* 437-465.

Rushton, J. P. (1976). Socialization and the altruistic behavior of children. *Psychological Bulletin, 83,* 898-913.

Rushton, J. P. (1989). Genetic similarity, human altruism, and group selection. *Behavioral and Brain Sciences, 12,* 503-559.

Rutherford, J., McGuffin, P., Katz, R. J., & Murray, R. M. (1993). Genetic influences on eating attitudes in a normal female twin population. *Psychological Medicine, 23,* 425-436.

Salovey, P., Rothman, A. J., & Rodin, J. (1998). Health behavior. In D. T. Gilbert, S. T. Fiske, & G. Lindzey (Eds.), *The handbook of social psychology* (4th ed., Vol. 2, pp. 633-683). New York: McGraw-Hill/Oxford.

Sampson, R. J., & Bartusch, D. J. (1998). Legal cynicism and (subcultural?) tolerance of deviance: The neighborhood context of racial differences. *Law & Society Review, 32,* 777-804.

Sandys, M., & McGarrell, E. F. (1995). Attitudes toward capital punishment: Preference for the penalty or mere acceptance? *Journal of Research in Crime and Delinquency, 32,* 191-213.

Schaeffer, A. M., & Nelson, E. S. (1993). Rape-supportive attitudes and sexual victimization experiences of sorority and nonsorority women. *Sex Roles, 29,* 767-780.

Schaler, J. A. (1995). The Addiction Belief Scale. *International Journal of the Addictions, 30,* 117-134.

Schaler, J. A. (1996). Spiritual thinking in addiction-treatment providers: The Spiritual Belief Scale (SBS). *Alcoholism Treatment Quarterly, 14*(3), 7-33.

Schein, E. H. (1956). The Chinese indoctrination program for prisoners of war. *Psychiatry, 19,* 149-172.

Schroeder, D. A., Penner, L. A., Dovidio, J. F., & Piliavin, J. A. (1995). *The psychology of helping and altruism: Problems and puzzles.* New York: McGraw-Hill.

Schultz, P. W., & Stone, W. F. (1994). Authoritarianism and attitudes toward the environment. *Environment and Behavior, 26,* 25-37.

Schwartz, S., & Ames, R. (1977). Positive and negative referent others as sources of influence: A case of helping. *Sociometry, 40,* 12-20.

Schwarz, N. (1997). Moods and attitude judgments: A comment on Fishbein and Middlestadt. *Journal of Consumer Psychology, 6,* 93-98.

Scott, W. D. (1908). *The psychology of advertising.* New York: Arno.

Seawel, L., Smaldino, S. E., Steele, J. L., & Lewis, J. Y. (1994). A descriptive study comparing computer-based word processing and handwriting on attitudes and performance of third and fourth grade students involved in a program based on a process approach to writing. *Journal of Computing in Childhood Education, 5,* 43-59.

Sellin, T., & Wolfgang, M. E. (1964). *The measurement of delinquency.* New York: John Wiley.

Sexton, D., King, N., Aldridge, J., & Goodstadt-Killoran, I. (1999). Measuring and evaluating early childhood prospective practitioners' attitudes toward computers. *Family Relations: Interdisciplinary Journal of Applied Family Studies, 48,* 277-285.

Shapiro, J. P., Dorman, R. L., Welker, C. J., & Clough, J. B. (1998). Youth attitudes toward guns and violence: Relations with sex, age, ethnic group, and firearm exposure. *Journal of Clinical Child Psychology, 27,* 98-108.

Shashaani, L. (1994). Gender differences in computer experiences and its influence on computer attitudes. *Journal of Educational Computer Research, 11,* 347-367.

Shashaani, L. (1997). Gender differences in computer attitudes and use among college students. *Journal of Educational Computing Research, 16,* 37-51.

Shaw, L., & Sichel, H. S. (1971). *Accident proneness: Research in the occurrence, causation, and prevention of road accidents.* New York: Pergamon.

Shaw, M. E., & Wright, J. M. (1967). *Scales for the measurement of attitudes.* New York: McGraw-Hill.

Shelton, C. M., & McAdams, D. P. (1990). In search of an everyday morality: The development of a measure. *Adolescence, 25,* 923-943.

Sherif, C. W., Sherif, M., & Nebergall, R. E. (1965). *Attitude and attitude change: The social judgment-involvement approach.* Philadelphia: Saunders.

Sherif, M., Harvey, O. J., White, B. J., Hood, W. R., & Sherif, C. W. (1961). *Intergroup conflict and cooperation: The Robber's Cave experiment.* Norman: University of Oklahoma Press.

Sherman, H. J., & Christian, M. (1999). Mathematics attitudes and global self-concept: An investigation of the relationship. *College Student Journal, 33,* 95-101.

Shim, S., & Bickle, M. C. (1994). Benefit segments of the female apparel market: Psychographics, shopping orientations, and demographics. *Clothing & Textiles Research Journal, 12*(2), 1-12.

Shneidman, E. S. (1980). Death work and stages of dying. In E. S. Shneidman (Ed.), *Death: Current perspectives* (2nd ed., pp. 305-311). Palo Alto, CA: Mayfield.

Shneidman, E. S. (1987, March). At the point of no return. *Psychology Today,* pp. 54-58.

Shultz, T. R., Leveille, E., & Lepper, M. R. (1999). Free choice and cognitive dissonance revisited: Choosing "lesser evils" versus "greater goods." *Personality and Social Psychology Bulletin, 25,* 40-48.

Sideridis, G. D., & Chandler, J. P. (1996). Comparison of attitudes of teachers of physical and musical education toward inclusion of children with disabilities. *Psychological Reports, 78,* 768-770.

Sideridis, G. D., Kaissidis, A., & Padeliadu, S. (1998). Comparison of the theories of
reasoned action and planned behavior. *British Journal of Educational Psychology,
68,* 563-580.

Simonton, D. K. (1990). Personality and politics. In L. A. Pervin (Ed.), *Handbook of
personality theory and research* (pp. 670-692). New York: Guilford.

Simpson, G. E., & Yinger, J. M. (1985). *Racial and cultural minorities: An analysis of
prejudice and discrimination* (5th ed.). New York: Harper & Row.

Singh, B. R. (1991). Teaching methods for reducing prejudice and enhancing academic
achievement for all children. *Educational Studies, 17,* 157-171.

Slininger, D., Sherrill, C., & Jankowski, C. M. (2000). Children's attitudes toward peers
with severe disabilities: Revisiting contact theory. *Adapted Physical Activity Quarterly, 17,* 176-196.

Smith, M. C. (1990). The development and use of an instrument for assessing adults' attitudes toward reading. *Journal of Research & Development in Education, 23,*
156-161.

Smith, S. C., Ellis, J. B., & Benson, T. A. (2001). Gender, gender roles and attitudes towards violence: Are viewpoints changing? *Social Behavior & Personality, 29,*
43-47.

Smith, W. S., & Erb, T. O. (1986). Effect of women science career role models on early
adolescents' attitudes toward scientists and women in science. *Journal of Research
in Science Teaching, 23,* 667-676.

Snyder, M. (1982). When believing means doing: Creating links between attitudes and
behavior. In M. P. Zanna, E. T. Higgins, & C. P. Herman (Eds.), *Consistency in social
behavior: The Ontario symposium* (Vol. 2, pp. 105-130). Mahwah, NJ: Lawrence
Erlbaum.

Sorge, C., Newsom, H. E., & Hagerty, J. J. (2000). Fun is not enough: Attitudes of Hispanic middle school students toward science and scientists. *Hispanic Journal of Behavioral Sciences, 22,* 332-345.

Sparrow, P. R., & Davies, D. R. (1988). Effects of age, tenure, training, and job complexity on technical performance. *Psychology and Aging, 3,* 307-314.

Spector, P. E. (1976). Choosing response categories for summated rating scales. *Journal
of Applied Psychology, 61,* 374-375.

Spector, P. E. (1988). Development of the Work Locus of Control Scale. *Journal of Occupational and Organizational Psychology, 61,* 335-340.

Spranger, E. (1928). *Types of men* (P. J. W. Pigors, Trans.). Halle, Germany: Niemeyer.

Stagner, R. (1985). Aging in industry. In J. E. Birren & K. W. Schaie (Eds.), *Handbook
of the psychology of aging* (2nd ed., pp. 789-817). New York: Van Nostrand
Reinhold.

Stanley, H. W., & Niemi, R. G. (1990). *Vital statistics on American politics* (2nd ed.).
Washington, DC: CQ Press.

Staw, B. M., Bell, N. E., & Clausen, J. A. (1986). The dispositional approach to job attitudes: A lifetime longitudinal test. *Administrative Science Quarterly, 31,* 437-453.

Steel, R. P., & Rentsch, J. R. (1997). The dispositional model of job attitudes revisited: Findings of a 10-year study. *Journal of Applied Psychology, 82,* 873-879.

Steele, C. M. (1988). The psychology of self-affirmation: Sustaining the integrity of the self. In L. Berkowitz (Ed.), *Advances in experimental social psychology* (pp. 261-302). Mahwah, NJ: Lawrence Erlbaum.

Steele, C. M., Southwick, L. L., & Critchlow, B. (1981). Dissonance and alcohol: Drinking your troubles away. *Journal of Personality and Social Psychology, 41,* 831-846.

Stenback, A. (1980). Depression and suicidal behavior in old age. In J. E. Birren & R. B. Sloane (Eds.), *Handbook of mental health and aging* (pp. 616-652). Englewood Cliffs, NJ: Prentice Hall.

Stephan, C. W., & Stephan, W. G. (1992). Reducing intercultural anxiety through intercultural contact. *International Journal of Intercultural Relations, 16,* 89-106.

Stephenson, W. (1953). *The study of behavior: Q-technique and its methodology.* Chicago: University of Chicago Press.

Stone, M. K., & Hutchinson, R. L. (1992). Familial conflict and attitudes toward marriage: A psychological wholeness perspective. *Journal of Divorce & Remarriage, 18*(3-4), 79-91.

Stotland, S., & Zuroff, D. C. (1990). A new measure of weight locus of control: The Dieting Beliefs Scale. *Journal of Personality Assessment, 54,* 191-203.

Subhi, T. (1999). Attitudes toward computers of gifted students and their teachers. *High Ability Studies, 10,* 69-84.

Swanson, J. E., Rudman, L. A., & Greenwald, A. G. (2001). Using the Implicit Association Test to investigate attitude-behaviour consistency for stigmatised behaviour. *Cognition & Emotion, 15,* 207-230.

Swim, J. K., Aikin, K. J., Hall, W. S., & Hunter, B. A. (1995). Sexism and racism: Old-fashioned and modern prejudices. *Journal of Personality and Social Psychology, 68,* 199-214.

Szybillo, G., & Heslin, R. (1973). Resistance to persuasion: Inoculation theory in a marketing context. *Journal of Marketing Research, 10,* 396-403.

Tannehill, D., Romar, J.-E., O'Sullivan, M., England, K., et al. (1994). Attitudes toward physical education: Their impact on how physical education teachers make sense of their work. *Journal of Teaching in Physical Education, 13,* 406-420.

Tannehill, D., & Zakrajsek, D. (1993). Student attitudes towards physical education: A multicultural study. *Journal of Teaching in Physical Education, 13,* 78-84.

Tasker, F. L., & Richards, M. P. M. (1994). Adolescents' attitudes toward marriage and marital prospects after parental divorce: A review. *Journal of Adolescent Research, 9,* 340-362.

Tellegen, A., Lykken, D. T., Bouchard, T. J., Jr., Wilcox, K. J., Segal, N. L., & Rich, S. (1988). Personality: Similarity in twins reared apart and together. *Journal of Personality and Social Psychology, 54,* 1031-1039.

Temoshuk, L. (1992). *The Type C connection: The behavioral links to cancer and your health.* New York: Random House.

Templer, D. I., LaVoie, M., Chalgujian, H., & Thomas-Dobson, S. (1990). The measurement of death depression. *Journal of Clinical Psychology, 46*, 834-839.

Terwilliger, J. S., & Titus, J. C. (1989). Gender differences in attitudes and attitude changes among mathematically talented youth. *Roeper Review, 11*, 128-131.

Tesser, A. (1998). Attitude heritability, attitude change and physiological responsivity. *Personality and Individual Differences, 24*, 89-96.

Theodorakis, Y., Bagiatis, K., & Goudas, M. (1995). Attitudes toward teaching individuals with disabilities: Application of planned behavior theory. *Adapted Physical Activity Quarterly, 12*, 151-160.

Thompson, E. P., & Kruglanski, A. W. (2000). Attitudes as knowledge structures and persuasion as a specific case of subjective knowledge acquisition. In G. R. Maio & J. M. Olson (Eds.), *Why we evaluate: Functions of attitudes* (pp. 59-95). Mahwah, NJ: Erlbaum.

Thompson, S. C. (1981). Will it hurt less if I can control it? A complex answer to a simple question. *Psychological Bulletin, 90*, 89-101.

Thurstone, L. L. (1928). Attitudes can be measured. *American Journal of Sociology, 33*, 529-554.

Thurstone, L. L. (1929). Theory of attitude measurement. *Psychological Review, 36*, 222-241.

Thurstone, L. L., & Chave, E. J. (1929). *The measurement of attitude: A psychophysical method and some experiments with a scale for measuring attitude toward the church.* Chicago: University of Chicago Press.

Tibon, S. (2000). Personality traits and peace negotiations: Integrative complexity and attitudes toward the Middle East peace process. *Group Decision & Negotiation, 9*, 1-15.

Tinsley, H. E., Hinson, J. A., Tinsley, D. J., & Holt, M. S. (1993). Attributes of leisure and work experiences. *Journal of Counseling Psychology, 40*, 447-455.

Tjaden, P., & Thoennes, N. (1998). *Prevalence, incidence, and consequences of violence against women: Findings from the National Violence Against Women Survey.* Washington, DC: National Institute of Justice.

Tobias, S., & Donady, B. (1977). Counseling the math anxious. *National Association of Women Deans, Administrators, and Counselors, 41*, 13-16.

Torabi, M. R., & Yarber, W. L. (1992). HIV Prevention Attitude Scale. *AIDS Education and Prevention, 4*, 172-182.

Torkzadeh, R., Pflughoeft, K., & Hall, L. (1999). Computer self-efficacy, training effectiveness and user attitudes: An empirical study. *Behaviour & Information Technology, 18*, 299-309.

Tougas, F., Brown, R., Beaton, A. M., & Joly, S. (1995). Neosexism: Plus ça change, plus c'est pareil. *Personality and Social Psychology Bulletin, 21*, 842-849.

Triandis, H. C., & Triandis, L. M. (1962). A cross-cultural study of social distance. *Psychological Monographs: General & Applied, 76*(21, Whole No. 540).

Trimpop, R., & Kircaldy, B. (1997). Personality predictors of driving accidents. *Personality and Individual Differences, 23*, 147-152.

Tuch, S. A., & Martin, J. K. (1991). Race in the workplace: Black/White differences in the sources of job satisfaction. *Sociological Quarterly, 32*, 103-116.

Tyler, T. R., & Schuller, R. A. (1991). Aging and attitude change. *Journal of Personality and Social Psychology, 61*, 689-697.

Urban, W. M. (1907). Recent tendencies in the psychological theory of values. *Psychological Bulletin, 4*(3), 65-72.

Urban, W. M. (1912). Values. *Psychological Bulletin, 9*, 260-264.

U.S. Census Bureau. (1997, December). *Census brief. Disabilities affect one-fifth of all Americans.* Washington, DC: Author.

U.S. Census Bureau. (1999a). *Health insurance coverage. Current Population Reports*, P60-211. Washington, DC: Author.

U.S. Census Bureau. (1999b). *In and around the home 1997. American Housing Brief*, AHB/99-1. Washington, DC: Author.

U.S. Census Bureau. (1999c). *Statistical abstract of the United States: 1998* (119th ed.). Washington, DC: Author.

U.S. Census Bureau. (2000a, September). *Money income in the United States 1999. Current Population Reports*, P60-209. Washington, DC: Author.

U.S. Census Bureau. (2000b, September). *Poverty in the United States 1999. Current Population Reports*, P60-210. Washington, DC: Author.

U.S. Department of Justice, Bureau of Justice Statistics. (2000). *Capital punishment statistics.* Washington, DC: Author.

U.S. Department of Justice, Federal Bureau of Investigation. (1999, October). *Hate crime data collection guidelines.* Washington, DC: Author.

U.S. Department of Justice, Federal Bureau of Investigation. (2001, February). *Hate crime statistics, 1999.* Washington, DC: Author.

U.S. Senate Special Committee on Aging. (2000, February 7). *Developments in aging: 1997 and 1998: Vol. 1. Report of the Special Committee on Aging, United States Senate* (pp. 211-244, 287-293). Washington, DC: Government Printing Office. Retrieved November 1, 2001 from the World Wide Web: www.gpo.gov/congress/senate/senate22.html

Valliant, P. M., & Oliver, C. L. (1997). Attitudes toward capital punishment: A function of leadership style, gender and personality. *Social Behavior & Personality, 25*, 161-168.

Vanman, E. J., Paul, B. Y., Ito, T. A., & Miller, N. (1997). The modern face of prejudice and structural features that moderate the effect of cooperation and affect. *Journal of Personality and Social Psychology, 73*, 941-959.

Van Overwalle, F. (1997). Dispositional attributions require the joint application of the methods of difference and agreement. *Personality and Social Psychology Bulletin, 23*, 974-980.

Vinick, B. H., & Ekerdt, D. J. (1989). Retirement and the family. *Generations, 13*(2), 53-56.

Vivian, J., Brown, R. J., & Hewstone, M. (1994). *Changing attitudes through intergroup contact: The effects of membership salience.* Unpublished manuscript, University of Kent at Canterbury, UK.

Vrij, A., Van Schie, E., & Cherryman, J. (1996). Reducing ethnic prejudice through public communication programs: A social-psychological perspective. *Journal of Psychology, 130*, 413-420.

Wade, T., Neale, M. C., Lake, R. I. E., & Martin, N. G. (1999). A genetic analysis of the eating and attitudes associated with bulimia nervosa: Dealing with the problem of ascertainment in twin studies. *Behavior Genetics, 29,* 1-10.

Waldman, D. A., & Avolio, B. J. (1986). A meta-analysis of age differences in job performance. *Journal of Applied Psychology, 71,* 33-38.

Walker, I., & Crogan, M. (1998). Academic performance, prejudice, and the jigsaw classroom: New pieces of the puzzle. *Journal of Community & Applied Social Psychology, 8,* 381-393.

Waller, N. G., Kojetin, B. A., Bouchard, T. J., Jr., Lykken, D. T., & Tellegen, A. (1990). Genetic and environmental influences on religious interests, attitudes, and values: A study of twins reared apart and together. *Psychological Science, 1,* 138-142.

Walster, E., Walster, C. W., & Berscheid, E. (1978). *Equity: Theory and research.* Boston: Allyn & Bacon.

Walter, H. M. (1997). *An investigation into the affective profiles of girls from single-sex and co-educational schools, as they relate to the learning of mathematics.* Unpublished master's thesis, University of Exeter, UK. (ERIC Document Reproduction Service No. ED 439 015)

Ward, C. (1988). Attitudes Toward Rape Victims Scale. *Psychology of Women Quarterly, 12,* 127-146.

Warr, P. (1992). Age and occupational well-being. *Psychology and Aging, 7,* 37-45.

Washington et al. v. Harold Glucksberg et al., 117 S. Ct. 2258 (1997).

Wasmuth, C. E. (2000). Euthanasia. In *Encyclopedia Americana* (Vol. 10, pp. 711-712). Danbury, CT: Grolier.

Wass, H. (1993). Gender differences in the workplace. In R. Kastenbaum (Ed.), *Encyclopedia of adult development* (pp. 171-174). Phoenix, AZ: Oryx.

Watson, D., & Pennebaker, J. W. (1989). Health complaints, stress, and distress: Exploring the central role of negative affectivity. *Psychological Review, 96,* 234-254.

Weaver, C. N. (1998). Black-White differences in job satisfaction: Evidence from 21 nationwide surveys. *Psychological Reports, 83,* 1083-1088.

Web-Based Education Commission. (2000). *The power of the Internet for learning: Moving from promise to practice.* Washington, DC: U.S. Department of Education. (Web site interact.hpcnet.org/webcommission/Professional_Development.htm)

Weber, M. (1930). *The Protestant ethic and the spirit of capitalism.* London: Allyn & Unwin.

Webster v. Reproductive Health Service, 492 U.S. 490 (1989).

Weeks, W. A., & Nantel, J. (1995). The effects of gender and career stage on job satisfaction and performance behavior: A case study. *Journal of Social Behavior & Personality, 10,* 273-288.

Weinberg, D. H. (2000, September 26). *Income and poverty 1999—Press briefing.* Washington, DC: U.S. Census Bureau. Retrieved November 1, 2001, from the World Wide Web: www.census.gov/hhes/income/income99/prs00asc.html

Weinberger, A. (1979). Stereotyping of the elderly: Elementary children's responses. *Research on Aging, 1,* 113-136.

Weinburgh, M. (1995). Gender differences in student attitudes toward science: A meta-analysis of the literature from 1970 to 1991. *Journal of Research in Science Teaching, 32,* 387-398.

Weinger, S. (1998). Poor children "know their place": Perceptions of poetry, class and public messages. *Journal of Sociology & Social Welfare*, *25*, 100-118.

Weinstein, S., Weinstein, C., & Drozdenko, R. (1984). Brain wave analysis. *Psychology and Marketing*, *1*, 17-42.

Weisman, A. D., & Kastenbaum, R. (1968). The psychological autopsy: A study of the terminal phase of life. *Community Mental Health Journal*, Monograph No. 4.

Weiss, K. R. (2001, January 22). College freshmen rate money as chief goal. *Los Angeles Times*, p. A3.

Weiss, M. (1994). *Conditional love: Parents' attitudes toward handicapped children.* Westport, CT: Bergin & Garvey.

Weisz, M. G., & Earls, C. M. (1995). The effects of exposure to filmed sexual violence on attitudes toward rape. *Journal of Interpersonal Violence*, *19*, 71-84.

West, R., & Hall, J. (1997). The role of personality and attitudes in traffic accident risk. *Applied Psychology: An International Review*, *46*, 253-264.

Westbrook, M. T., & Legge, V. (1993). Health practitioners' perceptions of family attitudes toward children with disabilities: A comparison of six communities in a multicultural society. *Rehabilitation Psychology*, *38*, 177-185.

Westbrook, M. T., Legge, V., & Pennay, M. (1993). Attitudes towards disabilities in a multicultural society. *Social Science & Medicine*, *36*, 615-623.

White, B. H., & Kurpius, S. E. R. (1999). Attitudes toward rape victims. *Journal of Interpersonal Violence*, *14*, 989-995.

Wicker, A. W. (1969). Attitudes versus actions: the relationship of verbal and overt behavioral responses to attitude objects. *Journal of Social Issues*, *25*(4), 41-78.

Wicker, A. W. (1971). An examination of the "other variables" explanation of attitude-behavior inconsistency. *Journal of Personality and Social Psychology*, *19*, 18-30.

Wiehe, V. R. (1990). Religious influence on parental attitudes toward the use of corporal punishment. *Journal of Family Violence*, *5*, 173-186.

Wiener, Y., Vardi, Y., & Muczyk, J. (1981). Antecedents of employees' mental health: The role of career and work satisfaction. *Journal of Vocational Behavior*, *19*, 50-60.

Williams, C. J. (2001, April 11). Netherlands OKs assisted suicide. *Los Angeles Times*, pp. A1, A15.

Wilson, B., & McCrary, J. (1996). The effect of instruction on music educators' attitudes toward students with disabilities. *Journal of Research in Music Education*, *44*(1), 26-33.

Wilson, E. O. (1978). *On human nature.* Cambridge, MA: Harvard University Press.

Wolins, L., & Dickinson, T. T. (1973). Transformations to improve reliability and/or validity for affective scales. *Educational and Psychological Measurement*, *33*, 711-713.

Wong, P. T. P., Reker, G. T., & Gesser, G. (1994). Death Attitude Profile–Revised: A multidimensional measure of attitude toward death. In R. A. Neimeyer (Ed.), *Death anxiety handbook: Research, instrumentation, and application* (pp. 121-148). Philadelphia: Taylor & Francis.

Wood, W. (2000). Attitude change: Persuasion and social influence. *Annual Review of Psychology*, *51*, 539-570.

Woodmansee, J. J. (1970). The pupil response as a measure of social attitude. In G. F. Summers (Ed.), *Attitude measurement* (pp. 514-534). Chicago: Rand McNally.

Woodrum, E., & Ventis, W. L. (1992). Moral Attitudes Index. *Journal of Empirical Theology, 5*, 70-84.

Wright, L. W., Jr., Adams, H. E., & Bernat, J. (1999). Development and validation of the Homophobia Scale. *Journal of Psychopathology & Behavioral Assessment, 21*, 337-347.

Wright, M. (1999). Influences on learner attitudes towards foreign language and culture. *Educational Research, 41*, 197-208.

Yeung, R. R. (1996). The acute effects of exercise on mood state. *Journal of Psychosomatic Research, 40*, 123-141.

Yuker, H. E. (1994). Variables that influence attitudes toward people with disabilities: Conclusions from the data. *Journal of Social Behavior & Personality, 9*(5), 3-22.

Zagummy, M. J., & Brady, D. B. (1998). Development of the AIDS Health Belief Scale (AHBS). *AIDS Education & Prevention, 10*, 173-179.

Zanandrea, M., & Rizzo, T. (1998). Attitudes of undergraduate physical education majors in Brazil toward teaching students with disabilities. *Perceptual & Motor Skills, 86*, 699-706.

Zeitz, G. (1990). Age and work satisfaction in a government agency: A situational perspective. *Human Relations, 43*, 419-438.

Author Index

Subject Index

About the Author

Lewis R. Aiken was born in Bradenton, Florida, and attended public schools in Florida and Georgia. He graduated from Florida State University with B.S. and M.A. degrees in psychology. Subsequently, he attended Emory University and the University of North Carolina at Chapel Hill and graduated from the latter institution with a Ph.D. in psychology. After receiving the doctorate, Dr. Aiken taught at the University of North Carolina at Greensboro, where he was also Director of Admissions and Placement Research. Other teaching appointments included Dana Professor of Psychology and Chairman of the Department at Guilford College and Research Educationist at the University of California, Los Angeles, and the University for Teacher Education in Tehran, Iran. On returning to the United States, he taught at the University of the Pacific and at Pepperdine University. Among the awards he has received are an NAS-NRC postdoctoral resident research associateship (U.S. Navy Research Laboratory and San Diego State University), a USOE postdoctoral fellowship (Stanford University and the University of Georgia), and a Fulbright research/lectureship. During his long career, Dr. Aiken has also served as a consultant for numerous educational, governmental, health, and industrial organizations and has worked in many different educational, clinical/counseling, research, and business situations. His major research interests are in psychological assessment and social and personality psychology. He has published books on psychological and educational assessment, personality, adult development and aging, death and dying, and general psychology. Dr. Aiken is a fellow in the American Psychological Association and a member of several other professional organizations, and he is listed in *Who's Who in America*. A father of two and a grandfather of four, he and his wife, Dorothy, have lived in Thousand Oaks, California, for more than 20 years.